The Well-Rounded Soccer Coach

# DEDICATION

For Neeta, Sunaina, and Shaylan—you are the loves of my life; thank you for all of the sacrifices as I coach, write, and teach.

For all my family and friends: thank you for continuing to love and support me.

For my closest soccer coaching staff friends: Keith Wawrzyniak, Dave Banks, and Ryan Spencer, your long-term loyalty is much appreciated; we had an incredible run, didn't we?

For Anson Dorrance, Jay Martin, Gloria Averbuch, Tim Crothers, Jodi Helmer, Manuel Morschel, Martin Meyer, Liz Evans, Thomas Stengel, and Jenn Grabenstetter: your belief, encouragement, and support throughout this writing process are much appreciated.

For my long-time coaching friends, you are among the truly elite in the country: Anson Dorrance, Jeff Tipping, Dave Lombardo, Hank Leung, Ken Krieger, Gene Mishalow; I have learned valuable lessons from your "doctorate courses."

For the hundreds of kind players and coaches whom I have had the good fortune of sharing positive experiences with on our soccer journeys: I know the memories and lessons will stay with us forever.

For the many coaches whom I have yet to meet: the ones who share my desires to take the time to teach skills effectively, strive for excellence diligently, maintain passion for the game selflessly, compete honorably, and contribute positively to player development.

For *Electra*, especially the Banks, Bartucca, Costantino, DeSimone, Gallivan, Grose, Lee, Smith, and Wawrzyniak families: many thanks and *Let's Go Get 'em!*

Ashu Saxena

# The Well-Rounded
# SOCCER
# COACH

Foreword by
**Anson Dorrance**

For U9-U19

Form Your **TEAM**. Plan Your **SEASON**.
Develop your **TRAINING**.

Endorsed by

Meyer & Meyer Sport

British Library Cataloguing in Publication Data
A catalogue record for this book is available from the British Library

Title of 1st edition: Soccer – Strategies for Sustained Coaching Success, Meyer & Meyer, Aachen, 2012
**The Well-Rounded Soccer Coach**
Maidenhead: Meyer & Meyer Sport (UK) Ltd., 2018
ISBN: 978-1-78255-142-3

© 2018 by Meyer & Meyer Sport (UK) Ltd.
2nd edition 2018 of the 1st edition 2012
Aachen, Auckland, Beirut, Cairo, Cape Town, Dubai, Hägendorf, Hong Kong, Indianapolis,
Manila, New Delhi, Singapore, Sydney, Tehran, Vienna

Member of the World Sports Publishers' Association (WSPA)
www.w-s-p-a.org
Printed by: Print Consult GmbH, Munich, Germany

ISBN: 978-1-78255-142-3
Email: info@m-m-sports.com
www.m-m-sports.com

# TABLE OF CONTENTS

## Training Sessions

# PREFACE

*"Each day is a little life." – Arthur Schopenhauer*

"Welcome to America!" shouted the tall, thin, blond, pony-tailed, blue-eyed, smiling 10-year-old girl. She was the first player to greet me on the first team that I coached in Fairfax, Virginia. Being an American all my life, I was surprised at the welcome, yet I had to smile at her energy and enthusiasm. She and her teammates had heard that I would become their head coach in August of 1995. I had just moved there in July from Clifton Park, New York. Having coached youth and high school soccer there, I was interested in continuing my coaching career immediately.

After a few phone calls and various offers from area clubs to take on teams, I was eventually introduced to Keith Wawrzyniak and Dave Banks, both parent coaches who were coaching and managing the Braddock Road Youth Club Electra Under 11 (U11) girls' soccer team. Little did I know then, I would go on to coach that team through their U19 year and that numerous families from the team, including Keith and Dave, would be among my closest friends to this day.

Keith, in his humorous way, poked fun at my Indian heritage and had told the girls I was Cherokee, Navajo or Sioux (I really do not remember). It did not occur to the girls that my parents are actually from India, the country in Asia. Thus, I was welcomed by the girl with the blond ponytail to a country I already knew and loved.

Some years later, that same player (CJ), her teammates, Keith, Dave, and I would celebrate numerous accomplishments. We were the Virginia State Champions twice, a Region I Finalist, elite performers at top tournaments around the country, and we were a team that demonstrated long-term player development. Electra, as the team was simply known, went on to develop highly successful, accomplished players at the club, high school, ODP, collegiate, and even national levels. Given our team culture, it is no surprise that several of the girls were captains of their various teams and leaders in life off of the field, too.

From modest beginnings as a player, CJ would go on to win a HS state championship, a collegiate national championship, and off the soccer field, she developed into a wonderfully graceful, compassionate person of tremendous strength. Many of us attended her and her teammates' weddings, and she is just one example of many Electra alumnae you will get to meet throughout this book. Those players and their parents are among those who lend powerful credibility to the strategies for becoming a well-rounded coach and experiencing sustained soccer coaching success that I offer in the pages that follow.

*Statement from a former soccer player (Cassandra "CJ" Grose):*

*"On the field Ashu stands out because of his commitment to the development of each individual player and his contagious passion for the game. Off the field Ashu stands out as a man of character, challenging those around him to live a life of integrity, kindness and continual personal growth. As a player for Ashu I certainly developed my skills on the field as he encouraged me to never be comfortable at the level I was at, but to continue to develop into a player with the complete package of technical skills, mental toughness and a refined understanding of the game. In looking back though, what I value*

most about Ashu as a coach were the life lessons I took away by "catching" his love for the game and learning about life in light of soccer. I still remember studying the flight patterns of geese as a team and discussing how it related to us on the field and in life. I have often thought back to and used those life lessons such as taking turns flying as the leader and flying in such a way that empowers the flight of those around me. I am forever grateful to Ashu that he took the time to coach us beyond just the details of the game."

— CJ Grose, BRYC Electra U11-U19 (Messiah College)

## WHY THIS BOOK WAS WRITTEN

*The Well-Rounded Soccer Coach* is a clear, credible resource by an experienced soccer coach who shares proven player development methods for attaining long-term coaching success. The experiences in coaching ages U9 to U19 for several years have been valuable in both shaping soccer successes and creating positive team cultures. In addition, my interests in education, psychology, management, current events, philosophy, global issues, and sports in general have enhanced the overall coaching experience for those who I coach and work with.

Given my long-term achievements, honors and credentials, along with having written articles and offered contributions to books, a growing audience became interested in what I do for teams on and off the field. In addition to BRYC *Electra*, there were highly successful stories that followed in BRYC *Attack,* BRYC *Blue Thunder*, and teams more recently in North Carolina (U16s, U15s, U12s). Additionally, the methods described in this book also positively impacted highly competitive high school programs in New York, Virgina, and North Carolina. What is it that leads to enduring excellence in coaching? There is a lot more to it than simply inheriting talent and winning matches. Thus, curiosity from coaches first inspired me to share the wealth of experiences because if it helps coaches, then it ultimately benefits those who matter most in this game — the players.

As I scanned the vast resources available to coaches in terms of books, periodicals, videos, DVDs, emails and various online materials, I realized that a lot of things appeared to be missing. I could not find a single resource that captured on- and off-field insights, practical full-session plans for a whole season, the college process for youth (and high school) coaches, and various other important features from a coach-as-educator perspective.

The topic of player development in soccer is critical at the moment, especially in America and the UK, and I feel a responsibility to contribute several valuable insights and help build a strong support system for all coaches interested in the topic. Thus, the attempt to raise the standards of resources in terms of connecting all coaching aspects is set; the key features of *The Well-Rounded Soccer Coach* include:

- proven methods and techniques
- an example of a complete season of training sessions
- explanations as to the "how" and "why" of selected exercises
- useful resources for coaches, players, and parents in a variety of areas on and off the field
- anecdotes from coaches, players, and parents that demonstrate objective results
- direct access to someone who is "in the trenches" of the coaching profession who focuses on player development

Lastly, I also wrote *The Well-Rounded Soccer Coach* to honor the many terrific players, families and coaches who I have been fortunate to meet along this enjoyable journey. It is a beautiful game, and I am glad to have had so many positive experiences that I can now share with a wider audience who will be able to use this book in many ways to benefit themselves, those they work with and those they coach.

## WHO THIS BOOK IS FOR

The primary audience for *The Well-Rounded Soccer Coach* is soccer coaches— both genders, all ages, all levels, all experience levels from rookie to veteran. Coaches in the United States as well as from other countries will find great value and usefulness since no other book like it currently exists. Especially with the release of the US Soccer Coaching Curriculum and additional articles regarding player development, coaches will find this book of tremendous value because I will share proven methods and sessions with detail, quality, and credibility that are unmatched in publications currently available.

Secondary audiences for the book include soccer players and parents, coaches of different sports, and directors of coaching/coaching education who lead other coaches or can offer *The Well-Rounded Soccer Coach* as an excellent resource for professional development.

## WHY ANSON

When I first contemplated writing a book on coaching soccer, there was only one person whom I wanted to write the foreword. If he said "no," then there would not be a foreword to this book I am sure there are critics who suspect I might have had a hidden agenda in asking Anson Dorrance to write the foreword to my book— a big name to sell more copies.

However, I am reminded of a quote, one of many quotes, that Anson has given to me during the years that I have known him (credit Aristotle for this one): "Say nothing, do nothing, be nothing." In essence, one cannot worry about what others think or say. Instead, one must choose a path that he knows to be right and true, take action and use the power of voice effectively. Thus, it is partly because of his inspiration that I have followed through on writing *The Well-Rounded Soccer Coach,* and it is because of his mentorship, loyalty, support, and friendship that I asked him to be a part of this adventure.

I first met Anson Dorrance in early December of 1995. He was presenting during the NSCAA symposium at the Carolina Inn during the NCAA Women's Division I semi-final and final weekend in Chapel Hill, North Carolina.

Like most people who followed women's soccer, I was curious about the amazing records already established by Anson and the *Tar Heels*. Their legacy was not just about astonishing statistics, but more so about the leadership skills, coaching knowledge, teaching ability, and management style. I had seen past championships on television, read a variety of articles about the Dynasty, and I was impressed with the stream of champions who had already played and were playing for the *Tar Heels—* Mia Hamm, Kristine Lilly, Tisha Venturini, Tracey Bates, Shannon Higgins-Cirvoski, Angie Kelly, Staci Wilson, Robin Confer, and Cindy Parlow to name a few.

In one way or another, I would eventually meet them all, and I never failed to be impressed by their genuine role model spirit (e.g., the latter three were players who signed autographs for the young

BRYC *Electra* team I had taken to the old Raleigh Shootout just a few weeks earlier); humility (e.g., Shannon and I coached opposing school and club teams in the DC area and though she was a legend, she invited me to join her and her famous coaching husband at a table for dinner at one of the NSCAA conventions some years later); generosity (e.g., Tracey more than once took time via informal introductions at events or via email to respond to questions); competitiveness (e.g., the first three were long-time US Women's National Team stalwarts who didn't just play the game, but competed with an unmistakable fury every minute to lead teams to NCAA, Olympic and World Cup championships); toughness yet approachable (e.g., Staci is still the toughest back I have ever seen play the game, yet she took time out of her schedule to do a session with the *Electra* team, and the girls loved her); insightfulness (e.g., Angie was one of BRYC *Electra's* first coaches at UNC team camp way back in 1996, and Robin always had good insights when she was approached about her coaching thoughts during the UNC girls' soccer camp sessions that we both happened to work at); and loyalty (e.g., Cindy would always come back to Chapel Hill during her various stints with national team duties; she served as an assistant coach on Anson's staff, and she continues to be a good friend who I enjoy chatting with about youth soccer and player development).

Of course, this list doesn't include the many talented and kind players who either came before or after these players and from whom I have also learned a lot regarding the UNC program: Marcia McDermott, Amy Kiah, Bettina Bernardi, Beth Huber, Susan Ellis, Heather O'Reilly, Angie Kelly, Anne Felts, Anna Rodenbough, Yael Averbuch, Mandy Moraca, Ashlyn Harris, Nicole Roberts, Susan Bush, Raven McDonald, Kacey White, Libby Guess, Ariel Harris, Sterling Smith, Nikki Washington, Robin Gayle, Cat Reddick, Nel Fettig, Helen Lawler, Laura Winslow, Lorrie Fair, Laurie Schwoy, Rebekah McDowell, Ali Hawkins, Beth Sheppard, Siri Mullinix, Sarah Dacey, Tiffany Roberts, Jessica Maxwell, Leslie Gaston and Jordan Walker just to name a few.

So, why the extensive name drop? To point out that they all played for and excelled at UNC (and some on the US Women's National Team) under Anson. Players are often a reflection of their coach and while all of these players certainly had other influential people in their lives, all are forever connected by one coach—Anson. In addition, Anson's current and former staff members, including Bill Palladino, Chris Ducar, Tom Sander, and Bill Steffen continue to be terrific friends and they have certainly been valuable members of the *Tar Heel's* successes. They also remind us that a coaching effort is a team effort and that loyalty, support, hard work, professionalism, knowledge, ability, humor, team chemistry, motivation, compatibility, respect and communication are among the most important features of group dynamics.

When Anson saw my teams, BRYC *Electra* in particular, show improvement at camp over the years, he was both pleased and surprised. Pleased that player development does take place at the youth level and surprised that a coach like me could take the route of non-recruiting in a competitive area such as northern Virginia and still find success without necessarily having the best athletes or top names, but by being focused on long-term player development. As a result, I have continued to work at UNC camps over the years, taking a particular liking to the team camp weeks.

When BRYC *Electra* was putting together a coach-of-the-year nomination for me, they approached Anson to write what I would later consider to be one of the nicest letters of recommendations that I have ever received. In addition, when Gloria Averbuch was looking to break down some of Anson's ideas and relate them to youth and high school coaches in the book she wrote with Anson, *Vision of a Champion*, he steered her to me. Lastly, when he and Tony DiCicco were looking to rustle up some proficient youth players in the making of two videos (*Playing the 1-4-3-3* and *Playing the 1-3-4-3*), Anson called on me and on short notice, I was able to provide five players who are, in the words of Anson, "forever immortalized in video soccer fame."

*As a huge underdog, Electra caps an amazing run at regionals, losing 2-3 in 2OT in the Championship.*

I have learned a lot from the man who is widely considered to be one of the greatest soccer coaches in the history of the sport. Despite his critics, Anson continues to share his knowledge by being active in the soccer coaching education community, explaining the UNC system at summer camps, clinics and conventions, demonstrating his ideas in books and DVDs, and without question, developing players throughout their careers for success on and off the soccer field. All along, he has shown character, compassion, competitiveness, and creativity in establishing a wonderful culture at Carolina. In addition, he has groomed and inspired hundreds of coaches, along with influencing coaching methodology and standards of play around the globe. Off the field, he is a devoted Sunday school teacher, and an incredible family man, serving in the roles of loving husband, father, grandfather, brother and so on. He has supported me and for that, I am appreciative. If you're going to learn, you may as well learn from the best; Anson is one of them, and I am proud to call him a friend.

Thus, the time has come for a book that considers coaching aspects on and off the field that are interconnected as both are critical for successful player development. Beyond all of the victories that a team can obtain on the field, it is the joy and satisfaction of seeing players develop lasting positive qualities as a result of the culture you lead that make coaching an incredibly valuable life-long experience. If a coach sets the right team culture, a team will produce players who:

- learn and improve technical and tactical skills along with physical and psychological qualities to reach higher competitive levels of performance
- grow into able problem-solvers
- mature into leadership roles and perhaps become future coaches
- be productive citizens
- retain strong friendships over many years—becoming so close that teammates consider each other family
- develop values such as hard work, faith, and integrity which will serve them on and off the field

Player development is critical in youth soccer, and it is an especially relevant, hot-button topic in the soccer world at present. What I share in this book has value for coaches at all levels because, in essence, if a coach is not striving for ongoing player development then that "coach" is not really coaching at all. There are many resources available to coaches, especially in this era of the internet and electronic communications. However, the mass email blasts and over-exposure of some resources can leave one wondering if the information out there is really useful at all while at the same time, it can come across as a disjointed collection of exercises that have neither congruence nor connection to a bigger picture: lasting player development and sustained success. Some resources also seem to offer exercises without adequate instruction or credibility that the user can easily identify. *The Well-Rounded Soccer Coach* offers coaches of both genders, all ages, all levels, and all experiences strategies that have led to objective, concrete results with great successes in player development, championships, and a continued passion for the game of soccer.

*"The fog's just lifting. Throw off your bow line; throw off your stern. You head out to South channel, past Rocky Neck, Ten Pound Island. Past Niles Pond where I skated as a kid. Blow your air horn and throw a wave to the lighthouse keeper's kid on Thatcher Island. Then the birds show up: black backs, herring gulls, big dumb ducks. The sun hits ya - head North. Open up to 12 - steamin' now. The guys are busy; you're in charge. Ya know what? You're a goddamn sword boat captain. Is there anything better in the world?"*

– Captain Billy Tyne, Perfect Storm (Produced by Katz 2000)

When you are able to lead a team on a journey, be it for a week at camp, a few weeks of training, a few months that comprise a season, one year, a decade, or more, there is something magical that can take place where the team is not just something that you are a part of, but that it is a part of you. With such a strong connection among all members of the team, there is something powerful that holds you together on the field through wins and losses and off the field through adversity; there is something inspiring that holds each player accountable when they are away from the team, whether to work on fitness or just basic standards of behavior; there is something genuine about feeling invincible, that together, the team can accomplish anything. Anything. You are a coach, coaching the world's most beautiful game—"is there anything better in the world?" **Let's Go Get 'em!**

The phrase *"Let's Go Get 'em!"* is how I used to end emails that I sent before match days to one of the earlier teams in my coaching career, *Electra*. In an era and location where teams changed composition, coaches, clubs, and colors, this team stayed the course and excelled in numerous ways on and off the field, as indicated throughout this book. Thus, this phrase is a nod to *Electra* with a sincere thanks to all of the players, families and key staff members Keith, Dave, and Ryan for an amazing journey that hasn't ended yet.

# FOREWORD

## By Anson Dorrance

In the summer of 1997, the U12 girls of the Northern Virginia BRYC *Electra* had journeyed into a week at the North Carolina Girls Soccer Camp with their young coach Ashu Saxena. They attended the Team Camp, a special week where the idea is to provide a soccer camp experience for the players in our player development methodology and expose the coaches of the teams to everything we know about the game. *Electra* was one of the youngest teams in camp that week but they genuflected to no one and returned twice in future years. Ashu coached *Electra* from U11 to U19, and I was honestly stunned at how much his team improved from one year to the next and how hard they trained. I was also very impressed with how they conducted themselves off the field, how they treated each other, and the clear respect and affection they had for their coach.

Anson Dorrance and Tony DiCicco send good wishes to one of Ashu's teams, Blue Thunder.

So to make a long story short, I hired Ashu to work for me in 1996. I wanted him to teach youth players and their coaches about player development, as well as about human development. Everything that was good about the improving level of girls' soccer in America and female empowerment was exemplified by this coach and his fine teams.

One of my favorite insights into the real value of the athletic experience for us who coach is in the story of Amos Alonzo Stagg. This extraordinary football coach at the University of Chicago, who when asked by a reporter following his 1913 National Championship what he thought of his team replied: "I'll tell you in 20 years."

Now, at the seventeen year mark from when I first met Ashu and he started coaching the *Electra*, part of the team was reunited in Orlando, FL. The core was supporting Ashu's marriage to the beautiful Neeta. One young woman had travelled all the way from Seattle to be there to honor Ashu; she is now a college biology teacher and has successfully coached and officiated youth soccer. This former player, Ashley, was a MAC Hermann Semifinalist (the top award for female college soccer players), NSCAA All-American, leading scorer, and captain at West Virginia University, reaching the NCAA "Sweet 16" as a team highlight during her career there. Previously, she also played varsity for four years at the high school where he coached, garnering NSCAA All-American honors and leading that team to two state championships. Another former player, Christina, has graduated from Princeton, after reaching the NCAA College Cup and serving as their soccer captain, and is now in medical school thinking of eventually becoming a surgeon or an oncologist. A third, Katie, is finishing up a University of Virginia graduate degree to teach and possibly coach and teach at some level (she went on from *Electra* to play at Boston College). A fourth, Jenn, is teaching, after a terrific playing career at UNC Wilmington, where she also served as their team captain. She coached a youth team with one of Ashu's *Electra* assistants, Ryan. All four players played for Ashu from U11 to U19.

Other former players attending the wedding played for the high school team where he coached (Crystal, who went on to play at Syracuse and now does some work with *ESPN*) and on *Electra*'s younger sister team, *Blue Thunder* (Jordan, who went on to play at James Madison University and has been accepted into a public health program at University of Pittsburgh; and Erica, a goalkeeper at perennial Division 3 power *Emory*). *Blue Thunder* was another team who visited UNC Team Camp and exemplified player development.

When they spoke to me of their coach, they all said he had a generosity of spirit, he made each of them feel special, he was principle-centered, and he cared about each of them as people first. He would show videos such as clips of *Braveheart* to teach them courage and standing up for themselves, and clips of *Breakfast Club* to show what it means to get along with people. He had individual conferences to try to get to know each of them and to show that he cared about them. One of them told me "he worked so hard for us, we wanted to work hard for him." When one tore her ACL during the peak collegiate "recruiting" season, Ashu was there to help her step by step and teach her about discipline, handling adversity, and achieving goals. He also taught them to become accountable for their own performance by keeping score in practice, but he never pretended that soccer was more important than their academic lives or the development of their character. Sportsmanship was also very important to the *Electra* and all of the former players said Ashu was insistent that it was always important how they represented themselves, their families, their club, their team, their league, their state, their region, and their country.

And yet, with all this "human development" going on behind the scenes, they came back every year better soccer players and a team focused on getting stronger. In addition, his coaching methods, philosophies, and contributions over the past 20-plus years led to club, high school, ECNL (Elite Clubs National League) and ODP (Olympic Development Program) successes in teams he coached before *Electra* in New York, in Virginia after *Electra*, and in North Carolina after he moved there, too.

Years ago, when Ashu asked me what I thought about writing this book, I told him he had to...he was already the individual I recommend to every youth coach who wanted to insert our system and philosophy into their youth development. Of course, our principles and philosophies are only a part of what he teaches. My email inboxes are filled with "best practices" that he has learned and applied successfully and that he has drawn from all over the soccer kingdom and innovated through his own experiences.

In a letter of support, unbeknownst to him at the time, by the request of his teams' players and parents, I stated that Ashu "has had a significant impact on a collection of young players that are developing the right way: becoming more and more technical every year I see them. In addition to helping his young players successfully through those necessary barriers of technical sophistication at a very impressive rate, he represents our game well. His manner is kind, his instincts thoughtful and supportive, his personality warm and generous. If I had a kid that age, I would love for her to be coached by Ashu. Not only would her game improve markedly, but I feel her association with Ashu would make her a better human being."

In *The Vision of a Champion*, the book I wrote with Gloria Averbuch to help the youth "navigate all the treacherous waters" of their sport, I referenced Ashu as someone to contact who had mastered it. I stand by that now as you explore and apply his vision and his time tested and practical ideas.

*Anson Dorrance*
*Women's Soccer Coach, University of North Carolina*
*21 Time National Collegiate Champions*
*NCAA 1982, 1983, 1984, 1986, 1987, 1988, 1989, 1990, 1991, 1992, 1993, 1994, 1996, 1997, 1999, 2000, 2003, 2006, 2008, 2009, 2012*
*AIAW 1981*
*USSF 1984*
*U.S. Women's National Coach 1986-1994*
*1991 FIFA World Champion*
*US Soccer Werner Fricker Builder Award*
*United Soccer Coaches Hall of Fame*

# CHAPTER 1

## PERSONAL STATEMENT, TEAM MISSION STATEMENT, AND COACHING PHILOSOPHY

*"Badness you can get easily, in quantity; the road is smooth, and it lies close by. But in front of excellence the immortal gods have put sweat, and long and steep is the way to it." – Hesiod*

What is your coaching philosophy? Do you have a set of values and beliefs to help guide your evolution and development as a soccer coach (and as a human being)? If someone asked your players and perhaps their parents what your mission statement is, could they define it? What is your team's style of play and is it congruent with your coaching philosophy? Whether you are a coach, director of a club, age group director of coaching, technical director, or any other member of personnel charged with player development, you must have a mission that drives your team, club, or program so that all members are motivated to unite for a common purpose.

A good coach has vision, works steadfastly in a framework of guiding principles, stays flexible to make appropriate adjustments, and develops a comprehensive coaching philosophy so that the journey of coaching winning soccer is successful. No matter what stage one is at in his or her career, it helps to think about one's personal value system.

If one can clearly define such a coaching philosophy, it follows that the coach can coordinate the development of a working mission statement for the group that he or she leads. The outcomes of taking such a step are: pride in the program, communication of principles that steer key decisions, connectedness among all members of the program, and lifelong skills that benefit all associated with your program.

Without defining such important characteristics, it is likely the team will lack focus and identity, and its play on the field will be disjointed. These weaknesses can be evident in a team at any level. This is an issue that the United States National teams have struggled with over recent years, and it is no surprise that the US is not developing many players at an elite level nor winning with as much frequency as desired or even expected, considering the large numbers of resources in the country. This issue is perhaps shared with other countries such as England, professional clubs around the world, youth clubs, college teams and high school programs where a clear vision for player development and a defined measure of success are unclear or clouded by a clash of philosophies and practices.

## PERSONAL STATEMENT

Though one needs to develop his or her own philosophy of coaching statement, I share mine in this section to help readers gather ideas. The components that follow are based on years of experience, and I continue to modify, improve and adjust ideas as necessary.

- DEVELOPMENT – I have had the good fortune of coaching ages U9-U19, mostly highly competitive club soccer, in addition to some mid-level club, state and regional ODP (Olympic Developmental Program), ECNL (Elite Clubs National League) and high school soccer in my coaching career. I firmly believe in creating a year-round culture of player development within my teams. Sessions are geared toward the development of technical and tactical skills where players are challenged to improve their ability to execute skills under pressure. Some exercises are very fundamental in nature while others are more complex. Coaches often ignore fundamental exercises by blindly following a "the game is the best teacher" model emphasized by many soccer "authorities." However, as it is clearly evident today, players in our national programs are lacking in technical skills and as such, fundamentals must be a priority in training sessions. One has to sometimes do the "boring" stuff to help players advance.

  *Note: Fundamental skill sessions are never boring if the coach is creative, teaches proper technique, sets high standards, encourages competition, and continually challenges players appropriately. I also firmly believe in other areas of development that are important from a personal standpoint for players: critical thinking skills (players have to be able to solve problems rather than be controlled every minute by a coach; asking players "Why?" often is a good start), social, emotional, psychological, behavioral, and physical development. As a coach, part of my mission is to equip players with the necessary skills to move on to the "next level," whatever it happens to be for each player, whether it is moving on to a regional/national team, college program, professional team, high school team, club/intramurals, adult league or other opportunity. Team development is also an important factor in individual player development. A difference between a coach at an elite level versus one who is simply average is that the elite coach strives for player development goals and improvements in every session, match, week, month, year, meeting, and is committed to it with resolve. In addition, an elite coach does not become complacent and instead strives for ongoing professional and personal development.*

- GOALS — I believe that defining goals and setting forth objectives to reach them is an important process from both an individual and team standpoint. I don't want my players to just hope for their goals to work out, but instead, to understand the effort that goes into reaching goals to appreciate it that much more when they do reach them. Players should set challenging goals and continue to set them as they grow. A coach must assist players in setting such goals, outlining steps to reach them and communicating regularly with both players and their support systems (e.g., teammates and parents). In addition, by evaluating progress and giving feedback regularly, it helps bring focus and an overall sense of mission for the long haul.

- TEAM — For the team to excel, it needs every player to be at their best, and likewise, when every player strives for improvement, it benefits the team. Players have to understand that they are a part of something bigger than themselves and thus, my teams are known for having a terrific culture where everyone wants to work hard for their teammates in positive ways. A common fallacy that has hindered player development is that of only focusing on individual progress; massaging the interests for a few and catering to the politics that sometimes go on in soccer are mistakes and have negative effects both on and off the field in the long-term process of player development.

- VALUES — Loyalty, teamwork, honesty, sportsmanship, class, integrity, hard work, faith, professionalism, dedication, responsibility, sacrifice, discipline, respect, commitment, and determination are just some of the values I believe in and try to make parts of my teams. I don't believe in cheating, foul language or cutting corners, and as a result, neither do our players. As an example, I do not encourage "professional fouls" like many coaches do and instead, I look to put greater emphasis on player responsibility. I often tell my teams that if they are called for a foul, it is because they had a mental lapse and we can't afford that; if they foul, it is because they didn't hustle to get in proper position, they didn't stay alert to engage themselves in the moment, they were lazy in the particular situation or they didn't focus to make a better play. I also expect my players to be just as hard-working in the classroom and value academics. Players know that they represent not just themselves, but also their families, the team, the club (or school), the state, the region, and ultimately the nation.

- FITTER, FASTER, STRONGER — The standards of fitness, speed, and strength are very high in competitive soccer, and thus, players are expected to work on these areas year-round. In addition, they know some of the skills that will be tested throughout the year, in addition to fitness tests. As a result, intrinsic motivation to improve needs to be developed rather than relying on extrinsic motivation. Nutrition, hydration, and appropriate rest are paramount in a year-round program for player development. I've noticed more coaches stray from fitness without a ball and they wrongfully declare that playing is enough fitness. That may work to some extent for coaches who recruit or are perhaps blessed with elite athletes, but it generally does not serve players well to ignore an emphasis on improving physical qualities. After all, we are developing fitness as a way of a life and not simply soccer players of present time. In addition, many recent articles indicate that cross-training helps ward off the negative aspects of repetitive-use injuries and burnout. An important by-product of working on conditioning, foot speed, agility, strength, endurance, and sprinting is team chemistry; by performing together, there are features of camaraderie, responsibility, accountability, and spirit that cannot be achieved as easily individually. Fitness with and without a ball are regular parts of my program starting at a young age, and as a result, the players I send off to college are usually better prepared than their counterparts. At the high school level, it is not even close, as players in my program are usually among the fitter players on teams. One can't simply recruit or hope for the best athletes; one has to set up environments for players to maximize their athletic potential and treat fitness as a necessity rather than a burden or punishment. Getting "fitter, faster, stronger" for soccer will ultimately help your athletes excel as they progress to higher levels and, more importantly, in life.

- COMMUNITY — Players are expected to build a healthy sense of community on the team. In addition, they are also to try to reach out to local and distant communities in various ways. Community service projects should occasionally be fit into the team calendar, and staying connected to the community in general is educational. I also believe players' families and friends are important parts of the sense of community we build on our teams. As a result, some of the teams that I've worked with for longer terms are often referred to as "families," and in a highly competitive arena where players change teams often, that is something truly special.

- PHOTO ALBUM — No matter how long I coach a player, I vow to give the player "snapshots" of much of the above in terms of skills, tactics, values, and experiences. Numerous players who have played for me always comment about how well stocked their "photo albums" were compared to other players because of the experiences we had together. If coached well, players will be versatile in terms of having a strong foundation of technical skill, good understanding of tactics, good discipline off the field in terms of training and getting "fitter, faster, stronger," and a desire to continue to be involved in the game. Fun should certainly be in all albums, and if you care about player development, strive to work on all areas for the players you coach.

- BIG PICTURE — Maintaining a healthy perspective is critical in all we do. Short-term ups and downs must be tempered with good vision and understanding of long-term goals and objectives. Such an approach helps players understand that success is indeed a journey. As a result, they will be able to respond to situations with greater resiliency and loyalty to your program. I can point to examples such as losing in a state cup semifinal or getting demoted to a second division where short-term vision caused our teams to go through adversity and lose a player or two who couldn't see the bigger picture. However, adherence to a long-term vision and maintenance of regular communication allowed those players who stayed loyal and worked hard to ultimately overcome such adversity and overachieve, winning state cup championships, developing skills, tactics, and passion for the game and ultimately playing at high levels on state, regional, high school, college, professional teams, not to mention becoming captains on their teams and leaders in life. Player development is a process and not something that can be fixed in the short-term or, worse yet, ignored altogether.

- PROBLEM-SOLVERS/THINKERS/DECISION-MAKERS — One area that is very important to me involves developing abilities in players to think for themselves. As a result, my coaching style is more like a guide than a dictator, an enabler more than an authoritarian. I strive to give players tools and ideas to succeed, but I don't try to orchestrate their every move. This is a big problem in youth coaching in particular. I've worked with older teams that supposedly won a lot at early ages but struggled later on to perform basic skills that well-trained younger teams could do. Invariably, the coaches of these teams didn't bother to develop skills, a passion for the game, discipline on and off the field, versatility in players or other important values listed previously. In addition, a coach has to manage parental influences. By communicating well with both players and parents, coaches are able to effectively use different positions and formations, as an example, to educate players that learning the game in different situations is important to developing better players. I encourage players to try to manage communicating with each other on and off the field to become better problem-solvers; this could mean allowing players to work out situations such as choosing their own positions/formations during scrimmages, what to do about forming team expectations, choosing what free kick play to try in a match, or choosing shooters for a penalty kick shootout. Controlling every movement and play on the ball is highly detrimental to long-term player development. Coaches need to improve their approaches to teaching and communicating, and people in administrative positions need to support improved coaching methodology programs. In my conversations with national team staff and other upper-level coaches, one area that is often raised is the player's struggle with problem-solving in match situations. A good coach can have impact by constructing healthy environments where players are forced to make decisions, be it small-sided games or encouraging options beyond just first options while training, rather than the coach controlling every play much like a puppeteer does. Another way to help with this aspect for player development is to encourage greater use of free play where players of different ages, genders, and abilities can come together and play without coach-centered sessions. Coaches should also encourage players to watch matches live and on television, as there is much to learn and knowledge can be enhanced by watching quality matches. Given that the soccer culture is stronger in other nations, we need to help encourage good ways to enhance the mental game of our players. If done well, our players will continue to excel as they move up in age and levels, rather than stagnate or, even worse, regress, or quit.

- CREATIVITY — Soccer matches are player-centered, contrary to many sports in America, such as football, baseball and basketball, that are coach-centered. Coaches cannot call timeouts in soccer nor do players play only offense or defense in pre-determined moments of matches. Thus, soccer training sessions should also follow a player-centered model. Coaches need to encourage players to problem-solve to enhance their creativity, otherwise this valuable resource goes largely untapped. In other words, sessions should include fundamentals and experiences of performing skills that may not seem useful as a regular part of games (e.g., a back heel performed while facing backwards, both "forehand" and "backhand" foot-volleys or scoring only with a behind-the-standing-foot shot akin to a Cruyff move). Players should be encouraged to be creative and coaches are responsible for creating a culture that allows for this. Juggling helps touch and creativity, 1v1 exercises encourage take-on ability, foot skill repetition allows players the tools to perform creative touches to get out of and exploit situations in matches — the list goes on. Allow players to choose point systems for scrimmages so that they feel it is okay to try some offbeat skills and get rewarded at the same time. There is no question we lack creative players at the highest levels of soccer in America. It is no secret that players in unstructured environments (e.g., "pick-up," "indoor" or "futsal") gain an edge when it comes to creativity. Watching soccer at the next levels or individual player video clips can inspire players to be creative. Coaches can do simple things in practice, such as requiring three-touches before passing, or a restriction that a player must take on or performing with flair before passing or shooting to foster creativity. One must identify creativity and allow it to grow, especially in younger players. One of the most creative players I coached (Ashley) often "struggled" as a young player since she was smaller than the other girls at the time and would get knocked over a lot. However, as she grew and continued to develop skills, understanding, and athletic qualities, she became a force to be reckoned with, scoring goals to lead our club and high school teams to state championships, and becoming one of the all-time leading scorers on her Big East college team, qualifying for national camp after having made the state and regional teams, and garnering high school and college All-American honors in addition to one of the most prestigious honors a college soccer player can attain—being named as a MAC Hermann Award Semi-finalist. One of her teammates (Claire) had a similar situation where she was on a strong team but was considered to be the number three forward in a two-front system. When she made the move to a team I coached, she excelled and went on to gain the same honors above (with repeats of All-American and MAC honors). Ashley and Claire are two very special players whose creativity may have not developed had it been up to other coaches who couldn't look past physical weaknesses at their early stages and raise the competitive challenges that would help them develop to the next level.

- WARRIORS — Along with having creative "artists" on your team, you also need "soldiers." Ultimately, a coach wants to bring out both artist and soldier qualities in players, but to truly reach an elite level, you need to develop a warrior mentality among your players. They need to want to go to battle for the team in every competition, but especially in the most competitive of situations. There is nothing greater in team sports than when your team competes with everything they have, puts everything on the line, and has nothing left to give at the final whistle. Some of these victories are among the most enjoyable experiences that my alums and I still look back on with joy, as in most cases, we were the underdog knocking off a nemesis. Developing a warrior culture takes work by a dedicated, savvy, knowledgeable coaching staff, constant communication (especially with team leaders), and attention to detail in rallying the players to demonstrate vigor, energy, courage, and competitive spirit not just in matches, but in training sessions. Thus, a coach needs to develop a healthy culture of player development, along with staying attentive to motivational strategies, being creative to bring out passion from each player and preparing players for their "big moment." If one does this well, then players will be immune to the extra pressures of such a major event and will be able to focus on performing the fundamental skills under pressure. That's not to say that they aren't excited, because they are and they are psyched. However, they are not so excited that they cannot perform, and they instead let the pressure of the moment get to them instead of using the pressure of the moment to take victory. We need passionate players with warrior spirits to compete; not just in the game of soccer, but in the bigger game of life.

- FUN/HUMOR/LAUGH/SMILE — Always remember that soccer is a game. Yes, we are passionate about it. Yes, we would like to win every match we play. Yes, we go through difficult times as hard-working coaches who care about our teams. However, soccer is still a game and if we don't allow our players moments to have fun, share humorous times and do simple things such as smile regularly, we'll lose them. I know my training sessions environments are perhaps more competitive, organized, player-centered, and focused than most other youth environments, but our players generally have fun because of the long-term approach we have in player development. You don't have to blur the line and sacrifice your core values to add laughter in your training sessions. Good-natured bantering is a positive life skill and helps ease the tension during stressful moments that all teams have at various times in the season. Some coaches go overboard and seem more interested making training sessions fun. They want to be popular with their players and parents, and while this approach may be good for a very young or recreational environment, elite players lose respect for such coaches because they want to be challenged. Remember to find humor in even the smallest of things and that players don't try to make mistakes; they usually try to do the right thing. Mental mistakes need constant attention, while physical mistakes sometimes just happen. Learn to manage this and move forward. Remember that in the "big picture," we should have fun as a coach and more importantly, the environment you create for your players should be an overall fun experience for them. Having staff members who complement your approach, style and philosophy helps, and for the good, loyal ones who I have worked with in my career, I am grateful. Find that balance of being competitive, driven, hard-working, and yes, fun-loving.

## TEAM MISSION STATEMENT

With each team I coach, I believe it is important to have some semblance of a "mission statement" for the team. Similar to corporations and schools, this statement runs parallel to your personal statement. To get more commitment, dedication and team identity, an individual team mission statement should ultimately come from the players, even if it is the main idea and not the specific words.

*As examples, I offer three mission statements:*

(1) BRYC Electra – The tryout ad created for this team ultimately became our work-in-progress mission statement. The girls had the chance to look at the ad each fall and spring season and offer comments; given that the parents were also an important part of that team's long-term successes, we invited them to comment on aspects of what ultimately one parent termed, our "*Electra* Mission Statement." We put some of these values on our team brochure, referred to these ideas during team talks, player meetings and tryouts, and ultimately the words in our statement became the basis for team philosophies of many future teams that I coached. An example of one of the teams was the BRYC *Attack*, a team I took over from a well-respected coach who did a terrific job preparing the team. After the change, the team went on a fifty-plus-match unbeaten streak, culminating in a state cup championship and regional semi-finalist placement (the team had not reached the final four of the state cup prior to this magical season). Much of that success was due in part to the *Electra* Mission Statement and the values easily transferred from one elite team to the next. Most of the statement is contained in this sample tryout ad:

*We seek team players who are hard-working, versatile, athletic and dedicated. Our program focuses on building soccer skills and developing positive character in our athletes. We maintain a stable team environment throughout the years – players, parents, and coaches get along and contribute positively for the good of the team. In addition, players receive excellent assistance with the college process due to the staff's vast network of college coaches and placements. Likewise, players have the solid backing of a top club that continues to place players into competitive programs across the country. Electra participates in top-flight, national-level competitions, and players are ODP participants at the state, regional, national levels, already being ID'd for higher levels of play.*

*Our environment is fun, challenging, competitive, spirited, and designed for players to improve and excel throughout the year. Players should understand that the team has long-term goals, and the team culture provides learning opportunities for success on and off the field. Our players develop an understanding of formations and positions at very high levels; they are provided the opportunity to play different positions in different formations. All team members are expected to maintain their fitness throughout the year and are provided with a fitness packet and training tips to ensure that they meet this goal. Interested players should be committed to compete at high-level competitive showcase and tournament events. Due to our training and development of versatility, all positions are welcome.*

(2) BRYC Blue Thunder – A "younger sister" team of BRYC *Electra* and *Attack*, BRYC *Blue Thunder* was another team that I coached for multiple years, showing player development progress each season. At one of our team meetings, I asked the players to write down a mission statement and list our core values for our team. Following are some of the ideas that they came up with:

*BRYC Blue Thunder's Mission Statement:*

- To be reverent soccer players with dexterity, with focused goals, and who illuminate themselves and everyone around them.
- To be a team that plays with skill and class, that people enjoy watching play because of the chemistry we have.
- To come together as a whole to work to our best standard and achieve our goals. We will battle through all 80 minutes, we will come out 100%, we will be a winning team.

*Note: The team was U16 at the time and played 40-minute halves.*

- To achieve and become a better team on and off the field. On the field, be on task and work together because there is no "I" in team. Off the field, we need to be respectful of each other and to be honest with each other.
- To strive to be the best we can be, to be the best physical and mental players out there with best efforts.
- To play the highest level of soccer in a competitive environment, while showing class and good sportsmanship.
- To maximize the opportunities to grow as players and teammates in all aspects that the game can provide.
- To come out and play our hardest, to ensure that we are the best we can be.
- To accept players into our family and raise everyone's game to the highest it can possibly be.
- To develop our skills as a player and as a team, build strong relationships with others, and essentially guide us through our next steps in life.
- To be a united force made of 18 talented athletes who play for each other to an extraordinary level to achieve a common goal, consistently out-desire, out-work, and out-perform every team we compete against, play to our best standard, enjoy the match and each other, and keep in mind that "if winning were easy, everyone would do it."
- To be fearless; play with energy, pride, courage; have the mindset that we are the best, believe everyone on the team is a winner; push ourselves and try our hardest; become leaders and motivators; become the best team that we can possibly become.
- To have fun, make long-lasting friendships, and to play the game of soccer at a high level.
- To keep up the competitiveness and intensity; keep the family, togetherness, sister-like qualities; work toward perfection; keep and improve the *Blue Thunder* "magic"; BT is ONE and a TEAM!!
- To be the best-skilled, hardest-working, and classiest team; push ourselves to bring soccer to a new level and improve on and off the field; keep the game in perspective and realize that there are people around the world who are in need; we want to re-define "champions."
- To win state cup at least two times; be a clean (no cards) team; continue to improve fitness and individual skills; play each other like we're "enemies" in practice to compete.

BRYC Blue Thunder's Core Values – hard work, determination, sportsmanship, commitment, respect, honesty, team spirit, cohesiveness, teamwork, responsibility, focus, class, friendship, skill, speed, courage, intensity, encouragement, unity, integrity, drive, readiness mentally and physically, team chemistry, competitiveness, motivation, support all teammates, playing our best, have a good time while getting the job done, love of the game and one another, perseverance, growth of skills, relationships, ownership, happy/fun environment, dedication, preservation of the "BT Family," champions, loyalty, compatibility, open-minded, accepting, confidence, team comes first, admit mistakes, friendly, friendships, caring, loving, always give 100% effort, pride, success, winner, leadership, perfection, creative, reach goals/dreams, trust, encourage individuality, fun, no "groups" or cliques," don't be average, faith, don't believe in "impossible," greatness, poise, condition, self-control, alert, initiative, intent, industrious, cooperate, enthusiasm, resourceful, adapt, ambition, patience, reliability, sincerity.

(3) NC U16/U15 R3PL/ECNL Teams – These are two teams that I coached after moving from Virginia to North Carolina in recent years. Working in a true club system, each team had a variety of coaches in their pasts and futures. Such a system has both strengths and weaknesses, especially when it comes to forming good habits and team culture at young ages. Thanks to the experiences and general frameworks of working with past teams, I was able to lead each team to new heights. However, it was much more of a challenge to encourage the same value system and positive team culture as with past teams since I inherited the teams at older ages. As an example of creating a "mission statement," I

encouraged the former team to write a lot in journals and meet often to develop a sense of unified purpose. As noted later in this book, the team went on to win a state championship.

With the latter team, I had the team choose five words that would help drive their season with me. I put the five words on every team email and referred to the words often to build a sense of a common "mission" for the players and their families. This particular team went on to take the previous year's state cup champion into an intense 0-0 overtime tactical thriller, only to lose in a PK shootout (the team had lost to this particular state cup champ 4-0 just two weeks prior).

It was a joy to see both teams grow through their respective seasons, be told by coaches and parents familiar with both teams from earlier seasons how much the teams improved in such a short time under my leadership and witness first-hand how each team formed a more positive team culture than perhaps what they had come in with. The words the latter team chose were:

Passion, Unity, Dedication, Discipline, and Effort. In addition, I coached a younger team in the club, and we established Team, Effort, Communication, Compete, and Focus as key words to measure our success.

## COACHING PHILOSOPHY

The third component that helps define a program is the coaching philosophy. In theory, this is how you directly manage your teams on and off the field. Based on your personal statement and your team's input regarding the team mission statement, you must be able to verbalize your coaching philosophy. One could argue that a personal statement and coaching philosophy should come before the mission statement, but I believe the three components should interact to form a powerful triumvirate upon which your program is based:

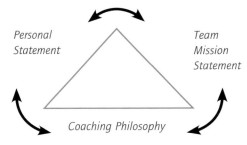

*Personal Statement*

*Team Mission Statement*

*Coaching Philosophy*

For example, if your personal statement includes integrity, do you follow your league rules regarding recruiting? If you value honesty, do you insist your players don't tug jerseys or commit so-called "professional fouls" in training sessions and matches? If you strive to improve the creativity of players, do you construct intentional training sessions that develop creativity or do you stifle their attempts at creativity by controlling their every move? If your team desires to be one of the "top" teams (e.g., win a league championship, finish in the top four in the state, or successfully place in national competitions), do you create highly competitive environments and maintain high expectations?

Coaches, teams and clubs are often quick to say their programs are about certain qualities that look good on paper when in reality, they are simply paying lip service to what they think other people would like to hear. I am sure many of you have heard the oft over-used and misused terms premier, advanced, elite, select, top-flight, etc. However, such "false advertising" coaches, teams and clubs eventually fade because their foundations of "coaching excellence" are hollow and flawed.

From my experiences, it is incredibly valuable to take an inventory of what your personal value system is about, what your team individually and collectively believes are important traits of a successful season and team, and what your coaching philosophy says about how you teach skills on and off the field, manage interpersonal relationships on the team, and ultimately, develop players to move to the next level, whatever that level may be. My coaching philosophy is fairly simple: long-term player development is the top priority. To support this philosophy,

*Electra & Blue Thunder compete in an event in Richmond, VA.*

developmentally appropriate training sessions are planned and executed with high degrees of expertise, teaching, and challenge. Players are kept active and are also expected to be responsible off the field with guidance toward fitness, nutrition, and skill improvement. Complacency and cliques are unacceptable so we are attentive, build solid team chemistry, and create a competitive environment where players are consistently challenged to be better. In addition, characteristics such as leadership, problem-solving, passion for the game, and community are all a part of the long-term player development package.

*Note:* *I include details on items such as style of play, substitution patterns, training session creation, coaching methodology, and communication in other parts of this book. Such items should not be but often are confused with coaching philosophy.*

If coaches have any difficulty constructing their personal statement, team mission statement, or coaching philosophy, then it is a good idea to talk with experienced coaches. Most coaches have a mentor of some sort who they can turn to for this exercise. The coach may or may not be involved with soccer, but that is not as important as grounding oneself with a value system on which to build upon. Other helpful resources can be various Code of Ethics statements offered by state associations and national coaching associations (e.g., United Soccer Coaches). One of my favorite resources that I have used with teams is John Wooden's Pyramid of Success (*They Call Me Coach*, Wooden/Tobin 1988); the pyramid hangs on the wall at my desk, as it has for several years. The Pyramid includes values and qualities that are presented in a good visual for coaches and athletes to understand excellence. Whatever your experience as a coach may be, it is a good idea to revisit these statements through periodic reflection and evaluation. A coach with an understanding of self and team visions is much more believable in the long-run (and more successful, too).

## Reflections:

- What values do you believe are important to maintain as a coach?
- What is your team's mission statement?
- What five values would your team consider most important?
- What is your coaching philosophy?
- Which coaches do you look up to most and what are their values?

# CHAPTER 2

## CREATING A TEAM CULTURE FOR PLAYER DEVELOPMENT

*"The strength of the team is each individual member...the strength of each member is the team." — Phil Jackson, retired NBA Basketball Coach*

I have been coaching U9 to U19 players and teams at several competitive youth levels since I began coaching in 1986. Two of the several teams that I have coached, *Electra* and *Blue Thunder*, exemplify long-term player development. Both teams were able to survive the highly competitive and super-saturated DC area youth soccer scene and ultimately flourish into very special stories.

As underdogs in a very competitive area of the country, neither team ever recruited players as other teams did, but rather focused on the players we had, offered tryouts and aimed to maximize each player's potential. That is not to say that we didn't attract good players because we certainly did, but we created an environment that players simply wanted to be a part of, not just for the many benefits of playing with our teams, but for all of the intangibles that they also received.

Ultimately, it was the team culture of player development that helped both teams over achieve in many ways. Holding steadfast to consistent desires to improve and reach for excellence, players not only developed skills, but they ultimately fed off of each other in terms of raising team standards to create a highly competitive, productive, enriching environment that was a lot of fun to be a part of, too.

BRYC *Blue Thunder*, which started in Division 5 (the "bottom") in their U11 spring season, reached Division 1 (the "top") at U14 fall and advanced into the state semifinals in their U14-U18 spring seasons with primarily the same core players. Essentially climbing over dozens of teams, including many who started early as powerhouses, was an achievement the players can always be proud of. The top two teams in their age group in the state were strong from an early age, and their recruiting machines could simply not be overcome for *Blue Thunder* to break through to a state championship. However, overcoming other teams and even being asked to merge with a couple of them were compliments of a much deeper level.

*Note:*   *We declined offers to merge and simply moved on as best as we could. Players went on to be successful on their high school, college, and ODP teams, and the team graduated from club soccer with success.*

Another earlier team that I coached that also demonstrated continuing advancement was BRYC *Electra*. This team began as a borderline Division 1/2 team at U11 and ultimately graduated over 25 players to competitive collegiate women's soccer programs. During our time together (from U11 to U19), the team won two Virginia state championships (perennial state semifinalist/finalist otherwise), became a Region One finalist, and achieved many, many successes on and off the field. *Electra* is a major reason why *The Well-Rounded Soccer Coach* was written.

Players from my club programs regularly received and receive honors on their college, ODP, and high school teams and consistently impacted those teams positively. What keeps teams like BRYC *Blue Thunder* and BRYC *Electra* together for many years, promotes high standards season after season, and contributes to the development of players who are successful on and off of the field? It is a team culture of player development. The impacts of creating the right culture are far-reaching, as indicated by an email that I received from a former player:

*".... Looking back on my soccer career, I was not naturally as athletic as many of my teammates. I am not saying this to be modest or self-deprecating; it is true that I was not as fast or strong or physical as many opponents or teammates. But what I did have, and what made me successful, was a work ethic and commitment that I now understand as heart. This "heart" was not unique to me. What I think set our team apart was that it was a collective heart, present in most of us as people and players, and fostered and encouraged by you and the example and standards you set. We loved each other but also the culture of our team demanded and supported heart. In that atmosphere of shared purpose we worked selflessly, tirelessly, productively to achieve our goals. There was something so comforting, so rewarding, so formative, in being surrounded by people who wanted and valued what you did and were willing to work for it. In collectively devoting our time and our energy, we threw our hearts into Electra and what I got out of it, and I hope you and my teammates did as well, beyond the wins and championships, was that sense of real and lasting satisfaction that comes from being a part of something that is so much bigger than yourself and demands so much.*
*Our team was incredible like that—it was a group of people who worked with you and for you; who helped you grow and grew with you; who shared your purpose and meaning and were willing to work for it; who essentially shared your heart.*
*I do not think I would have been able to fully understand what exactly it means to have heart and to live with heart were it not for Electra and for you. I also would not be who I am today and where I am today without you and Electra. And I surely would not have the clarity that I have now about what I want out of life were it not for my experiences with Electra. I think it takes time and some distance to truly appreciate this, and now, I really do....*                                                Katie #11

*[Katie was a Former BRYC Electra player who played/started on the team from U9 to U19; made her HS varsity team as a freshman where she was a two-year captain, competed successfully on the top state ODP team; and was ultimately recruited by several college programs before deciding to play at Boston College.]*

*Electra* and *Blue Thunder* are exceptions in that they maintained the same coach for multiple years, which has its own advantages and disadvantages.

*Note:* *Both of these teams competed before the ECNL and DA were developed. Thus, their tournament and state cup championship competitions included the top teams providing the highest competitive levels, making their numerous achievements that much more impressive and credible.*

Continuing growth should be the primary goal of youth coaches in particular, but in reality, every coach at any level should create an environment where players are challenged appropriately, taught effectively, and consistently improving in all areas. Examine any coach who is successful in any sport in the long-term and you will find a steadfast commitment to player development and attentiveness to role identification, team chemistry and ultimately, team culture. What follows are tips for creating a culture of player, social, and personal development.

Team Chemistry and Cohesiveness — Positive, healthy team chemistry is a foundation for everything the team does on and off of the field.

- CULTIVATE INTRA-TEAM FAMILIARITY: As a coach, lead players to change partners and groupings often during training sessions and match warm-ups. Encourage the players to choose different partners with whom to work during each exercise. To help the "mixing" process, use various "counting off" techniques to organize groups. These techniques include lining up players and counting off by twos, threes, fours, or however many numbers are needed to obtain the desired number of groups. Though it is possible to try something such as saying to the team, "get into groups of three," it often results in familiar groupings that can result in cliques if one is not careful to break them up. This takes attention, so be sure to monitor which players warm-up together and which players tend to gravitate to the same groupings when given the opportunity to self-select. Attention to this aspect will ultimately help form tighter bonds among teammates and lasting skills of cooperation, tolerance, respect, understanding, and appreciation of the need to be accountable to all team members.

One very helpful idea that assists in the random assignments of players to groups includes having players pick playing cards as they arrive at practice. Depending on the age of the players, there would always be a player who would ask if the team was going to play cards or if I was playing solitaire before they arrived. I chose the aces, twos, threes, and fours out of a standard deck of cards, which gave me 16 cards with all kinds of possibilities to divide the team into groups (for example, the twos can be in a group together or players with red cards can be on a team and so forth).

Colored beads, marbles, or poker chips (do not encourage gambling!) to randomly determine partners and groupings also work very well. In addition, such techniques eliminate players trying to stand in certain positions to be with their chosen team members. In fact, we vary groups so often on my teams that players quickly give up trying to predict where they should stand to be with a certain team member or two. Continually changing team partnerships allows each player to become comfortable working with all other team members, while forming tighter bonds throughout the team; the end result is akin to a well-constructed spider web in which connections among all players help strengthen all relationships.

Ultimately, every player should have been paired and grouped with every other player on the team several times. The lasting effect is that players will naturally feel very comfortable with any groupings that are put forth by the coach; in one respect, they look toward the surprise when being placed into groups. Players also develop confidence in themselves to associate with players that they might not initially gravitate toward, and they learn the important life skill of working with others in a team setting to benefit the team and themselves. Collaboration and co-dependence are strong positive outcomes by constantly mixing up the groups.

- ENCOURAGE "BUDDIES": "Buddy" activities can solidify budding partnerships and friendships on the team. For example, with the help of a coach or parent, each player draws the name of a "secret sister" out of a bag prior to a big match or tournament. Then, the sisters surprise each other with "psych-up" goodie bags before the big match. A similar technique of "secret Santas" could be applied using the exchange of little gifts for the holidays. Another idea is for each player to have a "buddy of the week." *Electra* implemented this system during one of the spring seasons when the team didn't train much together due to high school soccer. I wanted the players to stay connected as we had to prepare for regionals after the high school season was over. So, I implemented a "buddy of the week" program to allow the girls to remain close with each team member by sending emails, making phone calls, or going out to a movie or lunch with the assigned buddy of the week.

Below is a number scheme that you can use very easily. For example, if you have sixteen players, then assign a number to each player. Here is a sample rotation that you can use for "buddy of the week" or other desired groupings (such as a 1v1 ladder, pairs or groups for training sessions, Dutch 4v4 tournament or 4v4 summer/winter competitions).

| Week | A | B | C | D | E | F | G | H |
|------|------|------|------|------|------|------|------|------|
| 1 | 1-2 | 3-4 | 5-6 | 7-8 | 9-10 | 11-12 | 13-14 | 15-16 |
| 2 | 1-3 | 2-4 | 5-7 | 6-8 | 9-11 | 10-12 | 13-15 | 14-16 |
| 3 | 1-4 | 2-3 | 5-8 | 6-7 | 9-12 | 10-11 | 13-16 | 14-15 |
| 4 | 1-5 | 2-6 | 3-7 | 4-8 | 9-13 | 10-14 | 11-15 | 12-16 |
| 5 | 1-6 | 2-5 | 3-8 | 4-7 | 9-14 | 10-13 | 11-16 | 12-15 |
| 6 | 1-7 | 2-8 | 3-5 | 4-6 | 9-15 | 10-16 | 11-13 | 12-14 |
| 7 | 1-8 | 2-7 | 3-6 | 4-5 | 9-16 | 10-15 | 11-14 | 12-13 |
| 8 | 1-9 | 2-10 | 3-11 | 4-12 | 5-13 | 6-14 | 7-15 | 8-16 |
| 9 | 1-10 | 2-9 | 3-12 | 4-11 | 5-14 | 6-13 | 7-16 | 8-15 |
| 10 | 1-11 | 2-12 | 3-13 | 4-14 | 5-15 | 6-16 | 7-9 | 8-10 |
| 11 | 1-12 | 2-11 | 3-14 | 4-13 | 5-16 | 6-15 | 7-10 | 8-9 |
| 12 | 1-13 | 2-14 | 3-15 | 4-16 | 7-11 | 8-12 | 5-9 | 6-10 |
| 13 | 1-14 | 2-13 | 3-16 | 4-15 | 7-12 | 8-11 | 5-10 | 6-9 |
| 14 | 1-15 | 2-16 | 3-9 | 4-10 | 5-11 | 6-12 | 7-13 | 8-14 |
| 15 | 1-16 | 2-15 | 3-10 | 4-9 | 5-12 | 6-11 | 7-14 | 8-13 |

Again, the key here is to break down cliques while at the same time strengthen the bonds among all of the players on the team. The effects are powerful, allow players to understand that everyone matters, and extend to life skills outside of the team in terms of learning to get along with people of varying backgrounds, personalities and experiences.

**Examples of some good team-inspiring movies/movie clips (appropriateness depends on the age of your team):**

*A Few Good Men (1992)*

*Any Given Sunday (1999)*

*The Blind Side (2009)*

*Braveheart (1995)*

*The Breakfast Club (1985,)*

*Brian's Song (1971)*

*Chariots of Fire (1981)*

*City Slickers (1991)*

*Coach Carter (2005)*

*Field of Dreams (1989)*

*Freedom Writers (2007)*

*Friday Night Lights (2004)*

*Gladiator (2000)*

*The Guardian (2006)*

*Hoop Dreams (1994)*

*Hoosiers (1986)*

*Invincible (2006)*

*Jerry Maguire (1996)*

*The Last of the Mohicans (1992)*

*A League of Their Own (1992)*

*Lucas (1986)*

*The Mighty Ducks (1992)*

*Miracle (2004)*

*The Natural (1984)*

*The Patriot (2000)*

*Pelada (2010)*

*The Perfect Storm (2000)*

*Remember the Titans (2000)*

*Rudy (1993)*

*Seabiscuit (2003)*

*Stand and Deliver (1988)*

*Varsity Blues (1999)*

*Victory (1981)*

*We Are Marshall (2006)*

- "DO YOUR THING" – Develop customs unique to your team. *Blue Thunder* had a tradition in which all I would say is "do your thing," and the players gave every other team member a high five and a "good effort" at the end of training sessions and matches. It is another way for all players to bond, to realize that every player is valued and respected, and to both celebrate good moments or break the tension in more adverse moments. Other team traditions involve team meetings, match day warm-ups, team outings, community service, college mailings, taking team pictures, end-of-season notes, share time, tee-shirts, etc. If you continually inspire new ideas and creativity among your players, then you will also develop critical thinking, reasoning, and innovative skills in your players, all of which have important transformations onto the soccer field.

- CELEBRATE TOGETHERNESS AND COMMUNITY SERVICE: Promote regular team activities and get-togethers. "Team bonding" shouldn't be artificial or necessarily predictable; teams can celebrate events beyond just birthdays. The hope is that, ultimately, the team will want to get together naturally on their own and by their own volition. Just for fun, our teams have participated in team dinners, ice cream runs, bowling, roller-skating, beginning-, mid- or end-of-season gatherings just to get together, ceremonies, a whitewater rafting trip, an outdoor adventure program, a trip to an amusement park, picnics, movies, college visits, an Irish step-dancing lesson (which offers exceptional footwork and fitness cross-training during a lighter part of your season), a self-defense class (valuable for self-esteem, confidence, and an improved mentality on the field), players-only get-togethers, and community service activities.

One team took referee license courses together, which was not only another way to get together, but also a way to give back to the game together. Another team sought out teams in areas affected by adversities such as 9/11, hurricane and tornado disasters, and poverty and found ways to help from writing cards to donating funds and items. Our teams also sought out activities such as donating to a family during the holidays or volunteering to help less fortunate children with learning to play soccer, read, and so on. One of the teams participated in a Leukemia & Lymphoma Society benefit and as a result of being touched by cancer through family and friends, the team ended up being the top fundraising team in the DC/Virginia region. Another team "adopted" a child in Africa through an organization.

Some clubs and high schools have ongoing activities that also help teams come together for the good of service so it is worth asking around in case you are looking for other ideas. Some of these activities could include working with the Special Olympics, collecting gently used equipment to donate to those less fortunate, or volunteering time to clean up local parks, roads, and neighborhoods where teams may or may not train and play matches.

Setting examples through participation in community service activities helps players to understand the community and ultimately the world around them. As Millard Fuller said, "For a community to be whole and healthy, it must be based on people's love and concern for each other." What greater way to inspire teamwork and citizenship than to participate actively and regularly in community service together.

Every team is different; be sure to pick activities in which the whole team can participate. Involve parents and family members on occasion, too. Also allow parents time to get together; parents can contribute positively to a culture of development so fostering healthy connections among the parent body is important. Encourage parents to be unified on the touchline in support of the team. As a coach and leader of your program, you may have to consistently educate and inform parents about the need for unity and positive support of the team through regular communication. Strategies and suggestions regarding team management are also in this book.

Generally, the resultant team spirit of togetherness inspires players and their families to invite each other to their special occasions, too (e.g., birthdays, religious events, family celebrations, graduations, weddings, etc.), where more team community foundations are laid. Just as a staff that can get together off of the field, a team and all of its members that can get together in healthy, positive ways off of the field will help build experiences that ultimately translate to excellence on and off the field for life.

Communication – Regular communication is essential for players, parents, and your staff. Give feedback to players on their game in such a way that they feel comfortable seeking feedback on their own. My style is to remain calm and respond to situations rationally rather than emotionally. I believe that, through this approach, a player can learn to accept constructive advice, develop intrinsic motivation to improve, take ownership and responsibility of their game, and request suggestions for improvement. In general, an effective coach – and leader – empowers players to take charge of their experience through model behavior and communication. My staff and I try to give individual progress reports regularly in informal (e.g., evaluation sheets, occasional "report cards" and feedback notes) and formal settings (e.g., conferences, player-parent meetings). Please see the appendix for these evaluation tools.

We also give updates to parents. Invite parent involvement and share your long-term vision, big picture perspective and team philosophy with them. I write team families an occasional email update that sometimes includes a motivational quotation or story to help everyone maintain a healthy perspective. By modeling regular and effective communication, you will hopefully encourage positive communication among all members of your program, which includes staff, players, families, friends, fans, administration, and other community members. Positive communication builds team chemistry in the sense that everyone is engaged, has a voice, and will be listened to.

Communication is an important topic and is also included in other sections of this book because it is necessary in several aspects of coaching. Especially for youth players, it is important that the coach educates players that the "giver" and "receiver" of information must understand where each is coming from and not overreact nor create unnecessary drama. Thus, over-communication can also be a problem since you do not want to create a culture of panic, overreacting or continuing crises. For example, I regularly give examples to the team such as the following scenario:

During a match, Player A tells Player B to "step up and mark tightly." Player A needs to learn how to give urgent directives in a pressure situation in an effective and positive manner, while at the same time, Player B cannot be so sensitive as to think Player A is being mean or bossy. The two players are on the same team, we are highly competitive by the very environment we have chosen, and the bottom line is that we need to get things done and perform our roles to the highest of standards all of the time as we all strive for excellence.

Sometimes volume is needed to reach players farther away, but tone has to be monitored with commands given on the field. These are teachable moments that should be used regularly to foster healthy communication.

- GROUP PARTICIPATION: When we have team issues to discuss (e.g., attendance, community service choices, team goals and standards, role identification) or new players try out for our team, we find a way to involve all team members. Depending on your situation, you may or may not always have that luxury. However, I think it is a mistake in that so many decisions are left out of the very players whose input would actually help various situations and help teach players to make decisions, listen to each other's opinions, and ultimately become stronger individuals and teammates by both sharing their own voice and listening to what other team members are thinking.

Team meetings are excellent ways to listen to players' voices so everyone is used to hearing them on the field, too. Team meetings are also terrific opportunities to show video clips, read articles, share quotes, group-think, and more. Such meetings also proved powerful for several athletes who were far ahead of their peers when it came to participating in other environments such as ODP, high school, college, or regional/national events because they had a leg up on ideas such as communication, leadership, decision-making, team chemistry and problem-solving.

*Statement from a former player on team activities:*

*"The team bonding exercises you introduced to us in the hotels on long trips brought us closer together as not only teammates but also as a family. Even if the activities themselves were a bit random, we always ended up laughing and spending quality time with each other! Your sense of humor and your ability to relate to teens was unbelievable considering ...we could be a bit difficult at times!"*
— Cannon Clough, UNC-Chapel Hill '18

The power of having the team, for example, give feedback on tryout players is that when a selected player ultimately joins the team, she or he has already been accepted by her or his peers. On some of our club teams, our tryout process was generally a slower one, since we believe a first impression or reputation are not the sole basis for a decision; we evaluate whether the player and her parents understand our team culture and can add to it in positive ways. A mistake that I often see is that a coach simply makes a decision after a first impression, based on player reputation, or without any sense of how team chemistry may be affected adversely. In the case of a couple of situations where timeliness were issues, I know we sometimes rushed to decide yea or nay on a player when we really should have listened to the team, while at others, the team had wanted to stick up for a given player that may have not been a top choice among the staff. Another mistake I see in how club-wide tryouts are handled is that there is a loss of connection to team, and player placement is decided on one or two tryouts — if a player puts on a good show for two sessions, but flops for the season or if a player is perhaps affected by other factors for a tryout and has an "off-session," potential mistakes that affect individuals and the team as a whole can be made.

However, there is value in team input; a good coach can both listen and lead in matters regarding player selection with effective communication. Ultimately, the coach must communicate that it is possible that not everyone may be happy with every decision, but in every situation, decisions are made with a team-first mentality and the team must support the decision made. Additional information on tryouts and player selection/evaluation is given in this book. Please refer to the appendix for various worksheets used for team meetings.

Every player on the youth teams that I coach participates in each match and of course, this is a topic a coach must communicate well during all parts of the season (pre-, during, and post-) since various games and situations will come up that may not allow for every player to play as much as one would hope. There may be a rare occasion where a player might not get into a match for various reasons, but obviously playing time is increased promptly. Each situation is unique, but if a coach selects a player to play and that player upholds their responsibilities, then the player ought to play in matches.

We play a variety of formations, and we try to play players in more than one position. Full participation ensures that no player (e.g., ones who wouldn't otherwise have had an opportunity to play) loses interest or questions the point of working hard to earn playing time. If only the same eleven players participated in each match, they could become complacent. Alternatively, the team could suffer if one or two of the "starting eleven" were away (e.g., injury, illness, college visits). Thus, a good team will want to excel in player development, avoid complacency, encourage healthy competition, and strive for depth since it is incredibly valuable going deep into a season. So, coaches must inspire a healthy team culture where every player feels like a part of the team's results. Remind players that they represent their families, team, club, league, state association, and nation. Delineate individual roles and challenge team members to bring out their special qualities; I've used effective analogies (e.g., a potluck — what are you bringing to the table?) and just about any team-oriented life experience (e.g., a firehouse, emergency rescue team or a ship's crew) where each person's role is critical for the "team" to succeed.

Your active role as a coach is important too. Challenge players to be better — it can be tiring, but you will earn and maintain the respect of your players. See additional sections in this book for ideas such as testing players and keeping score to foster healthy, competitive environments. As a coach, go to courses and clinics to pick up ideas, but go further — find good mentors and learn from excellent coaches in soccer and in a variety of sports, read books and articles, watch matches, and more. It is ultimately your choice to grow, stagnate or decline in terms of your personal coaching development. Be active in striving for improvement, as that will inspire your players to do the same. With such actions, you will ultimately create and lead a team culture for player development.

EMPHASIZE TEAM, BUT RESPECT INDIVIDUALITY — Everyone is different and what is exciting about a team sport such as soccer is that it is a powerful feeling to come together from different backgrounds, experiences, strengths and weaknesses, character traits, likes and dislikes, and various personalities. It is part of the fun in terms of the "potluck" analogy in which everyone brings something to the table for everyone to partake in. Thus, a coach must bring that desire and spirit out of each player regularly and if successful, a healthy, winning team culture is created. If you are lucky to have a full team where every player is already intrinsically motivated, an exceptional human being, team-first oriented and actively seeking self-improvement on and off the field, then your only role as a coach is to get out of the way. However, most of us are not that lucky. With my teams, I use the potluck analogy often along with a quilt analogy in that everyone can control what they want their piece of the "quilt" to look like and if they make a good overall effort, then they will ultimately be rewarded.

During one of our winter "off-seasons," we kept a running points total during training sessions when we played 4v4 and 8v8 indoors and outdoors. Each player accumulated points based on assists, goals, headers, 50-50s, 1v1 battles, tackles, etc. At the end of the winter, we found a reason to have a team activity in which we had a potluck. The top eight players on the team were served by the bottom eight. The activity is just one example of many in which competition is emphasized in a healthy environment that results in a fun team activity that does not humiliate anyone. Proper communication along the way is important, while at the same time, the activity also reminded the team of our important potluck analogy.

Players on my teams have regularly gone on to win honors on their various teams (college, ODP, high school, etc.). Likewise, they have always attracted strong interest from college programs because of our excellent player development reputation. When any recognition is given, the team is always praised as it is each member's contributions that affect each other's standing, opportunities, and honors. Of course, my staff and I will also give individual praise separately so that the team and the individual are complimented appropriately.

Along with encouraging team-first systems, it helps to be creative in recognizing individual qualities in order to get to know the team better — this could be as simple as identifying player roles, traits (e.g., artist versus soldier), or strengths. For example, before a match, we may go around the group randomly and take turns saying what another player does exceptionally well. Coaches should be creative in recognizing individual qualities within a team construct. One such project that I produced for one of my teams is in the appendix.

LOGS AND JOURNALS — The power of the written voice is an exceptional tool that also allows players the opportunity to express themselves and for the coach to learn more about each player. It is critical that the coach understand and value each player for the person they are, not just for the particular soccer skill they may be good at.

I have used logs for training purposes, such as having players keep track of fitness and "off-season" workouts, or to meet certain juggling standards that the team expects. Please see the appendix for more specific ideas on training logs. Using logs holds players accountable and helps to create a positive team culture for player development since everyone is held to a high standard. Therefore, they will ultimately want to improve both intrinsically (to simply get better) and extrinsically (to not let teammates down or fall behind and risk loss of playing time).

With more recent teams, I have used worksheets and journals, going so far as to purchase journals and require players to keep them in their equipment bags where we could write in them or share what we wrote at training sessions, matches, or team meetings at traveling events. This is particularly handy in true club systems where coaches are rotated often and one may not inherit a group with the same team philosophy or individual accountability that I hold to very high standards. Thus, to get to know the players and understand team constructs, I quickly try to imprint my team culture via team meetings and written journals. Some of the topics that I have had players write and share include:

- Draw a picture of leadership
- Write your own letter of recommendation
- Top 3 Team/Individual Goals for this season/for soccer in general
- Why do you play soccer?
- If you dedicated this season to anyone, who would it be and why?
- Five words that describe the ideal family
- Design the cover of the journal
- Evaluate your performance (training session or match)
- List what you do exceptionally well
- Describe your role on the team
- Say one word about each player
- What makes a good teammate?
- Any questions for the coaching staff?
- Complete the sentence: The team is....

Other writing instruments can be created by the coach. For example, I often have a worksheet ready for team meetings with various statements and questions for players to work on (see appendix for examples of team meeting forms). It is important to listen to each team member's voice, rather than just the captain's or a select few. In meetings, for example, all members should be made to feel comfortable speaking up. However, the reality is that some feel more comfortable than others and thus, one can learn a lot by individual conferences and by writing exercises.

ESTABLISH TEAM VALUES — With the team members, determine a set of core values and standards; we have used UNC's set of values (see appendix for an adaptation), John Wooden's *Pyramid of Success*, and "*Lessons from Geese*" as platforms to build each team's respective identity in addition to maintaining a trademark of effective individual player and team development amongst my teams. These values should include lifelong qualities — loyalty, equity, teamwork, long-term vision ("the big picture"), integrity, character, discipline, self-improvement, respecting differences, sportsmanship, professionalism, punctuality, commitment, responsibility, decision-making, sacrifice, leadership, competition, and much more.

As an example, I asked one of my recent teams to decide on five words that they believed the ideal team should be about. Just giving the team this instruction alone was powerful in that it brought the team together to seek input from each other, listen to each other's thoughts and opinions, and ultimately to come together to decide on five words. The team decided on Passion, Unity, Dedication, Discipline, and Effort, and I used the words on every team email so that players (and their parents) would be reminded of our core values. It worked out well since we could always point to the words as standards that we met or fell short during various situations throughout the season.

Standards of conduct may pertain to eliminating swearing to keep a professional atmosphere and avoid getting into an unhealthy language issue that can result in a yellow card in a match or unnecessarily instigate poor behavior from opponents. We also encourage being on time for all activities, cleaning up after training sessions and matches, helping with equipment, recognizing referees and tournament staffs, reading books/articles, participating in community service, and more. Ultimately, the goal is for each player to become a champion on the soccer field, and more importantly, in life. Players who are true to the team's core values, keep up with the standards of play and performance, and contribute positively to team culture show tremendous growth as people; they're the ones who will be effective players, citizens, and leaders.

Former players confirm these ideals; some examples include that they regularly give back to the soccer community by officiating matches and coaching youths, they volunteer in numerous community service activities, and they become captains/leaders of their teams. In addition, I have several alums who are teachers and coaches themselves, and what a powerful legacy that is when your players continue the values that you implement and go on to add more of their own positive, constructive and healthy qualities.

Training and Match Standards — Be sure to plan your training sessions — have a theme, but don't be too rigid either. In planning training sessions, think about keeping all players active, ensuring fitness components, working on fundamental technique, and helping players execute skills under pressure. **Note:** In national credential programming, planning sessions emphasizes four pillars of physical, technical, tactical, and psycho-emotional-social components. Have players compete, personally try to impact the team's play, and reach out to each individual during the course of every training session. After players master a set of skills, teach finer points, increase pressure, demand speed of execution, and emphasize higher-level details of play. Remember, if you've run out of things to teach, then you've stopped being an effective coach and should pass your team on to someone who will take them to another level. Such a deficit in coaching, teaching, and leadership abilities is why many advocate for rotating coaches every year or every couple of years, but to me, that is a statement on the lack of ability of coaching staffs. Yes, it is nice to hear "other voices," as some advocates like to frame the rotation of coaches, but if the voices are not at a high enough level for player development, then that only shortchanges the player. I have coached teams successfully for multiple years because the experiences and abilities to teach advances and provides leadership for the long-term with effectiveness combined with the savvy to bring in "voices" and newness for continued growth; the results speak for themselves. However, as another elite coach who also has such abilities and credentials said, coaches like us are "dinosaurs," meaning we are reaching extinction.

Keep score and statistics often (as adapted from the UNC system) to encourage competition and track growth, and constantly strive to improve players' play and impact on the game. Additional information and numerous details are given in later sections in this book, in addition to easy-to-adapt charting sheets for training sessions.

One example of how these player development ideas had such a powerful effect was when I took on a U18 girls' team, BRYC *Attack*. The team was a strong team with several talented players, yet it had never reached the state cup semis in its career. With a lot of the ideas and philosophies described in this and other chapters of this book, along with only a few weeks in the transition to my coaching practices, the team went on to achieve several tournament accomplishments, a run of approximately a 50-match unbeaten streak, a Director's Cup National Championship, a USYS Snicker's State Cup Championship, and a semifinalist finish at the USYSA Region One Championships.

The same effect occurred when I took on a U16 team in North Carolina, as the team had been successful but never had won a state championship out right (i.e., without penalty kicks) and at U15 prior to me arriving, the team finished only as a state semi-finalist. Using many of the ideas and philosophies shared in this book, I again led a team to their first outright state championship along with several indicators of positive player development. The team beat their highly competitive and talented rival 1-0 in an intense state cup final, whereas our team had just lost to the very same team 3-0 earlier in the season.

Both of these two teams also followed in the footsteps of the older team that I mentioned, *Electra*, to place several players into highly competitive college (and even pro) programs and garner various successes in other environments such as high school and ODP soccer during their youth careers.

So, ultimately, whatever the program's mission statement (that you choose to define) will be, be sure it will have lasting, positive, powerful effects. If the philosophy and vision are strong, clear, and maintained, along with a healthy, active team culture for player development, then anything is possible.

*Reflections:*

- In what ways do you value team chemistry?
- How would you describe the culture of your team, including players, staff, parents, friends?
- How do you actively promote good team culture in training sessions, matches, and off of the field?
- What traditions does your program have?
- How do you choose teams for scrimmaging?
- Do players compete in training and strive for excellence?
- Do you treat all players equally?
- When it comes time for player input, do you listen to voices of all team members?
- What kinds of activities and service does your team participate in together?
- How effectively and professionally do members of your program communicate with each other, including players, staff, parents?
- What lasting qualities do you want the players whom you coach to leave your program with?
- Do your training sessions include goals toward player/team development?

# CHAPTER 3

## LEADERSHIP: MANAGING SUCCESS AND OVERCOMING ADVERSITY

*"Great leaders are almost always great simplifiers, who can cut through argument, debate, and doubt to offer a solution that everybody can understand." – General Colin Powell*

Leadership can make or break an organization. In the case of soccer teams, clubs and programs, sound leadership is especially important if the entity is to survive long-term. Along with understanding your vision and creating a strong team culture for player development as explained in the previous two chapters, a successful coach needs to develop his or her own leadership style that is effective while at the same time develop leadership in those he or she coaches and works with. With sound leadership, an organization can manage success and overcome adversity to continue to grow and reach its goals.

## UNDERSTANDING LEADERSHIP

Leadership is one of my favorite topics to both discuss and teach. There are plenty of resources available to acquire a textbook understanding of leadership and to be inspired to lead other people. However, one of the best teachers of leadership is certainly experience. One has to not just understand various theories associated with leadership, but he or she also needs to have a practical understanding of leadership. Minoring in management in college and ongoing reading involving the topic of leadership have helped me to have a very good understanding of leadership. In addition, the practical experiences of teaching and coaching for well over twenty-five years in each profession have been invaluable in helping me to become a leader in our sport. I regularly engage in conversations about leadership and other coaches have asked me often about issues regarding team management; I always point to qualities of understanding and teaching of leadership as immediate places to begin when assessing a team's health. Applying knowledge successfully is much more important than simply acquiring knowledge; not doing anything of value with this knowledge or worse, being ignorant about relevant practices and understandings and not making any attempt to seek out necessary knowledge to excel spells doom for any program.

In simple terms, leadership is accomplishing tasks; it involves motivating others to take action to meet goals that the leader wants to realize for the group he or she leads. Effective leadership gets others to understand why the actions must be performed, believe in their importance and demonstrate motivation to take action for the greater good of the group. In the situation of a team, each player knows that the team's success depends on his or her effort to take action.

All humans desire belonging and identity; thus, in the team construct, players need to know their roles and feel a sense of importance in the larger group. If players feel involved with decision-making and are given opportunities to be in charge, they will be motivated to live out the team's mission statement on and off the field. For example, if team loyalty is an important value, then a well-led team will have all team members, including staff, players, parents, and friends, speak well of the team not just when the team gets together, but in environments away from the team, too. A well-led team will stand together humbly when it reaches successes *and* in solidarity through adversity.

Likewise, a good leader will not only model good behaviors during the season(s) he or she coaches specific teams; other positive outcomes of a good leader include inspiring players to pursue the game at higher levels, give back to the game through teaching, coaching, officiating or other avenues, and continue on as a loyal, enduring member of the "family" he or she leads. It is always a joy to see current and former players work with current teams and to hear about their lives as they pursue playing and coaching as passions.

In addition, an elite-level leader will get involved to make positive change(s) in his or her sport, be a voice to stand up for what's right rather than politic to gain self-indulging advantages, and he or she will also contribute to coaching education so that other coaches benefit from his or her knowledge and experiences. Having a positive life-long impact and influence are much more meaningful by-products of effective leadership as compared to simply having a title of coach and being a self-proclaimed "leader."

## LEADERSHIP QUALITIES AND SKILLS

Think about leaders you admire. What kinds of qualities do they have that help them to successfully lead others? Chances are that if we took an informal survey of leadership qualities amongst all leaders who we admire, we would come up with the following characteristics: action, passion, determination, visionary, honor, integrity, commitment, goal-oriented, innovation, inspirational, resolve, community-building, values, trusting, look you in the eye, endurance, caring, knowledge, perspective, experience, wisdom, intelligence, humility, accessible, openness, equity, expertise, motivational, courageous, compassion, high standards, collaboration, strategist, competitive, encouragement, assertiveness, role model, provides direction, organization, empathy, problem-solver, decisiveness, confident, flexibility, dedication, sense of humor, consistency, discipline, magnanimity, good communicator, listener, accountability and effort.

A leader must have resolve and a steadfast commitment to what is best and what is right for the group, regardless of what others think or say if what he or she believes is indeed optimal in the big picture. One should not sacrifice nor compromise integrity, honor, valor or principles, but instead, he or she must be comfortable and secure to carry on. In terms of coaches, a lot of them remain average or even substandard because they are unaware of what it means to lead or they say/do what is perhaps convenient at the time, rather than what is right and enduring. I have seen many coaches, particularly inexperienced ones, be more concerned with risking popularity rather than staying focused on making tough decisions that keep the group moving toward genuine and sustained excellence. Some decisions are certainly very difficult, but it is the responsibility of a good leader to exercise decision-making appropriately with conviction. Ultimately, such a coach gains respect and chooses this path over popularity. A good leader also needs to remember that the greater good and what is right are important to stay aligned with throughout the journey of leadership.

Leaders who are in the public eye will sometimes have various challenges brought upon them by various factors including rumor mongers, jealous outsiders, the media and other assorted distractors. It is important to have a good support system to help manage such distractions that surely can drain one's energy or just be annoying. In the bigger picture, the leader with values will win; there is no question that the one who stays true to what he or she believes in, focuses on what matters and stays attentive to leading effectively will stay among the elite and the others will fade.

Perhaps the area that tests leaders most, including soccer coaches, is change and its assorted decision-making features. Leadership is all about change because to create a sense of urgency, one needs to get others to change, whether it is a small or large adjustment, their attitudes, behaviors or actions. If one is to feel a need to change, adopt the direction and vision of the group, navigate adversity, and rise to expectations, the leader must strive to manage change as effectively as possible. The higher the level of the leader, the greater the expectations become: the team members should not fear the leader or change, but instead embrace change and the competition to be stronger than the opposition.

Examples of change regarding coaching soccer include playing time, roster changes, position selection, formations, roles, captain choices, starting versus substituting, disciplinary issues and player-impact. Change can sometimes be difficult because of variables that include people's reactions, experiences, acceptance of change, empathy quotient, comfort-level, flexibility, understanding of team-first mentality and other assorted factors. However, a leader must do his or her best before, during, and after the change; sometimes it can get "messy," but ultimately people need to understand that challenging moments can be turned into positives and sometimes change is simply necessary.

Adversity tests all of us in our lives, and it is often said that one's character is revealed in adverse moments. Especially in the case of working with youths, change is a teachable moment that can be valuable in the bigger picture of life. Adults must take an approach that keeps everyone's self-worth intact and encourages empathy, responsibility and moving on. There is neither a need for animosity nor personal glory in terms of trying to prove who is right or wrong; trying to rationalize with the irrational is futile. The youth learns so much more when encouraged to try to take an adverse situation as an event to make one stronger and that ultimately he or she is in charge of his or her attitude concerning how to move on.

Certainly, we can all think back to situations involving change that made us stronger for it. Though it may have been difficult at the time, one can only try to look back at the problem-solving process, evaluate strategies that worked or didn't work, and move on. In many cases regarding coaching, some familiar phrases that help me when communicating with team members include remembering "the big picture," "the team comes first," and that often, "it is personnel; it is not personal."

It is important to note that these qualities, traits and skills are associated with leaders many people admire, such as Abraham Lincoln, Martin Luther King, Jr., Mahatma Gandhi, Nelson Mandela, or Aung San Suu Kyi. The same qualities could be attributed to coaches/managers many people admire, such as John Wooden, Dean Smith, Bill Walsh, Joe Torre, Sir Alan Ferguson, Anson Dorrance, Tom Landry, Jose Mourinho, Vince Lombardi, Bill Belichick, or Phil Jackson. Such lists of leaders and coaches are certainly debatable regarding greatness, but that is not the point here.

Looking at the list of characteristics, one can easily see common traits among these leaders. Obviously one can pick out skills where some of these leaders may have not been as strong when compared to others. When people talk about leadership, they also mention less savory characters who led groups with "success" if one measures success based on outcomes. However, it is not my interest to mention the negative aspects of humanity, as I would much rather focus on the positive to encourage effective leadership and professionalism in coaching.

A leader must also have good interpersonal skills to effectively assess what is being done, make adjustments as necessary to meet objectives, delegate responsibilities, and offer feedback to inspire excellence. Empathy and wisdom are important in understanding why people behave the way they do, their sense of values and what makes them tick. Communication is such a key factor and no matter how hard one tries to communicate, chances are there will be misunderstandings occasionally. However, one can always work on his or her communication skills, verbally and in writing, with individuals and groups. People will have different views, but I believe it is important to communicate honestly and not try to hide the facts.

This strategy can sometimes be difficult to hear for those who I work with since I can be blunt, but I don't believe in fluff or superficiality so the other piece of advice is to remember to stay true to what you believe in. Even if some choose to not want to listen to the truth, you are better for it in the long run if you adhere to your core values.

If one is to inspire others to take action, then certainly how one relates to others is a key feature of leadership. In addition to these qualities, a good coach should develop good teaching abilities, marketing skills as appropriate, and evaluation instruments to effectively assess not only players and fellow staff members, but him- or herself.

No one person is going to score high in all leadership qualities, but one can reflect often and seek appropriate feedback to continue to improve leadership skills. A good leader also knows where he or she falls short regarding leadership skills and instead of ignoring these areas, he or she tries to improve in these areas and hires staff that complements him or her well as a leader. Commentary on forming successful staff partnerships is included in the next chapter on team management.

## LEADERSHIP STYLES

First, a coach must understand good leadership qualities and the associated skills listed previously. The next step is to have an awareness of leadership styles and their associated strengths and weaknesses. There are many styles of leadership, but they mostly boil down to three:

Authoritarian (autocratic) — the leader is in charge of making all decisions and commanding actions taken by the group he or she leads.

Leader

Subordinates

Delegatory — the leader decides what needs to be done, assigns tasks independent from what he or she does and gives free reign for subordinates to execute plans.

Leader

Subordinates

Participatory (democratic) — active promotion of joint partnerships to participate in decision-making and task execution where the leader and subordinates are seen as equals; includes effective use of persuasion and motivation.

Leader

Subordinates

Of course, that offers a simplistic explanation of leadership styles, but it is offered as points to consider, rather than as a full course in leadership. Obviously there are other constructs to consider such as the notion of "co-leaders" and various intermediate stages of leader and subordinate functions.

It is important to understand leadership styles to reach understanding with those around you; such people include assistant coaches, athletic directors, board members, and directors of coaching. One must understand the decision-making focuses of each entity; as such, the leader does not need to micromanage but instead lead effectively to optimize the performance of each part of the overall organization. If you can, try to become familiar with coaches from where your players come to you and coaches to where your players are going upon leaving your program.

Reaching a consensus of which skills to apply to each situation is not always possible, but being aware of the leadership styles of yourself, staff and other coaches involved with your athletes helps one to better understand the psychological construct of the players you coach. Remember that, in general, a shared value system of common purpose and direction will be much more effective than one that is scattered and unfocused.

An effective leader will ultimately have to use various components of each leadership style based on experience, proficiency and situation. Striking an appropriate balance with thoughtful intent, effective communication and active reflection has a greater chance of succeeding in the long-term as compared to being uninformed, ignorant or deficient in leadership qualities, skills and styles. A few suggestions regarding when to use each style and assorted strengths and weaknesses of each style are listed in the following tables.

## POSSIBLE COURSES OF ACTION

| SITUATION | LEADERSHIP STYLE |
| --- | --- |
| Time is short, decision needs to be made immediately by the leader, experience and proficiency of subordinates are severely limited to produce desired results; leader may lack certain leadership skills such as communication, inspiring others, or willingness to yield control | Authoritarian |
| Time is available, decision is still in the hands of the leader but actions are taken by subordinates completely; subordinates have expertise and experience to carry out tasks; educating, trusting and building responsibility among subordinates to take action; leader encourages problem-solving through discovery and communication; leader may lack decisiveness, organization, and expertise in some cases so instead turns it over to subordinates | Delegatory |
| Time is available, good dialogue between leader and subordinates is always present; trust, expertise, open-door policy, consistent exchange of ideas, motivation via allowing for autonomy and decision-making within the team construct; constant exploration of finding balance between leader and subordinates in various aspects of team progress | Participatory |

## STRENGTHS AND WEAKNESSES

| LEADERSHIP STYLE | STRENGTHS | WEAKNESSES |
| --- | --- | --- |
| Authoritarian | Fewer viewpoints to consider, less dependent upon time, gives leader full command; gives appearance to subordinates as to who is in charge; pays homage to the old adage "if you want something done right, then do it yourself." | Limits creativity and problem-solving development; players are unable to make decisions on their own since they are used to having decisions made for them – they freeze when encountering new situations; develops fear in subordinates and can foster resentment, dislike and distrust; leader is distant from subordinates; lacks long-term positive effects |
| Delegatory | Allows leader to be in control of decision-making and task assignments so he or she does not have to worry about communicating vision; gets tasks off the plate of the leader and into the hands of the subordinates, inspires problem-solving situations for subordinates; trust is given by the leader and appreciated by the subordinates since they are free to get tasks done in ways of their choosing | Leader gives full reign to subordinates to carry out tasks without interaction – possible miscommunications, misunderstandings, and misconceptions may arise as to the details, expectations, standards of actions; may put too much control in subordinates' hands who may be inexperienced and give the leader (and in turn the organization) a bad result and reputation |
| Participatory | Leader and subordinates have a close connection, regular communication and strong rapport since the subordinates feel valued and respected; develops decision-making, problem-solving, and creativity which results in long-term adaptability when subordinates face new situations; greater motivation to excel since subordinates are accountable for decisions and actions; feeling of ownership leads to responsible actions and loyalty to organization; has long-term positive effects | If leader is not respected, can blur lines; can appear confusing as to who decides what and carries out what task if communication is unclear; inexperienced leaders lose respect in this environment since they lack expertise, decision-making, vision, or familiarity with managing success and adverse situations that may arise |

Please note that the terms "strengths" and "weaknesses" are used with the full knowledge that one may view a style's strength as a weakness and vice versa. It is important for coaches to reflect upon what they believe is appropriate, necessary and expected given various decisions, timeframes and situations.

### Types of Leadership Actions

Generally, leaders take action to make a transaction or a transformation. Both are considered rational actions by leaders and can be viewed as attainable by any of the three leadership styles. It takes a skillful leader to navigate the balance between styles and to bring forth leadership skills to keep the group moving forward. A leader whose choices are more of the transformation variety wwill ultimately create a healthier organization that succeeds in the long-term.

Transaction: If a person in a leadership position would like to get something done, he or she will effectively "give something to get something." For a coach, this translates into forming a system of rewards and punishments. As examples, consider the coach who uses naming a "player of the match" to try to encourage all players to go after being the best player in a match. Or, examine the coach who believes that punishments in terms of fitness exercises will motivate players to do something well or deal with the consequences. This form of leadership action may get things done, but it is not as lasting in the long run since it forms a more extrinsically motivated athlete. It is sometimes used with less-experienced teams, age groups that are more concrete in their developmental stages or groups that explore various actions, but need a more immediate change.

Transformation: A leader using this type of action is after long-term, positive and effective changes that ultimately help subordinates become proficient problem-solvers, team members and good leaders. Through regular reflection, role identification, assessment of strengths and weaknesses, participation in setting goals, open and honest evaluation, an aim toward developmentally appropriate standards, maintenance of high expectations, and encouragement of intrinsic motivation, the coach effectively transforms the athlete into a leader on and off the field.

There is no secret that transformational leadership actions are far more effective than transactional ones. As indicated in the previous chapter, having a well-defined, solid understanding of and commitment to a personal statement, coaching philosophy, and team mission statement forms a wonderful platform upon which to exercise transformational leadership.

To get people to do something they previously did not think was possible transcends transformational leadership and is truly extraordinary. People often ask me what makes my teams attain long-term excellence and sustained success on and off the field. Sometimes parents may ask what I may have said to inspire a particularly competitive training session or highly entertaining match. In both cases, I give credit to the program created by all of us, and I respond by saying that I was successful at getting into the heads and hearts of the players. Such a notion is critical for having a positive coaching impact and overall long-term effect.

## DEVELOPING LEADERSHIP IN OTHERS

For an organization to reach long-term success, an effective leader must learn to develop leadership skills in team members. In any team, some members may be better leaders than others and some may show greater capacities to lead than other team members. This is natural, but a coach can still assist with each individual's journey toward his or her leadership potential.

To teach leadership to players, it is important to give them a problem-solving model and real issues to work on. A standard problem-solving model involves the following steps: identify the problem, devise possible solutions, take action to solve the problem, and evaluate how effective the process was in order to make adjustments for future problem-solving situations. Such a model is useful in a variety of situations, whether solving a mathematics problem or trying to navigate through an issue on a team. Examples of situations on a team could be a problem in communication between two players, promptness in beginning training on time, or letting doubt creep in as to whether or not players are giving it their all for the team all of the time. A coach with good leadership skills will use these situations as teachable moments through discussion, writing, team or small-group meetings, or individual conferences. Helping players solve problems effectively will ultimately strengthen their leadership skills.

### Types of Leadership Roles for Players

Regardless of a designated captain position, players should be educated actively with intention on the types of leadership roles they can fulfill. Such roles include:

- Lead by example/role model
- Lead by action
- Lead by communication verbally (speech or writing)
- Lead at the front, back, or middle
- Lead on the field and off the field
- Lead by bringing people together
- Lead by coachability
- Lead by smarts, tactical skills or creativity
- Lead by fitness or strength
- Lead by technical skills
- Lead by caring or empathy
- Lead by effort/work ethic
- Lead by attitude
- Lead by perspective

A coach should also offer opportunities for players to make decisions. I feel very good about my style, which is complemented by my educational experiences, as I have helped develop leaders in life – not just as captains for teams they go on to play for, but solid citizens who impact communities positively.

## MANAGING SUCCESS

A team is surely bound to attain "success," whatever that "success" may be. Some teams handle success very well, while others clearly do not. A coach with effective leadership skills will help his or her team to manage success so that players strive to reach another level, rather than be content with what they have achieved and fade into complacency.

An example of "success" could be measured by a championship as certainly winning is associated with excellence. No leader of a program ever sets out to coach a losing team. However, there is more to success than just a measure of results. If a team wins a championship in soccer, was it lucky to have a good draw, did it catch a stronger team on a bad day, or have good things happen on the other side of the bracket to have a perhaps easier time than what might have been? Did the team employ good tactics, just hang around for their opponent's mistakes, or catch a break in a match that otherwise may have not happened? Did the team just have a good run with the right players and put things together for a few matches? Did the team win in penalty kicks? I am proud to say that every state or other championship we have ever won at whatever level was never on the basis of penalty kicks (PKs). Have we won on PKs? Absolutely, we have and several times in various matches throughout the years. In fact, one of the most memorable PK shootouts was to advance to the regional finals long ago. Yes, PKs are a part of the game and it is important to prepare teams for these situations. However, I have seen coaches who brag about wins and personally, I would rather not base successes on PK shootouts, which essentially are commonly thought of as no better than a flip of the coin and recorded as a tie in the NCAAs (National Collegiate Athletic Association).

This is not meant to take away from a team's winning a championship, but the intent is to understand that winning something of significance outright and more than once separates elite teams from other good ones; beyond winning, a coach should have greater depth to his or her team goals.

*A statement from a former player, one of the best "warriors" I ever coached:*

*"The character development Ashu taught me during my years with Electra have proved to be very valuable. I have started my own fitness company, and I think my success has been based off of my ability to relate, push, and encourage people to do physical things they never thought were possible. Ashu never let us believe we were capable of giving anything less than our maximum effort at all times, and that is a belief I carry with my own clients today. If you are always trying your hardest, you will always get results. Ashu never settled for half effort, teaching us never to settle for that with ourselves or others. Now my clients feel the same way."*

– Laura DeSimone, BRYC *Electra* U9-U19 (Elon University)

Sure, my teams celebrated championships and promotions to higher levels of competition – many of them, but we developed a humble culture that kept things in perspective. We never believed we had arrived at our best and thus, we cultivated a desire to be better as a team and as individuals. We challenged our teams to not just win one championship so outsiders could say we got lucky, but instead we worked hard to win a second or more championships. In addition, it is helpful to establish a culture that enjoys working hard for meaningful results so that success is appreciated and not taken for granted. As I had one team after another with successes of their own, it became expected that the next team would "win," but we had to fight complacency and help each team find its identity and appropriate challenges to avoid any sense of entitlement.

Just because one of my older teams won did not mean that one of my younger teams was going to win also; the success would have to be earned. In addition, as each player garnered several high school honors and college placements, we always shared the news with the team as an honor for everyone; as a result, we had much more joy on our teams when celebrating success rather than the back-biting, jealousy, and negative behaviors commonly associated with other programs.

More importantly, and perhaps the best piece of advice to give to coaches, players, and teams, is that we emphasized excellence every day, one day at a time. Although we had long-term goals that included an aim toward certain placements and championships, we also outlined objectives to reach those goals in addition to setting short-term goals and objectives along the way. If you coach, player development should always be a goal, and if your team's players are not developing, then success has not truly been realized. Thus, the information throughout this book is valuable in developing a winning mentality to create champions and not just winners of championships.

*A statement from former parents on leading a team:*

*"Player development - You have always focused on the long term. Not that short steps aren't important but what goals can be set for the long term - 1 year from now? 2 years? how about 5 years from now? For soccer players, is there a plan after club, high school, or even college?*
*Humility - For an elite soccer club, travel was a big part - competing at various tournaments. My daughter and family's first tournament was at Ottawa, Canada after moving to Virginia from California. There were others of course - Florida, Delaware, North Carolina, and Arizona just to mention a few. Ashu taught not only the players humility but even the parents. When traveling (he said), you not only represent the soccer club (Braddock Road Electra) but you also represent the state of Virginia. Humility went far for players and parents, as college recruiters watched matches and enjoyed the humble nature of the program. College process - Prepare the player as much as you can. Have the player ask questions to the college coach and not the parents. It is the player that coaches are recruiting, not the parents. Have the player talk with former players that have graduated from high school and are now playing in college about their process."*

– Wing and Sou Lee (parents of Erica, BRYC *Electra* U15-U19 & Boston University)

Before you begin coaching a team or before the season for a team you already coach, you should verbalize what success means for that specific team in increments.

Choose age-appropriate measures. Performing this exercise helped me coach teams for multiple years since I had several goals for each seasonal year, part of the season, training session, and match.

For example, success might be finishing with a .500 average, finishing top four in the state, or it may mean winning a particular championship. Okay, so what if the team accomplishes or does not accomplish one of those types of goals?

Does it mean the team was successful and is in position to continue to be successful? Has the team learned tactics, improved technical skills, enhanced passion for the game, become a powerful group that understands both individual effort and team concept? Has each player learned what it means to compete and be on a journey that ascends toward excellence and ultimately greatness? Are good habits formed and motivation sparked for each individual to become better on and off the field and for the team to carry their game to another (higher) level?

Clearly the better programs are ones that sustain excellence and to do so, they must manage success with grace, humility, clarity, vision, determination and dedication. Result-oriented goals are good, but surely they are only just one part of defining success. As legendary tennis player Arthur Ashe put it, *"Success is a journey, not a destination. The doing is usually more important than the outcome. Not everyone can be number one."*

Coaches must have development as a measure of success both in quantity and quality of players developed and who move on to next levels. In addition, coaches should not claim that they have developed players they have not really developed; otherwise it is just grasping, false advertising and ultimately shallow.

Elite clubs and coaches are ultimately not ones who simply recruit, buy, or inherit talent, but ones who lead sustained success in player development.

*A statement on humility and the big picture from a former soccer player on a HS team.*

*"Ashu made me want to be a better player and a better person. He leads by example and coaches with integrity. The influence he's had on me extends beyond the pitch. It's shaped me into the woman I am today. I always felt he instilled in his players a healthy balance of hard work and reward with the big picture in mind. It was roughly 99% hard work and 1% reward. But that 1% felt so good and kept us hungry and honest. Looking back now, I wish I had more of that mentality heading into college. I think I was given two contrasting schools of thought (Ashu's vs. my club coach's) and that both shaped me into the athlete and player I was, but his approach translated in the college world."*

– Crystal Thune (Syracuse University)

## OVERCOMING ADVERSITY

Just as a team will reach success, it will surely come across adversity, sometimes indirectly and in small doses, and at other times, head on and in full force. A well-led program will overcome adversity and its members will find strength in and support from each other. Adversity can take on many forms depending upon the team's composition and thus, when I coach a team, I try not to make certain situations any bigger than they need to be because there are just going to be life moments that have far greater importance than a soccer match. Too much of today's society wants to make everything seem like the greatest thing ever (hence the overuse of the words "huge" and "epic") or that the world is collapsing; everything is neither "the best" nor "a crisis." Save those labels for more meaningful situations and your team is likely going to be able to handle adversity well. Players, families, friends, and coaches should keep things in perspective, maintain a more even-temperament, and remember to emphasize the team concept as a family or community.

Common adverse moments that affect most teams at some point include situations such as a defeat, playing time, conflict, misunderstanding or miscommunication between personnel, relegation or demotion, changes in player or staff personnel through leaving or joining, and injury. Though one cannot control some people's reactions to such adverse moments, a coach should help the team prepare to deal with these situations as best as possible.

In addition to managing team adversity, coaches must help individual athletes through situations such as long-term injuries. Helping players to regain their mentality, confidence, team connectedness, physicality, competitiveness, and skills is a necessity. I have had some players on past teams get injured in activities outside of our club team's schedule (e.g., high school sports); as a result, I always worked hard to address all areas to bring the player back appropriately.

As an example, one club player I coached was a highly recruited, versatile athlete who sustained an ACL injury in a high school match during her junior year, a critical time in the college recruiting process. To support Christina, I had an older player who had gone through the injury phone and email her to offer reassurance that the injury was temporary and that her career was still alive and well. I phoned coaches and likewise, received reassurance for her that she had already been seen and will continue to be on the radar, as such injuries are common. Likewise, I was already familiar with the injury, surgery, and rehabilitation processes so talking with her was encouraging. Her family and teammates also provided the strong support necessary for her on the road to recovery. Per the doctor's and physical therapist's (PT) guidance, Christina began attending our team practices, even if all she could do was watch, then slowly jog and gradually get back into agility exercises with and without the ball. I remember her dedication in returning, as I would spend extra time between team sessions to throw in clock, mirror, and ladder exercises. She began to warm up with the team with confidence in performing exercises, and obviously she worked out on off-days with and without her PT. Eventually, the time for her first team training session arrived, and I made her play in a no-contact grid; her confidence grew as teammates passed the ball to her and she would execute skills to be a part of exercises. Her knowledge of the game stayed current as she was on the bench with us for matches and of course, reading the game improves when one is not just playing it, but also watching it.

The most emotional moment came when Christina played her first match with us after approximately eight months; she sat on the bench for the first half, and ten minutes into the second half, after warming up, she came to the midline where I was standing and said "I'm ready." Her teammates encouraged her during her shift and hugged her when she substituted out. She was all smiles.

*In Christina's words:*

*"I began playing soccer for Ashu at the age of 9, at the very start of my travel soccer career, until I was recruited to play in college. My teammates and coaches on Electra quickly became my family. Through these years, it is safe to say that Ashu was a foundational influence on my development as a competitive Division 1 athlete. What I remember most as a young girl playing for him was the commitment to practice, repetition, and training that he required of us. No victories were won without long hours and hard work. There were expectations of excellence and dedication, and of course loyalty and encouragement.*

*One of my personal memories and most challenging moments was recovering from an ACL injury during prime recruiting season in my junior year. There was a great deal of emotion for me during this time, as it was hard to ignore the uncertainty of what was to come, and how I would reach my future ambitions. I don't ever remember there being any uncertainty from Ashu. As I worked back to playing, he steadily guided me, preparing me, pushing me, and ultimately leading me back to competing at the level I had left. Fittingly, Ashu was there through the last stages of my career as well, and perhaps what I consider to be the pinnacle of my career and culmination of years of hard work. He traveled to Cary, NC for the NCAA Division 1 Final Four to watch me play for my Princeton team against UCLA."*

– Christina Costantino, BRYC *Electra* U9-U18 (Princeton University)

There are definitely moments that one cannot prepare his or her team for, and those situations remind us where athletics is in the bigger picture of life. Such adverse moments may include a player being taken off the field in an ambulance or other medical emergency involving doctors and hospitals, a death of a teammate, family member or friend, divorce of a player's parents, or other life moment that comes unexpectedly and affects people with a great intensity and depth of emotion. I am fortunate that the teams I have led have been able to survive such situations together and thank goodness for having positive team cultures to do so.

Regarding individual adversity, I know I have had moments where people did or said things that I certainly didn't agree with. Or in other cases, they were acting out of ignorance, malice, or jealousy.

Many of us who have been successful get hit with that, but essentially, it is garbage to be thrown out with the trash. A helpful image for such situations is from the movie *Gladiator* (2000) where Maximus is constantly antagonized by Commodus. Rather than stoop down to his level, take the bait or let evil enter his heart, Maximus stays strong, focuses on what matters most and moves forward with honor. Perhaps more peaceful images come from the great leaders Mahatma Gandhi and Martin Luther King, Jr. — two men who had every right to give in to hatred, but refused to because they believed love was the better path.

In addition to self-reflection, I recommend that coaches have discussions on leadership issues and connect with colleagues to have a clearer understanding of leadership effectiveness. Connect with coaches, teachers, business people, and leaders in a variety of other fields to educate yourself about what works and what doesn't. Along with a plethora of books and articles on leadership, there are many instruments available online to help one assess his or her skills, style and capacity to lead. The access to such information is easy, and I also encourage reading books and articles on the topic, whether directly, or by situational experience. In fact, because leadership is so crucial in a variety of arenas, full leadership courses are offered at universities, online, and as seminars. To help decide about specific leadership concepts regarding coaching a soccer team, I have included helpful ideas and materials in other parts of this book.

Two terrific stories of leadership involve teams that I coached for several years in Braddock Road Youth Club (BRYC) in northern Virginia, a highly competitive soccer region. Coaching teams for several years generally doesn't happen in club soccer anymore, for good or bad, as discussed in the chapter on player development. However, both teams demonstrate long-term successes as the result of highly effective leadership. One of the teams was BRYC *Electra* (U11-U19) and the other was BRYC *Blue Thunder* (U9-U17, which I continued to assist through Fall U18 after having moved from VA to NC).

### The Story of BRYC *Blue Thunder*

*BRYC Blue Thunder began playing travel soccer as a U9 travel team. Five of the U18 team members (thirteen since U12) along with staff had been with the team since its formation at U9, displaying commitment and loyalty that are often rare in youth soccer. The team entered competitive league play as a U11 team and was placed in the lowest division, Division 5, at the start of the spring U11 season. Even with such a start, the team persevered and adhered to long-term goals, including the development of technical and tactical skills, increasing opportunities to play at a higher level, and ensuring that players had fun both on and off the field. By the spring U14 season, the team had made it to the top division, Division 1, and into the Virginia (VYSA) State Cup Semifinals.*
*The team continued to develop and endured the competitive college showcasing process, much in the same tradition as "big sister" teams, BRYC Electra and BRYC Attack that I coached; these two graduated teams placed 50-plus players combined into collegiate programs around the country. More importantly, because of the way players were developed, they mostly played for all four years in college, garnered various honors, were selected to be captains, and excelled in college. The teams played in competitive showcases well-attended by college coaches, competed against college players/teams via scrimmages, and the numerous connections to collegiate programs also helped players attract multiple opportunities.*

*When Blue Thunder finished as U18s, the team was still in Division 1 and finished as a five-time VYSA State Cup Semi-finalist, along with winning/placing in numerous tournaments in addition to placing players in collegiate programs. Though the team may have not been as successful as their older sister teams in terms of state cup championships and numbers of players moving on to more competitive collegiate programs, Blue Thunder accomplished something exceptional in terms of conquering the odds of a team beginning in Division 5 and reaching the status of an elite team in the state in their age group, not once, but repeatedly. The team continued to grow and for us, it was not just about soccer; the experience meant much, much more. In addition to league and tournament accomplishments, the team performed community service activities together. We all were very proud of the girls for being the top Virginia fundraising team for the Leukemia & Lymphoma Society's Kick for Cancer Program. We also won the inaugural Vanessa Pean Invitational Cup, which was established to honor the memory of a young student and soccer player killed in a tragic car accident. The Vanessa Pean Foundation provides financial assistance to underprivileged children in Haiti so that they may obtain an education. In addition, the team helped teams in Manhattan (after 9/11) and in Florida (after hurricanes), along with wrapping gifts for underprivileged families in the local DC area. Lastly, numerous girls gave back to the game through officiating and coaching younger players.*

*Like their older sister teams, Electra and Attack, Blue Thunder was mentioned in* Vision of a Champion *(Averbuch/Dorrance 2002) and the* United Soccer Coaches Soccer Journal *which highlight long-term development success in youth soccer. The team was also recognized by UNC Coach Anson Dorrance at UNC Team Camp where he pointed to the team as a good story in youth soccer development. Due to my past involvement with Region One ODP, then-USWNT Staff Coach Jeff Pill did a training session with Blue Thunder. In addition, the team was selected to participate in studies by UConn (explosive exercises' relationship to physical improvement) and UVA (team leadership) doctoral students. The team won sportsmanship certificates in nearly every season of league play since U9, demonstrating the commitment to sportsmanship and positive citizenship on and off the field. The team participated in activities year-round, as we enjoyed our time together – as players, families, and friends.*

*Our final tryout advertisement read as follows: "BRYC Blue Thunder is a highly competitive U18 girls' travel soccer team based out of northern Virginia. Our emphases have always been on development, competition, fun, team chemistry, sportsmanship, effort, leadership, and long-term goals. We play up in league (Division 1) and travel the country to play in tournaments. Our girls are well-prepared to compete at high club soccer levels, in addition to College, ODP, and high school play."*

The experiences of leading two different teams each for seven-plus years was certainly a source of pride, a topic of conversation in coaching circles and had very positive effects on other programs and teams I have worked with throughout my coaching career. Of course, I share credit with the good staff members and families who were committed to the "big picture" vision I had and continue to have for the teams I worked and work with.

Unfortunately, I believe there are some people in leadership positions who have titles, but who don't lead, inspire action, nor are effective in making improvements and adjustments, or reaching for excellence. They run out of ideas or inherit positions they are not ready for. If they are not experienced nor tested in adverse situations, they are sometimes ill-equipped to lead. Similarly, there are well-qualified, competent coaches who are not always promoted into good positions and their valuable voices are not heard as much as they should be. It is always better to take the high road, accepting responsibility as a leader and choosing excellence whether one has a leadership position or not.

Some of the older readers of this book may remember the movies *Braveheart* (1995) and *A Few Good Men* (1992). In the former, there is an exceptional scene involving the leadership evolution of Robert the Bruce and his relationships with his dying father and the rising rebel William Wallace. Being a privileged noble, Robert comes to realize the effectiveness of Wallace's leadership style.

*Note:    This is not an endorsement for all of Wallace's actions.*

There is a scene in the movie where Robert tells his father that he admires Wallace's passionate fighting and ability to inspire others to fight for freedom. In another scene, Wallace teaches Robert that "men don't follow titles, they follow courage... If you would just lead them to freedom, they'd follow you. And so would I." The earlier scene where Wallace is on his horse giving the "freedom speech" is one I used with older teams in the past, as the scene is clearly one of the most inspirational in terms of taking important action now rather than having regrets in the future.

In *A Few Good Men*, the closing scene is one I refer to a lot when coaching athletes; in it, Kaffee tells Dawson that "you don't need to wear a patch on your arm to have honor." In much the same way, I never chose to give my teams the captain armbands so common, even at youth levels — perhaps it is an external symbol that attracts attention and holds deep value for some. However, just because one wears a captain armband, it does not automatically mean they are a good leader (or the only leader); I believe that good leaders don't need symbols suggesting that they are.

*A statement from former soccer parents:*

*"We are very thankful to have had Ashu as a part of our lives. He was dedicated to our daughters and to our team. He encouraged our girls to live up to their potential while always striving for excellence. The ultimate goal for Ashu, above winning and prestige (though that was an inevitable result), was always for each of his players to mature as people and soccer players who set high standards for themselves and constantly demonstrated the dedication, hard work, and commitment necessary to achieve them. We greatly appreciate Ashu's efforts and continue to see the impact of his efforts in our daughter's continued success."*

– Liz & Richard Gallivan, BRYC *Electra* U9-U19 (Katie, Boston College)

I am proud of the teams that I have been able to coach and, not to sound arrogant or cocky, they demonstrate excellent examples of leadership. My leadership extends to each player, involves the team as a whole: parents, friends, families, officials, coaches, staff, community, and all. We manage success and adversity well, and cultivating leadership in players is a strength of our program. Without being a good leader, my teams would not have come close to the number of successes that they have had on and off the field. Beyond championships and excellent player development, several players continue to give back to the game and coach; many are teachers. In this chapter, I have included just one example of background information about one of the teams, *Blue Thunder*, that I coached with effective leadership. I offer more examples, especially with *Electra*, throughout other sections in this book.

In summary, "listen to, learn from and lead" your teams. Set clear, attainable goals, empower people, know your strengths and weaknesses, accept that you may not know everything, know who you can trust, hold high standards of responsibility, accountability and integrity, find out each person's skills, encourage sharing of effort, results and credit, manage successes and adversities, communicate effectively, combat complacency and cliques, and continually strive for excellence.

*A statement from a former parent from BRYC Blue Thunder:*

*"Ashu Saxena: Coach, Mentor, and Friend. Some lessons are better learned years down the road...looking back and suddenly having that "AHA" moment. Many of Ashu's lessons have come to my attention in this way.*

*As parents we entrust to teachers, coaches, priests, etc., our most precious gifts...our children. Our strongest hope is that they may somehow value these children as their own. I remember being that parent so many of us are, thinking that the sun rose and set on my daughter (well didn't it?). In speaking with Ashu at some point during his tenure as her travel coach he said to me in so many words... "You have a favorite, it is your job as a parent and is expected, but I have no favorites here. I am responsible for all of these girls and their development." Although this seems blatantly obvious in retrospect, it was so earth-shatteringly significant at the time...and spoke volumes to me about the kind of coach we were fortunate to have mentoring our daughter.*

*Among the mini lessons, phrases, messages relayed by Ashu on a regular and consistent basis:*
- *His aim was the development of the whole player and whole person....development was always key. Other key phrases often heard and certainly branded in our memories as players and parents: The Big Picture, Balance, Team, Commitment, Integrity, and Sportsmanship.*

- *Our daughter was coached and mentored to be a skilled, thinking, team player by Ashu. She was treated with fairness, equity, respect, and consideration and modeled these same behaviors on and off the field. This was in sharp contrast to our son, two years younger, who was taught (by another less quality coach for a short time) to be a nervous, critical, selfish, and self-serving player and further encouraged to be demanding and deceitful in modeling the coach. Long story short: he lost his love for the game while our daughter flourished.*

*Ashu is many things and he conveys to his players many things...above all respect for each other and all of mankind. He builds confidence and character, independence, and perseverance in his players and this foundation is evident in everything they do on and off the playing field. Beyond my daughter's playing skills and ability, she was profoundly impacted as a person and teammate. This has been demonstrated and recognized in her experiences on her college team as well as with her classmates, workmates, friends, and family. We attribute a great deal of her positive molding to Ashu Saxena. He simply made parenting an easier, more rewarding endeavor."*

— Liddy Zarone, parent to Jordan Zarone BRYC
*Blue Thunder* (U12-U18, James Madison University)

*Reflections:*

- What does leadership mean to you?
- Who are the people you consider strong leaders?
- What qualities do you admire in leaders?
- How well does your leadership skillset mesh with your personal statement?
- What kinds of leadership roles and skills do you identify for and develop in your players?
- Does your team have strong leaders and if so, in what ways? Why?
- How do you prepare your teams to manage both success and adversity?
- Do you expect leadership from captains or do you try to bring out leadership skills in every player you work with?
- Do you have examples of teams you have led to achieve sustained success or are the successes one-time accomplishments?
- In what ways can you be a leader in soccer for your team, program and community?
- Do you take the perspective that you exist for your team or that the team exists for you?

# CHAPTER 4

## TEAM MANAGEMENT: PLAYERS, STAFF, PARENTS

*"A people that values its privileges over its principles soon loses both."*
*— Dwight D. Eisenhower*

A team needs to understand its mission, core values, leadership, and how each member is interconnected. In all soccer teams, there are special coach-player and player-player dynamics. If involved with a youth, high school or college team, then add in two more dynamics: player-parent and coach-parent. With most teams, at least one assistant coach is present so that system also adds to the overall structure that needs to be managed. What follows in this chapter are suggestions on how to manage those dynamics with commentary based on several years of experiences in a variety of situations. Some of the recommendations are perhaps obvious and some maybe not so obvious. However, it is my hope that the ideas shared in this chapter will help enhance your team dynamics and as a consequence, your team's performance. In addition, it is often valuable to have members of each group understand features of the other groups involved so I also suggest using the ideas below to have an honest and open discourse among all program members.

## STAFF

### *Selecting a staff for your team*

There is no question that a staff that can work together effectively can be the defining feature as to the success of the team. I have been in and observed a variety of situations; I cannot emphasize enough that key factors such as philosophy, values, experience, maturity, team-first mentality, reliability, credibility, knowledge, proficiency, expertise, loyalty, professionalism, humor, responsibility, respect, intellect and synergy are all important considerations when selecting a staff. You must consider your Personal Statement and Core Values, as explained in chapter 1, to assemble the best possible staff, especially when it is in your control. Each member will have varying levels of intensity in each area stated above, but hopefully the combination of talents of each staff member will provide a well-balanced and formidable unit to lead the team.

There is not a magic formula in assembling a staff since there are so many variables to consider: competitive level, age, emphasis (e.g., everyone plays significantly versus results first), season duration, and much more.

For example, if you are on your own in the coaching role, then you may have a team manager or other people who may be involved with team responsibilities. Or, take another case where two coaches are responsible for three teams in an age group for a club. Or, in the case where a coach leads the top team in a program (e.g., first team in a club or varsity in a high school), he or she will need staff members who are on the same page in terms of player development and day-to-day operations. The possibilities are endless.

A coach should understand his or her strengths and weaknesses along with his or her personality characteristics. In my opinion, the most successful coaching staffs are comprised of coaches who complement each other well, yet are still unified in moving toward common goals together. To use an analogy, it makes no sense to identify a destination if the staff members are moving in different directions — a group with good team chemistry will row as hard as they can for you, but if the mission is scattered and communication is unclear, then the journey is ultimately sabotaged, frustrating, and destined to be unsuccessful in the big picture.

Sometimes you may be limited in identifying personnel to comprise your "ideal staff" for all sorts of reasons: time, schedule, job, financial, credentials, requirements, location, and more. However, for me, what follows are two real examples of an "ideal staff," of which I had been fortunate to have for multiple years during my career while coaching club as a head coach and while coaching high school as an assistant. The grids below help to describe some of the qualities that, when pieced together, create a synergy that positively funnels to the players for a winning formula in more ways than one.

The ideas of role identification and complementary coaching are ones I believe in whole heartedly and have a lot of experience with; they are also concepts that all coaches should be aware of as they hire staff to form a program of excellence. The key idea is that differences are used to complement one another toward a common goal. Mutual respect, loyalty, and effort toward common goals are important to communicate about and demonstrate for the team and each other on and off the field. As examples of two very successful situations in my coaching career, consider the following:

Example 1: Club, Head Coach, three years in particular out of several years with the same coaching staff intact year-round; State Championship and Region One Finalist (lost in 2OT) among numerous other successes during the three "ideal staff" years.

| | Head Coach | Assistant | Assistant /GK |
|---|---|---|---|
| **Leadership Style** | In-charge yet open to feedback from staff and players. Steady demeanor, highly competitive, teacher. Psychological understanding/motivation. | Attuned to emotional excitements to balance steadiness. Adds pep and zaniness to balance intense, competitive nature. Communicate. | Diplomatic, focused, no-nonsense. |
| **Philosophy** | Team first. Player development is the top priority. Attractive & attack-minded play w/emphases on width and creating numbers for options off of crosses, combos, midfielder final passes. Creativity, technical/tactical skill development. Develop good thinkers/problem-solvers. Preparation for all situations via training is key. | Team first — "for the kids." Defensive focus on denying space/time and comfortable losing possession to clear balls out of defensive third. | Focus on GK primarily with added looks at shape in back and runs of forwards. |
| **Organization** | Planned/executed training sessions with adjustments as necessary, match warm-up, mini-camp charting, team meetings, player conferences, fitness packets, college process, handouts, worksheets. Parent meetings. Vision, constant assessment and preparation for the "big picture" to best benefit the players team-wise and individually. | Less organized, but able to maintain common vision and move toward progress for all players. Effective communicator for parents, too. | Not part of role so no need to put time in that aspect (and that is okay). |
| **Training/ Matches** | Active teaching/playing. Fitness. Fundamentals for all, as players play different positions in different formations. Compete. Mindset/goal-oriented at outset. | Spontaneous, repetition, drive to compete, lines or no lines develop. "Raise voice" if needed (emotion). | Balance in amount of planning and spontaneity. Player-mentality perspective. |
| **Substitutions** | Every player plays unless special circumstance. | Periodic subbing in shifts. | Sub as needed. |
| **Formation** | 1-4-4-2, 1-3-4-3 primarily; exposure to 1-3-5-2, modified 1-4-2-3-1. | 1-4-4-2 | 1-4-4-2, 1-3-4-3 |

Example 2: High School Varsity, Assistant Coach, four years in particular out of six years with the same coaching staff intact for pre-, in- and post-season; State Championship and numerous other successes during the four "ideal staff" years.

| | Head Coach | Assistant/GK | Assistant |
|---|---|---|---|
| **Leadership Style** | Authoritarian, but evolved toward consulting, open to ideas, suggestions, comments. Intense. | Easy-going, let loose, wild and emotional as necessary to balance intensity of situations and to offer different voice when needed. | Always prepared, offer ideas to support the staff, challenge team to consistently strive to be better; give emotional support to individual and groups of players as needed. |
| **Philosophy** | Defensive-minded, but flexible (e.g., some man-marking, some zonal). | Attack focus, especially generating out of center mid. | Shape in attack and defense; identify roles and responsibilities for individual players and lines. |
| **Organization** | Very organized on all fronts so assistants could focus elsewhere since both were outside of the school. | No need — outside of school. | No need — outside of school. |
| **Training/Matches** | Planned, teaching, a lot of choreography and set-play practice; had ultimate say, but good at consulting staff. | Mixture. | Small-group sessions, focus on lines or individuals and team as a whole. |
| **Substitutions** | Starters play, sub in reserves as needed; with staff input, evolved toward regular substitutions, which proved critical in keeping team fresh deep into season. | Quicker to sub players in/out with "mistakes," and comfortable with reserves going in earlier. | Did not have to manage this aspect, but encouraged use of subs for big picture/long-term vision of season, identify need for subs, prep players going in, debrief players subbing out as necessary. |
| **Formation** | 1-4-4-2 w/stopper-sweeper varied with zonal back four. | 1-4-4-2, 1-3-5-2 | Any; encourage constant improvement of focus, intensity, effort, desire regardless of formation. |

*Statement from a former player who played high school in a program I assisted with:*

*"Ashu has coached many successful teams. I had the honor of playing under him for four years at W.T. Woodson High School. We won two state championships and could have won four. Every practice Ashu reminded us that there was someone somewhere working harder. If we wanted to be champions we had to keep raising the bar in practice. There simply was no substitute for hard work and you could never be too fit."*

– Crystal Thune (Syracuse University)

Staff should meet at the beginning and end of the season, often during the season and off-season, and any other time when communication is necessary. Some issues to discuss include goals, ideas for training, formations, evaluations, communications and position considerations, and everything else that comes up during a typical season. Many of these issues are discussed in earlier chapters, and it is best to hash these out early and often to encourage effective communication and understanding. In addition to the characteristics and roles of each staff member, as given in the previous examples, one key issue to discuss is the area of responsibility – who does what to make the staff run as one cohesive unit?

### Staff responsibilities

Depending on your staff construct, your responsibilities will vary. As stated, when selecting a staff, each member should be clear on his or her role and specific responsibilities; the head coach must exercise good leadership to both communicate with and invite communication from all staff members in these areas.

Key components in the coach-player and coach-parent dynamics include evaluations, feedback, and meetings. Depending on each staff member's role, experience, level of involvement and skill, the head coach should determine how each of these components should be executed and by whom. For example, with some teams, I've been on my own and all responsibilities have fallen on me. In other situations, I have had capable staff members who didn't mind me taking charge because they simply did not have time to devote to these necessary, often time-consuming responsibilities.

In some cases, staff members may have not had the expertise to be as detail-oriented as I would have liked, and thus, I did it all. In any case, the head coach is ultimately responsible and thus, the quality, common language, precision and impact must reflect the coach's leadership toward the team's journey to excellence. Do make use of the talents of other staff members, as appropriate, as sometimes they may have a different voice, style, or manner that can positively impact players and be consistent with the messages you want to send.

Evaluations, feedback and meetings have greater impact when the staff takes on a team effort to execute each with professionalism and high standards of excellence. Coaches should communicate with each other so that everyone is on the same page and to avoid any misunderstandings. In long-term coaching situations, my players and their parents knew that my standards were at the very highest levels. Thus, they understood where my comments were coming from, regardless of the medium: evaluations, conferences, meetings, feedback, coaching points, and more.

Some of the challenges that I see with club situations is that common language, standards of excellence and objective ratings are lacking, particularly if the experiences of coaches varies from year to year. For example, a coach may think very highly of a player's skill, whereas based on my experiences, knowledge and expertise, I see the player as quite average or even below average given the age, level and player development progression I know should be occurring. Thus, improvements in club situations should be made to develop appropriate standards, expectations, common language and curriculum. In addition, club leaders must ensure the hiring of experts in key positions, education of coaches on how to teach skills at ever-ascending levels of challenge and continuous improvement of the overall level of player development understanding among all staff members.

On visits to professional clubs and their respective academies in England, such ideas of common language, expectations and curriculum are perhaps easier to attain for reasons offered in the chapter on player development in this book. In addition, there are some clubs in the United States that come close to this concept. However, we have a ways to go to develop; even experts in the UK believe improvements must be made there, too. With time, travel, communication, and exposure, forays into coaching education and player development in places such as Brazil, Spain, Germany and the Netherlands are increasing and offering other "solutions" for us.

### Evaluations/Feedback

With whatever situation you are in as a coach, you are in the fields of player development and player evaluation. Players must improve under your tutelage and likewise, you have a responsibility to constantly assess each player's progress.

I have been a coach of teams for several years, in addition to taking on the positions of mentor, evaluator for ODP (Olympic Developmental Program) and ECNL (Elite Clubs National League), as extra eyes for college coaches and camp coach; each position requires evaluations and feedback. It is important to communicate prior to, during and after the "season" in which you coach. Such communications involve what the coaching staff is looking for, ongoing suggestions for improvement and specific ratings used in various assessments.

When communicating with players (and parents, as applicable), I begin with "Ashu's Five Ss," a simple trademark scheme that I have used since very early in my coaching career with all ages and levels of play. The "Ss" stand for the essential qualities of a soccer player: skill, sense, strength, speed, and sportsmanship.

- Skills: technical skills in the general areas of first touch, dribbling, passing, receiving, finishing, heading, shielding, turning, tackling; being able to execute skills cleanly under pressure in a variety of situations with various body parts (left/right foot, as appropriate).

  *Note: I do not prefer to use the terms "strong" and "weak" foot.*

- Sense: tactical skills, decision-making, speed of thought/play, ability to read the game, creativity.

  *Note: Although creativity is often thought of as intangible or immeasurable, it is a trait that carries players to higher levels and one that we need to improve in player development programs.*

- Strength: physical toughness; includes but not restricted to athletic components such as size, strength, endurance, durability, vertical leap.

  *Note: I do not consider size a weakness if the other components of strength and the other Ss are sound enough to overcome lack of size or physical strength.*

- Speed: obviously, if everything is equal and two players are compared in terms of running on the field with (technical) or without (physical) the ball at distances of 10+ yards, then naturally the

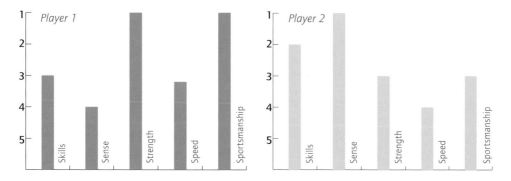

faster player wins out; speed impacts games and is perhaps more genetic than teachable so we look to that quality as highly desirable; quickness, agility and explosiveness are included.

- Sportsmanship: psychological qualities — respects self, teammates, coaching staff, opponents, officials, program; includes attitude, understands team concept, accepts role(s), gives maximum effort, competitive, intensity, dependability, responsibility, training mentality on and off the field, motivated to excel, able to do what's right not just when someone is watching; warrior.

An average player may be strong in two or three of the Ss, a very good player in three or four, and a weak player perhaps only one (or none). A truly elite player may be excellent in all five, or he or she may be off-the-charts exceptional in two or three of these areas and relatively strong in the others. Certainly we can think of well-known players who arguably rate exceptionally high in some of the areas: Xavi and Messi in all with perhaps physical size a "weakness;" Wambach in strength, skills and sportsmanship; O'Reilly in skills, speed and sportsmanship; Dempsey in sense, strength and sportsmanship; Rooney in skills, sense and strength; Ronaldo in skills, sense, speed; and so forth.

As noted in the chapter on team culture regarding the analogy of a "potluck," encourage players to optimize their gifts and skills, aim to maximize their special quality or qualities, improve secondary traits and bring their best of whatever they can to contribute to every training session, off-day practice and match. As coach, it is your job to develop players of varying levels of the Ss to a strong force as one team to compete consistently with maximum effort and intensity. However, it is also the player's responsibility to work on what he or she can control and there can be a variety of other factors that may affect development.

The way to explain the Ss to players (and parents, as applicable) is to give them a visual, using your hands moving up and down to various levels (one of the best visuals is that of the old stereo systems where various sound frequencies are given when a song is played; of course, with today's generation, they don't have stereos so use alternate visual examples). As an exercise, describe the following two players, their roles on the team and coaching implications:

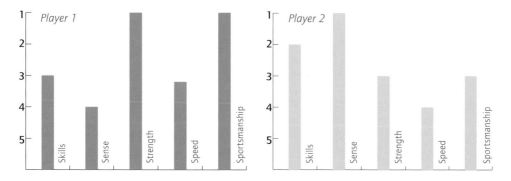

*Note: 1 is the highest (excellent) and 5 is the lowest (unsatisfactory).*

As players grow and develop, fluctuations in levels can also take place and thus, it is the job of a well-trained set of eyes with experiences at various levels to project such fluctuations through the normal course of events and to communicate with the player how he or she might improve in each of the areas to maximize his or her potential. In addition, the coach must design training sessions, occasional off-day small group sessions or off-day training guidelines to provide a roadmap for players to improve.

However, greater emphasis must be placed on the responsibility of the player to compete, improve, give 100% effort and understand their role in the player development process.

Another common communication device is explaining to players why they are on the field and what they need to do to impact matches. Hank Leung, a highly successful long-term coach at various levels, shared this thought process that I have continued to use with my teams for several years. Hank's essential framework helped break down the simple reasons why players should get playing time; my slight modification goes something like this:

- Score goals
- Create and produce assists and scoring opportunities
- Maintain possession
- Defend relentlessly when we don't have the ball to prevent the opponent from doing those things to us

Stepping outside my own general evaluation and feedback tools for a bit, consider evaluations in other arenas. ODP has long used player assessment schemes and standard evaluation forms, with the former implemented at district and state levels and the latter used at state and beyond. Sometimes, the initial assessments for sorting players into pools are no more than ratings of 1, 2, or 3 with 1 the top, 2 average and 3 the bottom. With the large number of players involved, this provides a quick, to-the-point initial sorting of players akin to what often occurs at summer camps to divide players into competitive, developmentally appropriate groups. However, is this the best method, is it precise enough and is there perhaps too much preference or bias toward certain players?

The Elite Clubs National League (ECNL) on the girls' youth side continues to develop its assessment tools and adjust various factors involved with player identification. ECNL uses a system whereby coaches scout matches to identify players at events, also known as showcases; their system rates players in the areas of athleticism, technical quality, attacking play, defending play, ability in the air, versatility, and overall with ratings of 1: State Team Standard to 5: National Team Standard.

*Note:* At the time of rewriting this second edition, US Soccer has launched the Girls' Developmental Academy. Because it is in its infancy, no commentary on its evaluation system is given here.

The challenge with such numeric schemes is obviously consistency, objective standards and experience. I have seen some outstanding coaches in both environments as a coach having worked in both. However, I have also seen some very average coaches with average players. Thus, if some coaches have not coached elite level players or are not experienced in player development, does that skew some ratings? The positive is that both US Soccer and US Club Soccer have realized that they need to send their staffs to more events and involve them directly in the identification and coaching phases. Both groups offer similar opportunities in terms of funneling top players to "training camps" or international trips where presumably the players work with strong coaches either on or closely affiliated with national staff coaches for the respective age groups. With smaller numbers, the feedback should be, in theory, much stronger, precise and detailed. When I have worked and work in these situations, I had always wished direct feedback could also be offered to players who didn't make the pool so that player development could still be the priority for all players returning year after year.

Perhaps US Soccer's Developmental Academy on the boys' youth side has an overall stronger system of evaluation since it covers both players and coaches, has existed longer, and puts the scouting in the hands of US Soccer staff. Richard Butler, DA Director for Charlotte Soccer Academy says, "We have a scouting system. Probably 80% of our matches are scouted by US Soccer per diem scouts. They look at individual players for the National team but also grade us (coaches) on style of play, coaching, discipline, facilities, attacking and defending play, team shape and how we deal with officials." Thus, part of the premise is that if coaches are held accountable, then the overall level of coaching rises, as does player development. Of course, the money inequity issue exists between the male and female sides in US Soccer, but even still, one wonders why US Soccer and US Club Soccer don't have similar programs that perhaps could unify evaluation processes. Regardless of the arena, helpful, lasting, specific, detailed, and individualized feedback needs to be provided for players in more uniform ways that help all players.

*Note:   At the time of writing this, the Girls' DA is just beginning, along with components of the ECNL on the boys' side. Thus, there are additional opportunities, yet further divisiveness on the youth soccer landscape. The coordination of player development remains to be seen.*

Obviously the player with the right mentality is going to work his or her best to continue to excel and if he or she is lucky, a year-round coach will be in that player's support system to continue to help progress player development year round. However, all players benefit from good feedback, as it is not only beneficial to improving play, it also provides valuable life skills in terms of accepting valid criticism, providing pathways to improvement and allowing players to make choices to better oneself. Be sure to give consistent, regular feedback verbally in training, conferences and meetings, but also use written evaluation tools because having commentary, objectives and goals in writing helps to keep a good record of progress. Lastly, a coach must use good judgment and discretion in terms of using evaluation tools; consider the age, level and experience of the team you work with.

*Please see the appendix for some evaluation tools that I use with teams:*

- Standard mid-season or post-season
- Match data
- In-season focus sheet #1: 54321
- In-season focus sheet #2: Improving/Raising
- Possession & self-rating
- Self-evaluation

Evaluations should also help coaches understand what they need to work on in training sessions in terms of player development. For example, throughout my coaching career, not only have I evaluated my own teams and tryouts, but I also have identified players for various situations such as ODP at regional, state and district levels, ECNL ratings at national events, assessments for mass player pool sorting, summer camp evaluations, feedback for coaching friends regarding their personnel and a variety of other situations.

Among the most common comments that I give to players include the need to develop and improve in the following areas:

- Passing/Finishing: power, accuracy, distance, surfaces (PADS) with both feet; consider pace, bend, spin/no-spin, texturing, angles
- 1st touch emphasis: being able to receive a ball with various body parts from a variety of situations (air, ground, bounces/no bounce, spin of ball, angles, speed, distance, etc.)
- Turning
- Tackling
- Shielding/back-to-pressure
- Vision: reading the game, decision-making, speed-of-play
- Being able to execute skills cleanly under pressure to keep a nice 1st touch control- 2nd touch flow rhythm
- Shooting versus finishing
- Dribbling/foot skills: developing one or two "signature moves," keeping the ball out of the opponent's tackling semi-circle
- Technical (with ball) and physical (without the ball) speed; foot speed, agilities
- Strength, power, quickness
- Heading, vertical jump
- Understand that improvement is within your control — attitude, choice, fitness, skills, communication, effort, determination, discipline, etc.
- Work-rate, effort, intensity, impact

Thus, it is no secret that training sessions are devoted to these areas from a very young age and all throughout a player's career.

## Meetings

The staff should be prepared and organized for team meetings. In short, off-field meetings should not be more than one hour for older players. On the field, fifteen to thirty minutes should be enough time to get your message across and if not, then plan an off-field team meeting depending on what you wish to accomplish. For example, if you are having a pre-match meeting or half-time, be sure that each staff member understands his or her role. One staff member might take on motivation and attacking, another goalkeeping and restarts, and perhaps another defending. Perhaps you may have a parent meeting, if applicable, and you may need to designate one person to talk about team-specific information while another staff member needs to focus on guidelines and roles for parents. Or, in many cases, you may be on your own and need to plan accordingly. In short, some things to remember for team meetings include:

- Be organized — begin and end on time; be professional — have an agenda and stick to it.
- Have a goal and a few objectives to accomplish.
- Be precise and have an impact in the message you give.
- Add variety by use of one or two of the following: articles, pictures, video, quotes, notes, diagrams, illustrations, music, worksheets, or whatever else you may have that is within your coaching toolkit; be effective in ways that show you care and have a point.
- Know principles from teaching regarding psychology, belonging, learning styles (e.g., visual, auditory, haptic, or kinesthetic).

- Understand people need to be motivated to return to your meetings, so be enthusiastic, focused, and respectful of their time; foster team chemistry so getting together is seen as a joy and not a task.
- Allow interaction — use partners and small groups to assign exercises, as necessary, but be sure you begin and end with the whole group.
- Vary the environment and have all members present.
- Give thanks for effort and support.

The meeting must have an impact and the message needs to be clear to all involved. Coaches need to understand that meetings build team chemistry and reinforce a positive culture that you establish. An example of topics covered in a pre-match meeting is given in the chapter regarding coaching methodology, as it is in the context of preparing a team for a state championship competition. Pre-match meetings should include areas of motivation and focus, tactics, brief scouting, team goals, objectives for lines (backs, midfield, forwards) and inspiration to maximize performance. There are many memorable pre-match team meetings, and it would be impossible to list all of them, as some of them are rather lengthy in addressing a variety of topics in motivation, personnel, tactics, brief scouting and much more.

However, some pre-matches have been as simple as showing a picture to the team at an appropriate time (e.g., family of ducklings crossing a road), sharing a song lyric, short reading of an article, mention of a poignant quote, or selecting a letter of the alphabet and encouraging that the players embody and exemplify qualities that begin with that letter during the match. For example, for the letter P, I have used pride, passion, power and precision. Or, with the letter C, use courage, creativity, composure and compete. Or, one can try an anagram such as PEAS, which might stand for Pride, Excellence, Attitude, Skills. Other ideas for team meeting sheets for players to work on during meetings that occur off the field that allow for positive interaction include ideas such as the following: "He or she is....": players fill out words for each player; at a future time, cut slips for each player with all of the positive comments.

| NAME | POSITIVE & PSYCHE-UP ADJECTIVES |
| --- | --- |
| Player 1 | gritty, never shies away from tackles, one of the top long balls on the team, fierce competitor |
| Player 2 | sweet, one of the funniest team members off the field, team player who likes to connect with everyone, great foot skills |
| • | |
| • | |
| • | |

- "I am the one who...": player fills out their qualities, then the coach can compile a list and see if the team can guess who each player is.
- Divide into pairs, work on a team topic (such as establishing team expectations); move to groups of four to compare and contrast player ideas; share with the whole team to come to an agreement.
- Goals and objectives for the team and individual players – write these out individually, but encourage sharing in pairs before discussion with the whole group.
- "Creating Community" peer evaluation – see appendix. This idea comes from UNC Women's Soccer, and its use has to be confidential and appropriate; otherwise, instead of building community, a coach may have a fractured team instead. Anson Dorrance and his staff are masters at using this concept with their women's college teams, and they adapt the version each year, per player input.
- Sit in a circle and take turns going around saying something such as a positive compliment to the person sitting to your left and right and one area that you wish to improve in about yourself.

**Parent meeting agendas that I have used include the following topics:**

- Welcome, reinforce team's five main words of identity.
- Brief positive comment about a recent training session or match.
- Main reason for meeting – pick 2-4 brief items (examples could be the need for volunteer positions, explaining playing time, season's goals, next few weeks' emphasis, college process or tryout information).
- Any club/program/team news.
- Upcoming schedule.
- Brief reminders about team mission/core values, how we can improve as adults, what players can do to have greater success, the need to continue to work together, communication.
- Thank you for the support, and remember "the big picture."

*Physical therapy, nutrition, training logs, etc.*
This is not a book regarding specific research and statistics in physical therapy, nutrition, training logs, or other such areas as there are numerous resources and professionals in these areas for such topics. The coaching staff should work together in determining an appropriate training program for exercises in and out of training and in and out of season to develop fitness, speed, and strength, as appropriate. Two main types of training are aerobic and anaerobic. In addition, coaches must pay attention to exercises with and without a ball, flexibility, agility, and power at varied levels of intensity to develop both aerobic and anaerobic capacities.

Note:   *As is often in youth soccer, there are various "trends," some of which endure longer than others. One such trend that we are in the midst of is to only focus on training with a ball, almost at the exclusion of being without a ball completely. However, there is also much research that indicates this lack of diversity in training has led to various detriments in terms of "burnout" and "repetitive use injuries." Thus, in various parts of this book, I have included what has proven to be successful in the long-term in terms of youth and high school programs that I have led and been a part of. Ultimately, you and your staff need to decide what levels of with and without the ball training fit in with your construct. No doubt, players in the US need to be touching a soccer ball more often to improve the overall level of skill, while at the same time, we should be conscientious that we are also preparing athletes for a lifetime of fitness, agility, and strength (in soccer and beyond). Lastly, there is something to be said of the mental toughness and challenges of endurance that various physical exercises without the ball provide.*

In high school, college, professional, and regional/national team situations, coaching staffs have "strength and conditioning" and related athletic training personnel on staff, or at the very least, they have someone on-call as a physiotherapist. Many club programs for youth soccer are often affiliated with a clinic so that coaches and families have access to their services. Coaches should identify appropriate personnel to help guide the team in the areas of nutrition, hydration, stretching, strength, fitness, speed, quickness, explosiveness, conditioning, first aid/CPR, injuries, rehabilitation, individual/team psychology and assorted other areas associated with exercise science.

There is so much information available via the internet, periodicals, videos, courses and books that coaches should learn as much as they can to improve awareness in these areas. Most coaches do not have medical training as doctors and thus, they should not try to take action in areas that they are not familiar with. At the same time, it is helpful to be aware of current information in a variety of areas to educate and connect with your athletes. Be sure the staff knows the requirements, regulations and expectations so that proper responsibility is carried out in managing these aspects for the team.

Personally, I consult with appropriate experts on occasion in the various categories, read and send out articles to teams, and refer just about anything to professionals in the field; especially in this day and age, one simply cannot risk liability so being aware of protocol is absolutely critical. However, I do motivate players toward getting "fitter, faster, stronger" regularly; information regarding this is found in the chapter about developing a year-round program for player development.

### Match reports, scouting, pre-match staff notes, post-match analysis, etc.

The coaching staff and personnel must know who is responsible for completing match reports after matches, devising pre-match notes, creating scouting reports, and documenting post-match analysis. Of course, the level of detail put into these items depends upon the level one is coaching at and on the staff available to assist in these operations. I have handled most of this on my own and make decisions as to the needs of the team and situation.

- Match reports should be relatively easy to fill out given good planning and completing items ahead of time. These items include the date, time, location, weather, field dimensions and conditions, personnel (starting line-up and substitutes), positions, formation, opponent information, and any other salient features. I have included an example in the appendix, and there are also others that I like to use. Be sure to have the diagram of the field handy, along with space for notations in each half of the match and over time, if applicable. Completing these reports promptly after each match helps gather information concerning what the team needs to work on, and the information gathered helps in scouting for when you meet the same opponent in future competitions.

- Scouting philosophy varies by coach, so be sure to understand what you and your staff expect in terms of scouting responsibilities. Depending on the age, level and particular competition, use scouting in a way that you are comfortable with. Too often, I have seen coaches go overboard and they concentrate so much on the opponent, they neglect to focus on their own team to properly prepare them for matches. While at the same time, I have seen coaches use scouting effectively wherein they point out formations, restart information, key personnel and strengths/weaknesses in simple, brief terms. The staff member tasked with this job should have a match report type of form available in which they can note this information, diagram line-ups, indicate substitution patterns and, when possible, chart information such as where shots are taken and by whom, pass distribution of key players, final pass trends and more. Obviously, video and computer software often play a part as does recruiting players when it comes to college, national and professional teams. Again, each staff member should know their roles in the scouting process and communicate effectively for the good of the team.

- Pre-match notes allow the coach (and staff) to anticipate situations in the match regarding personnel, formations, and an assortment of other variables. An example of a pre-match plan I used for a regional-level match with one of my teams is included here

*[Team name]: Notes for match on [date]; Coach*
*5:30PM, Location, Field dimension/condition*

FORMATION: Our team plays a 1-4-3-3 with one holding/two attacking triangle in midfield (1-4-1-2-3). The idea is to attack and make opponents adjust to us rather than the other way around. In addition, the two attacking CMs are not to be flat with each other, and out of the three CMs, one needs to show a bit away from the other two when we have the ball to change the point of attack.

*Note: I've told the girls that our formation is as such: when attacking, the triangle is one hold/two attack and when we defend, recover into two hold/one attack so that we have the mentality that we must get numbers behind the ball, eliminate outside shots/crosses, provide help, and delay the opponent's attack. However, given the personnel, match-ups, and match situation, we will occasionally invert the triangle to two hold/one attack explicitly.*

ALTERNATE FORMATIONS: Depending on the match situation, we can adjust into a 1-4-5-1 (withdraw the outside forwards from the 433 to help in OM) or a 1-4-3-1-2 (withdraw the CF to help in CM) — these are more defensive and counter attacking-minded formations for us. Can use these to protect a lead, withstand a barrage, or in fatigued situations. If we are behind and we have to just let it all out there for a goal, then we go into a 1-3-4-3 (a terrific formation for training and development, but we're not all there yet in terms of personnel, fitness, smarts) — we have used that effectively in a couple of matches thus far. Feel free to adjust, if necessary, but in any case, I emphasize with the girls that they have to be responsible, competitive, and intense in whatever formation we play and realize it's still soccer no matter what (they cannot shirk responsibility and dump a formation because they're not willing to work).

PLANNED STARTING LINE-UP AND SUBSTITUTIONS: I usually decide the starting line-up after the last training session of the week, and given that we still have training today (Wed) and Thurs, I will finalize a starting line-up on Friday.

*As of today, here is the plan for the starting line up in a 1433:*

| | | | |
|---|---|---|---|
| **Forward:** | LF: [Name] | CF: [Name] | RF: [Name] |
| **Midfield:** | ACM1: [Name] | | ACM2: [Name] |
| | | DCM: [Name] | |
| **Backs:** | LB: [Name] | LCB: [Name]  RCB: [Name] | RB: [Name] |
| **Goalkeeper:** | | GK: [Name] | |

*Early adjustment options:*

- Our DCM gets assignment of their highest ACM as well as cuts off passing lanes into the opponent forward's feet; our ACM2 gets the assignment of the opponent's more dangerous second CM since ACM1 is not as defensive-minded (though she's improving); invert the triangle so that DCM and ACM2 are the two DCMs and ACM1 at solo ACM, if necessary.

- Sub in [Name] to RCB, move RCB to DCM, DCM to ACM1 with ACM2, move ACM1 to RF (sub out); this may change due to LCB being sick today, but hopefully this gives us a good idea of the possibilities

- [Name] in to ACM1, ACM1 to RF (sub out).

- Switch LF and RF — put RF on the opponent's stronger OB to deny penetration ([Name] is fast, more defensive-minded), [Name] goes on the opponent's weaker OB to shred her and get to the goal.

- Regular substitution pattern:

- Optimal line-up has OFs [Name] and either [Name] or [Name] with CF [Name], [Name] and [Name] at ACMs, [Name] at DCM, [Name] and [Name] at CBs, [Name] and [Name] at OBs, and [Name] at GK.

- In this match, if the optimal line-up is in, [Name] or [Name] would substitute at OF ([Name] also at ACM), [Name] at ACM or OF, and [Name] at OB (or OF). [Name] is a smart player who provides a spark, and [Name] can play on either side in the B or F lines. [Name] or [Name] can go into CB, if necessary. [Name] is a good ACM also.

- If the opportunity is there, [Name] at CF (or OF), [Name] at ACM, [Name] at any F. However, all three cannot be in at the same time; give them a positive comment before they go in, tell them to RUN for the time they are in.

- If we are up at least by two with 15-10 mins left and things are going generally in our favor, then I try to find extra rest time for those with ailments, starting at the front and on down ([Name]-quads, [2 Names]-fitness, strength, [Name]-groin, leg soreness, [Name]-breathing, hips, back, [Name]-fitness, [Name]-knees, breathing) — can't be all out at the same time obviously due to numbers and so we still stay strong on the field to the end. An ideal win is 4-0 so we strive to get that, but given that we have a match the next day, the win is more important than a big score since we are not deep physically.

Not starting: [Name] (missed three training sessions since last match), [Name] (misc. ailments — breathing, back, hips, also missing Wed training where we are doing a lot of patterns/restarts), [Name], [Name], [Name], [Name]

Not playing: [Name] (injury rehab — not available)

Playing time: of the available players, [3 Names] are likely to not see as much playing time in this match and that is okay — they should be able to get some minutes in the first half, and that's fine, but we're going all out for the win, we can make up time in the following match, and they have not proven to be impacting players versus the more competitive teams. Of the three, [Name] has subbed in and proven she can be quite capable at CF — she's feisty, has decent speed, can find her teammates in one or two touches, and she shoots on frame well. Without those three, it leaves 13 field players who will get plenty of playing time.

Girls will meet at 4:30pm, take care of taping, cleats, shinguards, uniform, restroom, etc. They formally get together at 4:45pm, talk about instructions for the match, and then do our pre-match warm-up.

They should manage the warm-up on their own. I'll remind them about the routine and need for a proper, intense warm-up.

Parents: [Name] is the only one we will really talk with — she's our manager, has the cards/roster, etc., and she is a good one to ask if anyone has any questions. On the "negative" side, be aware of [Name's parents]. This team is still learning that not starting is not a punishment and not the end of the world.

Opponents: Basically, I don't really know anything about them; I don't let the history of scores/results influence me either. Like all regional opponents, they'll be strong and they have a few key players — one forward that is fast, athletic, crafty; two center mids that are likewise forces. I'll check with the girls/ DOC on specifics, but refocus their energies on today, not yesterday. They're starting to learn to take one match at a time the best they can so hopefully, we'll play well.

- Post-match analysis should be done promptly, noting areas for the team and each player individually to work on. Apart from assessing performance, look at effort, intensity, competitiveness as those are important qualities to evaluate consistently. Make good notes, recall specifics and be clear on how you communicate your analysis. As indicated previously, depending on staff numbers and level of coaching, you can delegate roles to staff members if the synergy and consistency of high standards are there to do that.

A note about the position of Team Manager(s): There are a variety of support roles that are covered directly by the staff, by support staff such as an athletic department or administrators or other layers of support such as in a club system.

In the event that you are in a youth situation where individual teams are responsible for administrative duties to keep the team running and a parent is needed to be a team manager, it is critical that you have a well-organized, responsible, team-first and objective person in this position to coordinate parent functions. I have been lucky over the years to have some very high quality adults in this role for my teams.

The role of team manager is too much for one person to do and thus, good leadership to encourage delegation and participation is needed. Make sure the roles are communicated to team members and parents before the season begins. With or without a team manager, some of the positions to coordinate for the team include:

- Manager: main person in charge of team administrative duties
- Treasurer
- Equipment/ball retrieval — occasional help at training/matches
- Team sportsmanship liaison — to help manage sideline, spectator behavior, communicate with the officials, if necessary
- Website
- Field coordination — scheduling
- Field set-up/take-down organization
- Fundraising — club and team-specific
- Uniforms/tournament tees
- Social (including team dinner/reservations)
- Team doctor, medical kit supplies, ice for matches
- Publicity
- Team history

- Community service
- Sideline "bench" or tent for the team during matches
- Hotel/travel coordinator
- Photographer
- Tournament applications/registration
- Directions
- Brochures for colleges

*Statement from a former team manager:*

*"Ashu,*
*You know how much I value your friendship and the fond memories of our time together on the soccer fields. I was especially proud to be able to be there with you in NYC when you were recognized by the USOC for your developmental coaching skills. It was a very special moment that I will always treasure. I always felt it was my job to ensure you could focus on coaching the girls while I made sure you had what you needed for practice or the match. That included being the "ball keeper" especially when Keith was punting the balls to the girls.*

*If there was one aspect that most impressed Sandy and me, it was your knowledge and preparation for the college process. The planning and preparation of the team handout, the mailing event to address and stuff envelopes and the handout and tracking process at tournament matches. Most of all was the result and reward of the process which achieved a very high success rate for girls going on to college. It all began with you setting high goals for the girls both on and off the field and for their parents to observe your high standards and expectations.*

*I feel like I could go on and comment on any subject. I still have all of the Electra documentation to include emails and would be willing to share it with you. Just let me know what you are looking for and I'll dig it out for you."*

— **Dave Banks, BRYC** *Electra* **Team Manager U9-U19**
**and father of Ashley (West Virginia University)**

I would not put a parent in charge of items such as match notes that are subjective in nature and carry sensitivity; coaching decisions need to stay as such. As leader of the program, you never want to be in a situation where if that person was not there, the team would fall apart organizationally. Likewise, you need to eliminate the appearance of favoritism, as perception versus reality can be tricky to navigate in this arena where parents are involved. Thus, as you get everyone involved appropriately, it builds the culture that you are creating in positive ways.

An example of a plan for home and away matches for high school (and perhaps some college) coaches could include the following:

*Note:* *This assumes the schedule has been set by the athletic director and all meetings prior to the season have taken place regarding coaches, players, parents, fans, school community and anyone else involved with the program. I also assume that schedules and short-form rosters have been forwarded to local media, colleges, clubs, stores and other community facets by the personnel assigned to that task (e.g., athletic/activities, sports information director, etc.).*

*Home:*

- Two days prior — contact visiting coach/athletic director, confirm match time, uniform colors, directions, parking, available facilities for meeting, changing, restrooms, seating, warm-up, etc.

  - Scouting report on opponent, if applicable (obtain earlier, if possible).
  - Confirm trainer availability.
  - Contact boosters to be sure parents are assigned to match for concessions.
  - Contact media regarding match information.
  - Confirm security and be sure supervision is available just before match until after the match when everyone has departed.

- One day prior — confirm announcer (PA set-up), confirm ball personnel, complete any tasks still outstanding, note any updates.

  - Remind team of time, location, attire for school day, travel, pre-match, match, post-match.
  - Remind team to spread word about the match.
  - Allow captains time with team for any miscellaneous announcements.
  - Review emergency procedures with athletic director/training staff.

- Day of match

  - First aid/medical kit, emergency medical forms, plus trainer availability if appropriate
  - Water and ice
  - Soccer balls for warm-up plus four match balls, inflated to specs
  - Pump, vests, discs, and any other equipment
  - Meet with captains, secure warm-up music plus National Anthem
  - Stadium, parking areas, field, access to lights, scoreboard unlocked
  - Match day rosters — original plus copies for officials, opponent, announcer

- Just before match

  - 60-70 minutes prior — pre-match with team
  - Greet visiting team and officials — direct them to appropriate facilities; remind opposing coach where to direct opponents' fans and any players needing treatment, if applicable
  - Greet announcer, concessions, ball personnel/coach or supervising adult
  - Just before match, send team and opponent full rosters to announcer

- During match

  - Security and supervision should be visible and be a presence, actively "sweeping" all areas (in front, sides, behind) facility
  - Announcer is on-target, alert, appropriate half-time announcements (ball personnel, thank sponsors, previous match, other school sport results, next match, etc.), music
  - Manager or staff keep match statistics on match report form

- After match

  - Thank opponents, officials, fans, ball personnel, dismiss
  - Concessions closed and monies deposited appropriately
  - Field clean
  - Equipment stored and put away, as appropriate
  - All spectators vacated from site

- Lights out, staff/security dismissed
- Match report completed
- Report scores to school plus media
- Note outstanding players from match (both teams)
- Debrief match with staff, if possible, and review key points for next training session

*Away:*
The away duties are generally simpler, though they also include the previous aspects, as appropriate. Nonetheless, here is a list of items to cover:

- Confirm date, time, location, locker facilities, warm-up space, uniform colors
- Rosters for opponent, officials, announcers
- Confirm bus departure and arrival times, check off with athletic director, team, families, fans
- Remind team of uniform colors, attire for school day, travel, warm-up, pre-match, match, post-match
- Water, ice, medical kit, soccer balls, pump, vests, discs, equipment
- Permission slips, emergency medical forms
- Greet opposing coaching staff and officials — note any updates, distribute rosters as appropriate
- Match report form — managers, coaching staff, or player
- Confirm travel to and from match — parents drive own child with written permission only on return if decided by coaching staff
- Thank opponents, fans
- Send match result and information to school and media
- Identify top players in match from both teams
- Debrief match, plan next training session

### Beyond immediate team staff

There are many structures beyond just coaching a team. For example, if you are a coach in a club, then it is important to understand how you connect to those around you — coaches of the teams above and below your team in the same age group, coaches of the teams above and below you across age groups, age group directors, directors of coaching, board members and other assorted constituencies that you must be aware of. The size of the club will influence communication structures and pathways to problem solving.

In addition, high school and college coaches have additional personnel to liaise with to keep things running smoothly for the team. As indicated in the previous section, there are program components such as the athletic director, boosters/fund raising, media, facilities, rules and regulations (e.g., NCAA compliance) and more. Coaches must understand the communication structures involved and protocols for each medium — phone, email, text, social media, letters and bulletins. If the program is on the same page regarding communication protocols, then misunderstandings and miscommunications are less likely to occur; thus, each staff member should be aware of the "what, when, why, who and how" of communication systems.

### Professional development

This is a necessity when it comes to coaching. My experience with coaches is that they often get locked into their own world of the game, whereas they would benefit greatly from learning from and working with others. I don't mean just consulting with other coaches on the staff you work with, but with others outside the immediate coaching circle. The challenge may be that sometimes, opportunities may not always be available due to time, money or quality. Thus, each coaching staff member should identify professional development opportunities early on, seek support to attend them and be held accountable for their education before, during and after the specific opportunity. Credentials, conventions, workshops, clinics and symposiums through United Soccer Coaches, US Soccer, US Youth Soccer, state associations and other organizations are terrific ways to further one's education in a variety of areas that are soccer-specific and soccer-related.

Coaches should also find time to observe elite coaches in action with their own teams in natural settings; such opportunities can often be much more valuable than the "circus ring performer" variety of sessions, and the observer can see where acquired information gets put into practice, how communication is used effectively and what intangibles an expert coach offers in his or her element. Professional development can also include teaching other coaches and educating the community you are in about aspects of your team to soccer in general.

Another way to develop is to seek feedback in the form of evaluations; such assessments could be informal or formal by other coaches, directors of coaches, age group coordinators or players. Self-reflection is another way to develop. Whether one takes courses, seeks feedback from others or self-reflects, I believe common themes to evaluate coaches in training sessions should include:

- **Organization**
  - Field spaces — appropriate layouts for exercises, objectives, number of players
  - Equipment — vests, discs, goals, flags
  - Players (numbers)
  - Time per activity

- **Session**
  - Warm-up, fundamental, match-related, match-condition, cool-down lesson plans
  - Progression from simple to complex
  - Active vs. inactive
  - Transitions, flow
  - Adjustments, adaptability
  - Stoppages — amount, content and conduct; interruption versus meaningful problem solving

- **Information**
  - Objectives
  - Presentation
  - Coaching points — show versus tell
  - Relevance, quality of explanation
  - Meaningful versus jargon

- **Impact**
  - Do players show improvement technically? Tactically?
  - Has the coach impacted the team's play?
  - What is the impact on the enjoyment, passion, creativity, enthusiasm of the players?
  - Has the coach taught some things to players to inspire effort, give confidence and make a difference in their play?
  - Appropriate challenge level
  - Transfer of knowledge, cues

- **Presence**

  - Coaching personality
  - Rapport
  - Professional – demeanor, language, attire, punctual
  - Body language
  - Engaged and engaging
  - Inspirational, motivational – player input?

- **Communication**

  - Clear
  - Non-verbal, verbal
  - Direct
  - Length of time to explain ideas
  - Responsiveness to player questions
  - Feedback
  - Ask "why?"

Teaching ability is so critical in the field of coaching, yet I believe it is often overlooked. One has to understand the psychology, methods, learning styles and various formats associated with teaching. My personal feeling is that coaching education platforms need to do a much better job of educating coaches in these areas. Ultimately, one of the best measures for a coach over the season(s) is whether or not player development has taken place, if improvement has occurred as a result of or in spite of coaching and if the player continues to play the game.

In addition, coaches should keep up with articles and information at the levels they are working with and higher; there is simply a lot of information available online, too much to not pay attention to some of the good resources. Thus, the staff should coordinate to make as strong of a commitment to professional development as possible. If a coach is not growing, then he or she will stagnate. In addition, players will be more inspired to grow, learn and develop if they see that you are going out to do the same.

## PLAYERS

*Note:* *This section is valuable and important for parents to read and understand along with their son/daughter on your team. Obviously this entire book refers to the people who matter most when it comes to coaching – the players. Everything that you, as a coach, do is essentially for player development, and by using the strategies in this book, you are also positively impacting personal development. By being attentive to issues such as core values, leadership, team culture, player development, execution of sessions, evaluations and developing a year-round program, you are not only trying to be a better coach (and person), but more importantly, you are also helping those you coach to be better players (and persons).*

One of the most important steps that a coach should take before setting foot on the training ground involves identifying the outcomes that the coach ultimately wants players to learn as a result of being coached in a particular program. These outcomes include individual and team objectives that the coach should not just idealize, but actually record; written goals and objectives are much more powerful than simply going over a few ideas in one's mind.

Thus, the coach needs to identify areas that he or she wishes to focus on. Examples are given in the chapter on creating a personal mission statement and such ideas can include values in addition to soccer-specific objectives. As another example, an individual goal may be to improve a player's first touch with both feet. The objectives, stated clearly and in such a way that the coach can assess them, may state that the player will be able to juggle the ball one hundred times with feet only, settle nine out of ten long-service flighted balls off of the first touch in such a way that the first touch prepares the receiver to pass or shoot on the next touch and receive twenty consecutive driven balls on the run with the inside or outside foot wedge.

Perhaps a team goal is to improve communication during matches. Some objectives that follow may state that the goalkeeper will successfully set up each defensive restart in a match followed by immediate acknowledgment and response by teammates, substitutions will involve direction along with stating "nice effort" given by the incoming player and "have a good match" stated by the outgoing player, and perhaps on every transition to defense, immediate communication by the first ("ball!") and second ("force right/left") defenders is expected.

Of course, the fun in reaching goals and objectives such as these is designing training sessions and setting a team culture that encourages, expects, and emphasizes excellence toward these identifiable and measureable outcomes. Coaches must focus on sustaining intentional player development, and by understanding how everything one does impacts players individually and collectively, the coach will have greater success in reaching his or her goals or better yet, the goals of the program on a grand scale. This is not a book on all of the intricacies of psychology and education, yet it is valuable for the coach to gather resources in these areas to serve as a guide on how to reach stated ideals to help each player.

One area regarding players that is not covered in other chapters of this book is in the area of formal "rules." Coaches should be clear on expectations, whether it is regarding punctuality, language, equipment, eligibility, attendance or any other number of issues where guidelines are necessary to have consistency, clarity and comprehension. Navigating through choices and consequences is an important step in the growth, maturity and development of athletes at all ages and levels. For example, with younger teams and high school teams, it is common to have "contracts" to help spell out a program's expectations so there is an agreement formed between the coach and each player. If using such a device, include statements about effort, being a good teammate, and other team values to inspire behaviors that foster intrinsic motivation. Personally, I do not like having a long list of rules and guidelines unless they are necessary, supported and can be followed through on. Rather, I prefer to focus on creating a team culture that encourages good behaviors, appropriate actions and most important, belief by all members of the program; if done well, then players act positively on instinct, habit, good decision-making and from within. Coaches are advised to consult with their program administrators for existing, suggested or required contracts.

*An example of guidelines for player conduct includes the following: Player Expectations*

**Soccer is a team sport and teamwork is essential to a good team. To build good team skills, players should:**

- Try hard and do your best at all times.
- Be a good listener when your coaches are instructing you.

- Be cooperative in training sessions and matches, try to learn new technical and tactical skills, and do expected off-day workouts to the team standard.
- Be willing to enthusiastically play different positions in various formations when the coaches think it will benefit the team and to enhance your soccer experience and player development; versatility is an asset.
- Be a team player instead of an individual; you will grow and develop individually within a team focus.
- Be supportive of your teammates and loyal to the team both on and off the field.
- Demonstrate good sportsmanship all of the time.
- Cheer on your teammates when you are not playing; be supportive and helpful, not rude or demeaning.
- Make a commitment to be at all training sessions and matches. Be present and engaged; training part time will make it difficult for the player to learn the plays, to build team chemistry, and to emphasize the individual skills and teamwork being taught. Expecting playing time without being present is unfair to the player and his/her teammates. Those players selected to a team are expected to participate in all training sessions, matches and scheduled activities. [Contact the coaching staff in advance to be excused if you have an unavoidable conflict and simply just cannot attend.]
- Inappropriate behavior can lead to suspension from activities.
- Be on time and arrive dressed appropriately with all of your equipment for all training sessions and matches.

### Some additional advice for players includes the following:

- Have patience – many players start out "successfully" at younger ages but peak and are unprepared to face challenges at the latter middle school and older ages; what happens is that some players may begin "slowly" at the younger ages, but because they are in environments dedicated to skill development they have the necessary skills to excel as they mature physically. The ideal scenario is to have natural athleticism and be in an excellent player development environment where you are challenged, taught well and supported to compete in healthy ways. The lesson is that "winning" early is not worth it if the outcome is an unskilled player unable to compete when it matters. Thus, if you are on a team that isn't winning at a young age but you are learning appropriate skills technically and tactically then be patient and work hard to continue to improve. Likewise, if you are on a team that is "winning" at the early ages, make sure you are learning, being appropriately challenged and not being controlled by a coach more intent on telling you everything to do during matches who is unable to teach skills and the ability to think on your own; growth in player development is critical.

- Avoid complacency – just because you're on a winning team does not mean you will make that team, start or play significantly the following season. Always work hard on and off the field to improve, otherwise just know there is always someone else working harder than you and that person could take your spot now or later; competition is an important lesson in life so embrace it in a healthy, positive way to be challenged to be better. You are replaceable so accept the challenge of working hard to avoid being replaced.

- Be coachable – you can learn something at every age; the moment you think you have arrived, then arrives the moment where you are defeated due to a less than positive attitude. Be willing to learn and improve constantly. Having to work for something difficult to obtain is much more valuable than being handed something just because you happen to be there. Have a positive impact in every training session and match, accept challenges willingly and don't run away from situations that are actually meant to improve your play. A negative "'tude" is detrimental to your and the team's progress so avoid it or be prepared to be displaced.

- Accept this definition of confidence — **confidence is successfully and consistently executing skills under pressure; it is not something you can blame someone else for if you don't have it or lose it.** Granted, there are those situations or people out there who may affect your self-belief but have faith in yourself, work hard to execute skills well, take responsibility as to your success rate of executing skills, and seek help from your coach for feedback and instruction. Thus, repetition of skills in training sessions and on your own are critical to gain confidence; do not just hope for scrimmaging all of the time at team training sessions — you need skills.

- Understand that the team comes first — if you choose to miss a team activity then it should be for a good reason, or the "big four" as I call them: family, religion, health and academics. Part of being a member of a team is sacrifice — you will need to sacrifice other things for participation on a team, and that is ordinary, not extraordinary. If you are overscheduled then there may come a point where you will have to make a choice as to what you can honestly devote your best effort toward. If your commitment to the team becomes an issue, understand that your coach has the team as the focus, not your other activities; they will try their best to work with you and hopefully support you in positive ways. However, understand that having too many activities on your plate can cause unnecessary stress, fatigue, other health issues, team chemistry challenges and a decline in performance because ultimately if you are not practicing something, you are likely to be passed up by others who are. You put your coach in a difficult position when you choose to miss training sessions or matches, so accept that there may be consequences — these decisions "are not personal, they are about personnel."

- Communicate effectively regarding absences — it is important to be responsible, honest, proactive, willing to make up training time and request rather than demand time off, should the need arise. Learn to balance need versus desire — if your goals in soccer are very high, then some of your desires may just have to wait. Likewise, if you experience a disappointing situation such as limited playing time, don't have an outburst on the field, but instead, wait 24-36 hours and find a calm way to discuss the situation with your coaching staff. By you discussing the situation face-to-face rather than someone else for you (e.g., a parent), you strengthen the coach-player dynamic and eliminate the "parent-as-agent" syndrome that can ultimately backfire as a long-term approach for your growth. It has to be your game and interest in seeking feedback, not your parents. Depending on age, level and experience, you won't always have your parents to "fight your battles" so look at it as an opportunity to learn how to solve problems.

- Be a good teammate — give 100% in training and matches; you owe that to your teammates and ultimately, you all benefit when the team excels so you may as well do your fair share. Don't backstab or partake in cliques — you are expected to be loyal to your entire team, including coaches, on and off the field. Rather than leave "weaker players" out, include them and even better, help them to improve since you ultimately depend on them as much as everyone else in the program. Likewise, sometimes some players may just be better than you and it is not your coach's fault or anyone's for that matter — just try your best and there's something rewarding by staying with something challenging should the opportunity arise.

- Don't let the "uncontrollable" get to you — though you can work hard to leave positive impressions, you cannot depend on other people's opinions to provide your value as a player. If you don't make a team or a starting position, work harder so that next time they have no reason not to take you; if it doesn't work then try again or adjust expectations and move forward.

- Win with grace, lose with honor. Play fair and compete with integrity. Experiences with success, failure, challenging moments and adversity all provide opportunities to learn. Be a part of the process to move forward positively. You can always be "fitter, faster, stronger" and improve your skills, knowledge and ability to compete at a higher level.

- Be attentive to feedback and evaluations — take criticism in a positive way; if your coach didn't care about you, then he or she would not offer feedback about what you can do to be better. As frustrating or disappointing as the advice may be, understand that they are challenging you to be better and you should accept this with gratitude. If you are unable to keep up with the level of your team then being moved to a situation where you can find greater success is not such a bad thing — it is a part of life and you can choose how you react to such a challenge.

- Playing multiple sports through the youth years can have some advantages in the very early ages since "cross-training" and transfer of competition and various tactics are beneficial. However, as you get older, be wary of the attendance issues described. Also understand that playing multiple sports and participating in various activities is a part of American culture that is not so much a part of other cultures around the world — be fair to your teammates and seek support through communication to manage your choices effectively.

- Accept individual honors with your teammates in mind — they work hard to help every member find success and thus, they are a part of your successes. Appreciate your honor, but don't let it be your sole identifying characteristic over your value system and who you are. Medals, certificates and trophies eventually fade, but character is forever. If you have to compete in other environments away from your teammates, represent your program well and be grateful for the opportunities you've earned — don't take the opportunities nor your teammates for granted.

- Being successful in soccer is challenging, as it takes hard work, dedication and plenty of skill given the highly competitive nature of the sport. You ultimately have to choose how far you want to go with it, but rather than look at the sport as a means to an end, learn to value the process and enjoy the journey. The value of being a part of a special team with terrific experiences is priceless, and the skills learned will transfer to life experiences forever.

## PARENTS

A charter helps to convey the common goals and ideals that we aspire to as a team. In effect, it is a mission statement. Members of a program should point to a set of common core principles that define a team regularly throughout the course of the year as a standard of excellence. Information about mission statements along with an example that I produced with one of my teams are included in chapter 1. When the mission statement and core values are derived from the players, they take greater ownership of them and want to hold each other accountable with greater responsibility and dedication.In coaching high school and college soccer, the rules and regulations are clearly spelled out in handbooks and cover a plethora of topics: discipline, playing time, drugs, alcohol, substance abuse policies, conduct, sportsmanship, fees, overnight trips, and more. In addition, I regularly try to give articles to parents that help them understand their roles on the team because especially in today's society, regular reminders and communication are important. As examples, readers can find two articles from US Soccer ("Parents" & "Dear Parents"). I also include timeless articles regarding parenting and its effects on adolescents that are available online that I refer to and expect parents to read:

1. A Nation of Wimps: *www.psychologytoday.com/articles/200411/nation-wimps*

2. Coach Fitz's Management Theory: *www.nytimes.com/2004/03/28/magazine/28COACH.html*

3. The Growing Backlash of Over-Parenting: *www.time.com/time/nation/ article/0,8599,1940395,00.html*

4. What If the Secret to Success is Failure? *www.nytimes.com/2011/09/18/magazine/what-if-the-secret-to-success-is-failure.html*

These links are on my website, and likewise, I suggest coaches include links on their program's websites, along with various other links to good articles and resources. The articles are some of the more poignant ones of today's society and address various challenges associated with managing today's parent group. Though generalized, the articles are excellent resources. Of course, you don't want to overwhelm parents, so limit what you put out there for them as you are trying to help them be aware of parenting roles and not cause them to take such critiques as personal attacks. In addition, I hold regular meetings with both players and parents to continue to communicate what we are about, how the team is doing, what is coming up, and basically to continue to try to establish as healthy of a team culture as possible.

As far as potential grievances, generally the player and parent are encouraged to talk with the head coach/coaching staff directly first. This should be done at least 24-36 hours after a match and done in person as a priority, or at the minimum, over the phone. This should not be done via email or text as such mediums too often lead to misinterpretation and miscommunication. When possible, encourage the player to communicate directly first, then the parent with the child so it is seen as an instructive approach rather than "oh no, here comes another parent trying to interfere/'fix' a player issue that is a coaching decision." If the issue is not resolved, the player/parent would be encouraged to speak with the age group director, athletic director/director of activities or director of coaching/soccer programs, whoever is most appropriately the next level of supervision in the program. Include the coach — the biggest mistake is leaving the coach out of the mix, and it does not set a good example for the child to go over someone's head rather than solve an issue directly. During parent and player meetings, we regularly communicate about the need to eliminate whining, complaining, back-stabbing, witch hunting, rumors, dishonesty, and individual agendas, and instead encourage positive behaviors and support of the team.

As for a contract, clubs and schools have their respective general forms that include a waiver of liability, physical examination by doctor, medical release/emergency information, and more. For an example of a contract for the team, including players and parents, consider the following:

*Note:* *Coaches may want to have an attorney look over any contract deemed official or at the very least, appropriate club/academic personnel should be in such a position to have contracts reviewed.*

*<Team name> Parent Contract — please sign, date, and return to coach <name> by <date>*

## Parents' Expectations

Positive parent participation is an important part of our team's success. The following are examples of the types of participation that all parents are expected to adhere to:

- Display appropriate behavior on the sidelines at all times.

- Encourage the players with cheers and positive comments.

- Demonstrate good sportsmanship.

- Do not harass or verbally abuse anyone, including players, coaches, spectators of both teams and officials (referees, assistant referees).

- Do not coach along the sidelines or behind goals; do not interrupt team activities such as pre-match, warm-up, match, half-time, or post-match.

- Ensure players arrive to training sessions and matches on time.

- Encourage your son/daughter to notify the coaching staff directly in advance if a player cannot attend a scheduled training session or match.

- Ensure that the child fulfills his/her responsibilities to the team.

- Be on time to pick up players from matches and training sessions.

- Support the coaches, especially regarding lineup choices and discipline, regardless of where your son/daughter is placed.

- Provide assistance in fundraising for special events as needed.

- Focus on effort, improving competitiveness and player development, not on results. Your child may not be developing as fast as you or the coaching staff would like, but it is important to accept reality and understand the staff is doing what they can.

- Provide environments which help the athlete to obtain proper rest and energy preservation (e.g., no sleepovers or swimming before matches or tournaments).

- Communicate with the coaches, but NOT during, before or after matches (apply 24-36 hour rule).

- Support the team concept and team mission statement/core values.

- Schedule vacations and camps around the soccer season.

- You are responsible to ensure that all family members and guests that you bring with you to the matches are aware of this code of conduct.

- Inappropriate behavior can lead to suspension from activities.

- Treat officials and guests teams with respect and as guests of our club. Negative actions or remarks are inappropriate. Failure to comply with the above requirements may lead to you being suspended from matches and training sessions. Any fines incurred by the club due to your actions will be your financial responsibility.

*Electra parents breathe a sigh of relief after a tense over-time game, securing another state championship title.*

### Additional recommendations for parents:

- Instill a work ethic in your children; today's society has altered what it means to work hard and it helps your child in the long run if they understand what it means to give 100% effort. Too often, coaches are frustrated with the lack of work ethic and competitive fire from today's athletes; yes, coaches will try to foster it, but you, as parents, must support it. Instead, parents often make excuses for their children and it only hurts them (and you) in the long run.

- If you always bail out children with new items when they lose their soccer ball or a piece of stitching goes bad on their cleats, then your child loses a sense of responsibility and appreciation; instead, they learn to feel entitled that they will always be bailed out by you so what's the point in looking after such items?

- Don't base the quality of coaches on winning or losing. Too often, I've seen parents rave about a coach because the team is winning, only to undermine a coach when the team loses. Player development, learning useful life lessons and continuing to progress in and play the game are much more important factors. Likewise, some youth and high school coaches have good records that are due more to recruiting and athleticism than coaching; if they are not emphasizing player development, then be wary since other teams will overtake them eventually.

- Be realistic, have patience and show support; your son or daughter may not be progressing as fast as you may like as compared to other children. Athleticism, skills, speed, strength, sense and maturity are developmental and as a result, their growth rates vary per child. There are many variables involved, but understand that if your child was successful at a young age due to physicality then they may not be as successful at older ages unless their technical skills grow appropriately, too.

- Allow disappointment and challenge yourself to include good features (i.e., teachable moments) of athletics rather than become overprotective and "bubble-wrap" your child to keep them from feeling what are incredibly important feelings to learn to process in healthy ways.

- Ask yourself if you'd rather have your child pick up lots of trophies and medals at young ages U9-14 or still playing the game, progressing and "winning" when it counts in terms of making regional, high school, college and professional teams at older ages, U15 and older. This is a no-brainer for educated, knowledgeable coaches, but unfortunately, parents are often causes for teams to experience unnecessary turmoil because the team isn't "winning" enough. Yes, you may have to eat "humble pie" sometimes, but it is far better than having your son or daughter burn out or get passed up by other players whose parents had the right mentality and exercised patience.

- It is a game, and it is the child's game, not yours. Don't try to find ways to impose your will on the team, but instead, create healthy ways for your child to impact the team positively. Too often, parents are too caught up in what is just a game; instead of valuing the child who happens to play the game, they value the player who happens to be their son or daughter. Your child needs your love more than anything else; your coach can assess the game and your child's effort. Likewise, your child does not need to relive every moment of training sessions, tryouts and matches with you. Move on.

- Be a problem solver, not a problem creator; coaches are incredibly thankful to parents who are positive life forces, are good role models, are helpful to the team, understand that the team comes first, see that the team does not revolve around their child, are savvy enough to know there are many, many players who are very good, and yes, even better than their child, and maintain professionalism in their support of the team. Coaches don't try to tell parents how to run their family or how to do their jobs; so, parents should respect the coaching staff and not try to tell them how to do their jobs.

- Remember that players and coaches are never trying to lose a match; they're trying their best to win. In the same way, coaches understand that you are not trying to be a bad parent, but sometimes some decisions just don't sync with what each would prefer to do. Be respectful and again, remember that soccer is a game. You should not be making decisions that are coaching/program decisions; even if you are paying money, that action does not entitle you to make coaching decisions. In addition, just because you watch soccer or attend matches, that also does not translate into some sort of "authority" to interfere.

- If you're always hanging around training sessions then understand that it may cause undue stress and pressure on your child. Have healthy relationships with other parents; be a unified force in supporting all members on the team, not just your son or daughter.

- Good coaches often leave the game, be it at the club, high school or even college levels, due to parents. Their reason for leaving the game is that they "cannot stand the parents." Thus, thank a coach for their efforts, regardless of the results; they are probably working very hard for very little pay considering the number of hours spent on behalf of your child and the criticism they take.

- Remember that parents can make or break teams and likewise, a child's passion for the game. Coaches need to be held to high standards of teaching ability, role modeling for children and player development, but they must also be supported in their endeavors to do so. Your child is the most important person on the team for you, but the coach does not have favorites because he or she needs to take care of every player's interests, not just yours.

- Be sure to read everything your coach suggests that you read; help your child to take on this responsibility, too. Encourage communication between your child and the coach, rather than dominate conversations; learning how to communicate and solve problems are terrific life skills that we want all children to improve in.

Additional information is given throughout this book that will help parents understand how best to help their children move forward in his or her soccer journey. In addition, coaches should recognize the importance of parents and include them appropriately; it is a mistake to admonish parents for taking an interest in the game. Instead, choose to support parents and understand their important role in working together to support each child.

*From a former soccer parent:*

*"During an ECNL event in Texas, Ashu surprised me by asking my opinion on how the weekend went. Ashu coached my daughter's U16 women's soccer team (in NC). I was surprised because very few coaches have ever asked my opinion as a parent. Like most parents, I was excited to have this opportunity to speak 1:1 with Ashu. More importantly, Ashu helped me understand his vision for the weekend for both the team and for individual players like my daughter. After our discussion, I came away with a very positive feeling that Ashu cared deeply about all his players and strove to balance winning with the long-term goal of helping each player continue their development. Ashu was objective, thoughtful and respectful toward both the players and their parents. He recognized that parents were an integral part of team and player success. I wish all coaches had this philosophy."*

— Charlie Robinson (father of Hannah, Middlebury College)

*Reflections:*

- What does your team management structure look like?
- What roles do you consider the head coach's? Assistant coach's? Manager's? Player's? Parent's?
- Do you plan your meetings and have purposeful, meaningful talking points and activities for team members?
- What does your plan consist of for match day in terms of people involved, equipment, spectators, transportation, media and opponents?
- How do you educate staff members, players and parents about the game and their roles?
- Does the team have any particular rules and expectations in writing? Why?
- Does the program use player and parent contracts? Why?

# CHAPTER 5

## THE COLLEGE PROCESS

*"It is very important to generate a good attitude and a good heart, as much as possible. From this, happiness in both the short term and the long term for both yourself and others will come." – Dalai Lama*

Youth and high school coaches have a responsibility to develop players to the next levels, and one of these levels involves success in collegiate soccer. Especially in America, college soccer is a major objective for youth and high school players. Certainly youth soccer has several "next levels" in terms of progression of challenge (e.g., higher division, ODP/DA/ECNL, state, regional, national teams, college, professional) or natural chronology (e.g., high school, college, club or intramurals). Depending on the level of player, high school may be the goal of a youth player, but for many players, opportunities exist to play in college and they want these options.

For many players, college soccer can also be an avenue to professional soccer. Simply put, soccer has evolved to a point where a player cannot begin playing soccer in high school and expect to pursue a highly competitive college program. Thus, strong player development must take place from a young age and be a continued area of focus for coaches.

I have been fortunate to coach several players who aimed high and reached their goals of moving onto their next levels, including college soccer and beyond. I am proud of our programs that have successfully provided players with numerous opportunities to compete in college and given families lasting and terrific experiences of enjoying watching their children grow into young adults through the college experience. Our teams often placed more players in collegiate programs in comparison to our competitors in our and other age groups. It was always a great source of pride for players and parents to know that their patience, hard work and goal-setting benefitted them much more than their opponents.

In addition, our players survived and excelled in their college pre-seasons and careers for four years, whereas players on other teams who once had promising youth careers often did not make it. It frustrated me and still frustrates me that coaches who like to tout how successful they are do very little to help their athletes; they don't spend the time to help others, they overrate their players and lose credibility, or they are ignorant to the process of promoting players to the next levels. Because of the many successes and popularity of collegiate soccer in America, I include this chapter to help coaches, players, and parents navigate the college process. I have shared much of this material with my teams, various players and their families, and other coaches/clubs throughout my career, but hopefully this information proves beneficial to an even wider audience.

Preparing players to play in high school and college has been relatively easy for me because of long-term vision and expertise in player development. In fact, a strong club team that is developed well often plays "better" soccer at U14-15 than a high school team and at U16-18, "better" than a lot of college teams. Of course, this is a generalization and depends on the area one coaches in and levels of high school and college teams involved.

However, this was often the case for the teams that I coached, as some of the best soccer played was in those latter youth years. It showed all members of our programs that the years of teaching and emphasizing player development paid off and, as a result, it was no surprise that college coaches came looking for our players at the events that we attended. It should be noted that our preparation was at the highest level, but there are other factors involved with gaining a position in a program, as indicated later in this chapter.

As coaches, we need to consistently ask ourselves if we are focused on short-term goals and the current season, or long-term goals and player development that equips players to be successful beyond the lifespan of our teams. The short-term method is a common and destructive force in our sport. I comment on this aspect of coaching in the next chapter regarding player development. To help put players in the best possible position to continue to play the game in college and beyond, I offer several tips in the chapter on developing a year-round program.

What follows are helpful tips for coaches, players, and parents for the college process. All parties are encouraged to engage in regular dialogue so that the player has appropriate opportunities and can pursue his or her goals when the time comes. This information is based on several years of successful experiences in helping players to have multiple choices and helping them to find their "best match" in terms of their educational and athletic experiences. Remember, it is a process that is unique to each player/family, so take a deep breath and remember the "big picture." Also note that it is okay for a player to not be sure about one's major, type of school desired, etc., early on since he or she will learn more and more through the college process.

Perhaps the most important advice to give a player who hopes to pursue a position in a collegiate program is to remind them to give their best effort toward athletic and academic preparation. Players have these two factors in their control so they should work hard to be the best soccer player and academic student that they can be.

As a player moves up in level, physical characteristics of speed and strength increase in importance. Certainly, executing skills under pressure becomes that much more important, too. By managing academic responsibilities, the player demonstrates that they are less of a risk in terms of balancing athletic and academic responsibilities.

### A comment regarding scholarships

With scholarship money being limited for college programs, a player and his or her family should not expect substantial amounts since full scholarships are reserved for the truly elite players by the particular coaching staff's assessments. Partial to no scholarship money for the first year of college is more likely to be the case in soccer. In addition, a coach may be able to help families find academic money if the student athlete's profile contains favorable grades and board scores. That way, the coach can save athletic money, if available, and spread it around among a greater number of players depending on the situation. Another consideration that a college coaching staff will determine is in-state versus out-of-state tuition, sometimes offering just enough to beat out an athlete's in-state tuition costs for an out-of-state school or if the student is in-state, then not offering an amount the first year could be a course of action taken by the college coach. Players, parents and youth coaches should not get into a situation where they are dictating terms to a college coach, but rather follow the tips as to how best to pursue discussions involving financial matters. An athlete's value to a prospective coach is not simply predicated upon the amount offered; the scholarship situation is much more complex than that.

Parents and players should know that a fully funded collegiate soccer program has nine to fourteen athletic scholarships for its entire team depending on the division and gender (not every team is fully funded); note that athletic scholarships are not available at the division three level. Check with appropriate coaching staff and organizations for current year allocations of scholarship numbers. In other words, the number may stray from 9 to 14 depending on decisions not in one's control. Families should also consider that a college roster is larger than what the player may be used to, with numbers up into the mid to high twenties. If a few players are able to obtain full scholarships, then that leaves that much less for a coach to spread around. First-year student athletes are often not offered as much so that there is an incentive in terms of performance and showing improvement rather than locking up money into an athlete who may or may not pan out at the college level. This has happened in more recent years due to how early college programs and athletes commit to each other; a lot can happen between sophomore high school age to freshman college age. Lastly, a family should not simply decide on a program depending on whether or not a college scholarship is offered. There are just too many other factors to consider.

### Player profiles and coach recommendation forms:

Perhaps before beginning the college process, the player, parent and coach should consider the types of information often found on player profile and coach evaluation forms. This helps ground the player and makes him or her aware of the engagement necessary to try his or her best to stand out as a potential college student-athlete. Likewise, it also helps emphasize the need for honesty and credibility from coaches and parents in moving forward in the process. Following are several items often requested of coaches in assessing a player for potential at the collegiate level.

*Sample 1: Coach's Commentary*

Player's Name: ............................................................ Graduation Year:

Coach's Name: ............................................................ Club Team:

Coach's phone .............................................................

Coach's Address: ...................... City: ...................... State: .......................... Zip: ...............................

Coach's Email: ............................................................

Have you coached any players who have gone on to play at Division I Schools?    Yes ☐    No ☐

Please list some of the players and the colleges they attended: ................................................

Which Division I or II teams have you seen play? ................................................................

What is the highest level that you have played?...coached? ................................................................

Explain what you feel that this player's strengths are in as much detail as possible: ......................

................................................................................................................................

_____

Why do you think we should recruit this player? ................................................................

Explain what you feel this player's weaknesses are in as much detail as possible: ........................

How does this player interact with his/her teammates? ................................................................

Is he/she coachable? Does he/she accept criticism? ................................................................

_____

When will this player make an impact on a top 10 Division I team?

Freshman ☐                  Sophomore ☐                  Junior ☐                  Senior ☐

_____

List some colleges where you feel she could be a starter: ................................................................

_____

Please return to :

If you have any questions or comments, please feel free to contact us by phone or by email.

*Sample 2: Prospective student-athlete questionnaire to be completed by soccer player and soccer coach*

*Soccer Office Head Coach: Asst. Coaches: Address: fax: email:*

**PERSONAL**

Name: Last, First ............................................................................................................

Address: Street City State Zip ............................................................................................................

Home Phone: ...................... Cell Phone: ...................... E-Mail: ......................

DOB: ...................... Ht. ...................... Wt ......................

**Parent Name:** Occupation .................................. **College:** ..................................................
**Parent Name:** Occupation .................................. **College:** ..................................................

## ACADEMICS

High School .......................................... GPA .......................................... Class Rank ..........................
SAT Component Scores: ..........................................................................................................
Critical Reading Writing Math Essay ......................................................................................
SAT Subject Test(s) & Score(s) ...............................................................................................
Subject Score Subject Score ..................................................................................................
ACT Scores: ............................................................................................................................
Composite English Math Reading Science Reasoning Writing ....................................................
Intended School of Study or Major: ........................................................................................
Other Universities in which you are interested: ........................................................................

## ATHLETICS

Club Team
Upcoming Tournaments
Club Coach ........................................ Email .............................. Phone ..............................
HS Coach ........................................... Email .............................. Phone ..............................
Highest ODP Level Attained: ......................... Coach .......................... Phone ..............................
Position ........................................ HS Career: Goals/Assists ............................. GAA ......................

## COACH'S RECOMMENDATION

Developmental Academy or Elite Clubs National League experience:
Player's Name ....................................... Today's Date ..............................................
Coach's Name ....................................... Club/HS Team ............................................
Email address ....................................... Cell Phone ................................................

*Please rate your player in each area using the following scale:*
*1 = Excellent, 2 = Good, 3 = Fair, 4 = Poor*

**Field player**

| | | | | | |
|---|---|---|---|---|---|
| 1st touch | .......................... | Agility | .......................... | Game sense | .......................... |
| Passing | .......................... | Speed | .......................... | Field vision | .......................... |
| Shooting | .......................... | Quickness | .......................... | Work rate | .......................... |
| Tackling | .......................... | Endurance | .......................... | Enthusiasm | .......................... |
| Shielding | .......................... | Strength | .......................... | Leadership | .......................... |
| Heading | .......................... | Athleticism | .......................... | Team player | .......................... |

**Additional Comments:** ..........................................................................................................

**Goalkeeper**

| | | | |
|---|---|---|---|
| Hands ·············· | Agility ·············· | Game sense ·············· |
| Footwork ·············· | Quickness ·············· | Mentally tough ·············· |
| Punting ·············· | Strength ·············· | Concentration ·············· |
| Throwing ·············· | Vertical jump ·············· | Leadership ·············· |
| Technique ·············· | Athleticism ·············· | Team player ·············· |

**Additional Comments:** ····································································································

*An approximate timeline for the college process based on player's year in high school*

In each year, focus on improving soccer technical and tactical skills, increase fitness base and physical strength, strive to play at more challenging levels through environments, such as ODP, DA, ECNL, or guest playing up if appropriate, attend college games to get an idea of the speed and physicality of the game, visit college campuses and work hard to have as strong of an academic profile as possible. Research college programs online — investigate the rosters to see the number maintained, physical characteristics, level of player recruited (e.g., ODP, DA, ECNL, national youth teams), schedule, academic programs offered and any other information of interest.

Grade 9/U15: Identify two college camps to attend during the summer after your grade 9 year of high school. Strive to make the varsity soccer team, but if not, then strive to be the strongest player on the junior varsity team. As a high school player, set goals of improving skills, competing for playing time, organizing your time effectively to balance soccer five to six times per week with a challenging academic load, and having an impact in every match. As I tell players on my teams, strive to be one of the top three players on the field for either team in every match by competing with a 100% effort to have a positive impact. In addition, high school provides the opportunities to demonstrate leadership, compete with a range of ages, and represent your school in a positive light. While some high school programs and coaches may be good in the player development process, others may not be and thus the player needs to make high school soccer as positive an experience as possible.

The player may write to college programs, but due to NCAA rules, they will not write back to you. However, in doing so, this is the beginning of promoting yourself as a prospective athlete for their program. Thus, have your parents and club coach proofread your initial letter and email so that it looks professional. If the team is U15, the club coach should be sending out general mailings to coaches before major college showcasing events, though most college programs will be watching U16 and U17 teams. Likewise, the club coach may write a brief note in support of the athlete before any college camps are attended, assuming he or she is given enough notice beforehand by the player. Thus, team and individual communication are good starts to the process.

The player needs to make a strong first impression, and his or her individual letter should not be of the "cookie cutter" variety nor should it be from the parent. Some good examples of communications are provided later in this chapter. During the second semester, set up a meeting with parents and college guidance counselor to establish contact and perhaps begin to identify a few potential programs of interest. At this stage, the athlete is still young and his or her interests may change; that is okay and the player should not feel overwhelmed, stressed or anxious.

Grade 10/U16: This is an important year, particularly on the girls' side since the college process has been accelerated over the years. The club team will hopefully attend good showcases and tournaments where college coaches go to scout players. The player should write to college coaches before each event, the club coach and manager should be sure that club team members fill out team/player profile books for coaches at events, and the club team should have good team brochures available for mailing and handing out in person at tournaments. Likewise, the team may have player information available on a club website, but pay attention to security and privacy issues. The player should begin to research programs in earnest online and by talking with people (coaches, players, parents, known current college players, club alums and former high school players, etc.).

Pick two college camps if possible for the summer after grade 10. By the spring semester, identify a potential "Top 10" list of tentative college choices and send a formal letter and resume to each program. The player may attend spring mini-camps if possible at desired colleges – get a feel for campus, stay overnight for an "unofficial" visit, take the college tour, and along with a parent, initiate a discussion with the college soccer program staff. Fill out online player information/profiles as necessary by going to the program websites. Meet with school guidance counselors to stay on track regarding core courses and colleges of interest. What follows is a more detailed description of the sophomore year because it is such a crucial time-frame for athletes and their parents. The language is written in the format in which I addressed some of my teams in more recent years. In addition is a form that families can use to make notes about college programs that they research.

August – ongoing: explore various programs and gather information.

- Consider education and academic information – after all, that's why you're there and those features pertaining to education will help you in having career options in the long run. What courses do you like? What careers are you interested in? Can you think about one or two majors you might be interested in? What are the school's academic strengths/weaknesses? Since majors are often changed, how flexible is the school with changing majors?

- College profile: small/medium/large, location/distance from home, divisions (NCAA DI, II, III, NAIA, NJCAA), climate, student: professor ratio, male:female ratio, 4-year versus 5-year programs, academic support (tutors, study halls, advisors), living situations, familiarity with students already there/will be going there, type of campus, newer/older buildings, car allowed or not allowed on campus, graduate school/career placement, accessibility to professors versus teaching (graduate) assistants; **does it have the balance of academic, athletic, and social that is right for you?**

- A sensitive issue, but one parents will need to strongly consider: finances. How is the tuition, room, board, etc., going to be paid for? Does the student qualify for any particular financial aid, scholarships, academic monies, etc.? Remember that a D1 program may have a total of 9-14 scholarships to divide among its entire roster. In other words, a partial scholarship could be likely and a full one is going to be very rare. In addition, coaches may not offer any scholarship and instead go on merit – you earn money through the years if you progress as expected. Again, the goal is to find the best match for the student and not make a decision simply based on the "name" of a school or how much money one is offered. Explore athletic and academic assistance. See additional information for D2, D3, NAIA, NJCAA.

- Watch soccer matches live and on TV to develop a sense of style of play, type of athlete recruited, coaching style and competition. Visit the campus and facilities. Talk with coaches, players, former players and other students to get a feel if a program is within reach, a stretch, or comfortably possible based on knowledge at hand.

- Soccer-team specific: coaching style, playing style, team chemistry, your impact on the team, playing time – playing immediately versus not playing immediately or even for a couple of years, stability of coaching staff, academic support for athletes, facilities, conference, travel, development versus win at all costs, and more. Again, research the school thoroughly because if you didn't have soccer or if the coaching staff changes (which is likely in the four years you are there), would you still be happy at the school?

- Maintain a good filing system of mailings that you will receive from a variety of programs. In addition, keep track of communications between you and the school to refer to during the process.

- Explore sites such as ncaa.com, topdrawersoccer.com, and more to gather information about programs.

Searching online will allow you to find schedules and conferences in addition to finding links directly to men's and women's soccer programs (these websites have rosters, schedules, coaches' information, contact information, directories, player profiles and much more). The sites are particularly useful for finding staff mailing and email addresses along with phone numbers.

Tip: When naming some schools you are interested in, look up schools in that particular school's conference. Conferences contain schools that are often grouped together because of overall profile, competitiveness, size of school, academic offerings and other features. So, if you are interested in a particular school, then you might find yourself interested in other schools that you had not originally thought about.

October – November: Identify a list of ten schools you are interested in – this list will likely change throughout the process and that's okay. This step is just a start to get an idea of the types of programs you may wish to pursue. The list also gives all involved with the process an idea of the type of schools you are interested in as youth (and high school) coaches interact with various college coaches on your behalf. Be sure to pass this list on to your coaches so they can stay in touch through miscellaneous connections and communications for you. Your list should contain your ideal, "stretch," strong potential fits, and "comfortable" programs. I don't list schools as "safety" since there are just too many factors to consider any opportunity a "sure thing." In addition, be realistic and fair; don't overshoot a program nor mislead a program as that is just a waste of everyone's time and effort.

| NAME OF SCHOOL | ANY CONNECTIONS TO THE SCHOOL? | MAIN REASONS FOR BEING INTERESTED IN THE SCHOOL |
| --- | --- | --- |
| 1. | | |
| 2. | | |

Compose a brief letter and one page (one side) soccer resume/profile – the player should compose these documents, write the letter with their name on it and create a professional, spell-checked and grammatically correct document. The parent should not do the writing, though obviously the parent is helping to oversee the process. Be sure to check items such as spelling, name of school and names of coaching staff. A good, supportive coach familiar with the process should also be happy to help you edit the letter and resume. See the section "Suggestions for Letter and Resume" for ideas regarding format. Mail the letter and resume to coaches so they can begin a file on you (and to offer an alternative to email, of which coaches receive hundreds). You will likely get a response saying due to NCAA Rules & Regulations, the coaches cannot respond to you until September 1 of your junior year. However, they will likely send back a player profile form, possible coach's evaluation form and an address to return the form; do this promptly. Likewise, some player profiles are done purely online; search the soccer program sites of the schools you are interested in and look for the links for "prospective athletes."

*Intermilan captures a regional title and moves on to Nationals.*

**November 15 – onward:** As college playoffs begin to wind down and club events such as showcases and tournaments begin to pick up, email head coaches and cc assistant coaches prior to events you attend. Send emails to your list of schools in addition to any other programs you have a vague interest in, and who may or may not appear on the "registered coaches" list prior to each event.

- What to include in the email: your name, class year, expression of interest in school, brief explanation of why interested (e.g., major, have seen them play, connection). Invite them to please come watch your team, stating the full team name and abbreviation that may appear on the match schedule, the division the team is playing in, the match schedule (time, field #), and state that you look forward to future communication (use your voice and your own words that make most sense). Again, the email should come from the player, though you ought to use a parent over a personal email address. You may mention your coach's name if you would like, especially since they may know the coaching staff or have former players at the particular school. This aspect was and is highly beneficial for players I have helped and continue to help through their college processes.

- Tip: The more emails (within reason) from players on your team, the more likely the coach will try to find time to come watch the team play. If coaches know that you are interested then they are more likely to watch you play so be proactive and communicate effectively and professionally.

- After each event, send a brief follow-up email to coaches you emailed to thank them for attending your match(es) — a team manager or "college brochure hand-out person" will need to find out which coaches attended and which match they were there for. Your coach should send an email out to your team to indicate the list of coaches in attendance at each match. You might even follow up with coaches who you did not originally write to whom you found out came to watch the team play and you have an interest in. Depending on how interested you are, you might mention your next event, request additional information about the school, request spring mini-camp or summer camp information, or indicate that you look forward to the next steps in the process (for sophomores, the coaches cannot do a lot of communicating, but they may send out information, a general reply, etc.; for juniors, they can do more communication with you).

**February – June:** Plan additional visits to schools, get on campuses (e.g., many colleges offer spring weekend "clinics" or "camps" that make it convenient to both see the campus and be seen by the staff), and obtain feedback about where you may stand in the process. Unofficial visits are good ways to interact with the coaches/players — ask questions and gather information. Visits in the spring can still be productive, as most teams have an abbreviated spring season and the coaching staff will likely be happy to show you the facilities, introduce you to team members, and answer questions. Decide if a summer college camp or college combine makes sense in your particular case. It won't always make sense and they do cost a lot of money. Consult with club coaches as they can sometimes get an idea from college coaches about your potential fit relative to other recruits.

Obviously, continue to manage what you have control over — get "fitter, faster, stronger," improve technical and tactical skills, challenge yourself to take your game to a higher level and of course, make your academic profile as strong as possible. When playing high school soccer, strive to be among the top three players on the field for either team during a match, as previously noted. Set goals and make your high school play meaningful so you don't lose your edge gained from club play. You will follow similar email and communication processes for events in the spring through the summer. As always, contact coaches for information, questions, or concerns. It is likely that your club coach will meet with you and your parents at least twice for individual college process discussions, in addition to providing ongoing evaluation and feedback.

Grade 11/U17: Before beginning the school year, you will likely go to one or two college summer camps. Again, proactive communication with coaches should help steer you through deciding which camps to aim toward. It is also likely you will gain additional exposure opportunities through competitions such as regionals/nationals, ODP, DA, ECNL, or other identification camps that are attended by college coaches (e.g., some college combines where you know coaches will attend can help if your club team is limited on exposure). If your team gets optimal exposure then it is likely that time and money will limit the need for additional camps.

Continue to gather feedback from club coaches and college programs as appropriate (September 1 of your junior year is the official date that college coaches may contact you once per week). Continue to express interest, keep coaches posted, request visits (especially during home match weekends), research the program and similar programs (schools in the same conference may have similar profiles) and communicate effectively with programs. Meet with college guidance staff to begin the process of certifying that you meet all NCAA Clearinghouse requirements, investigate financial aid or scholarship information as appropriate, and seek assistance with beginning the college admissions application process. Do your best on standardized testing; stronger scores help everyone involved in the process.

Follow the detailed guidelines given here regarding research and communication. Depending on the situation, you may likely go to one or two college camps during the summer after grade 11. The appropriately named "big year" usually culminates with the athlete gaining an understanding of where he or she is going to pursue their collegiate career; this could happen early or late during the junior year through a verbal commitment.

Grade 12/U18: After July 1, coaches may phone the athlete directly, but continue to initiate contact, set up visits and consult with parents and coaches about the opportunities at hand. Even if you would like to commit "early," still take official visits as time permits in order to visit the campus, team, staff and all aspects of the school. Ask questions, gather information, include parents on financial considerations, and interact with coaches/players from the various programs you are considering. Be sure to exhaust all efforts, connections, and resources if you have not received opportunities. Most competitive student-athletes are effectively verbally committed by the end of junior year, but each person's process is unique and a commitment could happen well into the senior year. Over the years, I have often had college coaches ask for information regarding uncommitted players since they may have lost a player or more due to a variety of situations (e.g., transfer, injury, eligibility) or financial circumstances suddenly open up forming an unexpected opportunity. Or, it is possible a coaching change takes place and the recruiting for that particular program is late relative to other programs.

The official signing (in writing) date that officially commits the player to a college program occurs in February. Be sure the player, parents, club and high school coaches and any other friends enjoy the occasion. Seniors who are committed are expected to participate in all events through the year, as their future college coaches want to assess their progress, project them into their pool of personnel for the coming season and be in a good position to help set goals for the off-season transition to collegiate soccer. In addition, it is a strong showing of loyalty and team commitment to follow through on playing all the way to the end of one's youth career.

In any case, the athlete should continue to compete in showcases, be seen, ask for feedback, and seek out the collegiate program's off-season training packet in the spring/summer. It is a huge mistake for the athlete to commit early but do very little to prepare for the demands of college soccer. If the player comes from a good player development culture then he or she will likely be motivated to continue to excel and not just be another number on the college roster later that fall. Instead, the athlete will strive to work hard to compete for a starting position, come in fit, improve skills, and train appropriately during the spring and summer to transition into the college program.

## COMMUNICATION GUIDELINES

You may phone and email college coaches if you are interested in their program, intent on making a visit, or for other situations. Do not become a burden, but do it purposefully and with good reason. Remember that you are representing yourself, family, team, program, club, high school, and ultimately state so making a good professional impression is important. Coaches like to communicate with players so they know there is genuine interest and that it is not a situation where the parent is acting as their "sports agent." However, parents should monitor communications and help the player through the process — this is obvious because it is a major decision, there are finances to consider, and it is a big step for any family to send a child off to college. Coaches may not always respond due to NCAA Rules and Regulations, but you can initiate contact. At the same time, they may not always talk with you during an event so do not take it personally if they do not communicate as readily due to communication regulations. For various NCAA rules, restrictions, regulations, follow some information links on the website: www.ncaa.org/student-athletes/future/scholarships.

Included here are some good areas to research and good questions to ask throughout the process, especially as the player becomes more interested in collegiate programs.

- Player
  - How is the team chemistry?
  - What positions are being recruited?
  - Based on what you've seen, where do you see me in your program?
  - Would I play during my freshman year? Could I start?
  - How will the staff help me develop and improve as a player during my career?
  - Does the coaching staff plan to stay intact over the four years that I would be there? When and what were the most recent changes?
  - Based on the current personnel, where are most of the players from? What class years are the players? What positions? Note: Much of this specific information can be gleaned from rosters listed online.
  - If I am a goalkeeper, what is the goalkeeper coach able to do to help me improve? Do I train with the goalkeeper coach or the team?

- What opportunities might there be for me to play in the "off-season" or after my career? Professional? National team?
- What is the coaching and playing experience of the staff?
- What is the style of play?
- What are the coaching styles of the staff?
- How do you offer feedback to players?
- What criteria do you use for deciding about playing time?
- What percentage of players plays for all four years?
- May I meet some players in my intended major?
- Any notable alums?
- May I watch an upcoming training session?
- May I attend an upcoming match?
- What facilities do you have for soccer?
- What are the expectations during the "off-seasons" of summer, winter, and spring?
- What kinds of support does the university have for academics? Career placement? Job opportunities? Semester abroad?
- Could I take a campus tour and attend classes?
- What kinds of fitness testing does your program include?
- Do you have a training guide for the off-season or incoming athletes?
- What events does your staff plan to attend to recruit soccer players?
- Will you be able to attend any of my upcoming events and offer feedback on what I need to work on?
- Do you have any suggestions that would help me to be both a successful applicant for admission to your university and a strong candidate for your soccer program?
- What conference and non-conference matches are on your schedule?

*Note: Depending on the time of year, the program's schedule should be updated online.*

- What are the main adjustments from being a youth/high school player to being a player in your collegiate program?
- If applicable, could I play soccer and still participate in:
  - Another sport?
  - Intramurals, club sports, etc.?
  - Greek life?
  - Work? Internships?
  - Special majors such as architecture, nursing, etc.?

- Parent (see player questions also)

  - How can I best support my son/daughter during the college process, including now and during his/her career?
  - What is your coaching background in helping players develop?
  - What are the main adjustments from youth/high school to college soccer?
  - What kind of academic support do you offer for athletes?
  - How does traveling impact classes and academic workload?
  - How does the team get along with each other? Your staff? You?
  - At an appropriate time (if appropriate at all) but not the first visit, what types of financial support are available through academics or athletics? Is your program fully funded?
  - Do freshmen qualify for any scholarship monies? Does the amount usually increase during the player's collegiate career?

- How do you support the athletes when they aim for playing goals such as professional soccer or a national team?
- What does the college experience at your university entail for the player? Parents? Families? *Is there a good balance of athletics, academics, and social life?*

## SUGGESTIONS FOR LETTER AND RESUME

*Letter:*
- Business letter format, names, addresses, date.

- Two or three maximum short paragraphs; make use of bold face or italics to make your letter stand out from the rest.

- 1st paragraph – who are you? What club team and positions? Why are you interested in the program? When did you see their team play, attend camp, or get seen by them?

- 2nd paragraph – brief summary of one or two achievements, mention where you'll be seen next for club and ODP events; any particular goals with soccer (and academics)? Indicate if their program aligns with those goals based on information you may have (only if you have it); have you filled out a player profile?

- 3rd paragraph – state that you have enclosed a resume, are interested in the next steps in their process, look forward to future communication, and be sure to end with a "thank you."

- Sign off professionally, and be sure to include your resume.

*Resume:*
- See formats that follow for examples; a picture helps identify the person and adds a personal touch; it is encouraged but not absolutely necessary.

- Formatting is somewhat flexible, but information is not as flexible: name, address, phone, email, DOB, HS name, class year, club, ODP/DA/ECNL, HS, academic info; there are various ways to communicate all of this, but make sure it is clear, concise, and not too "busy."

- Names of references should include phone number and email (be sure to get their permission beforehand). You will want to mention key coaching references, especially ones with a solid reputation for player development and ones who may know a lot of the coaches or have former players to refer to also who can be good points of reference.

*Both letter and resume:*
- Be consistent with the font you choose.

- Check grammar and spelling carefully (this includes names especially). Have your parents proofread your documents so they know what you are writing; a good coach familiar with the process will proofread for you, too.

- Keep your coach in the loop since they should have lots of contacts, players, and others, to help you through your applications, and they are the person who the college coach (your potential next coach) will contact regarding your potential as a fit for their program.

- Make sure the letter and resume are in your voice. It is easy to copy such pieces from examples, from the internet, or other people's work, but it comes across as more of a "cookie cutter" model than your own voice.

- Keep in mind that coaches receive hundreds of letters/resumes, so make yours among the best! If you were looking at hundreds of letters and resumes, would yours stand out, look professional, and be one you would want to keep toward the top? Most coaches (and business people in life) will look at a letter and resume for maybe a minute, but you can grab their attention with good information, formatting, and even effective use of bold/italics/underline/font size, as appropriate. Of course, be honest and your information should be of substance over fluff.

- Check your club and high school packets for more information, and look online for additional information on exploring schools.

- Always write brief emails before and after events to the entire coaching staff; recognize that the head coach may or may not be present to see you play since the assistant coaches are often the ones who attend more events to recruit.

There are several examples of letters and resumes available, as I have dozens from the college processes of players I have helped. I include just a few to offer ideas, though the player should adapt as necessary and appropriate.

*Sample Letter #1 (format to one page)*

[Player's Name]
[Address]
[Phone Number]
[Email]

Date

[Coach's Name]
[School]
[School Address]

Dear Coach _____,

My name is [Player's Name], and I am a rising [grade

classification] (Class of ****) at [High School]. I have a combined interest in attending a strong academic institution such as _____ and playing soccer for a Division 1 program.

I am a starting Midfielder for my club team, [Club Name/Abbreviation]. My team competes in the Region # Premier League and also in the Elite Clubs National League (ECNL). I have extensive ODP experience as you can see on my enclosed resume. This summer I attended Region # ODP Camp and was named to the Region Pool. As for high school soccer, I was a Varsity starter as a freshman and led our team in [Key statistic]. I was named to the All-Conference team.

I have included my resume, along with a schedule of my tournaments and ECNL events for the upcoming year. I hope you or one of your staff members are able to watch me play. Thank you for your consideration.

Sincerely,

[Player Name]

Enclosures.

*Sample Letter #2 (format to one page)*

[Player Name]
[Address]
[Phone]
[Date]

Dear Coach [Name],

My name is [Player Name], and I am very interested in learning more about my potential to play soccer at [College/University]. I am seeking a school that offers both academic and athletic excellence.

I am a [Class designation] at [High School] in [City, State], enrolled in the International Baccalaureate (IB) program. I am ranked in the top 2% of my class, which consists of [Number] students.

I currently play for the [Club Team]. We have competed in the Region # Premiere League for three years and have won three of the last four [State] State Championships. My primary position is center midfield, but I have had a lot of experience playing both outside and center back over the course of my career. I have been selected for [State]'s ODP 1st Team every year since [Year] and invited each year to the Region # Camp. This year, I was elected by my teammates to be co-captain of my club team.

I admire your commitment to [College/University] and your extraordinary accomplishments (e.g., [specific honor]). I welcome the opportunity to have you or your assistant coach, [Name], attend one of my team's soccer matches in the future (see below). My coach, [Name], can be contacted at [Phone number] or at [Email].

Thanks for your consideration of me as a student athlete at [College/University].
Sincerely,
[Name]
[Email]
H.S. Class of [Year]

Upcoming Tournaments:
[Event Name, Location, Dates]

*Sample Resume #1 (format to one page)*

[Name]                                                        Class of [Year]
[Address Line #1]                                            [Photo]
[Address Line #2]
Home:
Cell:
E-mail:
DOB:

                  Height: ' "        Weight:
                  Positions: /

**Academic**

[School Name]
[School Address Line #1]                                    SAT:
[School Address Line #2]                                                    ACT:
[School Phone Number]                                                      Class Rank:
Current GPA: , Honors (if applicable)

Honorary Clubs/ School Interests
[Name of clubs, years, volunteer work through school, etc.]

**Athletic Achievements**


Club Soccer
[Club team name, year]                                          Jersey #
Team Website:
Coach:                     Phone:                     E-mail:
Team Highlights: 2x State Cup Champions, Finalists, Semi-finalists [Years]
Competes in Region # Premier League & Elite Clubs National League

ODP
[Years, State] ODP Team, Region # Camp              [Year] Region Pool
[Years, State] ODP Team Captain                     Region # Team Events TBD
[Year] Super Y National Camp                        Region # Championship

High School
[Years] Varsity Soccer (Freshman starter)
[Years] All-Conference Team
Led team with [Key statistic]
Coach:                     Phone:                     E-mail:
[Other high school athletics information]


**Other**
[Other activities]
Volunteer Work:


*Sample Resume #2- Player Profile type (format to one page)*


**PLAYER PROFILE FOR:** [Name]            **POSITION:**

**Team Information**

[Club team name]
[Club team location]
Coach: ; Cell: ; Email:

[Year] [Event] [Accomplishment]

**Player Information**

Name:                                          Jersey #:
Address:
City/State:
Telephone:
DOB:
Height:                                         Weight:

High School:                                    Grad Date:
*[High School address]*
Coach:
Class Rank:      / +
Un-weighted GPA:                                Weighted GPA:
SAT:            Not taken at this time          ACT: Not taken at this time
College Major:   Undecided
Extracurricular Activities:

**Soccer Achievements**

HS Varsity Soccer:
Club Soccer:                     *[Year]* State ODP team, Region # Camp selection
                                 *[Year]* Super Y OPD National Camp
                                 Voted Club Team Captain in Seasons

Camps:                           *[College]* Skills Camp [Year]
                                 *[College]*-selected to Camp All Star team *[Year]*

*[College]* Skills camp *[Year]*

## TEAM BROCHURES/TEAM WEBSITES

Through the years, much of team marketing has gone via the route of the internet on club and school websites or on team websites. However, I still prefer my teams to have a team brochure during the U16-U18 years. It is nice to mail these to college coaches at least once a year, even via email attachment, and especially good to have handy at events that the team plays in.

Although coaches often receive team and player profiles at showcases, it is handy to personally give coaches a profile about your individual team. This gesture makes the marketing of your team more personal and individualized, along with making it very easy for coaches to spot your players at the particular match they are viewing.

In addition, the team information included on such brochures is readily available and easily accessible. Thus, teams should include brochures as part of their budget items in the advanced club years.

The brochure layout varies, as different teams and clubs have their preferences. What worked best for teams that I coached was a color tri- or quad-fold document with the following format:

- Front panel: club team name, location, year; team picture, brief highlight of key team accomplishments.

- Inside panels: 3 to 4 players per page with key individual information. This information includes: picture, name, class year, jersey number, position(s), parent email address, ODP/regional/national team, honors, school, GPA, extracurriculars.

  *Note: Be consistent with individual pictures – uniform, background, and with player information – approximately all equal in length.*

- Back panel: coach information (picture, phone, email, credentials), information about upcoming team events; thank you for watching the team play.

Our brochures often received rave reviews from coaches for the simple design, key information access, and professionalism. We also had good team parents who we relied on to hand out the brochures and record the match and list of coaches in attendance. The majority of coaches who attended our matches were largely there because of the hard work we did to promote our players and obviously because our players were being developed at an elite level, no matter what their aspirations in the game. Sometimes there may have been as few as a half-dozen coaches, while on the average 25-35 per match were in attendance during peak times at multiple events with an all-time high of approximately 85 coaches (at just one match).

Following is a sample letter that I often attach when mailing brochures, adapting the letter for the specific team that I am promoting:

*Dear Coach,*

*Enclosed is a brochure about our U18 girls' team, Braddock Road Youth Club (BRYC) ELECTRA. We have juniors and seniors on the team*

*Note: I would include their class years.*

*All of the girls plan to pursue higher education, and all of them desire to play college soccer. We emphasize development and versatility on ELECTRA, so it is normal to see players substitute in and out of matches and play various positions. The girls' strengths as players also show in their ODP participation and their numerous accolades from their high school teams.*

*As indicated on the brochure and team data sheet (see website for details), ELECTRA has several noteworthy accomplishments in a number of highly competitive events. Last year's team won the State Championship and played well at Regionals (2-1). Although this year's team has some new players, we are off to a good start this season, having advanced to the [Tournament/Showcase] Quarterfinals (lost to eventual champion 1-0) and we won the [Showcase] tournament.*

*Our upcoming tournament plans include [listing of key fall events; name, location]. Some current plans for the spring include [listing of key spring events; name, location]. We hope to continue our success in these competitive events, in addition to help showcase each player. We have placed twelve ELECTRA graduates into college programs so far, and we look forward to providing similar opportunities for the current roster of players. We are also interested in college-club events for the spring and summer, such as scrimmages, 8v8 games, camp games, etc.; we would appreciate being notified of such opportunities in which we may participate.*

*As indicated on the brochure, the players have been recognized for their club, ODP, and high school play. They are also capable in various other sports, and several players have ODP District, State, and Regional level experiences (Region One tournaments/mini-camps, Houston/PDT Shootouts, Region One Camp, etc.). The girls also participate in various high school and community activities; they set high goals, work hard, compete with intensity, and are a terrific group of people to be associated with. We look forward to your interest. This is our last go-around, so we thank you and your staffs for all of the support through the years. Best regards.*

*Sincerely,*

*Ashu Saxena.*

## Additional opportunities for exposure

If available, players should take advantage of other opportunities to be seen: ODP events, guest-playing for grade-appropriate/higher-level teams within the club, state, regional and national competitions, college camp scrimmages and miscellaneous other opportunities that benefit the players. Communication with appropriate college soccer staff regarding the events is encouraged. Other opportunities listed here are especially important if the player is in a "soccer desert," which essentially means the player plays on a team that might not get seen at the high-visibility showcases

- Combines

- Guest playing (with coach's permission) for other teams in a position for improved exposure (at U16/sophomore year and older)

- Potential walk-on situations

## Additional tips for high school coaches to promote players

*Note: Club coaches will have their share of promotion media via brochures, college coach player booklets at events, website player profiles, and more.; the tips below can also help club coaches with the process of promoting players.*

- Establish connections with local colleges – invite coaching staffs to your matches and training sessions, contact coaches before players from your program attend their camps, have alums return and sell both your HS program and the one from the particular college that they go to.

- Have a brochure handy for fans, media, visiting college coaches, etc. Just as club coaches should do, consider mailing the brochures of your program out to a variety of college coaches.

- Since the media often covers HS sports more so than club, make use of the media by promoting your HS name, location, players' interests in college programs, and more. Even if just a blurb, it helps to have your program visible in the local papers, websites, and news programs; likewise, it helps to grow the game of soccer.

- Promote special matches to increase the atmosphere's positive energy (e.g., homecoming, rivalries, playoffs) beyond just championship matches.

- Establish positive connections with local clubs, especially since your players will feed into your scholastic program from these clubs. You can have ball girls/boys from the younger teams of local clubs run the sidelines at your matches; have the announcer say their team name over the public address speakers in front of the fans as an example.

- Do community service — it is good for the students to be seen in a positive light off the field in the community and again, the visibility ultimately helps promote your players. In addition, participating in community service is a terrific team bonding activity, along with positive, impacting service to nearby surroundings.

- Consider running a mini camp in which your players are counselors (make sure the players actually coach and maintain high standards). Perhaps have players take referee courses and give back to the game via officiating.

- Thank sponsors regularly with announcements, signage, visits, etc.

- Very important: establish positive relationships with club coaches because most of the college process is done via club soccer; work together toward player development, preparation for each season, and promotion to the college game so that everyone benefits.

- Support players in their pursuit of youth national and regional teams, ODP, Super-Y, ECNL, DA, W-league, professional teams, etc., play as appropriate and allow them to play in college showcases/camps (without conflict in neither schedules nor over-scheduling). Their sophomore and junior years into their senior fall seasons are prime college exposure times.

This is a helpful grid for club and high school coaches to help keep track of the college processes for their players. Be sure to communicate regularly with the player and his or her parents, along with the college coach as appropriate.

## TEAM NAME COLLEGE INFO

| PLAYER/GRA-DUATION YEAR | COLLEGES PLAYER IS INTERESTED IN | COLLEGES EXPRESSING INTEREST IN PLAYER | COLLEGES PLAYER HAS VISITED | COLLEGES PLAYER HAS "OFFER" FROM |
|---|---|---|---|---|
| POTENTIAL AREA OF INTEREST | | C: Directly to Coach<br><br>P: Directly to player | | CONFIDENTIAL — FORMAL OFFERS MAY ONLY BE MADE PER NCAA RULES |
| (Player's name) (Area of interest) | | C:<br>P: | | |
| (Player's name) (Area of interest) | | C:<br>P: | | |

This is a sample record-keeping scheme used by the parents of a highly recruited soccer player I coached in both club and high school, Ashley Banks.

*Statement from a former player who went on to be one of the most successful players and leaders ever coached:*
*"One of the most memorable moments I have had with Ashu didn't come on a soccer field, but rather when I celebrated my wedding day with him along with 10 other Electra family members. I grew up with this family and soccer took me very far, but the friendships I have created truly are lasting a*

*lifetime. Ashu instilled in me a work ethic that I have carried into the collegiate level, my academic career and my personal life. Without him pushing me to goals I never knew were possible for me, I would not be the player or person I am today. I owe him a great deal of gratitude for opening my eyes to the world of possibilities and for teaching me that I should strive for nothing less than what I aspire for and not to give up until I reach it."*

— Ashley Banks, BRYC *Electra* U10-U19 & WT Woodson HS/West Virginia University
4-year varsity (NSCAA All-American for HS and College, MAC Hermann semi-finalist)

**Colleges and Universities
(Bold indicates schools the
athlete returned questionnaires to):**

1.  Auburn
2. Barton College
3. Boise State U
4. Boston University
5. Bowling Green
6. Brown University
7.  Columbia University
8. Dartmouth
9. Doane College
10. Duke University
11. Duquesne
12. Elon University
13. ETSU
14. Florida State University
15. George Mason University
16. Georgetown U
17. Georgia State U
18. Hamilton College
19. Hartwick College
20. Haverford
21. High Point University
22. Iona University
23. Jacksonville State
24. Kent State
25. Kenyon College
26. Lehigh University
27. Manhattanville College
28. Marywood University
29. New York University
30. North Carolina State
31. ODU
32. Penn State University
33. Princeton University
34. Providence College

35. Randolph Macon Women's College
36. Sacred Heart
37. Seton Hall U
38. Sewanee University
39. Siena College
40. Swarthmore College
41. St Joseph's University
42. The Citadel
43. Towson U
44. Tri-State University
45. Tulane
46. U of Colorado
47. U of Connecticut
48. U of Delaware
49. U of Florida
50. U of Iowa
51. U of Maryland
52. U of Miami
53. U of Michigan
53. University of Scranton
54. U of Miss
55. UNC Charlotte
56. UNC Wilmington
57. U of Penn
59. U of South Carolina
60. University of Virginia
61. USNA
62. Vanderbilt
63. Villanova
64. Virginia Tech
65. VCU
66. VMI
67. Wagner College
68. Wake Forest
69. West Virginia University
70. Wheaton College
71. William and Mary
72. York College

These are some results of the college processes of some of the players I coached into collegiate programs. With well-led programs, a focus on the "big picture," a good understanding of the college process, and long-term commitment to player development, excellent results are achievable, as indicated below.

*College placements*
BRYC *Electra*, *Attack*, & *Blue Thunder* college placements (teams coached by me in VA), along with placements from teams directly working with since moving to NC; does not include the multiple exposure opportunities, offers, visits and choices each player had:

- **Akron**
- **Appalachian State University** (x5)
- **Arizona** – NCAA D1 playoffs, Captain; NSCAA Top 25; ODP State Team/Regional Pool
- **Armstrong Atlantic State University**
- **Belmont Abbey College**
- **Boston College** – NCAA D1 playoffs; NSCAA Top 20; ODP State Team
- **Boston University** – NCAA D1 playoffs, Captain x2, Soccer Buzz East Region All-Rookie Team; NSCAA Top 25; ODP State Team
- **Bucknell**
- **Campbell** – NCAA D1 playoff, Captain
- **Catawba College**
- **Christopher Newport U** (x2) – NCAA D3 playoffs, USA SouthAll Conference Team (as a freshman), Defender of the Week, Tournament Team; NSCAA Top 25
- **Clemson University**
- **Coastal Carolina** (x2) – ODP State Team/Super-Y National Pool
- **College of Charleston** (x4) – ODP State Team
- **Concord** – Captain
- **Converse** – All-Conference
- **Cornell**
- **Dartmouth**
- **Delaware**
- **Duquesne** – Captain, MVP Defense; ODP State Team
- **Eastern Carolina** (x2) – NCAA D1 playoff; ODP State Team
- **Eastern Kentucky**
- **Eastern Tennessee State** (x2) – Captain
- **Elon** (x2)
- **Emory** x (2) – NCAA D3 playoffs including Elite 8, All-Rookie Team; NSCAA Top 25, Player of the Week
- **George Mason** (x2) – NCAA D1 playoffs; NSCAA Top 25
- **Georgia** – NCAA D1 playoff; NSCAA Top 25
- **Georgia College & State U** – NCAA D2 playoff, Peach Belt All-Conference 1st Team (as a freshman); NSCAA Top 20
- **High Point University**
- **Hofstra** – NCAA D1 playoff; NSCAA Top 25
- **Jacksonville** – Captain x2
- **James Madison University** (x2) ¬– NCAA D1 playoff; NSCAA Top 25; ODP State Team
- **Lee University**
- **Lehigh**
- **Lipscomb**
- **Longwood** (x3)

- **Mary Washington** (x2) – NCAA D3 playoff, Capital Athletic Conference Rookie of the Year
- **Massachusetts** (UMass) (x2)
- **Messiah** – NCAA D3 Champion, Finalist, Semifinalist; NSCAA Top 10
- **Middlebury**
- **North Florida** – ODP State Team
- **Penn State** – Captain, WPS Washington Freedom reserve; NSCAA Top 10; ODP State Team
- **Pittsburgh**
- **Princeton** – NCAA Division 1 Semi-finalist; NSCAA Top 10; ODP State Team
- **Queen's (Charlotte)**
- **Radford**
- **Richmond** (x2) – Captain, Grad Assistant coach; ODP State Team
- **Rider**
- **Samford University**
- **St. Joseph's**
- **Tennessee** – NCAA D1 playoff; NSCAA Top 20
- **Troy University**
- **University of Alabama**
- **University of Louisville**
- **University of Maryland at Baltimore County (UMBC)**
- **University of Mississippi**
- **University of North Carolina at Chapel Hill (UNC)** (x2) – State/Regional ODP, former National Pool
- **University of North Carolina at Charlotte (UNCC)** (x3) – Captain; NCAA D1 playoff; NSCAA Top 25
- **University of North Carolina at Wilmington (UNCW)** (x3) – Captains; NCAA D1 playoff; ODP State Teams
- **University of Pennsylvania**
- **University of South Carolina** – State/Regional ODP, former National Pool
- **University of South Carolina Upstate** – State ODP
- **Villanova** – NCAA D1 playoff; NSCAA Top 20; ODP State Team
- **Virginia (UVA)** – All-time leader in career matches played, WPS Washington Freedom, NCAA D1 playoff including Sweet 16; NSCAA Top 10; ODP State Team/Regional Pool
- **Virginia Commonwealth (VCU)** (x3) – CAA First Team, Captain, NCAA D1 playoff; NSCAA Top 25; ODP State Teams
- **Virginia Tech** (x3 – NCAA D1 playoff; NSCAA Top 25; ODP State Teams
- **Washington & Lee**
- **Wellesley** – All-Rookie Team
- **Western Carolina**
- **West Virginia** – MAC Hermann Semifinalist, NSCAA College/HS A-A, Captain; ODP U16 Regional Team/U23 National Team; NCAA D1 Sweet 16; NSCAA Top 10; ODP State Team/Regional Pool
- **William & Mary** (x4) – MAC Hermann Semifinalist x2; NSCAA College A-A x2; NSCAA HS A-A, Captain; NCAA D1 playoff; NSCAA Top 25; WPS Washington Freedom/Boston Breakers; ODP State Team/Regional Pool

*Note:* *This list includes players that have actually played on my teams for sophomore or older years during the college process, and only players that played for teams I coach. Many of these players played for me at much younger ages for several years, too. It does **not** include the numerous players not on my club teams who have been helped along in the college process, been counseled, sought out recommendations, etc. The list also does not include some players who played on my teams at younger ages and also went on to play collegiately.*

*Lastly, the list includes some honors, but not all (e.g., many received all-conference, region, state high school honors of various types, many were Captains; several played in their college conference playoffs). The above list does not include additional players helped through my involvement in high school, ODP, a few guest players in past years, U19 teams, any coaching experiences prior to 2000, etc. Nonetheless, the list of programs (from just a few teams) indicates solid player development success and excellence in promoting players to next levels.*

Through the high school years, regardless of how high you aim toward pursuing college soccer, recognize that every player has areas to work on so no player should ever be complacent. Encourage every player to strive to improve technically, tactically, psychologically, physically, athletically, and socially to be the absolute best player (and person) that he or she can be. Playing and practicing competitive high school and club soccer effectively are obviously important parts of preparation for college soccer, but so are watching the game at the highest levels (World Cups, Champions League, Premier League, La Liga, Bundesliga, Serie A, Liga MX, MLS, NWSL, etc.), reading stories about inspiring athletes, and accepting constructive criticism from knowledgeable coaches. Playing pick-up small-sided games with older players, if possible, will enhance development, and if extra opportunities such as ODP, ECNL, DA, or elite identification camps are available, then players may consider those options, too. There is also no substitute for logging hours of proper exercises in running intervals and other fitness areas in addition to strength training. Playing other sports for cross-training can help athletes grow physically and psychologically if they can manage them into their schedules in as healthy a manner as possible. A player's biggest asset can be his or her work rate on and off the field so when you run training sessions, encourage all players to go for it!

Note: *One of the issues of the current system in the US is that players are often seen at the youth levels with and against their age group only. As high school, college, professional and national teams are of mixed ages, it is important for coaches in player development functions to expose players to different age groups.*

*"Over the years, Ashu has consistently been one of the top trainers/coaches for girls' youth programs. He has a knack for getting the best out of each player and having them understand how to play effectively as a team. They are always fit, organized and find ways to earn a result."*

— Dave Lombardo, James Madison University Women's Soccer Head Coach.

## Reflections:

- What are the next levels for the players you coach?
- How do you promote players/teams?
- Are you connected with local club, high school, ODP, DA, ECNL, college coaches?
- Do you know where your athletes wish to pursue college and in what area(s) of academic interest?
- Do you meet with your players and their parents to give an accurate picture of where the players stand regarding their pursuit of collegiate soccer?
- Do you promote watching college soccer (live and on television)?
- Do you market your team via use of letters, email, brochures, websites?
- Do you have a team manager or other personnel to help you hand out brochures at matches and maintain a list of college coach attendance at events?

## CHAPTER 6

## PLAYER DEVELOPMENT: WHOSE RESPONSIBILITY?

*"Come Together, Right Now" – The Beatles*

United Soccer Coaches, US Soccer, USYS, USSF, ODP, DA, US Club Soccer, USYSNL, ECNL, id2, PDP, RPL, PDL, Super-Y, SuperClubs, HS, NCAA, NAIA, USL, W-League, WPS, MLS, USL, NWSL, NASL, etc. It is no wonder that our US National Teams often lack cohesion on the field and struggle to play as one passionate force. With several organizations claiming to be an avenue to player development without a unifying mission or practical acceptance of "second-tier" status, we are a disorganized country in philosophy yet an organized country of many soccer structures. I chose the quote for this chapter with intention. It is part of a message the Beatles received when they were searching for greater cohesion when they experienced dissension and a growing rift amongst band members. First off, I am a proud American, and my intent in this chapter is not to offend anyone but rather to find greater "cohesion" of philosophy and practice in what we do as soccer coaches to raise the level of international competitiveness for our country's players and teams.

In addition, my long-term coaching experience is primarily on the girls' side at highly competitive youth levels including "club" (or travel, select, classic, elite tournaments/showcases, ECNL, regional leagues, etc. – get my point?), ODP, and competitive high school, so I don't profess to be an expert on the boys' side by any means. However, player development is a strength of mine so I have fairly strong views and opinions. Because we in the United States have access to so many resources, I believe that we should produce a greater number of quality players and our men's and women's teams should perform at higher levels internationally. On the men's side, it is no secret that we don't have American players consistently starting on what most in soccer would consider the elite teams of the top international leagues. If we want to be more competitive in the international arena then we need to "come together right now" to embrace what is good in America, work together and start improving player development, not just talk about it or create yet another organization. Otherwise, we will continue to lag behind other countries in soccer's "bigger picture." Hopefully after a United Soccer Coaches Convention theme of "The Best of US," we have been rejuvenated and re-energized toward reaching for excellence in American player development. In addition, with a change in leadership and other systemic changes in US Soccer, improvements in the areas of player development and coaching excellence will finally begin to bear fruit on the global stage. We already know that other countries are excited about player development and have mechanisms in place to find success. However, we all can do better, regardless of our backgrounds and experiences.

Perhaps the release of US Soccer's Coaching Curriculum documents and hiring of additional positions on the women's side provide proof of actions as steps in a more common direction. We still have a long way to go on both the men's and women's sides, so hopefully all coaches will look more closely at the player development piece of our profession. In addition, one of the stated challenges (in the US at least) has been a lack of depth of truly elite coaches able to affect player development that contains both breadth and depth in scope. Some of the hurdles include funding, location, schedule synchronization and more. The important goal for all organizations involved with player development, in my opinion, is coordinated coaching education, player development, and vision, as opposed to what currently goes on in terms of ego, money, and disjoint factions.

*"**SOLIDARITY** — "sol-i-dar-i-ty," noun: unity (as of a group or class) that produces or is based on community of interests, objectives, and standards."*

— Merriam-Webster Dictionary

Although mottos such as "Indivisible" and "Pressure Makes Us" were selected for the men's and women's national teams in past years, I hope that we can come up with a term or phrase that has greater depth and inspires far-reaching actions in the future of soccer in America. Not that solidarity needs to be it, but perhaps it is a strong statement that soccer has lacked among those people in charge of leading various soccer organizations; player development needs to be a transparent central philosophy and mission, rather than simply creating yet another business structure to add to the fray.

To make improvements and strategize toward progress, any entity must evaluate itself objectively and ask questions that guide its mission statement. What is our mission statement when it comes to American soccer? I am not talking about individual mission statements by the United Soccer Coaches, US Soccer, nor US Club Soccer, but more importantly, a driving force that helps guide coaches toward excellence in player development, coaching education and evaluation, and a unifying spirit in knowing that we are all a part of something bigger than our individual teams, clubs, states, and regions. We need solidarity, rather than divisiveness and factions, when it comes to putting our best foot forward.

We need a unifying motto that everyone in America can be proud of: "You'll never walk alone" is Liverpool FC's and "More than a club" is Barcelona FC's. When traveling on the NSCAA (now the United Soccer Coaches) Master Coach Diploma England trip, guided by former NSCAA Director of Coaching Education, Jeff Tipping, I was very impressed by the academies/clubs that we visited in terms of immediately getting a feel about what each club valued and emphasized, be it family, teamwork, development or "excellence," however that may be defined. In particular, Chelsea FC proudly displayed words all over its facilities that the Blues hold dear in day-to-day operations: integrity, excellence, style, unity, leadership, pride. In addition, if one scans various club websites, one can see what qualities certain clubs value and they are not afraid to say it. For example, Barcelona FC clearly states "mes que un club" on all of its pages and in the case of describing its youth programs, the site states the values of "tolerance, respect, solidarity, comradeship, citizenship and integration" as values to transmit during the Barca experience.

I am sure there are many of us who regularly create mission statements, core values, or mottos for our teams, but how about our leaders in the game do the same for us as a country? A club mission statement is perhaps easier than forming a national statement, but we need unity now more than ever as a country. Certainly we don't need to copy anyone just for the sake of having an identity, but we may as well learn from successful organizations and countries; we are a country that likes to be considered a "leader" so let's put our best minds together and move forward, not politically, but practically for the common good. In addition, mission statements and mottoes are just words if they are not believed, embraced, supported, and modeled; however, they are a beginning.

A strong characteristic of America is its diversity. We have a diverse country in terms of ideas, economics, climate, geography, culture, ethnic backgrounds, and enthusiasm from all ages involved with the game. I am not convinced when people suggest that our country is too big to unify since America definitely has advantages over other countries in terms of infrastructure. In addition, I am not suggesting that we need a nationally dictated system or style of play, such as the suggested 1-4-3-3 (1-4-3-2-1/1-4-2-3-1) system indicated in the USSCC. That is far from the point. I believe it is important to celebrate differences and experiences while allowing for creativity, autonomy, and varied methods from experienced coaches. However, we need to find the best of our positive qualities so that we have at least some common landmarks along the journey of player development. Otherwise, we are all just building metaphorical roads without a common purpose, vision, or destination.

We need to also "diversify" away from pay-to-play structures at the top levels. As an example, consider that there are some elite players on DA /ECNL teams, but there certainly some existing players who may not have such opportunities but who may be stronger. We need to find ways to emphasize player development instead of simply projecting business models into the game. Just because a player plays or a coach coaches in DA, ECNL, college, high school, or club does not automatically translate to "better" or "worse," as there is simply no hierarchy in our country. I can find good players and coaches in various organizations and cannot say all of the "best" players and coaches are in one organization.

Instead of finding common ground, it seems as if we are a country divided on so many fronts that it is no surprise that finding a common mission statement for a soccer coach in America is somewhat convoluted. As an example, at the competitive club level on the girls' side, we have US Youth Soccer that runs a National League, along with State Cups and Regional Premier Leagues, which eventually lead to regionals and an eventual national championship competition.

However, US Club Soccer offers their own version of a "national championship" for club teams in addition to a Super-Y "national championship" competition for summer play (USYS had or has a Director's Cup "national championship" for the summer, too). USYS's ODP also has a national championship competition run over the course of a few "tournaments" each year. US Club Soccer's Elite Clubs National League (ECNL) has emerged as a league to identify potential girls for youth national teams that ideally feed into the full national team, and you guessed it, they have their own "national championship." Do we really need all of these championships, especially at young ages? We need to develop the champion within players rather than simply provide players with more "championships" to play.

Having coached teams and seen competition in all of these environments, I am not convinced that player development is the top priority among the organizations leading to "national championship" competitions. Perhaps that will begin to change, but at present, they seem to exist simply as structures and systems with words available should one want to try to find a theoretical philosophy, yet in practice, player development lags behind goals in that area. Results are obviously important in player development since youths need to experience what it means to compete for something challenging, but with so many "championships," a bit of the passion is lost since it gets confusing to players as to what a "championship" actually is. In addition, if one is not at a level to win one kind of championship, then they can just go and find another. Is that good? Well, maybe in terms of having different levels of soccer championships available for recreational, average club, and elite club levels. However, for an overarching player development theme for our country, it is not.

I don't believe that a national program should dictate every aspect of the game, especially if experienced coaches are above the standard being set. However, coaches should have better support systems, especially those who need it. Positive indicators are symposiums, such as what ODP and DA have done for several years and ECNL has begun to do (I am still not sure why they can't work together toward true elite-level player development regarding standards of play, quality of players, liaising with club/home programs, scheduling, improving coaching standards of education, conduct, evaluation, etc.).

Why is player development not occurring at the breadth and depth needed in America? Perhaps if we identify the issues and have a dialogue about them then we can better tailor our efforts toward the challenge of player development. I know it is "not my job," as there are others in key positions to address player development, but perhaps the ideas below serve as points of discussions so we can all move forward, especially since the need for us to come together for the people who matter the most in all of this — the ones who play the game — is greater than ever. So, who and what are currently responsible for player development in America? What are possible solutions to improve the current landscape?

- Soccer issues

    - Who is in charge (nationally)? It would seem that there should be a natural hierarchy or organizational structure just as there would be at a club at any level, but there is not. I am glad that members from various entities met at the FIFA Futuro conference in the fall of 2010 and at the Player Development Summit in the spring of 2011. However, I still do not see an identifiable or logical structure to soccer in America. We have two different organizations that offer coaching education (United Soccer Coaches and USSF), at least two organizations that offer "player development" opportunities for identified players (e.g., ODP, PDP and id2), two organizations that are separately trying to be the leader in player development for boys and girls (DA from US Soccer and ECNL from US Club Soccer), and even in the one organization that runs the national programs (US Soccer), there is quite a disparity in its staffing, procedures and finances dedicated to both the men's and women's sides. Shouldn't we hear more often from a central organization in terms of vision, or is the USSCC document going to be it? Or, should we have a stronger connection to our regional and state staff (e.g., Directors of Coaching)? With technology and social media available, there is certainly a lot of information available, but it can seem overwhelming and disjointed to various entities including players, parents and coaches at all levels. It would seem rather easy to disseminate information that all coaches could access to help improve player development. Again, there is a lot of useful information available online, but there is not enough from a clear centralized philosophical perspective.

- **Do coaching education courses and promotional structures need revamping?** Again, we have at least two different organizations involved and while improvements have been made over the years, perhaps a stronger expectation and higher standards should be placed on coaches coaching higher level players. Just because one has a driver's license does not make one an excellent driver, and that is the same for those who complete coaching education courses. It is terrific that both organizations (United Soccer Coaches and USSF) are offering courses at a variety of levels to address the needs of coaches who coach at various levels and, as a result, coaching has generally improved in our country. However, if Daniel Coyle's "10,000 hours" hypothesis for sustained excellence in *The Talent Code* is to hold true, perhaps coaching education should be geared more toward building experiences that lead toward sustained excellence rather than the ability to pay a fee, have the time to go away for a week and put on a few short coaching sessions with little to no follow-up once the coaches leave the facility where the course is held. In addition, Coyle emphasizes that excellence comes from certain features: having a spark in terms of being motivated to pursue an area, improving skills through deep quality practice, developing experience via master coaching, and fostering the drive toward excellence by creating a culture of success (*The Talent Code*; Daniel Coyle 2009). Thus, the United Soccer Coaches Master Coach course structure makes more sense since candidates are paired with a mentor, there is an application process in which demonstration of commitment to soccer coaching excellence must be presented, there are requirements beyond the usual training session evaluation and submission of a couple of sample sessions, match analysis, and the like, and long-term evaluation is a component that supports coaches and creates an opportunity to excel. Of course, the cost and time of all courses prove to be barriers for some that also need to be adjusted, since again, just because one pays a fee for a course does not mean that they have reached excellence in coaching. This concept is akin to coaches saying that just because a parent pays a fee for a player that a player is excellent and/or should receive x minutes of playing time. Though some credentials require annual certification enrichment units, clearly we are not where we would like to be in terms of developing a greater number of top-level coaches. More needs to be done to mentor coaches for long-term professionalism and success, while at the same time organizations need to be more careful in identifying coaches with experience, commitment, and objective results to promote into key areas, especially when it comes to leadership and decision-making regarding player development.

- **Should there be greater continuity among professional, college, high school and club programs for the benefit of players (and coaches) at local levels?** It seems as if many soccer coaches, for good or bad, try to emulate academy systems from overseas. However, a youth club that has its ending point at youth soccer and is disjointed from professional or college programs (e.g., higher or "next" levels) seems to be more of an independent entity in the bigger picture of player development. It is clear that we do not have the finances or the pure soccer culture to have full-time academy programs that exist in the same way as they do overseas. So for now, it would appear that greater consistency in raising the overall standards of coaching would be in our national interest. In addition, the barriers to coaching education also need to be lifted, as such hurdles of time, money, and location often prevent some coaches from continuing to reach higher levels. Even if a club offers the DA or ECNL programs, it runs the risk of "recruiting" versus developing talent and that aspect needs attention. As the DA has been around longer, perhaps it is further along than the ECNL in existing for those who can pay just as much as for those who can play. Note: The two are not always mutually exclusive either. In addition, coaching education and evaluation need to be greater priorities to advance coaching systems at all levels. We lack a coaching hierarchy and that alone is confusing for players and parents, two groups obviously heavily involved in the bigger picture of establishing player development cultures. As examples, there are club coaches who are much more talented than high school and college coaches, especially in the area of player development, and there are college coaches who are stronger in developing players than some who hold positions at the national and professional levels. Likewise, there are some high school and club coaches with greater expertise than some at the ECNL/DA levels.

*Note: Another point to consider is the DA supposedly dictating players to not play any high school sports. Yet, elite athletes in various sports and researchers have often suggested success has been attributed to participation in multiple sports, while burnout, false or inflated self-views, and repetitive use injuries tend to increase with single-sport specialization. I also feel it is unfair to mandate 1000s of players to not play high school soccer for the sake of only a relative few who are selected for national programs. Seemingly, some of these organizations have tried to justify their high school ban by increasing number of events and "national camps" (which seem to increase the business aspect over the development aspect again). High school sports do have value – learning from other coaches/players, representing your school, competing (over just "showcasing"), playing with different ages, setting new goals, playing every day, opportunities to lead, and much more. In addition, aren't there benefits to soccer athletes from other sports? There just doesn't seem to be any absolutes that can be taken in our current systems yet – should there be? Certainly there are strengths and weaknesses to each environment, but it's a shame when some falsify their statuses and importance. We should all look after the players from both a scheduling standpoint and from a "bigger picture" perspective.*

- **Can player pool programs, such as ODP, PDP and id2, have greater connection to player development at youth levels? Are the DA and ECNL providing the high level of training and development intended?** There is no question that we need to create quality environments where properly identified players who excel have additional exposure to greater levels of challenge, as developmentally appropriate. These need to occur often enough so players improve steadily, rather than sporadically. It is terrific to see this concept beginning to take form in terms of training sessions in clusters of clubs around different regions in the country. In addition, the concepts of DA and ECNL are geared toward having exposure to supposedly better training and more competitive players on a more frequent basis. Is it working? As the DA has been around longer, it would appear that there is still work to be done given how our national teams are performing (or not) and developing players (or not). The ECNL still has a long way to go, as there are lopsided scores, some very average players on teams, and coaching education still needs greater cohesiveness, direction and follow-up. Coaching education by such systems is a good thing to support and continue, but can the level be raised and the frequency increased? Obviously there are some good intentions, but perhaps funding is one major challenge of raising the level. In addition, with the development of academies via MLS and NWSL programs, there will hopefully be greater forays into development (and not just into business models).

- **Pay to Play.** Perhaps one of the biggest differences of soccer development and an overall soccer culture is the current system in America of "pay to play." It creates all sorts of challenges in terms of coaching, player development and inspiring a culture of only playing or training independent from when there is an "admissions fee." Many other less affluent societies don't have all of the resources that we do; they just go out and play. Or, their academies have sponsorships and funding from other sources (e.g., national associations, government, sponsors), which allow coaches, directors of coaching, and other qualified personnel greater decision-making freedom. In recent years, it is terrific to see the development of "pick-up" style environments and actual futsal courts to provide greater accessibility to play the game in less-structured formats.

*Blue Thunder in the early years of competition*

- **Confusion for the average fan regarding soccer media.** For soccer fans and non-soccer fans alike, there is a lot of confusion regarding player promotion and team expectations. For example, why does the media lead us to believe that we should be excited when one of our men's players goes abroad to play and, at the same time, be happy when a foreign player past his prime comes to play in the MLS? Have we accepted that the MLS is a second-tier professional league and will remain as such? What would be the incentive of a non-soccer fan to go to a match if it is already billed as being inferior to other leagues? It is terrific that MLS has been in existence for over twenty years and has expanded. However, is it doing all it can to develop high level players? Obviously the EPL, La Liga, Bundesliga, and Serie-A all have loads of talent, years of experience and money and the overall level of soccer is much higher from playing, coaching and entertainment standpoints. However, if we don't see American players playing regularly at the highest level and we accept that the MLS is not the highest level, do we have a chance to further the sport? In addition, why do soccer television broadcast announcers overdo the positive, feel-good reporting and not enough of the critical examination needed to place a higher level of expectations on our teams? I believe our teams are very good, and they can continue to improve. As examples, I recall a USMNT match where we had lost to Brazil 1-0 years ago in a competition and the media raved about how terrific of a performance that was. Most countries go in with the mentality of expecting to win and are disappointed with losing. I imagine the media in Brazil covered that "win" as a disappointment. In more recent years, especially with the failure of the USMNT to qualify for World Cup 2018, there have been some more critical of our current system (e.g., Taylor Twellman, Alexi Lalas, Eric Wynalda, etc.); we need this criticism to avoid complacency and comfort with soccer simply as a business. Or, consider the Women's World Cup of 2011 where the media lavished praise on the USWNT for battling back versus Brazil short-handed and called it a "courageous" effort after losing the final to Japan. However, given those two countries' lack of player pools, resources, training facilities, and finances, we should have never put ourselves in such positions. We should also examine NWSL and ask if it has player development structures on the women's side, as some players are choosing to play internationally rather than in the US. On the men's side, Mexico has come back from years of inferiority to the US and seemingly passed us up, as indicated in the Gold Cup final of 2011 or recent qualification for WC18. Yes, they have the culture, but why have we seemingly stagnated to such a standstill if we have the DA and a host of other improved resources?

- **Whatever happened to Project 2010?** Anyone remember this program that was initiated in 1998 to put the USMNT in a realistic position of winning the World Cup in 2010? Supposedly millions of dollars were spent but only two programs still exist from their original plans: Generation Adidas, previously known as Project 40 when run by Nike, and the U17 residency camp held in Bradenton, FL (which only just ended in March 2017). I can recall when one of the prominent USMNT members was asked about Project 2010 and he apparently laughed off the question, suggesting the US would be fortunate to win a WC by 2050. Yes, US Soccer came out with the DA and the USSCC, but much more needs to be done to improve soccer in America on both the men's and women's sides. In addition, if the USSCC took that long to produce and that is all it amounted to, then surely that is a disappointment for highly skilled, knowledgeable, experienced coaches who have contributed much more to our own player development programs than was produced in the colorful, organized document. The document is certainly informative, but the level of information and number of practical training sessions for coaches are lacking. Perhaps another document with more advanced ideas is on the way? Yes, it is a start, and we should recognize those who produced it in a positive light for their efforts; the build-up and the reality of the document were good for newer, less-experienced and perhaps average-level coaches. Some of us just have greater expectations and have developed players with far less support than such a document would seemingly provide. Is there another "Project" national goal in place for both the men's and women's sides? Which organization will lead this charge and will it be supported by all organizations?

- **Coach, DOC, age-group coordinators, etc., roles.** Could these roles be better defined? Might national organizations offer greater support to people in these roles? Too often, clubs are forced to cater to "business interests" and less to "soccer interests." Clubs should be encouraged to make decisions and moves based on player development rather than cash flow or politics. Perhaps with a more unifying energy, whether among states, regions or the nation as a whole, a better culture for player development can be formed? Is it possible for our professional, semi-professional or even college teams to be better coordinated with local clubs to ensure a strong player development culture? Or, is it best left to clubs to figure it out for themselves? In addition, who are executive directors, directors of coaching and other administrative personnel accountable to? What if they are not the best people to make key decisions regarding player development? What if other coaches are more experienced, dedicated, and committed to player development than those who are supposedly in charge?

- **Proclamations.** Debatable examples include "must rotate coaches or players every 2-3 years," (what if a coach has the talent to keep a team going for a longer period of time where there is a dearth of quality coaches for the particular group of players?); "1-4-2-3-1 is our system," (a good guideline perhaps, but what if that is not the best system to develop players? Shouldn't players be taught the game regardless of positions and formations?); "position-focused players/coaches," (position training à la football, not futbol); names of teams ("elite," "premier," "classic," "advanced," "gold," etc.); tryout ads with accurate versus inaccurate information that try to proclaim being "the best."

- **Trainers and other support personnel.** With so many changes in society's climate, trainers and other personnel, such as strength and exercise coaches, have grown in terms of being a part of the player development picture. It is incredibly valuable to now have access to such people as strength and conditioning experts who have access to the latest medical information and exercise equipment to develop player's physical qualities. The scientific research, technological advancements, and expertise of many in physical and exercise science have improved greatly in recent years. In addition, soccer trainers are similar to tutors for classes for those players who either would like to "catch up" or "get ahead." However, at the youth levels, have such personnel also affected the athlete's intrinsic motivation to construct his/her own training environments? Have they hampered psychological development by instilling a mentality that the player can only improve with an externally organized, paid session? How does this affect the player in a match where psychological toughness is needed? Granted, if the youth has a coach who is inexperienced or if the youth needs an extra voice in healthy ways then perhaps the extra sessions serve as a benefit. However, if the psychological and physical tolls of extra sessions keep the player from performing at their best, then perhaps such systems need re-evaluation.

The bottom line is that we generally do not have control over other people's motives, so everyone involved with the game should be encouraged and expected to do the right thing, not just what will make the most money or put one's name over everything else. There has to be a willingness for all groups to evaluate and reflect on what is best for the bigger picture of player development, rather than be dug into their own foothold for the sake of ego, money or whatever other agendas.

- **Outside factors:** There are numerous influences worth considering when addressing the issue of player development in America. Some are perhaps not in our control, while others may be in more of our control than we think; I contend that these issues affect player development directly and indirectly. Nonetheless, these ideas provide points of discussion for leaders involved with player development and by being aware of the factors listed below, perhaps we will forge clearer paths to successful player development. In addition, these points are often thought of as negative influences (as many of them are), yet a good exercise would be to try to glean positives from such issues to help player development in soccer.

  - **"Professional" sports** Consider numerous trades and firings (even at midseason!), lengthening of seasons and thus reducing the quality of regular season play, difficulty in maintaining loyalty to team colors when the colors keep changing, sponsorship logos on uniforms being bigger than the actual team logo, scandals, influence on college and high school athletics, ongoing ownership battles, "win at all costs" mentality, marketing and imagery over substance and long-term value, influx of professional players playing on Olympic teams, lack of funding for women's professional opportunities, pro players influencing coaching/management decisions (e.g., rosters, coaching, personnel), players being labeled as a "franchise," recruiting and trading to win versus development and the vast inequality between teams with and without money. In addition, youth and high school sports are not "professional" sports. However, numerous adults treat such sports as "professional" through recruiting, scholarships, sponsorships and media exposure at tremendous costs to all.

  - **Athletic directors.** Are they the best people to make decisions regarding player development? Also consider the pressure to "win now" at college and high school levels, control of decision-making by athletic directors with boards, funding, alumni, boosters and other influential bodies.

As an example, every year's "musical chairs" in the college coaching circles brings about curious changes in staffing. If one observes such changes over the years, one can begin to understand the varying philosophies and levels of stability (or lack thereof) of the programs.

- League administrators. These positions are often filled with volunteers who are obviously very busy people when it comes to scheduling matches, assigning fields, assigning officials, and structuring divisions. As such, they may or may not be highly knowledgeable about soccer issues such as competition, development, patience and vision. Unfortunately, some are behind when it comes to making decisions regarding player development. In addition, some personnel are so wrapped up in the "politics" of soccer that they forget about who and what matters most. It is no surprise that many clubs and teams have left long-established leagues over the years to go to newer situations where key player development decisions can be made by experienced, knowledgeable and visionary soccer coaches. As such, there are too many leagues operating independently of a unifying player development model, but at the very least, such changes have caused many to examine policies and procedures in an effort to improve player development and competitive structures to stimulate growth in soccer.

- Media. Certainly the media plays a huge part in athletics. Consider the sheer entertainment value of sporting events such as the Olympics, Super Bowl, World Series, Stanley Cup, NBA Finals and NASCAR. Without the media, soccer would not have grown to the level that it has in America, as events such as the World Cup, Champions League, Euro Cup, EPL and MLS are for the most part, mainstream covered events. Hopefully the women's side of soccer can be supported by the media to a level where it is a part of regular coverage versus just covering big events. However, soccer's challenges are still tremendous, as football, basketball, baseball, NASCAR and other sports are much more popular than soccer in the US media. In addition, it is quite a sad statement that college and high school level sports are covered to such an inequitable extent that even a global sport such as soccer has to fight for minimal coverage. The media has the capacity to bring about awareness of events through advertising and influences to promote sports in good ways. On the negative side, the media often influences the public toward superficial glamorization, egotistical characters versus team identity, lack of values, blaming of others versus self-responsibility, sensationalism versus core values, and temporary hype versus long-term contribution. Not every contest can be "epic" or "huge," can it? Certainly just these few influences of pop culture have lasting impacts on youths, parents and society as a whole.

- Social media. Such media are valuable in terms of exchanging ideas and connecting people around the globe. However, consider the influence on attention spans, ability to think critically and reason abstractly, need for immediate gratification and lack of communication skills such media also feed. We must have responsible leaders who offer guidelines of proper use and etiquette in addition to understanding social media's potential ramifications.

- Competition. In many ways, pure competition has changed wherein people seem to need a reason to compete instead of competing for the love of competition. Contracts, pay, rankings, bonuses, short-term means to ends maneuvers, lack of consequences or enforcement of rules, and an apathetic shadow are constants when it comes to competition in sports. In addition, some parental influences and their necessity to "bubble wrap" children from healthy competition have shaped youths into believing competition is bad. Instead, we need to promote healthy competition for long-term growth and development. Instead of keeping the wrong parents from dominating decision-making scenarios, leaders need to include the healthy-minded parents who support vision, commitment and values and highlight them instead of having to cater to the ignorant.

- **"Territorial" disputes.** There is far too much "ownership" of youths in athletics today and this is not restricted to any one group in particular. For example, some clubs are too busy fighting over players when they don't have the players' best interests in mind. Or, consider the high school coaches of various sports who like to blame club coaches for soccer being a year-round sport, only to turn around and recruit players of various sports to their programs, run "off-season voluntary" conditioning sessions or clinics, and exaggerate rather small accomplishments to sway parents and players. It really is sad that adults play such games at the expense of children. No one should be treated like property and no child or parent should ever be taken advantage of for some egotistical "coach" of a sport.

- **Sociology/Psychology.** In many ways, there has been a lowering of standards, expectations, and responsibilities when it comes to working hard to be good at something. Instead of saying "no," society often enables people to believe they are better than they really are. This happens in sport, academics and just about any field where people are told they are better than they are in the name of "self-esteem." Then, when the person, still a child in most cases, runs up against a person or situation that offers greater challenges, has higher expectations or has to give the child the truth about where they are relative to others, the child and consequently his or her parents have an exceedingly difficult time facing reality. The research in this area is extensive and I encourage everyone to read up on the topic (I offer a couple of article resources in chapter 4, but there are many resources available in a variety of mediums). In addition, I like to use a good definition of confidence of substance rather than the rather empty meaning people misuse. Confidence is the ability to successfully and repeatedly perform and execute skills under pressure versus the externally controlled "stuff" that parents and society often want to say it is. Similarly, excellence is about performing ordinary tasks extraordinarily well. We should praise good effort and encourage improvement rather than lower expectations and reward mediocrity.

- **Business/Economy.** Capitalism is thought of as a good thing, particularly among western societies. The idea of opening a business and being in charge of your own destiny is a large part of the American dream. There is no secret that many who run clubs or training clinics are in business for themselves with benefits that hopefully find their way to those who are part of the club. I have had many friends in coaching who suggest that many coaches coach here simply because they see the US as a business opportunity – to make money on the masses where soccer is still seen as a sport from abroad. While some clubs excel in the area of player development, many exist as independent entities seeking to make enough profit to pay staff and if other factors such as enjoyment of the game, improved technical or tactical ability and providing a home for teams to play under come along as consequences of the club's existence, then the club is considered a successful business. I understand that coaches need to "put food on the table" as the expression goes, but sport should be so much more than just a business. It is difficult to see club leaders run sports as solely a "business", but if it makes them money legally then no one is really going to suggest it is wrong of them. After all, they see an opportunity, they have paying customers and no one is really evaluating them in terms of values, conduct and success. That is, if parents are willing to pay and they don't know any better, then that's just the way it is. In addition, this idea of "pay-to-play" hinders player development across the country.

Hopefully, soccer will continue to grow in this country without simply being about business. It is wrong to make decisions purely based on business, such as keeping unruly parents in a club because they happen to pay the bills, but clubs do it regularly. I have often seen positive uses of business and soccer and can only hope the negatives eventually decline. In addition, the lack of soccer being enough of a "business" financially keeps a lot of good coaches from being full time. In other words, many full-time coaching opportunities do not provide adequate benefits in the areas of healthcare, retirement, life/disability insurance policies, etc. Unfortunately, there seems to be a growing disparity between part-time and full-time coaches; just because someone is coaching soccer full-time does not mean they are better than someone who is part-time. In fact, one of the challenges of my coaching career is that I haven't given up my "full-time" job of teaching because I never wanted soccer to be all about business for me, and I have always wanted diverse intellectual challenges in my life. However, given my successes and honors, it is easy to see that I often spend much more time on soccer teams as compared to coaches who classify themselves as "full-time." I've been more passionate and helpful to players and their families than many coaches who are full-time, and it pains me to see families spend ludicrous amounts of money for very average coaching and no extra benefits of experience, college process or long-term vision.

In addition, a lot of good coaches won't go "full-time" into soccer because of the lack of job security, benefits and funds. I have seen a lot of terrific full-time coaches, but unfortunately, I have seen a lot of very average ones who are simply in it for business and who are elevated in parents' eyes simply because they are full-time. Likewise, I have known excellent part-time coaches who should be promoted into key positions and salaried appropriately but just aren't. There is no doubt that soccer as a business needs evaluation and support. While many make good money off of soccer who deserve to, there are many who don't or in many cases, who just won't. Alas, the entrepreneurial aspect of soccer business is alive, while some structures, such as national programs for both males and females, are under-funded.

- **Rankings.** It seems as if society has an infatuation with rankings, however problematic they are. Logically, how can one ever truly rank all of the teams playing a sport when it is obvious that not all teams play each other? I have coached both club and high schools that were "nationally ranked" in the top 10 in their categories. In addition, my teams have knocked off teams that were "nationally ranked." What does such a ranking really mean? Were the teams considered to be very good among teams in the same age group? Absolutely, and it is always nice to have an outside entity take note of a team's accomplishments on a national level. When one looks at ranking schemes, however, one has to look at the obvious facts that:

  - not all teams are included as some are excluded by not competing in the same events or number of events.
  - some teams have media and other influences on ranking systems while others do not.
  - in the cases of youth/high school teams, if the "success" is largely a result of recruiting then why reward that? Is that a good thing in youth sports? Inflating a youth team's "status" has some rather negative long-term ramifications.
  - if a program doesn't play other members in the ranking, they fall under the radar, so how accurate can such a ranking be?

To help my teams, I used team rankings in the following ways (if the topic needed to be addressed at all):

- If our team was the one ranked (most of the time I had no idea until after the fact!), then I cautioned the team against complacency or celebration since there were more matches to play. I reminded the team that a ranking is just a number – in any given match, the score begins 0-0 and the opponent will want to prove a team unworthy of any ranking. Soccer is a game where there are too many variables that can affect the game: size and conditions of field, officiating, injuries, and even if we outshoot the opponent by a huge margin, we still have to get more shots into their goal than they do in ours. The only ranking that ever mattered, if any, was the final end-of-season ranking.

- If our team was the one not ranked or ranked lower then I used that as an incentive and encouraged the team to believe an opportunity to play such a team is one that a true champion goes after – it is much more fun to defeat a quality team than one that is inferior. In addition, each team will play with the same number of players, rules, field conditions, and ball. So, the message would be to believe you can win, play hard, focus on executing fundamentals, be alert, work together and, regardless of the result, be happy with the effort you give when the match is over. I relish the underdog position but have also had numerous situations where we were the "favored" team on paper, too.

We will probably not get away from rankings in this lifetime, but I am sure you can tell how I feel about them – they are mostly useless when it comes to "national rankings," especially in youth sports. If one is using rankings within a team or club structure, however, then I feel differently as healthy competition kept in good perspective is rather useful.

- "Traditional" sports culture. Football, basketball and baseball still have holds on the general sports audience in America. Add in golf, NASCAR, gymnastics, skating and to some extent, ice hockey, it follows that soccer has a lot of competition when it comes to generating a larger fan base. While MLS is still in existence after its predecessor (the old NASL) failed, the WPS folded (after its predecessor, WUSA, folded) and is now the NWSL. Men's and women's leagues have improvements to make, but this is not a book on professional leagues. Both leagues should continue to be involved with player development; the MLS has taken visible steps in that direction and that is a terrific growth area to watch. Having a true club system can help player development if administered and supported in the right way. Around the globe, soccer is often among the top sports, if not the top sport. In America, we have the participation numbers in soccer, but our soccer culture is just not what it is in other countries in terms of regional rivalries, passion on and off the field, and national pride. Perhaps the soccer culture will improve as time continues.

  *Note: This is not to advocate the violence associated with soccer in other countries – we certainly do not want that.*

The solutions to player development issues are complex, as entities of different size and stature continue to compete at various levels. However, there are encouraging signs that point toward possible united efforts. Some of the solutions that could be put into effect for all coaches include:

- Expect higher standards in training, encourage competition, teach skill performance under pressure, measure performance standards objectively to mark improvements made and needed.

- Identify, support and allow experienced coaches to lead player development systems and structures. Centralize some themes, yet allow for creativity, experience and variety to bring the best out of coaches and directors involved with player development.

- Hold everyone accountable, including people in leadership positions, coaching school graduates, league administrators, coaches at all levels, directors and others involved with player development decisions. They should have resources to support them that ultimately excel player development rather than be tied down with bureaucracy. With technology, it would be easy to share ideas from the top levels. Some examples could be published training sessions or focused themes identified by scouts. For example, one major issue in American soccer is the need to raise the standard to enter the attacking third (or even attacking half) in possession with the expectation to come away with a shot. Or as another example, set a professional standard to eliminate "professional fouls" and expect this of coaches rather than avoid dealing with it. Greater expectations of coaches and players can lead to greater successes in the long run. Of course, we must have coaches capable of not only teaching skills and ideas to execute this, but coaches who can maintain such a high standard without giving in to outside factors or pressures.

- Encourage greater education pursuits by all, not just coaches. Improve coaching courses by involving education concepts in courses. There are many who may know particular skills and have valuable experiences, but they sometimes need stronger formats to teach knowledge and have a lasting impact. In addition, make such courses less dependent on time and money, while at the same time, hold standards very high so that we don't create average coaches who get promoted into higher positions without proving themselves.

- Expect organizations and leagues to have soccer-knowledgeable coaches versus soccer-political coaches in key positions, reduce travel at younger ages, inspect matches, assess coaches and hold them accountable, and support coaches who can coach and lead player development.

- Expect media support in terms of covering soccer at various levels around the world, but especially when it comes to our soccer athletes. Encourage attendance in communities at all levels to create a soccer culture that people want to be a part of, rather than as seeing it as a means to an end.

- Obviously, money is one of the key factors on all soccer player development fronts. In addition to money, ego plays a part, as people must come together for the good of our players. The power of sport to affect lives positively will always endure, but hopefully soccer has that much more to say about it globally.

*Reflections:*

- What does player development mean to you?
- How do you contribute positively to player development?
- Is soccer a means to an end for you? Is it primarily for business purposes?
- How do you impact the teams you coach in terms of promoting the game to players, parents, families and community members?
- Who are the people you identify as leading player development in your community?
- What obstacles to player development do you face? How can you overcome them?

# CHAPTER 7

## DEVELOPING A YEAR-ROUND PROGRAM

*"Hard work does not guarantee you success, but without it,
you don't stand a chance." – Pat Riley*

To develop a culture of player development, a coach must establish a year-round program beyond the timeframe of the primary season of play. This is particularly important in competitive club, high school and college programs. The rhythm of the season is established by league guidelines and the specific program's leadership that sets the timeframe permitted for activities. For most coaches in these situations, there is a lot of time when players are out-of-season and must buy into alternative training to continue on the path of player development. Examples of year-round programs for club and high school coaches are included in this chapter, but it is important for coaches to stay informed through soccer coaching organizations as guidelines and formal recommendations begin to take shape (in the United States); these organizations include US Soccer/Developmental Academy and US Club Soccer/Elite Clubs National League. In addition, coaches must consider the level of competition, age, season, extra participation (e.g., ODP, camps), and other factors to modify these examples to fit player needs. There is much debate about how early a child should specialize; adults must be realistic, empathetic, visionary, and supportive on all sides of ongoing discussions in this area. Again, the hope is that the following examples provide skeletal frameworks for coaches to work from.

For a club team example, I have chosen a situation where the State Cup is in the fall for a team that plays in the U15-U18 age groups. U13-14 age groups often have State Cup competitions in the spring (except for U19). Of course, the year-round programs of the Developmental Academy and ECNL are operating without State Cup competitions and therefore teams in those arenas will have varying needs depending on the mandates of those organizations.

- **Early August to end-of-August: Pre-season block of three weeks** – skills and fitness testing; includes 5-day high-intensity mini-camp, 6 regular training sessions, and 2-3 match-condition scrimmages. Mini-camp descriptions and score sheets are given in later sections.

- **September – early November:** Regular season with an average of three training sessions and one match per week; State Cup play in some weeks increases matches to two per week.

- **Mid-November – mid-December:** Showcasing season with one week off during Thanksgiving; generally 2-3 training sessions per week with 2 showcases as match-play competitions. Players will work on getting "fitter, faster, stronger" with and without the ball after taking days off to rest.

- **Mid-January – mid-February:** Saturday morning "off-season" conditioning with and without a ball (fitness, agilities, jump-rope, games); one day per week of indoor training (focusing on technical skills and playing small-sided games with fluid play/limited instruction) and sometimes an additional day per week for futsal or indoor soccer league play (not for anything more than playing the game, getting touches, skill development, maintaining match sense, decision-making, and team chemistry). Skill and fitness testing given at the beginning of February.

- **Mid-February – May:** high school soccer pre-, regular, post-season; very limited club play; once per week for maintaining level of play (if that at all; often, no club sessions of any physical taxation since players are training/competing five days per week), skill development to higher standard, and staying "in tune" for showcasing, early summer play. Note, many of our players were the strength of their high school teams and because they played a lot, rest was needed for players since high school goes at least 5 days per week. Thus, sometimes, the one meeting during the week was just simply to meet, connect, and continue to build on individual/team qualities. May often involves tryouts, which again depend on age, high school play, and level.

- **Mid-June to early July:** gather team to train at club standard and prepare for regional/national play. If applicable, build toward any showcases, prepare players for other playing environments (college, amateur, pro) or next season; usually 2-3 training sessions per week plus one scrimmage on occasion. Fitness packets given to players to offer good workouts and guidance toward maintaining year-round fitness base (see appendix for the actual training packet that I give to my teams). Skill and fitness testing before sending players off on their own.

- **Mid-July to early August:** Once per week small-sided games, no training sessions. Players continue to work off of training packets to be "fitter, faster, stronger." Note: At club level, during the "off-season" workouts and sessions, attendance often varied and that is common for club teams. Generally, "if in town, then make the session" was our credo.

*Note:* *In-season training sessions are approximately 105 minutes and off-season training sessions are usually limited to 60-90 minutes. A weekly club training rhythm for in-season may look like this:*

| | |
|---|---|
| **Monday:** | Training session – match recovery, technical training, position-based possession, restarts or shadow play for attacking/defensive shape; light fitness/agilities. |
| **Tuesday:** | No team session, light workout on own; watch soccer highlights on television. |
| **Wednesday:** | Training session – high-intensity technical/tactical training, small-sided games to full-sided scrimmage; speed training, medium fitness. |
| **Thursday:** | Training session – high-intensity possession game to full-sided scrimmage, restarts, shape; high fitness. |
| **Friday:** | Day off. |
| **Saturday:** | Light workout on own; watch soccer live or on TV (or match). |
| **Sunday:** | Match (or light workout or day off). |

For a high school team example, I have chosen a situation where the season of play is in the spring to offer a contrast to the club rhythm example given previously. It is difficult to believe that our country still has different states playing high school soccer in the fall, winter or spring, but perhaps that is an ongoing debate for soccer bodies to work on. My recommendation would be to place high school soccer in the fall to align with collegiate play, but such a decision is not up to me.

I have coached in high school programs that play soccer in the fall or spring so the following plan can be tailored to meet the needs of a specific program. Because my most recent high school soccer coaching experiences have been in the spring, I have geared this section to that timing. In addition, with the number of players who play club soccer year-round, it is also important to take that under consideration when devising such a plan.

When coaching high school, I never tried to dictate out-of-season training for high school, but unfortunately, such practices are very common across many sports. Lastly, a high school coach should allow athletes to participate in other sports, as that is a part of the experience and ultimately, players and their families will select what is best for them at the time and in the long run. Communication of expectations is vital to success, while at the same time, adults need to be wise in working together for the health, well-being, and safety of each child.

Approximately 7-8 weeks prior to the season: For athletes not playing a sport prior to soccer season (or on a club team that is active during this time period), use a 6-week suggested training program as a framework to build endurance, strength, and skills. Approximately 4-5 days per week, the athlete will do workouts, such as the ones from the training packet guide offered in the appendix. Obviously, this depends on the condition of the athlete and other activities; thus, the coach cannot work directly with the team and cannot make such sessions mandatory. The reason for leaving a 1-2 week cushion is to taper down to the season, where the last week or so before the season, the athlete should just do shorter slow or light interval running (20 min.) along with plenty of stretching. The athlete is encouraged to work on foot skills and other technical areas (dribbling, passing, receiving, heading, finishing, turning, etc.), as appropriate.

The athletic department will also send out a confirmation of receipt of an appropriate physical examination by the athlete along with appropriate signatures on the form, which also serves as a medical release/emergency form.

*Note:   If the athlete is playing a winter sport, then they would not use the 6-week training program since they are already training / competing at least 5 days out of the week, and we cannot afford to overload the athlete's physical capacity.*

In addition, if the players in the high school program play in an indoor league that consists of one indoor small-sided game per week or if they play pick-up soccer once or twice per week in these weeks leading up to the season, then the 6-week training program can be used, but athletes should only be actively fitness-basing four days out of the week instead of five.

Approximately two weeks prior to the season: Team captains run fitness/ball skill sessions among players 2-3 times per week. This helps to get the rust off and develop program cohesion, spirit, and chemistry without making the sessions mandatory nor driven by the coaching staff. Make it clear to all personnel that no one should feel bad nor made to feel bad about missing any of these sessions.

Tryouts/pre-season: The first few days generally involve the following format, of which is a bit of a "mini-camp" format to help all players in the program and set standards/expectations from the beginning. As an example, consider the outline:

**Day 1:**   foot skills/dribbling, 1v1, 4v4; 100s

**Day 2:**   passing/receiving, 6v6, 11v11; cones

**Day 3:**   long balls, heading, 8v8; 300s (6x50 yard shuttles)

**Day 4:**   crossing, shooting/finishing, 11v11; 50-100 shuttles

**Day 5:**   program match warm-up, 11v11; no extra fitness

*Note:   Each day also includes proper warm-up/cool-down dynamic stretching and competitions in the skill, small-sided, match condition phases of the training session. Detailed descriptions, testing, and ranking schemes are explained in later sections of this book.*

Given the spring season of play, we only run one session per day for high school and the duration of tryout sessions is usually 120 minutes due to the large numbers, need for rest periods, and opening day paperwork, announcements, and activities. Brief program meetings are conducted at the beginning and end of each session, but they are kept to a minimum as we want to demonstrate to the players that we expect intensity, yet we also respect their schedules. If we can fit in a scrimmage versus another program, it would usually be on Day 5 or Day 6, with naming of the teams by Day 6 or Day 7. Teams are told in-person, using one-on-one staff-player mini-conferences, if possible (especially for the border-line JV/Varsity players) and then a formal announcement before the teams separate.

In-season: The rhythm generally consists of 3-4 training sessions and 1-2 matches per week from March through May, with one week of spring break off somewhere in the middle of the season depending on the school calendar. No weekend training sessions or matches are expected, especially since many of the athletes may have one club, ODP training or, in a rare instance, scrimmage/match during the weekend. Thus, a typical high school weekly training rhythm may have the following emphases:

| | |
|---|---|
| **Monday:** | technical plus fitness (depends on personnel) |
| **Tuesday:** | technical, tactical |
| **Wednesday:** | match |
| **Thursday:** | recovery, tactical |
| **Friday:** | match |

Pre-match is usually in a classroom 75 minutes prior to kick-off, and warm-up on the field begins 45 minutes prior to kick-off.

At the beginning of the season, on the first day when the teams are separated into JV and Varsity, a vote for captains is established where the players put down three names confidentially, and it is announced that the coaching staff will let the team vote, though the staff has the right to determine if 2 or 3 captains is appropriate for the team. A standard leadership discussion is used before such a vote takes place and the boundaries/responsibilities of being a captain are explained.

The captains meet with the coaching staff weekly (usually on the field before/after a training session or during the school day if a mutually convenient block of time is available and does not impact the student's schedule heavily). The captains also help organize dress-up days, music for match warm-ups, spirit wear if necessary, what to wear on match days, psych-up activities such as secret buddies (motivational note and small piece of candy), and pasta dinners, which provide a social outlet for the team. Though the captains are the primary leaders on the team, all members are given a brief orientation on social media, how to communicate with the media, and a general briefing on representing the team, program, and school on and off the field.

Some form of community service will also take place during the season. Various sheets are used throughout the season to help the player get the most out of the experience, help the coaching staff get to know the players, or stimulate team chemistry. In addition, the athletic department also has a form that each player must sign and get signed by parents; the form is essentially the program's code of conduct.

Throughout the season, weekly feedback is given to each player by the coaching staff. Players are encouraged to watch other matches and occasionally scout another team if appropriate; maturity and professionalism must be maintained to the highest standards. After each of the first and second thirds of the season, player evaluations are given to help the athlete continue to improve. In addition, because of the length and intensity of the season, one or two days off, and one "fun" day off of the field are included, and an occasional training session gets replaced with a team meeting. Such decisions help keep the players "fresh" and motivated throughout the long season. Juniors organize the "Senior Day" match, which involves preparing a brief bio on each senior, organizing gift-giving and parent involvement, and liaising with the announcers on match day.

Post-season: Conferences take place after the season, usually beginning two days after our last match. An evaluation, goal-setting, and future plans are included in the discussion. In addition, all school equipment must be returned (e.g., uniforms, warm-ups, etc.). At the end of the school year, one meeting for interested players for the following year will occur. This is an organizational meeting where we get an idea of our numbers, reiterate expectations, offer summer training ideas, and get a feel for other sports played and club participation, as appropriate, so that we avoid overtraining yet encourage an appropriate amount of activity. We also expect the athletes to attend one strength training session given by the athletic training staff before they leave, unless they have already taken a strength training physical education class or are taking one in the fall season. A meeting with rising seniors also takes place after the season to encourage a strong foundation for the following year. Depending on the school situation, one meeting with rising ninth grade students may occur to essentially give the same organizational information and physical activity expectations. College process talks are given, as appropriate, though most college recruiting is done via club soccer.

Summer: Training largely depends on the athlete and what their schedule looks like. However, the player is encouraged to be active 6 days out of every 7 on what I have developed as the 1-2-3 plan (1 day of cross-training such as rollerblading, tennis, swimming, cycling; 2 days of harder interval-training; 3 days of medium interval-training or soccer skills/pick-up). Two to three days each week are also devoted to strength training if the student is a rising sophomore or older student athlete and has permission from parents, athletic trainer, and doctor.

Again, if the player is participating in club or other summer events, then some modification is necessary. In addition, we encourage the player to attend one or two camps, particularly if they don't have any club or other events. Essentially, all returning players are given a summer calendar/training log and are expected to fill it out daily. They then turn in the logs in person on the first day of returning to school, re-establishing the personal connection and accountability. Note: As technology improves in the areas of online and apps, it is possible to record data and have it automatically sent to the coaching staff.

Fall: This time period involves another 6-week block of fitness-basing if the athlete is not participating in club or another high school sport. In addition, a strength training class should be taken if the athlete is not participating in another high school sport. We meet during the second or third week of school to determine this time-frame for each athlete and review expectations of the soccer program. Generally, most players are participating in club or another sport so we don't have to manage their physical activity until the winter season.

*Statement from a former soccer player:*

*"Ashu's coaching style and Electra's core values and morals laid a very powerful foundation for me to excel and succeed in the real world today and for that I thank him. Ashu always focused on the fundamental skills — dedicating time during each training session to repetitious patterns to enhance muscle memory. Ashu had a coaching/teaching style that involved technical and tactical learning, which gave me a clear understanding of how to break down the game of soccer, which allowed the Electra to strategically execute its match plan. Ashu was more than a soccer coach. He cared about our overall success as students, which was reflected in taking the Electra players on a 'College Tour.' One of my most memorable moments was filming an instructional video with Anson Dorrance and Tony DiCicco near the campus of UNC on 'how to play the 1-4-3-3'"*

— Erica Lee, BRYC *Electra* U15-U19 (Boston University)

Readers are directed to the appendix for several pages that make up a training packet that I give to club and high school players. I hand the packet out in a meeting where I can discuss purpose, benefits, expectations, and precautions with parents and players together. There is so much material available on the internet, of which coaches ought to supply their families with links on websites. In addition, sports medicine professionals, such as doctors, strength and conditioning coaches, fitness experts, nutritionists, and athletic trainers, should be consulted to support your program.

Coaches should schedule regular meetings with such personnel so that the team has the necessary resources to make good decisions collaboratively and with balance to improve individually. The idea is to get "fitter, faster, stronger" to instill a culture of health, expectations, lifetime wellness, responsibility to self and team, and accountability. Note: Also please stay attentive to previous notes about fitness with and without a ball, cross-training, avoiding repetitive-use injuries, encouraging endurance for life, etc.

In addition to conditioning, I also include other vehicles to help enhance year-round player development. Please see the appendix for self-training suggestions and a juggling grid as examples that coaches can use. Likewise, online tracking services are growing in number that may also help coaches and players document growth and objectives. Many other components of a successful year-round program are described throughout this book; such areas include team chemistry, evaluations, feedback, and the college process.

## FINDING A BALANCE FOR PLAYERS

Apart from all of the materials in this chapter and the appendix, coaches must assist players (and parents) in finding a balance of soccer with the rest of their lives. Family, religion, friendships, health, and academics must be in check, rather than putting all of the proverbial "eggs in one basket" in terms of pursuing just one sport, be it soccer or any other sport, at the risk of jeopardizing other areas. While it is true that pursuing team athletics has so many positive aspects, one also needs to make sure that the environment is healthy, challenging, and meaningful toward life in general. Beyond the match on the field, we want the player to be a champion in life. Thus, as much as organization and planning are parts of excellent coaching, remembering to be flexible, versatile, and balanced are key elements for long-term success. On the other hand, as noted in books such as *The Talent Code* (Daniel Coyle, 2009) and *Bounce* (Matthew Syed, 2010), if one wants to be an expert in something, then one must invest the time in terms of hours upon hours of deep practice. Thus, it makes sense for many to pursue soccer year-round supplemented with thoughtful activities, though great care must be taken to have a challenging, developmentally appropriate, stimulating, healthy, supportive, and positive culture to avoid stagnation, overuse injury, and burn-out. Every high achiever will note inspiring figures in their lives, and thus it is possible (and likely) that you are one of those people for the players you coach.

*Statement from a former player regarding having a balance:*

*"One of the best things I remember is the fact that you never made me choose between two sports. Having a strong passion for field hockey and soccer, I was a bit scared at first, that maybe I would be benched or asked to choose between the two, but instead, you were understanding and worked along with me and the busy schedule I led."*

— Cannon Clough (went on to play soccer at UNC-Charlotte and UNC-Chapel Hill)

*Reflections:*

- Do you have a year-round program for the athletes you coach?
- How do you hold players accountable for off-day and off-season workouts?
- Do you help players structure their weekly workouts year-round in such a way to highlight peak and rest periods?
- How do you keep your players "fresh" for training sessions and off-day training year-round?
- What performance standards do you maintain for the team in terms of fitness and skills tests?
- How will national standards impact your program?

## CHAPTER 8

# COACHING METHODOLOGY

*"Winning isn't everything, but the will to win is everything."*
*— Vince Lombardi*

## BASIC DEFINITIONS

"Soccer is a simple game." Many people have said this, and it is a good tenet to remember when coaching. Some coaches often overdo it in terms of making the game more complex than it needs to be. This complication arises from any number of areas, including misplaced enthusiasm, lack of confidence, an overwhelming need to seemingly be in charge and at the center of attention, and because "someone else is doing it." Be sure to remember a few of the universal basics that hold true in whatever formation one chooses to follow or which play one chooses to run off of a restart:

- Time/Space — we want as much of these resources when we attack, and we want to eliminate these for our opposition when we defend.

- Attacking/Defensive shape — the contrast between expansion on attack and compression/compaction on defense.

- Seam — the passing channel between players; look to play through-passes in these lanes on attack, and deny this space when defending (i.e., close down passing lanes).

- Gap — the space between lines of play in a formation (e.g., between forward and midfield, midfield and back); find these gaps in the opponent's shape to exploit on attack, close these down when defending.

- 1st, 2nd, 3rd Options/Vision — encourage players to see all options including what is near (1st), mid-range (2nd), and far (3rd). Too often, players are not coached very well in terms of vision and as a result they play too predictably on the attack. Expectations on players in terms of problem solving must be raised for player development to occur. If coaches improve a player's vision, then they are moving in the right direction.

- 1st, 2nd, 3rd attacker — player with the ball (1st), players in support of the ball in all directions (2nd), and players stretching and threatening deep areas in the opponent's shape (3rd).

- 1st, 2nd, 3rd defender — often referred to as "pressure-cover-balance" and defined by the player on the ball (1st), covering players in support of the player pressuring the ball (2nd), and balancing players maintaining defensive shape for extremes (3rd).

- Squeezing/Pressure points — moments in the match where high-pressuring opponents literally squeezes the ball out of them through "hungry wolf" or "wild dog" defensive intensity.

- Rhythm — linking passes in a match where players are in sync and moving the ball the way they want to against an opponent.

- Momentum — despite always desiring this in a match, there are moments when we lose this; teams need to be able to understand the ebbs and flows in a match and how to ride and withstand such moments. To create momentum, we play to get up 3-0 in matches, understanding that the third goal in any match is a huge momentum statement.

- Compete — effort, attitude, and desire are essential to developing competitive players and teams.

- Culture — regardless of the team's performance, a coach must establish an enduring healthy culture that emphasizes player development, promotes players to next levels, assists players in growth and improvement, strives for excellence as a habit, remains humble and fights off complacency, unites to form a force greater than any individual, values loyalty and responsibility to the team on and off the field, encourages players to give back to the game, and appreciates victory with honor and integrity to have lasting success.

## TRAINING SESSIONS

To plan any training session, a coach must articulate goals and objectives, and design exercises that positively impact the game. Too often, I run into coaches who are either disorganized and their sessions reflect wasted opportunities for improving players, or coaches who can organize a session, but lack the expertise at executing the session to have optimal player and team development. Thus, one of the best suggestions that I can make to coaches is to write out goals and objectives for each training session in the areas of topics covered, psychological, social (team), physical, technical, tactical, and any other descriptive term to elevate the positive impact of the session.

Regarding the choice of topic, please also note that I do not always adhere to the "one-topic-only" philosophy, as I believe that if you are an effective coach, you have to not just be organized at running a training session, but also remain flexible. If players are underperforming in an area that is not your main topic for the day then you have no choice but to correct behavior so that play is improved. Too often, players are uninformed, and they get away with bad habits because coaches lack the knowledge or desire to make corrections. Thus, write out the session and approximate duration for each exercise, along with grid dimensions, number and color of vests, number of balls required, player numbers, and specific exercises with coaching points. However, also be comfortable to adapt appropriately, not to confuse players or be disorganized, but to impact play each day so that every player is accountable, challenged to excel and performance is elevated. In the sessions that I describe in the next chapter, you will see that some sessions include not only main topics, but also other exercises that need attention, even if not directly on point. My emphasis on the fundamentals is key, regardless of the topic. The basic format for training sessions follows a simple format:

- Warm-up (WU)

- Beginning words (BW) – in addition to the main topics for the day, offer brief comments to set the tone, bring focus, lighten the mood, or offer a memorable quote, share an article, or show a picture to connect with the team.

- Fundamental (FL) – technical skill emphasis.

- Match-related (MR) – technical and tactical emphases under pressure with competitive elements, directional or targeted.

  *Note: This may or may not include full-sized goals and maximum numbers; in terms of numbers, this could be 1v1 through 8v8.*

- Match-condition (MC) – technical and tactical emphases under pressure with competitive elements and simulation to full-match environment; play to full-sized goals, numbers from 8v8 to 11v11 (ideally); attention to restarts and other parts of the match are also worked on.

- Cool-down (CD)

- Final words (FW) – final words before dismissing, in addition to brief summary for today, leave with a few words that maintain a connection to the team and keep players looking forward to returning to the next session, be it training, a match, or other team activity.

In addition, I add **Pure Fitness (PF)** on occasion; this is fitness without a ball and done purely to build each player's fitness base along with mental toughness. Please note that fitness with a ball is emphasized to some extent in every training session and the coach must set high expectations for competitiveness and intensity so that fitness is naturally occurring in training sessions, too. Your team's level, age, and schedule will determine the regularity and amount of PF needed in sessions. Please see the training packet section in the appendix for examples of PF exercises.

The standard warm-up for training sessions may vary, but my teams have used the following general framework, to be completed prior to the main part of the training session:

- Dynamic Stretching/Agilities: Players jog across the field a couple of times to warm up the body's muscles, establish a comfortable mindset, and connect with teammates. This is followed by a series of agilities. Please see the agility warm-up exercises in the training packet section of the appendix for specific exercises.

- Ball skills:
  - Individually, players should do **foundational foot skills** prior to beginning the above dynamic stretching, if possible. If the culture is set, players will automatically do simple skills as they wait for the formal training session to begin, but if this is not the case, include some simple exercises with a ball after the agilities. I have my teams begin with the following exercises: 50 step-ups (toe-taps on the ball with the soles of the feet), 50 ping-pongs (lateral taps of the ball with the insides of the feet), 50 triangles (form triangle with the ball by pulling ball to self with the sole of one foot, cut across the body with inside of the same foot, then push out with the inside of the opposite foot; do 25 in each direction), 50 see-saws (lateral movement while facing forward throughout the exercise, push ball away with the outside of the foot, bring it back with the inside of the same foot; repeat on opposite side), 100 foot juggles (instep/laces, no spin). To keep these exercises fresh, sometimes I pick one day where players perform the exercises relatively stationary and another day moving around the field. I also challenge players with variations off of the main foundation skills — adding an extra explosive touch, combining skills, add in moves behind the standing leg for increased coordination, and other simple enrichments to make the exercises fun, challenging, and effective. See juggling grid in the appendix for variations on juggling challenges. The benefit of performing these touches is that each player has logged approximately 500 touches on the ball before the main training session begins.
  - **Dribbling moves** to improve foot skills — see the appendix for various moves. Have players practice moves in "traffic" so they have to make good decisions and good touches in realistic situations rather than in isolation. Add in surface restrictions, body part stops, ball exchanges, and unrestricted creative moments. Remind players to pay attention to looking up, change of pace, change of direction, size of touch, exploding into space, tighter touches in traffic, and to dribble at match speed.
- "Toss"-and-settles: each player has a ball. Encourage the players to accelerate by performing a dribbling move after settling the ball — do not allow players to "trap" the ball but keep the ball moving with thought as to direction, angle, speed; the player flicks the ball up with either foot about head height (or use hands to toss depending on skill level since the player must get enough repetitions) and settles the ball with either foot using:
  - **Inside of foot wedge** — use the inside of the foot to wedge the ball between the inside of the foot and the ground as soon as the ball hits the ground.
  - **Outside of foot wedge** — use the outside of the foot to wedge the ball between the outside of the foot and the ground as soon as the ball hits the ground.
  - **"Roof"** — use the sole of the foot to cushion the ball as soon as the ball hits the ground.
  - **"Elevator"** — use the top of the foot to carry the ball downward to the ground (no bounce); the key is to lift the leg to catch the ball in the air and then move the leg down with the ball so there is barely any sound as the ball is settled to the ground.
  - **"Cruyf" settle** — catch the ball with the inside of one foot behind the other leg, as if doing a Cruyf move; this is basically an inside wedge behind the other leg. Players need to bend the knees slightly and keep a wide stance to perform this skill.
- With a partner, work on partner juggles (example, forced 3-touch, or vary 1 and 2 touches depending on command), passing techniques (short distance on the ground, medium length bending balls and chips, long drives and lofts/flighted balls), heading.
- Small-group possession: The next phase of the warm-up usually involves some form of 3v1, 4v2, 5v2, 6v3, 4v4 +2, or similar small-sided possession game. My preference is to have a few smaller

games going on, though on occasion, I'll have one large game depending on the needs for team chemistry, complexity, and connectedness.

- **Regularly used first exercises:** It is a good idea for the coach to have a set of core warm-up exercises to use to provide variety and teaching opportunities. At the same time, these exercises are generally for the whole team and can provide good opportunities to establish team spirit, connectedness, and chemistry, along with occasional recreational moments with fun as the main objective. The coach should rotate these exercises frequently while demanding proper technique during each phase. Some exercises of this nature that I use include:

  - **Circle exercises:** half of the team around the circle with a ball while the other half is in the middle without a ball; players in the middle check to a player on the outside, perform an exercise, and then return the ball to the same player or a different player. This is a good exercise to work on many technical skills, usually a few each time so the execution of the exercises stays sharp. I have players on the outside move side-to-side to keep them active and also to make the inside players look for a teammate to improve vision. Outside players are encouraged to settle balls with good technique when receiving a ball from an inside player. Outside players also will toss balls with and without spin to keep inside players on their edge. In addition, I always have players give a teammate a "high-five" as they switch from outside to inside roles, or vice versa, to maintain spirit, team chemistry, and communication. Sample circle exercises include:

    - 1-touch pass back to the same player
    - Turn, find another player within 3 touches
    - Turn, explode using a dribbling move, find another player
    - Volley/half-volley, chest-volley, headers from tosses; encourage players to leave the ground, as appropriate, to work on balance, coordination, competitive mentality to win balls in the air, and to improve power. A sample variation is to have the outside player toss the ball, the inside player volleys back to the outside player, the outside player volleys again to the inside player, and the inside player settles ball back to outside player, all while on the move from distance. Note: Consult your colleagues, directors, or medical personnel regarding heading the ball in terms of technique, age, development, concussion potential, etc.
    - Work wall passes, take-/fake-overs, double passes, and overlaps to improve combination play with outside players.
    - Have players "partner up" in the middle to receive a ball, combine with each other before passing to an outside player; can also use volleys in pairs in the middle for added technical skill options.

  - **Pingers:** (a.k.a. "Brazilians" or "Peles") Players are in pairs, sharing one ball, approximately one yard apart. The coach can decide to do these exercises in place or while moving halfway across the width of the field. If done while moving, then remember that the person going backward is the "server." Be sure to rotate roles.

    - Right foot to right foot
    - Left foot to left foot
    - Diagonals and straights — one partner always passes diagonally (e.g., right foot to partner's right foot) while the other partner passes straight (e.g., right foot to partner's left foot).
    - Clocks — 2-touch where the player receives with the inside of one foot, brings ball across body to inside of the opposite foot, and passes straight to partner's foot, forming a narrow rectangle; players go counterclockwise for a predetermined time and then switch to clockwise. Encourage players to "hang in the air" while performing the two touches.

- Half-volleys/volleys — use "adjust-plant-punch" 3-step technique (a la the Irish step dancing rhythm mentioned earlier in the book); use for single foot strikes and headers, and for foot-foot, thigh-foot, chest-foot, head-foot combinations. For foot skills, be sure to practice inside "forehand" as in tennis), instep, and outside ("backhand") techniques.

- **"Chinese Coervers":** Players are in pairs, sharing one ball, maintaining approximately a two-yard distance apart. Perform 3-touch exercises where the rhythm is receiving touch-preparation touch-pass back to the partner on the ground with an aim toward bisecting the partner's feet. Both feet are used, depending on the particular combination of inside and outside of foot used. Players move up and back in synchronized movements — as one partner is coming forward in the touch-touch-pass rhythm, the other partner is moving backward, trying to maintain the two-yard distance. This is a good technical skill and speed exercise that also brings fitness and agility with a ball into the exercise. The possible arrangements of inside- and outside-of-foot touches and passes include:

  - Inside-inside-inside
  - Inside-inside-outside
  - Inside-outside-inside
  - Inside-outside-outside
  - Outside-inside-inside
  - Outside-inside-outside
  - Outside-outside-inside
  - Outside-outside-outside

- **"Brazilian" 3-touch:** Two players share one ball and are approximately ten to fifteen yards apart; passes are on the ground and again, they consist of inside- and outside-of-foot combinations of a touch-touch-pass rhythm (see "Chinese Coervers" for arrangements). The idea here is that the first touch is used to receive the ball laterally away from the body, the player steps past the ball throwing a fake (e.g., dipping the shoulder, throwing the arms, nodding the head) for deception, brings the ball back to the center with the next lateral touch, and then passes to the teammate with the third touch, again aiming to bisect the teammate's feet so the teammate can begin the pattern with either foot. Remind players to be light on their feet and to move their feet quickly to make adjustments depending on the use of the inside or outside of the foot.

- **Shuttles:** Players are in groups of five to seven, depending on numbers available. Each group has players facing each other on either end of an imaginary 15-20 yard line. One ball is needed per group. Generally, the player performs a skill, then runs to the end of the opposite line, usually running at the player on the opposite side to challenge bad touches. Some exercises that can be used include:

  - 2-touch passing — inside-inside both feet, outside-inside same foot (be sure ball does not roll backward on the outside touch), and inside-outside same foot.
  - 3-touch passing — use ideas from the "Brazilian" 3-touch exercise, focusing on inside-inside-inside to simulate receiving touch to space, looking up to see that the passing lane is closed, bringing the ball back in the opposite direction laterally, and then passing through the imaginary open passing lane.
  - 1-touch passing — good for focus, technique, speed.
  - 1-touch passing involving wall passes; player who passes across the distance makes bent run to open up body to player who receives — form wall pass and pass across the distance to keep

1-touch rhythm going. Encourage good technique by using the "far foot" to execute the return pass in the wall pass combination.

- Throw-ins across distance to receiving teammate who deals with bouncing ball with a run-through or settle (also spin and skip balls along the ground for added improvement to first touch) and speed dribbles back to the other line; rotate to high arc throw-ins so the receiving player can practice taking the flighted ball down with a foot settle (see above "Toss"-and-Settle exercises).

*Note: Depending on the situation, you may want to have the goalkeeper punt or throw balls across a longer distance to help players improve their first touch from flighted balls.*

- **Team handball:** an active, fun game to use on days when the main training session topic involves flighted balls, headers, volleys, or crossing. The rules of the game vary from coach to coach, but I have stuck to the following with good success:

  - Divide the team into two equal teams, use an area of approximately 30 x 50 yards, with goals at each end.
  - Play is directional, as in a regular match.
  - The ball is passed by the hands among players on the attacking team; they may bump (as in volleyball or rugby) with a fist, roll on the ground, or use a legal throw-in to pass to a teammate; except the next player cannot pass the ball in the same way it was passed to them (thus, mental skills are being worked on, too).
  - A player may carry the ball with at most two steps.
  - The attacking team turns the ball over if the ball drops, is batted down (from a bump or throw-in pass), or is intercepted.
  - The defending team can come within arm's distance of an attacking player to try to block the ball and is unlimited in number of steps while on defense.
  - A goal may only be scored with a header into the opposing team's goal.
  - Coaches should reinforce the good by-products of this game with the team: communication, quick thinking, movement off the ball, combination play, rhythms of changing the point of attack and short-short-long, transition, going to goal, and of course, fun.

- **2 up/1 down:** Divide the team into two equal teams. Team A possesses one ball on the ground using their feet to pass the ball. Team B has two balls that they may pass with their hands until they can throw one of the balls at the ball that is possessed by Team A. The teams switch roles when the hit is made. Make it competitive by keeping time as to how long a team can maintain possession of the ball. Or, play to a certain number of passes. Vary the size of the grid and restrict touches depending on the skill level of the group you are working with.

- **Tag games:** there are many tag games to use as a recreational warm-up. Obviously, you don't want to spend a long time on these, but use them sparingly for variety in how training sessions begin. Some tag games include:

  - Freeze tag — use a ball to pass through the frozen player's legs for releasing the player.
  - Railroad tag — vary the game to make the chased player have to tag one of four cones before laying down for safety.
  - Pinnie tag — Players are paired up with one ball between them except for two players (or four, depending on numbers) who are attached by holding a pinnie. These players who are "it" try to tag any player without a ball. Thus, the partners who are in the field try to work together to save each other by communicating and passing the ball back and forth.

There are many other core exercises described in the next chapter that contains sample sessions for an entire season. Such exercises include topics on additional foot skills, long balls, bending balls, finishing, passing, receiving, shielding, turning, and heading. It is critical that coaches involve technical training in every training session and assign homework so that players may also practice skills on their own. Please see the appendix for additional skills to use for player development.

For training session and match cool-down exercises, use simple agilities, such as jogging cross-widths of the field, or dynamic stretches used in the warm-up, such as sideways shuffles, grapevine, light skipping, diagonal running, S-curves, and other movements. Players will also take time to stretch on their own and in partners. Be sure to build time in so that players have this opportunity to slow down their heart rates, stretch to prevent soreness and tightening up, replenish fluids, and to regenerate for the next session.

One major theme for training sessions is that they need to be competitive in positive ways that bring out the best in players and impact the constant climb toward excellence in player development. Please see the score sheet samples in the appendix; use these for mini-camp and training sessions throughout the season. The positive effect of the score sheet is that it raises intensity and focus when used occasionally throughout the season, yet it is not as useful if it is only used for mini-camp or conversely if it is used for every training session.

Another key idea for training sessions is that the coach must lead the group in developmentally appropriate exercises that challenge, stimulate, and improve players in the areas of technical, tactical, physical, psychological, and socio-emotional quality. Remember to increase or decrease the difficulty level of the exercises through good decisions regarding use of time, space, dimensions, numbers, and touches on the ball. In addition, coaches should not micromanage every move that players make, but instead, inspire and stimulate creativity, decision-making, and problem-solving through effective communication **(remember to use why, how, where, what, and who to engage players)**. Stay attentive to different learning styles as you explain exercises and options on the field – players will have strengths and weaknesses with your visual, auditory, and haptic teaching methods. *Make sure they do things because they understand the importance of what to do, not just because you tell them to do it.* If players take ownership in their learning, can train in an environment that doesn't freeze them for fear of doing something "wrong," and can make sense of their connectedness to the bigger picture of player development, competition, and the team/program, then they are much more likely to develop with your coaching methodology.

Likewise, motivate players consistently toward intrinsic motivation so that they will want to improve on their own during and outside of your training sessions. Thus, consistently strive for self-improvement and be attentive to the team's needs, as players will feed off of your passion for the game and caring of them as individuals and as a team. By making decisions and using good training sessions with the intent of player development, your team is much more likely to obtain lasting positive impacts as a result of the experience under your coaching leadership. Thus, you are building relationships and core values in every training session – this is one of the most important methodologies in coaching any sport.

Lastly, coaches should remember that they have access to an abundance of exercises from a variety of sources. One can collect all of the exercises they want, but there are greater needs in the areas of knowledge, experience, assessment, evaluation, and understanding to fully commit to improving player development. Thus, a coach needs to positively impact player development through coaching leadership whereas a set of exercises is just a set of tools that provides a beginning point. Have the highest standards for yourself as a coach, and not to just improve aspects of the game for the player but to also contribute to the development of the person as a whole.

## RESTARTS

Coaches need to determine a framework of ideas for restarts that have enough variations to keep players interested and maintain tradition, yet not contain an overabundance of intricacies that end up making the restarts unnecessarily complicated. The most important mantra that I use for my teams is **"sprint first, rest second,"** as this gets players in the proper frame of mind after a restart is signaled (e.g., the ball goes out of bounds or the referee calls a foul). Players must sprint into shape, being aware of an opportunity for a quick restart whether on attack or defense, and then briefly "rest," in terms of collecting oneself in the brief moment preceding the instant when the restart is actually taking place. The "rest" does not imply the player shuts down but that the player engages to read and react for the ensuing play. An additional comment that I make to my teams is that "just because the ball goes out of bounds does not mean your brain does." Of course, use judgment when making such a suggestion, as I am rather blunt and direct with my comments.

Coaches need to work on attacking and defensive restarts in training sessions regularly so that the plays become automatic with high degrees of understanding and execution. Some coaches like to control every player decision on restarts, whereas my philosophy is to arm players with a variety of restarts to choose from. Ultimately, players learn to make decisions and appreciate the opportunity to test out restart variations of their choosing. In addition, it helps players learn how to work together, discover what works and what doesn't, understand and appreciate the roles and identities of their teammates and become stronger problem solvers. We want our players to take ownership and responsibility so this is one area where an effective coach can lay a strong foundation for growth and maturity in decision-making, leadership, communication skills, and cooperation.

Of course, teach and help guide the team as to when each variation is appropriate and likely to have a greater chance of success. The appendix has examples of restarts that are trademarks of my teams. It is impossible to cover every variation in detail, but readers are encouraged to examine their personnel, identify roles, and create variations, as appropriate. As a reminder, the examples provided in the appendix are snapshots of:

- Attacking and defending corner kicks

- Attacking free kicks

As an example of adapting to age-appropriate restarts, consider the youth player who is U9-U12 playing on a smaller field with smaller numbers. For attacking corner kicks, I always encourage the quick short corner using the 2v1 advantage (most opponents don't catch on and, if they do, they only send one player to defend the corner).

For the two players on the ball, remind them that the player closest to the end line touches the ball and overlaps wide of his or her teammate to get a good shooting angle and as an attacking shape to take advantage of the 2v1. The player on the ball dribbles along the end line and decides whether to give the ball to the teammate who made the overlapping run or to use a late cross to feed teammates making runs to goal.

As the reader will notice, my teams and I use words for the attacking restarts that have some meaning or correlation to the particular play or team. Coaches will want to develop easy-to-remember code words that help team members to remember the plays. In addition, given the limited training time with the youngest players, there is no need to spend excessive time on restarts — just teach a few of the basic ideas and instead, gear training time toward maximum touches on the ball.

For defensive corner kicks, I have included one formation that I use often when coaching girls soccer (youth or high school). We use a basic "3-4-3-1" framework that includes the goalkeeper plus two post players (3), strong flighted ball winners just a step from the six yard box (4), players just steps off of the penalty spot (3), and one roaming player (1) who protects the short and our counterattacks as necessary. We use a combination of zonal and man-to-man when defending corner kicks. However, I don't go into depth here because the coach needs to decide what is best for the team based on gender, level of play, age, personnel, opponent, size of field, and perhaps other variables that require situational decisions. However, the framework has worked very well for several years, considering how few goals were ever conceded on corner kicks in hundreds of matches. Note: As a critique of this formation that I prefer to use, some may say that players might be wasted on the post(s). However, sometimes, clogging the box creates a lot of potential defensive issues (e.g., miscommunication, getting into each other's way, etc.). This is the "chess match" of soccer in terms of decision-making.

As with attacking restarts, be sure to practice your defensive postures, identify roles, rotate players to prepare for situations that are bound to cause players to make decisions and adjustments quickly, and constantly ask players "what if?" questions to improve their on-the-field problem solving skills.

Additional restarts that need attention in training sessions are throw-ins, goal kicks, kick-offs, and goalkeeper distribution.

*Note:*   *Though the latter is a pause in the match rather than a dead ball restart, you must teach your team how to manage this vital part of the game. I include brief comments on each of these situations here:*

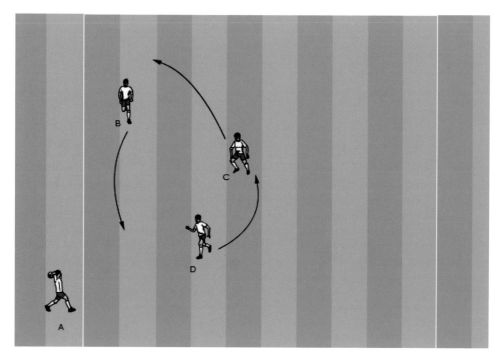

- Throw-ins

    - **Attacking** — For most throw-ins, we use a set of three options off of a basic set of movements. We expect each player to be able to throw in and receive the ball effectively, and thus we incorporate throw-ins into the match warm-up and into training sessions on occasion. Thus, all players are proficient on both ends of the throw-in. If we have a particularly long throw-in specialist, then we devise plays off of that special quality and use it depending on the situation. Generally, our outside backs take throw-ins, though we often look for a quick restart so it is not unusual to see midfield players or even forwards throw the ball in, especially as our style is to play up-tempo and high energy. Lastly, if we are in a particularly tight match then we do not allow our outside backs to take throw-ins in the attacking third of the field. Three simple options can be used off of the following basic movements.

**Note the basic roles of each player:**

A- Player throwing in the ball

B- Checking run, staying out of the "alley" (approximately 2-yard channel from the touch-line)

C- Deep run, high into space created by B's checking run

D- Spin to make run into space created by C's deep run, also makes space for A

Option 1:   A throw-in to B, lay ball back to A for a chip to C into space (replicates the short-short-long rhythm of play)

Option 2:   A throw-in to C who looks for support from A or inside to D

Option 3:   A throw-in to D who looks to combine with C or support from A or B

*Note:* *There are many variations that can be used, depending on personnel, age, level of experience, situation, distance from goal, etc. Coaches must train initial deceptive movements that come before the primary runs and then they must teach second and third runs. Have fun, be creative, and be sure to practice all aspects of throw-ins in your training sessions.*

Coaches working with young players should work on throw-ins in terms of techniques of throwing and receiving. However, an even bigger mistake perhaps is that coaches working with older players neglect this important part of the game, as it is an opportunity to work on upper body strength, coordination, flexibility, and range of motion, while at the same time throw-ins provide good opportunities to work on first touch.

- **Defending** — It is particularly important that players are trained to mark players appropriately tight. Train players to mark against the throw-ins meant to be flicked on and the throw-ins played to feet. Likewise, don't allow players to get spun and burned by opponents who are good at using their physical presence and back-to-pressure qualities. Mark extra-long throw-ins by fronting and backing a designated target player. In addition, we will always pull a forward back to mark the thrower, or at least be a presence so the opponent does not consider playing a ball off of a throw-in back to the player throwing the ball in. I am shocked at how many teams at all levels do not mark the thrower, which then results in the thrower often receiving a ball back and serving a dangerous cross into the box or combining with another player to threaten the goal.

- Goal kicks

  - **Attacking** — This aspect of the game also depends on the age, level, and experience of the team. Our preference is to play out of the back with a high percentage pass rather than a long flighted 50-50 ball served into a group of players. We only have our goalkeeper take goal kicks since we expect our goalkeeper and backs to be able to pass effectively at whatever range distribution is required. Thus, our basic shape is one in which we set up players to provide short and mid-range options for themselves or teammates. If those options are not on, due to the opposition marking up tightly, then we go to a more traditional long goal kick shape in which the target area is a triangular region just off of the center circle (the side is the same as the side that the goal kick is taken).

The basic shape for a goal kick taken on the right is given in the diagram, though coaches must understand that if we go for the long option, then the backs will move forward in support of the long ball played. In addition, coaches must train the resulting movement off of the ball when any of the options is played. Lastly, the coach must help the goalkeeper understand how to read what the options are based on how the opposition is marking the goal kick.

Option 1: pass across own penalty area to opposite-side outside back (opponents rarely mark this option, and the goalkeeper must be deceptive in setting up this option)

Option 2: pass to outside back on same side if opponents are marking deep and mid-range options

Option 3: pass to central midfield player if opponents are marking deep and short options

Option 4 pass to target players in long-range triangle set up on the edge of the center circle.

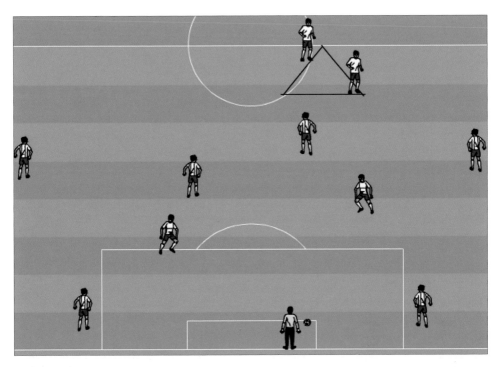

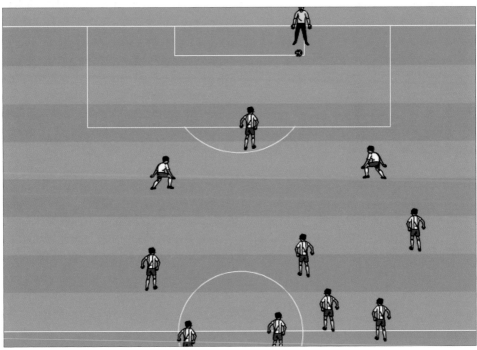

- **Defending** — As with any restart, there is a lot to consider when setting up a defensive shape against an opponent's goal kick. Basically, we try to prevent our opponent from playing any of the options that we use on our attacking goal kicks. Remind players to make up ground as the ball is played and not to react too late after the ball is played.

Our philosophy is to "bait" or invite an opponent to try shorter options but then to pounce on the short option immediately. Obviously, by following this strategy, we are more likely to win the ball closer to our opponent's goal and create a good scoring opportunity. However, this is because my teams were often shorter on the average as compared to our opposition. It is not that we didn't have good ball winners in the air, but more so because we tried to outsmart our opposition rather than rely simply on physical characteristics.

Some teams certainly do not oblige to play into your trap, so you also have to prepare to defend against the long option. After all, if the team is serving up a 50-50 ball, then it is also a terrific opportunity to win the ball back. In addition, I am surprised at the number of youth and high school teams that still use a field player to take goal kicks. Thus, we often post a player at the top of the box because if we win the ball, we have an on-sides target player to play to immediately.

The defensive shape for defending goal kicks and punts from the opposing goalkeeper is often likened to the shape of an umbrella, with somewhat curved shapes at the forward and midfield positions. Such analogies are useful for players of all ages since they help with visual imagery. Make sure each player understands the role necessary from each position; this includes understanding defensive shape, pressure-cover-balance lines of defense, communication, and how to respond if the ball is or is not played in a particular area.

- Kick-offs

  - **Attacking** — In keeping with the focus on player development, it is important to offer a few options for players to choose from so that they become comfortable with making decisions under pressure. Each restart is an opportunity for players to solve problems, so encourage a few options on kick-offs, too, rather than perhaps stifling players' minds by giving only one option to play from.

*Note:* *I respect different philosophies regarding kick-offs and the impressions they can make on teams. For example, the long kick-off to a designated side of the field suggests an immediate attack on the opposing team's backs and a potential opportunity to win a throw-in close to goal. Or, the "always go forward" mentality that may suggest a confidence in dribbling or passing skill to send a message of "here we come, deal with us." Or, the simple back-pass that suggests the mentality "we play out of the back regularly with confidence in our execution."*

Thus, I don't include a diagram for our attacking kick-off sets. I respect each coach's choice of going with some of the aforementioned options to set the tone for the team(s) they coach. However, if coaches are not working on kick-offs, I suggest teaching a few options so players are prepared for this aspect of the game.

When working with younger teams, I often offer three options for attacking kick-offs, giving animal names to each one so they are easier to remember for the players. By teaching multiple options, you are also helping the player to understand the beauty of the game: that there are very few absolutes in soccer and making choices that have consequences is a part of learning and growing.

Note:   *With the change in rules for kick-offs, teams often use one player on the ball to pass to a teammate. I prefer keeping two players on the ball, though perhaps more space between them as compared to the past.*

**The three basic options are all based off of beginning with the traditional two-player set at the center of the circle. The first player taps the ball and the second player plays to the following options.**

Option 1:   play forward through a seam to an outside player making a run into the gap in the opposition's shape (the gap may be between their forward and midfield lines or their back and midfield lines).

Option 2:   play diagonally back to a midfield player who next plays through a seam to a player making a run into the opposition's gap between their forward and midfield lines.

Option 3:   play straight back (midfield players let the ball run) to center back where options are chosen from playing out of the back are used. The idea here is that by playing the ball back, the opponents will come forward and thus expose more space and options to exploit.

- **Defending** – Defending kick-offs is fairly easy in terms of setting up the team to protect against the long ball, clog up the middle to shut down passing lanes, bait outside play to pounce on, and maintain good overall defensive shape. Coaches should put players on the edges of the center circle to chase the opponent's back-pass, but I also see this as a neglected teaching point. The opportunity to put in the element of a surprise tactic is there to use and though it may not always reap benefits, a player often can win the ball back quickly or at the very least, force the opposition into rushing a play that they don't want to do. Of course, coaches must also teach their players to keep play on one side of the field and make passes predictable upon which the team can build their defensive posture.

- Goalkeeper distribution

  - **Attacking** – our team shape is very similar to how we begin our attacking goal kicks. Essentially, we have the goalkeeper declare one side of the goal with the ball, and we work out of a basic shape in which short, mid, and long options are provided. A few key points to remember:

    - In most instances, encourage your goalkeeper to save a ball from going over the end line since the goalkeeper can run the ball up to the 18, rather than have to begin from the 6.
    - Teach your goalkeeper to expect good supporting angles from outside backs – it is poor shape when backs tend to be at the front corners of the penalty area instead of flattening out, level with the 6.
    - Go over supporting angles and runs once the ball is distributed.
    - Don't allow the goalkeeper to be predictable – encourage good reading and reacting to exploit weaknesses in the opposition.
    - Empower the goalkeeper to be the person to change the point of attack (i.e., if they receive the ball from one side of the field, look to relieve pressure by playing to the opposite side of the field) and to start counterattacks. The goalkeeper should look for the highest option possible, but not force it depending on the situation.
    - Be sure the goalkeeping coach (in some cases, it is directly your responsibility, even if you are not a goalkeeper coach) teaches proper technique of distributions with the feet and hands and tactics to make good decisions for the team. Include the goalkeeper in field player sessions to improve foot skills, passing and receiving, reading situations, and also to stay connected with the team through communication and simply being a presence.

- **Defending** — our team shape is also very similar to how we defend goal kicks. However, the coach must teach players how to make adjustments if the opposition prefers to play out of the back, throw to mid-range options, or punt long. A key reminder for the team is that the back line should not get caught flat. As one player goes to win the ball in the air, another player has to drop behind to play a miss or accidental backwards header. In addition, consider the strength of the goalkeeper, wind, size of field, and other circumstances affecting the goalkeeper's ability to distribute the ball.

- Penalty Kicks

    I only include brief commentary on penalty kicks: coaches should take note of the basics regarding penalty kicks taken during regulation versus in a shoot-out. For the shooter, I've mostly kept to a simple philosophy of beginning the run-up at the 18 and then passing low and firm to a corner. For a right-footed, player, I encourage shooting to the right low corner (when facing the goal) unless during the run-up, the goalkeeper moves toward that side. In that case, the shooter has enough time to adjust and place the ball into the lower left corner. Coaches need to educate all players about the natural curve of the ball's path when striking the ball with the inside of the foot and how to pass firmly without spin, whether using the inside or instep of the foot. I discourage high shots for the average player since the tendency is to strike the ball at hand-height of the goalkeeper (resulting in a save) or worse, the shot misses over the crossbar.

Other considerations to keep in mind include the order of selecting kickers for a shootout, choosing to shoot first in a shootout, and selecting a PK shooter during the run of play (the player who earns the PK by getting fouled versus a player who may be the team's "sure-shot" PK taker).

One of the most memorable moments in my coaching career was when one of my teams pulled off an upset at regionals via a PK shoot-out, advancing to the final over a team loaded with talent. Our team calmly made all five shots.

For goalkeepers, I defer to the goalkeeper coaches, as they often tend to have conflicting views about guessing, cheating to one side, or reading visual cues offered by the kicker. As a simplistic piece of advice, encourage them to go after the ball and get a piece of it; by telling the goalkeeper they don't need to make a catch, you empower them into believing the job is that much easier in terms of just trying to deflect the ball from going into the goal.

In general, offer a few tips but remember to keep things simple regarding the ball — for shooters, get it in the net, while for goalkeepers, keep it out. Coaches should take note that penalty kicks allow for good opportunities for decision-making (an easy skill to self-practice and test), communication, and for leadership. With most teams, I prepare field players and goalkeepers by regularly involving penalty kicks in training sessions. Thus, technique, preparation, psychological edge, and confidence are strengthened during the course of a season, and as a result, I can think of several instances where the team came out on the positive side of pressure-filled shootouts. However, there are many variables regarding shootouts and no team that plays several matches at a very high level over the course of many seasons is going to win all of them.

Coaches need to incorporate restarts into training sessions to develop as good a mentality as possible, individually and as a team. Such a mentality includes the key traits of communication, recognition, decision-making, problem solving, and leadership. Because player development involves all of these aspects, coaches owe it to players to train restarts effectively. However, the coach must find the right balance so as to not devote an excessive amount of time on restarts since having training sessions that are active, meaningful, and abundant in touches on the ball needs to be the primary objective in player development, especially for youth players.

## FORMATIONS

Given that this is a book more focused on player development than analyzing the strengths and weaknesses of systems of play, my only suggestion regarding formations is to expose players to multiple formations and positions. Depending on the level of play, moving players from one position to the next can be a challenge. However, if we are focused on player development (at the youth levels especially), we must find appropriate times to teach the game to players under match conditions. Part of my success in player development has clearly been the training of players to understand that no matter what formation or position the player is in, knowledge of the principles of the game is essential to move to higher levels of play. Versatility is a good trait to have as I have had numbers of players who may play primarily in one position in one or two formations for my team, yet they've gone on to play different positions in different formations for other teams they were a part of. The ultimate compliment to a coach in the area of player development is empowering players to move on to next levels of play as a result of the impact you had on their development. Conversely, there are numerous examples of players who weren't developed as players on other teams and they stagnate, have a difficult time adapting to position and formation changes, and they ultimately struggle to progress as players.

When choosing a system to play, coaching directors should help coaches who need guidance to choose formations that are meant to develop players. With coaching experiences and expectations being varied at next levels, it is also important to not let coaches stagnate the growth of players by adhering to only one system.

By teaching players to read the game, understand different game situations, and exploit weaknesses in the opposition, you also keep players on edge by changing formations on occasion. However, do not let such an approach backfire where players are blindly giving credit to or blaming a system of play for results rather than understanding the bigger picture of the game and remembering that effort, desire, focus, energy, responsibility, and competitiveness are important in any system of play. Thus, leadership as a coach is absolutely necessary, as communication, education, and impactful training sessions influence player development through systems of play.

There is a lot of debate about systems of play, and we have to remember that different formations help player development in ways that may be appropriate for different situations involving level of play, age, experience, situation, and personnel. On the women's side in America, for example, the 1-3-4-3 is a tremendous system for player development, as championed by Anson Dorrance. Examining systems of play, one also recognizes this formation as critical for player development for both genders by the Dutch. Likewise, Tony DiCicco successfully implemented the 1-4-3-3 system, also on the women's side. On the men's side, many coaches successfully use the 1-4-4-2 and 1-3-5-2 formations, though the latter is not as common due to the 3-back system being a challenge to play with. The US Coaching Curriculum has emphasized the 1-4-3-3 formation with variations of 1-4-2-3-1 and 1-4-1-2-3, along with the diamond midfield in a 1-4-4-2.

For my teams at the competitive youth level that played 11v11, I've had great success with player development by focusing on the 1-3-4-3 and 1-4-3-3 systems of play, but I've also used a sprinkling of other formations depending on the team and circumstance. As examples of a few different top-level teams that I've coached, they played 1-3-4-3, 1-4-4-2, 1-3-5-2, 1-4-2-3-1, and 1-4-1-2-3. All of the teams had very high levels of success, especially at the older ages where it matters more in terms of promoting players to next levels. Thus, when you know the game, train players effectively, and train skills thoroughly, you can create magic with teams of varying personnel. It also should be noted that many professional academies around the world have a primary formation that they use from the youngest to the full professional team. Such an approach has its strengths and weaknesses and depends upon several variables. Ideally, it would be super if our country could emphasize a formation as it has tried to, but there are so many variables associated with player development in our country that it just isn't happening, and I'm not convinced that it necessarily should.

As a sample situation, consider the case where someone from a central office demands all teams must play a given formation, but at the local level, the coach's expertise, knowledge, and experiences are superior in terms of player development. For individual clubs, perhaps it is easier to maintain continuity and consistency, but for a large country like ours, it is quite a challenge. In addition, we have a long way to go in developing players and there is more to it than simply choosing one formation. For teams playing 8v8, I have used a few formations that I feel develop younger players effectively: 1-2-3-2, 1-2-4-1, 1-3-2-2 and 1-3-3-1, each with perhaps a couple of wrinkles to add an extra layer as in the 11v11 systems of play. I see the last one listed used almost exclusively at this age, but without player development as a focus. Thus, the lack of vision to play a formation simply because it is considered easy rather than play a few formations to accelerate player development could be actually hurting players at young ages, though the negative impact may not appear until older ages. Again, I choose variation over stagnation to begin teaching shape, decision-making, multiple emphases in terms of width, attacking out of the back, runs in support of a target player, combination play, and much more. Thus, my training sessions are geared toward developing every player rather than locking players into a certain position in a given formation. Why limit player development when you can enrich and excel it?

As a helpful guide, this chart helps coaches to choose 8v8 systems of play that complement their respective 11v11 counterparts.

| 11v11 System of Play | Equivalent 8v8 System of Play |
| --- | --- |
| 1-4-3-3 | 1-3-2-2 |
| 1-3-4-3 | 1-2-3-2 |
| 1-4-4-2 | 1-3-3-1 |
| 1-3-5-2 | 1-2-4-1 |

## STYLE OF PLAY

Coaches should choose a style of play that not only suits their personnel but also has player development as a primary objective. Of course, at the highest levels, it is not as much about a style of play as it is about getting results. The obvious argument is to suggest that a team's style of play should lead to a result if executed well, and that is often the case for highly successful coaches at all levels. However, soccer has many variables so coaches focused on long-term player development as the top priority should pick a style that reaps benefits in the bigger picture rather than simply getting results for the moment. It troubles me when I see coaches encouraging players to use short-term tactics, such as "kick ball" (not direct play, but actually kicking and chasing), stalling (overuse of substitutions), and a robotic choice of style of play that yields neither player development nor results.

If I had to describe the style of play I use for my teams and the style that creates maximum player development then I would describe the actual style of play as an active, attractive, attacking style of soccer that involves possession with a purpose on attack and defending with a high-energy, intense pursuit of the ball. The "attacking" piece means that we actually create a variety of scoring chances with intent as best as we can, as opposed to others who say their style is attacking, but their play doesn't yield quality opportunities or the attacking is created by simply serving balls in the box hoping for scoring chances. The "attractive" component is a trait that actually comes from people describing our style as entertaining rather than us having to say it. Possession is a key element, as it allows us to attack, but it also is a tremendous defending scheme, too, because if we keep the ball, then we are defending by reducing the opportunities on goal by our opponent. The "high-energy," "active," and "intense" characteristics describe our passion for the game, demonstrate our commitment to fitness, ability to play at an up-tempo pace, and responsibilities by all members of the team. Going deeper into describing our style of play, we emphasize connected shapes on attack and defense, use of the whole field in all directions (especially width), engagement in problem solving and decision-making by all players through communication, and encouragement of creativity in executing skills. Specifically, we try to play maximum 3-touch and keep the ball on the ground, except for situations that include some final passes, early crosses, and clears.

## MATCH WARM-UP

A sample match warm-up is in the appendix. We partake in an active warm-up, and the key emphasis that has helped improve player development is that we look at the warm-up as an opportunity to improve our skills. Rather than just letting players go through the motions, be sure to coach your team in warm-ups so if players are not meeting a competitive standard in terms of effort and execution you can offer coaching points to keep them on track. Though situations may differ regarding the type of match being warmed up for, maintain high expectations so that the culture of your team is positive and enriches player development. Be sure to offer key words before, during, and after the team warms up. I always offer coaching points at key moments during the warm-up with specific goals for the team, position groupings, and individuals. Though pre-match meetings set the table for the match, as indicated in the chapter on management, the warm-up connections and vibe that we establish are critical as we enter the moments before the first whistle.

During the warm-up, it is absolutely critical to inspire confidence in your players to manage the field and surrounding conditions. Players should warm up well regardless of the sun, wind, thickness of the grass, size of the field, rain, cold, heat, etc., but it is the coach's job to teach players to eventually identify key factors and make adjustments accordingly. For example, in muddy or snowy conditions, passing on the ground is out of the match plan and, instead, lofting the ball becomes more critical. Or, on a worn turf field, passing balls to feet is more critical than into space. I like to have our teams go against the wind during the first halves of regulation and overtime (if not sudden victory), but there are certainly coaches who might choose differently. There is not one right or wrong way, but based on experience, I usually choose as such.

Likewise, coaches should remind players to play the match inside the field, regardless of the spectators, lights, media, and whatever else is outside the lines. In addition, I often tell our teams that the officials are just like the weather, as we don't have control over them and to therefore focus on playing the match, giving 100% effort, executing our match plan, communicating with each other, and staying focused to engage in responsibilities on and off the field. Keep it simple, but show the players that you are with them.

Just before the match, after the captains return from the coin toss, and after a brief water break, I have my team do a short series of 7-8 yard "there-and-back" sprints to get the blood flowing, calm any nerves, channel excitement, prepare physically and mentally for the intensity necessary, move as a team with focused energy, and subliminally stimulate the competitive juices as the players strive to be first. Then, after giving the line-up, if not already given, and a few key words to focus on, I allow the team to gather together, communicate with each other about the importance of such concepts as teamwork, maximum effort, intensity, competing for every minute, or the like, finishing with a team cheer that stays constant for tradition, ownership, and connectedness.

## DURING THE MATCH

During the match, coaches must manage a variety of key moments. Though seemingly obvious, coaches need to be attentive to all aspects of the match at hand. Communication is obviously at the core of all of these moments, and the stronger the culture you develop with your team, the better off they will be in terms of exercising greater independence and inter-dependence to play the game together. As I have often told other coaches I work with, the players are "on stage," and therefore the coach should not feel a need to be the "star" or at the center of attention. It is detrimental to player development for coaches to control every movement and decision of players, akin to a puppeteer manipulating puppets during a show. Coaches must find the right balance of offering effective instruction and feedback versus simply spewing out ineffective words that players eventually tune out. Communication needs to be specific, brief, instructive, and appropriate. Coaching language should be consistent and have a positive impact.

Several of these key match moments have been commented upon throughout this whole book, as player development involves so many of these aspects that are handled well by a healthy culture that you establish through your leadership as coach. Of course, as coaches, we try to emphasize some of these key concepts in every training session so that certain ideas are ingrained in our players, so it is rare that we would ever be harping on every detail throughout the match, at least out loud. Personally, I am super critical whether I am coaching or watching a match, but I choose moments wisely and that in itself is an art for coaching mastery that has so many variables regarding age, experience, level of play, comfort, personality, confidence, situation, and so much more. Following are a few additional comments to be attentive to, per the given situation during a match:

- Substitutions — be aware of substitution rules per the given competition your team is in; do not misuse substitutions to stall matches, bail out players who are unfit or unable to make good decisions, as you are trying to teach players the value of a high standard of match fitness and the necessity to advance problem-solving skills. I believe every player should play, but there are certainly different levels of play and situations that invite consideration as to how to find the right balance of playing time through the course of the season. Plan ahead and communicate effectively before the start of the season. During the match, you need to be allowed to limit your conversation and discussion since you have the whole team performance to consider in the match. So, as leader of the program, be sure to set a healthy culture where players understand your substitution patterns and accept your decisions in positive ways — the same goes for parents. For me, no one is guaranteed a starting position, as it needs to be earned, and I do not accept complacency, while at the same time, a player should not get a starting position just because they simply show up. Thus, my team culture is a healthy, competitive one whereby we make the right decisions rather than the most convenient ones. Player development is key and using substitutions wisely can lead your team deeper into the season with maximum depth in your player pool.

- Run of play – some common characteristics to assess performance involve the following: link passes, focus on execution, ask questions, find numerical superiority, rhythm, communicate, good-better-best decision, reading the match, timing of runs, first touch control-second touch flow, first-second-third option, vision, first-second-third runs, attacking and defensive team shape, individual body shape, spacing, angles, transition, increase speed of play in the final third, time and space, stay connected, face the ball, movement off of the ball, pass with a purpose versus pass for the sake of passing, attention to detail on restarts, passing to the proper foot, using correct surface and pace on passes, intensity, compete, effort, and various other snapshots of match play.

- Restarts – Coaching points include: readiness, details, communication, speed in which reading and reacting are taking place, execution of each piece, anticipation, positioning, body shape, match-ups and special adjustments. As noted elsewhere, restarts are a critical piece of the game that must be trained and understood by every member of the team.

- Half-time – During the first half, the coaching staff notes areas to emphasize during the half-time talk. Often, the standard is to limit comments to three points on the assumption that players cannot handle any more. However, I believe this aspect is largely a function of the team culture that you promote. While one cannot list every possible critique of the team at this time, one should use the time wisely to have the best chance of having an effect. Use assistant coaches effectively and appropriately (e.g., they may be assigned a focus on goalkeeping, interaction of the center midfielders, or movement of the forwards). Consider what the players are thinking so that they become active problem-solvers (I usually ask them how they think the match is going regarding various areas and given the culture that we create, they often grow and mature into very capable coaches). Some ideas to comment upon include the following:

  - Positive – note a few positive, specific things the team is doing well as a whole.
  - Assess effort, competitiveness, intensity, execution, focus – regardless of tactics, these are important characteristics to win.
  - Match analysis – offer critiques on how the team can improve; sprinkle positive commentary without fluff or irrelevant coach-speak; offer specific information to improve play:

    - Attacking and defensive shape, movement as a whole.
    - Specific information for lines – forwards, midfield, backs, goalkeeper.
    - Formation of and key players on the opposition.

  - Psychological – momentum, going after the third goal, playing to the end, raising play to another level of excellence.

*Attack wins the Director's Cup National Championship competition.*

*Statement from a former soccer player:*

*"Of everything I have been able to take from Ashu, he has one quote that I've never forgotten and always keep in the back of my mind during the match. He told us at half-time of one of our U16 matches, 'The third goal is always the most important.' Anyway we looked at it, he was right. It showed us that whoever got that third goal changed the dynamics of the match. That simplistic quote taught us never to give up. Even today, at U18, my teammates still find ourselves using it in a half-time talk. He taught us never to slow down or to give up, to get the third goal and just keep playing."*

— Hope Walker (College of Charleston)

- Adjustments — Again, coaches should offer communication throughout the run of play, and if adjustments are needed then coach them. These issues could include certain match-ups, changing who is taking long free kicks, playing quicker through the midfield, adjusting center back positioning to deal with the opponent's play, speed match-ups, formation changes, and so much more. For formation changes, we normally devise a simple code to communicate rather than broadcast it to the entire "stadium." As an example, we used a number scheme in which we subtracted thirty and the result gave us the number of backs and forwards we were going to play with (e.g., 73 meant we were going into a 1-4-3-3, 63 translated into a 1-3-4-3, and so on). As coach, you should feel comfortable making adjustments as necessary, while at the same time, you do not need to inundate your team with changes to the extent that you are trying to control every phase of the match and trying to be at the center of attention just to do so. What you should do in this case is focus more on your training sessions so that your team is better prepared. In addition, use the players as an effective resource to communicate adjustments to each other. One area that is always good on my teams is communication — coaches often compliment us on how good our communication is and how professional our team environment is.

After a match, players should do an appropriate cool-down. Post-match talks are generally brief, as players just want to get going. There may be times where a lengthier talk is needed, but it is good to keep things brief and address various issues at the next training session. I don't believe in getting too high or low after a match, as the lesson is to learn from the match regardless of the result and move forward in the journey of competition. Offer team or individual feedback as appropriate and necessary. For example, if there was a serious injury sustained or a card given, then appropriate follow-up is necessary. Or, to make a point about disappointment in a certain facet of the game, perhaps an immediate attention to detail and demand of expectations needs to be addressed. On the positive, if advancement to the next round of a major competition just occurred, you may need to offer brief praise and immediately get the team focused toward moving on to the next challenge. There are just too many variables to have a "cookie-cutter" post-match talk. In addition, depending on the age and time before the next session, you may want to offer a few ideas toward self-training, self-evaluation, reflection, performance analysis, skills "homework," and forming goals for upcoming training sessions.

## WHAT TO DO ON EITHER SIDE OF LOPSIDED MATCHES

As a coach, you will sometimes find your team on either side of a blowout. There are certainly different viewpoints, as the game of soccer is largely about opinions, isn't it? There are also so many variables to consider. Thus, what follows are simply a few suggestions, but certainly prepare your teams for either situation.

(A) **Losing greater than 4-0:** This has rarely happened to teams that I have coached over the past three decades, but in those moments, we've never given up. We've emphasized pride in oneself, competing, learning opportunities, breaking down plays to prevent certain situations, challenging players in the areas of executing technical skills under pressure, fitness, tactical decision-making, mental strength, and more. The keys are to instill belief in your team, break the game down into smaller time intervals, don't belittle your team, plan for the next training session, give players a brief moment to process what is needed, renew commitment to improve, and move on. It is also important for the players and the team as a group to maintain true to their mission statement and values, so take it honorably, strive to improve, and desire another opportunity to play.

(B) **Winning great than 4-0:** Note that, unfortunately, some competitions still exist where teams are encouraged to max scores to 6-0 or 9-0 or boost goal differentials to greater numbers. My teams have often been on the "positive side" of lopsided matches. Thus, we've used them as opportunities to train and continue the never-ending quest to improve. After all, if the opponent is not providing enough of a challenge, then it is our job as coaches to find ways to improve player development, fight complacency, and maintain competitiveness. Thus, some examples to try include: changing positions for players (out of their normal 2-3), play a different formation, maximum two- or one-touch on the ground, one-touch on the ground everywhere except two in transition, can only score off of 1-touch or a full volley or a header, have to maintain possession in each corner of the field before going to goal, every player must touch the ball before going to goal, three one-touch passes completed in each third of the field before going to goal, can only score off of a restart, play a player (or two) down. I know some coaches take the view that "an opponent should provide the competition and if they don't, then tough luck so go ahead and bury them." I just don't subscribe to that point of view since a "win" without challenge is a very meaningful. Do more for your players than simply coaching them to win the scoreboard.

## EXAMPLE OF PREPARATION LEADING UP TO A BIG MATCH

Every now and then, the team is going to have a particularly big match to prepare for. That is not to say that every match isn't important, but with effective coaching and strong player development, the team is likely to advance to a competition where the stakes are higher. Be it a league, state, regional, or national championship, the opportunity to play in a given competition's championship match is a special one. I have many memories of such competitions so it would be quite a challenge to share the preparation that went into each one. However, I share one real example in this section. As a head coach, it is a fun and rewarding challenge to take on match preparation for a particularly major competition and what follows are actual training sessions and commentary I used. The particular competition was a fall state cup semi-final and final weekend with a team that I had just taken on that previous summer. Though the team had not ever won a state cup championship outright (and only made it to the semis the year prior), under my leadership, I was able to guide them to higher standards of play, improve knowledge of the game, and elevate the team culture to one that the players and parents still talk about fondly to this day. Here was my approach for the week leading up to the big weekend:

**Saturday:** I made notes after our state cup quarterfinal match that helped me prepare for the next weekend (state cup "final four") in terms of planning training sessions and noting coaching points to review with the team, with lines (GK, B, M, F), and with individuals.

- Rhythm — runs in support of passes

  - anticipate; get the timing, body position, and preparation cleaner overall
  - touch to space to keep flow going (e.g., 3rd man runs)

- Communication — assertive, effective, prepare
- 1st/2nd/3rd options — vision, runs off ball, find seams/gaps in opponent's lines
- Possession under pressure — focus on better decision-making (no square passes!)
- Restarts — need to set up quicker on both att (attacking)/def (defensive)
  - Def tracking
  - Att positions/runs
- Smaller games within the big game: 1v1 att/def, 1v2 def, 2v3 def
- Denying turns
- Step up and out of GK box to defend with greater intensity, mindset to close space, deny shots, and clear
- PKs — practice, become deeper as a team with confidence and execution
- Outside/secondary range finishing
- CKs — both att/def
- Technique — improve execution with reps on clearing, heading, crossing, longball
- With ball, make better decisions as to when to turn and when to play the way you face — support must be present; communicate throughout
- Attacking stance on turns, next run, where support comes from (timing, angles)
- Playing versus different formations (1-4-4-2, various 1-4-3-3)
- Use game during week: 2 targets on end line for each team — helps imprint rhythm of looking for, and playing high target, and making runs in support of the ball (can be possessional or directional with goals)
- Potential exercises for training sessions this week:
  - Tuesday: Possessional game to 21; PKs knockout
  - Wednesday: Longball/Head; Crossing
  - Thursday: Posses w/focus on attack; Restarts and PKs

Sunday/Monday: Day off, rest, take care of academics (catch up, maintain, and get ahead).

Tuesday: Plans changed and with club philosophy, we go with the decision made by the age group director. Thus, the team had a joint session with the teams one year older and younger who were also heading into the state cup "final four."

However, I was able talk with the team at the beginning and end of training to commend the team on moving forward, state the need to focus especially well this week and raise the levels of intensity and competitiveness to execute well. I was able to use the possession game from above as a warm-up before joining with the other teams.

In addition, I reinforced to my team's players the importance to uphold team focuses throughout the mixed scrimmages to offer coaching during the joint session: Attack — 2-/3-touch restriction, play the way you face (not to be predictable, but to improve body stance and positioning), vision and movement to keep flow going, shoot more, create and take advantage of opportunities; Defend — communicate, opponent cannot complete more than 3 passes, keep ball on one side to deny switch and to make the field small.

Basic outline of the training session: warm-up with regular dynamic stretching exercises, 7v7 + GKs, followed by PK practice at end and cool-down with regular dynamic stretching exercises.

Wednesday: Focus on speed of play/transition, along with various points from the notes made on Saturday (see above); exercises were scrambled and brief to revisit some exercises the team was comfortable with and to have a psychological advantage of dealing with situations in an unpredictable order, rhythm changes and maintain intensity/focus.

- BW: Happy, excited; brief scouting report of opponent

- WU: jog, dynamic, stretch

- FL:

  - 3 teams of 5 each/1ball per team — random movement/ordered passing
  - Progression: open up, max 2-touch, sprint four steps after passing, flighted ball every other pass. CP: timing, touch, 1st touch control/2nd touch flow

- MR: 3 teams of 5 each

  - Transition game — B attacks A to goal
    - A tries to gain middle zone
    - A attacks C, continuous

  - Crossing/finishing — crossers/chasers on flanks, 3 att v 2 def in box to goal
  - Brief technical/possessional concentrated focus: 5v2; pairs longball/settle and longball/head, game in rectangles — 1-/2-touch mandatory rhythm, then unrestricted with 2-touch max in center rectangle
  - 1-4-3-3 (1-4-1-2-3) choreography
  - Team trains the GK

- MC: Scrimmage

- CD: dynamic, stretch

- FW: *Lessons from Geese* discussion — TEAM

Thursday: rained out — had to cancel training; instructed players to get a light workout in, rest, and set some personal goals for the weekend, and enjoy the "day off." Looking back, I am glad I was thorough in my notes and plans to get in what I could during the previous two sessions. I sent the team a sheet that I have traditionally used with teams before the quarterfinal stage of any competition. The sheet is titled *Lessons from Geese*, and it is a powerful statement about teamwork.

Friday: sent a team email about the upcoming weekend.

*Hello All,*

*My daily commute takes me past a church. This morning as I drove past the church grounds, guess what I saw on the front lawn? Yes, several geese! I obviously thought of the team immediately (attached is the handout from yesterday). We have worked hard for several months from tryouts in May to practices in July to preseason practices in August to the League season to now: State Cup semi/final weekend. We have an opportunity before us to put together not only what we've worked on in training in terms of skills and tactics, but also what we have encouraged along the way well beyond soccer: teamwork, competing, responsibility, sacrifice, knowledge, accountability, reliability, honesty, composure, perseverance, loyalty, trust, understanding, faith, perspective, effort, humility, versatility, focus, respect, and more. In the bigger picture, these life skills will hold you in good stead for years well beyond your soccer career.*

*As a forty-something, I reflect on various aspects of life, including my teaching and coaching careers. The highlights in these careers are certainly those moments in seeing young people grow up and grow together to achieve something worthwhile through hard work and the qualities above. This can happen at any moment and often, both of which make both careers enjoyable. As you know, I am also a firm believer at looking at where one is now and having a vision about where one wants to be in the future, not just looking and wishing, but being active in one's pursuits and without excuses, complaints, whining, or blame; being willing to accept challenges, stay focused, and rise up to meet them. This is not always easy because if it were, then "everyone would do it; the hard is what makes it great" as quoted in the movie A League of Their Own. Perhaps another quality stands out even more when it comes to the bigger events: passion — being passionate about the game and having a love for one's teammates. Among the most memorable team championships are those in which every player is passionate, driven, engaged, and understands what competing as a team really means: bringing together everyone's special qualities into one goal, one heart, one pulse, one champion. Knowing that you've given everything you can possibly give to the team in whatever role it means you have to do (think of the "ship analogy" from past team talks): running faster than you ever have to run down a ball for the team, skying higher than you ever have to win a header, following through on a clean tackle to deny an opponent, taking responsibility in striking lasers on goal, knowing that the strike-converts-to-finish can happen at any moment in the match, believing and supporting each other throughout the match, maintaining strength even when some things don't go our way, tracking players defensively with a legal suffocating stance, anticipating an air ball early and making it do what needs to be done, drawing up energy when you thought you had none left, communicating with teammates to encourage and instruct, having an urgent yet composed calm in competing minute by minute, willing the team to victory. We have such a chance to win a championship this weekend, approaching one match at a time as we always do. Regardless of the results, let's work hard and have fun together; let's be champions!*

*Thank you for all you do for the team — I am proud of you for competing on the stage we do. Rest, hydrate, and eat well today — see you tomorrow in flats by 11:15am at the field.*

*Thanks, have a nice weekend, everybody, and I hope all is well.*

*Take care,*

*Ashu.*

Saturday (Semi-final): Travel to site of the semi-final match (some traveled the night before). We had a brief team meeting, connected with each other, got used to the surroundings (looking at our match field), walked through some simple dynamic stretching exercises. Then, the team had a rest period just to loosen up, be together, hydrate, have healthy snacks, and take care of whatever they needed to. The team had a decent warm-up, but played with nerves in the semi; though they played overall better soccer than the opponent, the team narrowly won the afternoon state cup semifinal match by a score of 2-1. After the match, it was a huge relief and the team watched the end of the other semi-final, then went back to the hotel. The players were on their own for dinner (though most ate together with and without parents).

That same night, we had a 9pm Team Meeting:

- *Lessons from Geese*

- Commend team on winning the semifinal earlier today; explain that the team has been going straight for several months and that late in the season matches can be especially tight regardless of the opponent.

- Tomorrow's match provides an opportunity to see what we're about, how we deal with the excitement of the event, measure ourselves against a strong opponent (the defending state champion) who defeated us 3-0 earlier in the fall in league play, reach team goals we had set earlier in the year, overcome adversities of injury, transition, challenges, and to win a state cup championship.

- Went around in a circle and had each player say something positive about the person on either side of them. This was particularly meaningful.

- Elicited team goals for tomorrow's match:

  • Win in regulation
  • Score early (helps get our intensity and confidence going earlier in the match)
  • Earn a shut out
  • Flicks need to be purposeful
  • Stay focused
  • Strive for positive communication — the giver and receiver look at each other, acknowledge, be on the same page, understand competitive environment and situation
  • Don't worry about the "uncontrollables"
  • Play with intensity, leave it all out on the field
  • Don't get down, maintain composure, don't panic
  • Win the 50-50s
  • Box organization on attack/defense — get in position and decide quickly
  • Play soccer — "keep it on the floor," and play how we've trained to play (à la Barcelona — 1-/2-touch on the ground unless final pass, cross, shot)
  • Play and compete for the whole match
  • Be positive with each other (have each other's back)

9:30pm Meeting with GK/Bs — the full-team meeting was very positive, and I held the backs and goalkeeper over for a few extra minutes; challenged them to be united and defend as one solid force, covering for each other, avoid getting caught flat (the issue in the day's earlier match), basic movement and shape, and psychologically, accept the challenge of gaining redemption as compared to the previous match against this particular opponent (in which we lost 3-0) earlier in the fall. I left them by stating communication is very important among each other and for the team as a whole throughout the whole game.

*Statement from a former player regarding State Cup motivation:*

*"One of the most memorable times was the time during State Cup when you broke out with Miley Cyrus's "The Climb." It was a creative way to connect with us and motivate us for the match we were*

*about to play. I enjoyed all the laughs and smiles that brought our team closer together and made us
into an unbreakable bond that still even to this day cannot be separated."*

— Cannon Clough (UNC Charlotte, UNC Chapel Hill)

Sunday (Final):

- Pre-match (60 mins prior to kickoff)

  - Review team goals briefly
  - PKs during match and if shootout: requested anyone interested and feeling good about them to tell me during warm-up (six players let me know, and I let them know they could talk among themselves about order whenever they felt best — when the time came or ahead of time)
  - Restarts — attacking FKs: 1st one within striking distance is a hard shot on frame anywhere and the rest were situational — briefly review names of them; CKs on att/def; FK def — tracking through to the end of the play
  - On attack, realize the opponent plays with a SW, be sure to stay high to pressure and bent (correct surface) final passes away from her will be key
  - On defense, shade play away from their LF
  - Midfield work together — no flat lines
  - Forwards — timing of 1st/2nd runs
  - TEAM — compete, respect, passion, and at the end of the match, be sure that we all gave it our all

- Just before match (2 mins prior to kickoff)

  - Att: 2-touch, movement, play the way you face, take advantage of opportunities — good things can happen if you strike on frame; what happens if you don't — nothing
  - Def: No more than 3 passes, but it's okay if they get them in less dangerous areas while we regroup/reshape to win ball back; HFW (High Far Wide) clears; tracking
  - Take match 1 minute at a time and be one

- During match (coaches from other two teams competing that day joined the sideline, too) — numerous points made during match to players on and off field, I made it a point to stay standing (not to be nervous, but to be up and moving with the team); before the match, I marked down times on a sheet of paper to break down the match into smaller blocks of time (for each half, 10, 15, 25, 35 minute marks w/40 minute halves and 2 x 15 minute OT periods and PKs, if necessary). This was a huge match in many, many ways, so breaking it up helped all of us read, assess, adjust, etc.

- Half-time (with score 0-0):

  - a few comments regarding positive things we were doing in the match (limiting their opportunities, communicating well, playing well when the ball was on the ground and we moved it in 1-/2-/3-touch max rhythm, creating good opportunities in second 18 and off of crosses).
  - challenged team on taking advantage of opportunities and box organization to come away with more shots and hopefully a goal; diagonal dribble on attack to create space; get numbers up similar to training with 3rd man run combos and target play, play feet, spread field more, and show to the ball completely (finish the run).
  - defensively needed to position body better to avoid getting beat on turn or by hesitate move; be aware of #10's long throw-ins — back and front target player.

- reviewed a few positional emphases and technical corrections with individual players, a few tactical ideas with lines.

- Post-match: complete elation as we won the match 1-0!

In general, regardless of the coaching methodologies that you choose, be critical, communicate effectively, maintain high expectations, encourage players to be sharp, focus on high levels of execution and effort, and constantly teach to excel in the areas of technical and tactical skills, physical coordination, agility, and endurance with and without the ball, psychological strength, maturity, and confidence, individual role, and team power. By concentrating on effort, intensity, strength, execution, competitiveness, and focus, you are sure to elevate player development for your team and for each player you coach.

## Reflections

- What is your coaching methodology in areas of training sessions, match play, and match preparation?
- What are your core exercises and emphases throughout each season you coach?
- Why do you choose the formation that you do for your team? Is it about a program philosophy, personnel, development?
- What style of play do you emphasize for your teams? Why?
- How often do you include restarts in your training sessions? Do you train just free kicks and corner kicks, or do you work on other restarts that are also parts of the game?
- How do you plan your training sessions? Do you stay with one structure or do you add variety on occasion to keep players fresh?
- What outside features do you bring in to teach lessons that improve team dynamics?
- Are such features parts of your regular planning for training sessions?
- Are you as demanding in training sessions and match warm-ups as you are in matches or do you only "coach" during matches?

# CHAPTER 9

## EXAMPLE OF A FULL SEASON OF TRAINING

*"A small body of determined spirits fired by an unquenchable faith in their mission can alter the course of history." — Gandhi*

This chapter is perhaps one of the main reasons most readers will refer to *The Well-Rounded Soccer Coach*. What follows is an example of specific training sessions for a team's season. Readers will also want to refer to chapter 8 on coaching methodology and chapter 7 for additional ideas to develop a year-round program for player development.

Some key points regarding the exercises:

- Suggestions are offered regarding turning up the level of challenge or toning down the level; a good coach will set the bar appropriately high for his or her age group, level and experience.

- Comments are included regarding ideas on how to adapt the exercises, offer coaching points and explain reasons behind choices of exercise elements; there are many variations and options for coaches to go in their own directions, as appropriate for their teams.

- Coaches will ultimately have to make decisions about the sessions they choose to run and the duration of each exercise to use in their training sessions.

- The sessions in this chapter are not intended and mostly not appropriate for the youngest of ages (ages four through nine; e.g., it is suggested to not begin "heading" until at least age 12), nor do I include a lot of exercises that involve more stationary exercises such as shadow play. My choices of exercises are more in line with my player development philosophy in terms of keeping everyone active appropriately due to the fact that I had on average only three sessions per week during the main season and one during the off-season. Coaches at various levels will have more training sessions per week, which obviously translates to the need for adapting sessions appropriately. In addition, coaches will ultimately need to do shadow play per their personnel, formation, expertise, level, etc.

This is not a "be all, end all" series of training sessions, but rest assured, these are real exercises used with credibility laying in the vast numbers of successes regarding player development. Coaches who use these exercises need to understand their own responsibility in adapting exercises to be developmentally appropriate for the ages, levels and experiences of the players who they work with. In addition, I chose several training session models based on both the need to develop players and the need to advance the team based on their performances. Likewise, space limitations require me to give brief comments about exercises, and the reader needs to understand that coaching is not simply copying down a set of exercises, but leading the team toward consistent training for excellence.

As noted elsewhere, my first five opening season sessions (along with various other sessions throughout the season), are heavily influenced by the UNC Competitive Matrix model. Some of these opening exercises are the same or very similar to actual exercises run by the UNC coaching staff under Anson Dorrance, while many others are adaptations or of my own development and creation (which may or may not be similar to various other exercises out there). Inspiration for several exercise ideas come from resources such as the United Soccer Coaches Conventions, various periodicals, observations at symposiums, camps, etc. The key is that the coach must be knowledgeable in making decisions about setting a curriculum that will optimize player development. For my teams, the pre-season opening sessions became a tradition where players understood what was going on in terms of ranking players for feedback, objective comparisons, setting team standards and highlighting individual strengths and weaknesses.

My preference for pre-season is to have a "mini-camp" for the team(s) that I coach. If I coach multiple club teams, the preference is to give each team their own mini-camp to focus on each team; by giving 100% attention to each team, the message is also sent that the coach is fully committed to each player individually and each team that he or she works with. At the same time, if the two club teams are closer in age and competition can be used to push each team then I encourage joint sessions. A coach must decide what is best for each team and not simply what is convenient for the coach's schedule or paycheck. In the case of a high school team, I would run the entire group of varsity and junior varsity athletes together since tryouts would essentially occur during this mini-camp timeframe. In either case, the beginning of the season is absolutely critical for establishing a culture of competitiveness, chemistry, conduct and character that sets the tone for the season.

The five-day mini-camp scenario is particularly valuable when I am in control of training curriculum and scheduling; its effectiveness is in running the five days consecutively and not over the course of a couple of weeks. At the end of the previous season, I would write to the following season's team members regarding various "tests" that would be assessed during the upcoming pre-season in addition to details of the first five days of competitions.

*Note:* *In the case of younger players, I emailed the parents in addition to the players to improve all lines of communication and understanding. Depending on the situation, we had double sessions with a 60-minute morning fitness session followed by an evening 105-minute soccer session (this is recommended when players are able to get themselves to training). This situation allowed for optimal performances in each session since a long rest period between the sessions permitted players to re-fuel and in many cases, naturally created team bonding and interdependency. Or if players were in a situation where I knew some team members would be unable to make the morning fitness sessions, I felt that this would be less helpful to the team bonding than what I was after so I would decide on only one session per day instead. I gave players the fitness workout that they were to do on their own in the morning well before our evening sessions. A sample of this information includes the following:*

Day 1: Olympics — various skill tests, followed by competitive scrimmages

**Fitness: "Cooper Run"** — run 8 laps at a track, record time; also note where you are at 12 minutes (round to the nearest 1/4 of lap). Abs workout: crunches, leg lifts.

Note: *Though the Cooper Run is primarily an aerobic exercise and soccer is generally an anaerobic sport, I still believe in the positive mental and physical benefits of the Cooper Run, again with the bigger picture of lifetime activity in mind.*

Day 2: 1v1

**Fitness: "Cones" on grass** — set markers at a starting line, 5, 10, 15, 20, 25 yards; sprint to the 5 and back, 10 and back, etc., to the 25 and back; repeat 10 times, you have the balance of sixty-five seconds to rest (i.e., the sprinting and rest totals sixty-five seconds), with an extra 15 second rest after runs #4 and #7; record number of "misses" (meaning not able to start within the time allotted — if you miss one, don't stop, just rest for a bit, and continue to complete all 10). Upper body: push-ups.

Day 3: Passing/Receiving

**Fitness: 110s on grass** — set markers at a starting line and 110 yards; sprint to the 110 yard mark and jog back to the start in the remainder of a one minute (i.e., the sprint and return to the start totals one minute), repeat 10 times (resting an extra 15 seconds after runs 4 and 7), record number of "misses." Abs: seal walk, side and back bridges.

Day 4: Long Ball/Head/Volley

**Fitness: 50-100 Super Sets on grass** — set markers at starting line, 50 and 100 yards; run to the 50 and back, immediately followed by 100 and back; rest for one minute after you return; repeat 6 times; record total time of sprinting. Resistance exercises (partners) and extended push-ups (diamond, one-hand, leg up).

Day 5: Finishing

**Fitness: 10 x 40 yard sprints on grass** — record four fastest times, followed by medium-pace 20-minute run (on grass or track). Abs: extended seal walk, side and back bridges.

If we were in a situation where players had to be responsible for morning fitness sessions on their own then I also included the following note:

*"All players are expected to complete the fitness workouts on their own (in the morning preferably), record what is asked (please give the results to me on a sheet of paper or email them to me each day), and compete in the evening team sessions, too. For the fitness workouts, be sure to take a short jog or perhaps do the PEP warm-up, stretch well, etc., before you do the indicated workout. Be sure to accurately measure distances and record times (use a stopwatch). Also do appropriate warm-up and cool-down exercises. If you can work out with a teammate and have an adult handy to time you, then that would be super."*

In addition, I also sent out information about some of the types of testing that we would do throughout the season, but especially in mini-camp. Thus, a player would be held accountable since there was an immediate "test" to prepare for and the process of communicating tests ahead of time gave players intrinsic motivation to meet team standards. Otherwise, without any guidelines toward expectations, a player would not know where he or she stood until it was too late. This idea also has huge long-term ramifications in terms of getting players ready for not only your club or high school season, but college and beyond also. Some information that I send out regarding testing and target goals includes:

*"Players will be tested in a variety of exercises throughout mini-camp week. Some tests that players can use as benchmarks for their summer training are given next. Players testing successfully in these areas during mini-camp stand an overall better chance of contributing to the team's success immediately, impacting play competitively, and helping the team get off to a good start — it is our hope that everyone strives to be that kind of player!"*

## FITNESS:

Cooper Run — 7.5 laps (without rounding) in 12 minutes, with a goal of 8 laps.

120's — make 8+ (out of 10); sprint 120 yards in 20 secs, return to start in 30 secs, rest at start for 30 secs (repeat 10x).

*Note:   In the section previously noted, we used 110s. Adjust according to age/level of athletes.*

## SKILLS:

Juggle — 100+ (no specific body part more than two consecutive; body parts include — head, chest, each shoulder, each quad, each of the following surfaces L and R feet: laces, inside, outside, heel).

Longball for distance — combined distance of 75+ yards, sum of one each kick with right foot and left foot.

Finishing — start at 22, weave through two discs, finish from behind the 18, alternating posts — make 7+ out of 10 (score if ball passes through space between post and disc one yard inside goal).

Longball for accuracy/Heading — with partner, serve ten each from at least 30 yards, head back 20+ yards, make 7 times out of 10.

## COMPETITIVE:

* win at least 3/4ths of 1v1 games (cones + grids).

* lead team to win at least 3/4ths of full sided scrimmages.

*Statement from a former player regarding the Cooper Run:*

*"Every March, my teammates on Blue Thunder and I would journey to the Woodson High School track to participate in our annual Cooper fitness test. Although these Cooper tests, for the most part, blend together into repressed memories of trying to pass, one year truly stands out to me. I was on my last lap around the track and struggling to finish, when Ashu ran across the field to the opposite side to run with me on the last curve until the timer hit 12:00. Why does this memory stand out so much? It completely reflects how much Ashu invests in the kids he coaches, and how he truly wishes for them to succeed and push themselves to the best of their ability. It also demonstrated that there are people who support me through every step of the last sprint, people who care every bit about my success as an individual, and in the big picture — as a teammate. Nine years have gone by since that moment, and I am now competing in the NCAA. Despite the fact nearly a decade has passed since that Cooper test, if I ever need an extra push during fitness or fitness testing, I still think of Ashu's effort to support me in my final strides of those 12 minutes. This is just one anecdote of many that demonstrates how impactful Ashu was as a coach; it provides a representation of the time, effort, patience, and faith he put into us as athletes and Blue Thunder as a team."*

— Erica Stein, BRYC *Blue Thunder* U9-U18 ( Emory University)

Lastly, I do not list details on the standard warm-up and cool-down for each training session since the expectation is that those components are essentially the same for any session and do not need to be repeated in each session description. Coaches will have their own ideas and should adapt accordingly, and likewise, clubs, high schools, colleges and professional teams are likely to have their specific program routines — it is good to maintain tradition, as indicated early in the book. Readers may refer to Chapter 8 to find ideas for my teams' general warm-up and cool-down. So, with that background information regarding mini-camp forming a foundation on which to build, we are ready to begin the season and move forward. Note that sample score sheets to rank players, summarize results for individual players and the team, and to offer feedback for the first five days are given in the Appendix. Coaches are encouraged to produce similar sheets for their teams to use throughout the season, as appropriate, and as commented upon previously in this book. What follows are sample sessions for an entire season:

Sessions 1 – 5 are described in detail, as they comprise the first five consecutive-day training sessions for the team during "pre-season." These sessions require extra explanation due to the nature of the exercises, scoring points and need for understanding the sessions that set the tone for the season. Enjoy!

## SESSION 1:

Pre-season mini-camp day 1: "Olympics" (inspiration credit: Technical Olympics concept used by UNC women's soccer program)

- 1 ball per player; testing of skills without pressure; players have opportunities to warm-up before each skill is tested, but there are no "re-do's"

  - **Juggling:** record total of one try each at each of the following patterns; the trial is over if the ball hits the ground or a body part out of the pattern. [Importance: 1st touch, ball-mastery, focus, concentration.]

    - Foot-foot-thigh (FFT)
    - Thigh-thigh-foot (TTF)
    - Feet-only: encourage use of laces, "C-position/crunch abs," no spin; "low" is defined to be lower than knee-level, "high" is defined to be above head height.

      » Low-low-high (LLH)
      » High-high-low (HHL)

  - **Longball:** record sum of distances of one strike each of right and left foot. [Importance: longball distance assesses strength, secondary-range shooting, power, reminder to players to work on both legs/feet.]
  - **Throw-in:** record sum of distances of best two out of three throws. [Importance: throw-in technique is a neglected skill; develops ability in all players, assesses strength and technique.]
  - **Shooting:** begin at 18, one-touch to prepare ball to shoot behind 12; alternate shots to right and left low corners of the goal (mark 1 by 1 yard square targets). In this event, the player may choose foot to strike with (obvious variation is to restrict foot usage). Record number of finishes out of ten tries. [Importance: finishing to low corners off of a moving ball is realistic, going to goal encourages players to attack yet maintain composure when finishing, finesse rather than sheer strength and accuracy are key elements in finishing, shooting in low corners helps develop a mindset to not shoot the ball into the opposing goalkeeper's hands or worse, missing the frame over the top.]

- **4v4 small-sided games to goals; suggested dimensions:** narrow grid with full-sized goals and goalkeepers is 50 x 20 yards and wide grid with small goals without goalkeepers is 40 x 25. Testing of skills under pressure. Have soccer balls handy in all areas around the game grids — restarts are kick-ins and the coach should encourage taking all restarts within a 2-second count (count "one-thousand-one, one-thousand-two"). Player missing the frame on a shot must sprint to retrieve the ball and re-enter the game.

  - **Game 1:** all players on each team must touch the ball before scoring; start over if loss of possession occurs
  - **Game 2:** forced 3-touch
  - **Game 3:** maximum 2-touch

- **8v8 scrimmage;** competitive (see above guidelines, but play is unrestricted)

  The scoring for the 4v4 and 8v8 games is by team (3 points for a win, 1 point for a draw, 0 points for a loss) and by individual (+ 2 for a goal, + 1 for an assist, + 1 for a 50-50 ball win/tackle for possession, goalkeeper save, accurate goalkeeper distribution that results in assist or shot on goal). The important features of these games are developing the use of skills under pressure, a competitive mindset, speed of play, style of play, team chemistry, understanding that every player impacts the outcome of matches, and offering incentives for key components of the game.

## SESSION 2:

Pre-season mini-camp day 2: Foot skills/Dribbling/1v1

- **Skills "without" pressure**; 1 ball for every two players (note that "without pressure" does not mean that the standards are not high – demand attention to detail and excellence in execution; the pressure comes from timing, keeping score, or distance/spacing considerations rather than from the opposition).

  - **Figure 8s:** player weaves in and out of two cones over an 8-yard course using the following restrictions; total time in seconds of all four runs (fastest time is highest rank). [Importance: agility with a ball, technical speed, use of big and small touches, proficiency with both feet.]

    - Inside of feet only
    - Outside of feet only
    - Right foot only
    - Left foot only
    - Any foot or surface

  - **1v1 shield:** two players each with one foot on the ball or back to back with ball between players' backs to start; size of each grid is 10 x 10 yards. Play 3 x 40-second games. Player with possession of ball in-bounds is winner (+ 2 points). If game is called with no-one in possession or ball is out-of-bounds, then no winner and zero points awarded. Restarts with opponent having to begin position opposite side of grid that the attacking player starts from. Change opponent after each game. [Importance: shielding, back-to-pressure, getting out of tight situations, dealing with physical contact and aggressive play.]

- Skills with direct pressure – 1v1 emphases. [Importance: developing a mentality that each player is accountable and must compete to win his or her 1v1 battles; 1st attacker/defender roles, imprinting a competitive mentality, intensity, agility, fitness with a ball, decision-making, psychological belief that the player is in charge, whether on attack or defense; pushing oneself physically and mentally through fatigue.]

  - **1v1 in 10 x 10 grid**, directional, stop on line to score; 3 x 90-second games, rotate partners after each game. Scoring is 3 points for a win, 1 point for a draw, zero points for a loss, +1 for each goal scored.
  - **1v1 in 10 x 10 grid**, directional, score on ground through staggered or "diagonal" facing 1-yard goals; 3x 90-second games, rotate partners after each game. Scoring is the same as above.
  - **1v1 to goal:** defender serves accurate longball from behind end line to attacker who is waiting at the bottom of the circle near midfield; defender sprints to close down space while attacker concentrates on making a good first touch to beat oncoming defender to attack full-size goal (live GK). Players take two runs each on attack and defense; scoring is given to each player on each run as follows: Attacker 4/Defender 0 if attacker scores goal, A 3/D 1 if attacker gets shot off onto the frame of the goal, A 2/D 2 if attacker beats defender and shot goes wide (below goal height), A 1/D 3 if attacker side-steps defender but defender blocks shot, A 0/D 4 if defender stuffs shot so that ball does not go forward on the attacker's shot or if defender

does not let attacker get by or get any shot off. Only one 1-touch rebound shot is allowed, if appropriate. Goalkeeper gets 2 points for each held save made and 1 point for a punch, tip-over or dive deflection away from goal. A few key points: for the **attacker**, attack at speed so that the attacker has another gear to accelerate to beat defender, go at the defender, use a move (preferably a "signature move" that the player has worked on) and take chances, attacker does not have to get completely by the defender but rather engage the defender, don't get caught turning around and having back-to-goal or too wide where the shooting angle is poor, try to use a feint or two and attack the defender's front foot; for the **defender**, sprint to close down space to keep the attacker farther away from the goal, slow down about two big steps away from the attacker to avoid getting beat by attacker's accelerating touch ("the last step forward is the first step back"), use proper defensive stance, stay low, on balls of feet, one foot in front of the other, bend knees for mobility, keep eyes on ball, tackle the ball when the attacker's foot is off the ball (avoid "sticking"); for the GK, communicate to defender, encourage taking away the preferred foot, making tackles just outside of the 18, etc.

- Competitive games: the important features given above play out dramatically in the following games, lead the players to strive to ascending levels of competitiveness, intensity and effort.

  - 4v4: 3 mini-games, change restriction for each game, rotate players into different "positions," so players understand fundamentals of "kite" shape (penetration, width, support).

    - Player must take on or engage nearest opponent before passing.
    - No forward passing (except shot on goal); advance ball only by dribbling.
    - Only forward passing to advance ball but no turning — thus, a player needs to learn good body positioning to see the field behind, laterally and forward.

  - 8v8: unrestricted. The coach may layer in a restriction in case the attacking theme fades, but in general, this should be a fun game to play and watch for the whole team. Scoring for 4v4 and 8v8 is by team (3 points for a win, 1 point for a draw, 0 points for a loss) and individual (+2 for a goal, +1 for an assist, beating a player 1v1, defensive tackle or dispossession of opponent, +1 for GK as in Session 1).

## SESSION 3:

Pre-season mini-camp day 3: Passing/Receiving

- Skills without pressure, the importance of passing and receiving technique is especially valuable and must be trained well; some key points include receiving with a "high-to-low" action of the leg and foot, cushioning to settle (not trap) the ball with the inside of the foot (this action helps to keep the ball from skipping up or taking a bad bounce and going over the receiver's foot), player should be on the balls of his or her feet, taking small steps to adjust to the oncoming pass; for side-of-the-foot passing, player should use the "fatter" part of the sides of the feet (toward the heel rather than the toe) for greater surface area and maximum contact with the ball, follow through the ball rather than stabbing at it and following through into the ground; "punch" the ball with foot following through up in the air, as in a next step (with younger players, I encourage players to exaggerate the follow-through, almost putting the knee up into the mouth); non-kicking foot should be approximately alongside the ball, contact should be with the "nose" of the ball, meaning in the center horizontally and vertically, as the emphases are on ground passes.

- **2s/1 ball, passing/receiving through gates** — players are each 10 yards away from a central gate; alternate feet, 1 point for every pass cleanly through the gate, change partners but carry individual score through, 1 minute on each passing and receiving pattern:
  - Inside-inside both feet, 2-touch; receive inside of first foot, touching ball across body to second foot, pass with inside of second foot through gate to teammate
  - Inside-outside same foot, 2-touch; receive with inside of first foot, touching ball across body toward second foot, pass with outside of first foot
  - Inside-inside-inside both feet, 3-touch; receive with inside of first foot, touching ball across body toward second foot, player looks up and imagines that his or her passing lane is closed off, player touches ball with inside of second foot back toward the first foot, pass with inside of first foot
- **4s/1 ball, passing/receiving off the dribble through gates** — two players on each side of the station, player receives ball through one gate on back line, dribbles toward other gate and must pass before reaching the front line. Next time the ball arrives through the gate, the opposite player repeats so that the two players on each side are alternating. Ball moves counter clockwise (right-footed passing), use inside of foot and laces; go for 80 seconds each, then repeat going clockwise (left-footed passing).

- Skills with pressure

- *2v2 in 12 x 10 yard grids,* stop ball on line to score; points are awarded for each duo (3 points for win, 1 point for draw, 0 points for loss, +1 for any wall-pass, overlap, or take-/fake-over combination) and individual (+1 for goal or assist). Play three 90-second games; the coach may set up a ladder where the winning team moves toward the top grid and the losing team moves down toward the bottom grid or scramble the match-ups or pairings, as desired.
- **2 teams of eight players each; group possession** — two simultaneous possession games of 6v2 in approximately 15 x 15 yard grid (adjust per skill level); three games of 2 minutes each: first game is max 3-touch, second game is forced 2-touch on the ground, and third game is 1-touch; 4 passes = 1 point for attacking team, two passes completed by the defenders = 1 point. Depending on the level of the team, make each game on the ground only; coach technique in addition to tactics, decision-making, speed-of play, supporting angles and distance, rhythm

and tempo. With effective teaching points, the impact should pay off in competitive games and future sessions.

- Competitive games

  - **4v4 games only** (as a variation on the middle day of an intense week, this session does not end with a full scrimmage); scoring is for team (3 points for a win, 1 point for a draw, 0 points for a loss) and individual (+1 goal, assist, combination, +1 for GK as in Session 1).

    - 2-touch on the ground and minimum three passes before shooting on goal, encourage execution under pressure, movement off the ball, timing, speed-of-play and competitiveness.
    - Unrestricted – though the players may first show signs of fatigue at this point in the week, remind them that they are more than halfway through the mini-camp, you are proud of their efforts and that the team needs each player to give it their best effort. Thus, although fatigue is a mental obstacle to get through, we will need to have an enduring quality of competing for the whole game, every game, deep into the season.

## SESSION 4:

Pre-season mini-camp day 4: Longballs/Heading/Volleying

- Skills without pressure – be sure to encourage players to stretch extra after the team's usual warm-up, especially given the fourth day of an intense week; 2s/1 ball, longballs over 30-35 yards (adjust per level), briefly review techniques of striking longballs (non-kicking foot slightly behind ball, striking ball in the middle of the "mouth," follow through, friendly "back-spin" service) and receiving flighted balls (see ball early, get into the line of flight, adjust body to cushion, etc.). Rotate so that players are paired with different partners for each exercise. Duration is 2 minutes per exercise. If players are proficient in skill, then alternate right- and left-footed serves; otherwise, use a 2:1 ratio. In addition, for this session, you will want to go through a fundamental heading progression (cobra, knees, crabwalk, standing, rotating beginning stance of feet, jumping, attacking v defending headers; heading arc, "peeking through the window," trunk, etc.). Note: Consult medical personnel regarding concussions and other potential head issues before training heading technique.

  - **Longball-settle:** Player A pushes the ball away with sole then serves a flighted ball to B. If B can take ball out of the air with any body part on first touch and settle ball with foot on second touch, then both players receive 2 points. If B settles with only one touch, then only one point is awarded. B now serves to A, repeat.
  - **Longball-head:** Player A pushes ball away with sole and then serves flighted ball to Player B. If B can head ball past where A is serving from, then award 4 points to both players. If the header goes past one-half the distance between A and B then award 3 points. If the header goes forward, but is less than half the distance, then 2 points. Because serving accurately to the head and heading in general is weak, award one point for any other header. Switch servers at 1-minute mark.
  - **Longball-off grounders/rolling ball (e.g., backpass):** Player A serves ball on ground to Player B, Player B one-times ball back to A in the air who attempts to settle as in Longball-settle (points are the same). Encourage use of the inside of the foot and laces/instep for the one-time pass.
  - **Longball-clear:** Player A serves flighted ball to Player B who attempts to clear the ball with any body part over head-height over distance back to A. The points are the same as in Longball-head.

- Skills with pressure

  - **2v2 Head-volley game:** 8 x 12 yard grid, attacking players begin on their end of the grid and begin play with a toss, the teammates have one-touch each to head or volley — passing back and forth, advancing up the field, the shot must be taken with a head. If the header goes below shoulder height of the defending team (who must stand on their own line, but may block the shot with any body part except their hands), then a goal is scored; award 2 points for a goal or 1 point if the shot is taken "on frame" but blocked. Restart with opposite team attacking. Transition also occurs if the ball hits the ground when a team is attempting to advance up the field.
  - **2v2 Longball-service game:** Set up two 5 x 5 yard grids approximately 25 yards apart (adjust according to skill level); each team is in their respective grid. A player from Team A serves to Team B; if the serve is accurate (i.e., the ball would land in the target grid), then award 1 point to Team A. If the receiving team player can settle the ball and pass to his or her teammate with 1-touch and that player returns the ball for the original receiving player to serve back into the target grid, then the receiving team earns 2 points.

- Competitive — 8v8; scoring is earned by team (3 points for win, 1 point for draw, 0 for loss) and individual (+2 goal, +1 assist, accurate long ball pass, header accuracy, 50-50 flighted ball win, +1 for GK as in Session 1).

  - Max 3-touch, must be one long service (coach's decision) before shot on goal is allowed (start over after shot).
  - Unrestricted; continue to encourage vision to check third (longer) options, technique of serving and receiving flighted balls, and runs in support of longballs — movement off the ball should dictate play rather than simply reacting (I like to say to the team, "the run comes before the pass").

## SESSION 5:

Pre-season mini-camp day 5: Finishing

- Skills without pressure — warm-up with a simple shooting progression after the team's usual warm-up, again, encourage extra stretching due to yesterday's session on longballs and in preparation for today's session on shooting. This session is generally for finishing closer than 25 yards and thus, secondary-range finishing is done in a separate session. Ideal set up is to have two goals facing each other over distance, each with a live goalkeeper in it (the coach should still place discs one yard inside each goal post to encourage low-corner finishes). Points for this section are for the shooter — 2 points low corner, 1 point any other goal, -1 for any shot missed over crossbar and, for the goalkeeper — 2 points catch, scoop, or dive save (or if deflected tip/punch from any corner that requires leaving both feet; it has to be a spectacular save), 1 point for any other, -1 for allowing goal through body (hands, legs, etc.) or near post. Attacker is allowed only one 1-touch follow on rebound and earns 1 point for any rebound-finish.

  - **Power** — set shooting distance from 18 to 25 yards depending on level; set up power-shooting variations off the dribble, wall pass, overlap, lay-off, half-volley; emphasize proper technique: point of contact, laces/instep, non-striking foot alongside ball, toe down/turned inward slightly, ankle locked, body in a C or K position, head down, shoulders/chest/knee over the ball, "snap" of knee versus bad habit of using upper leg, run through the shot on the follow-through, both feet come off the ground, land on shooting foot.

- **Finesse** — set shooting distance from 15 to 18 yards; set up finesse variations off wall pass, overlap, take-/fake-over, turn, crosses on ground; emphasize technique with inside of foot.
- **Volley/Head** — same distance as above, but organize servers from wide positions and two attackers at a time running at goal — 1-touch finishes only and only one 1-touch rebound shot allowed. Emphasize techniques, especially "half-swing" on volleys, heading downward for shooting on goal, and "knocking the ball back where it came from" off of crosses.
- **PKs** — four attempts each; encourage finesse, beginning at the 18, good follow-through, low laser, confidence, patience, pass with pace.

- Skills with pressure — 4v4 games, one field has GKs in goals with any kind of finish allowed, the other field has goals with upper and lower corner targets — must finish off of 1-touch or hit the net on the fly into any corner. Can shoot at any time, but must take a shot after completion of third pass, no matter where the player is on the field. Points awarded for team (3 points for a win, 1 point for a draw, 0 points for loss) and individual (+1 for shot on frame/miss, assist or defensive snuff of opponent's shooting attempt, +2 goal, +3 any volley/head one-touch goal, +1 for GK as in Session 1).

- Competitive — 8v8, no restrictions, points as above, but also reward any 50-50 win, defensive tackle for possession, targeted header. For an extra push, encourage forward passing only with restriction of must shoot after third pass, if applicable, or shot must take place within 5 seconds of entering attacking half. This is especially valuable to practice on the big field with numbers similar to the full-sided game. End with no restrictions if using this incentive.

Now that mini-camp is over, the players are required to take the next day completely off as rest. The following day is a light 20-minute run with appropriate warm-up and cool-down exercises. No other activity is required, as the players will benefit from rest, paying extra attention to hydration, nutrition, and sleep. In addition, if they can watch one half (or a whole) of a high-quality match on television, that would be super mental training.

The following sessions are mostly based on having three training sessions per week with one match at the end of the week. In addition, these sessions are selected based on actual sessions I have used successfully measured by both player-development and results in terms of championships. It is important to note that I do not do the same training sessions every year in such a sequential order, as there are many variables involved such as age, level, experience, calendar year, schedule of matches and other competitions, climate, and additional considerations. The sessions include both a platform for ideas that need to be emphasized regardless of performance and also a selection of exercises based on how the team performed in matches. Throughout my career, I have generally had 18 players to work with (16 field players and 2 goalkeepers). Thus, coaches should adjust the numbers, per their specific team construct.

*Note:   I do not include training sessions or parts of training sessions that are more static in nature in terms of shadow play, choreography, formation-based, and other topics that perhaps depend more on specific programs, and therefore are less active. I leave that to the reader who must choose to sprinkle in such sessions in regular training sessions or as part of separate training sessions deemed as "functional," "shadow play," or "formation choreography." In addition, I do not list every technical skill or tactical skill in each training session, as an assumption is made toward the reader having at least a fundamental understanding of the basics. Likewise, if the reader has an advanced knowledge of topics, then he or she will want to advance some exercises by limiting time and space, reducing touches, and adding other similar challenges that are developmentally appropriate for the level of play. Lastly, coaches should feel free to combine sessions and/or choose them out of the order that they appear.*

## SESSION 6: FIRST SESSION AFTER TWO DAYS "OFF"

**Main topics:** 1v1 defending; roles, technical, tactical (note that 1v1 attacking was covered in Session 2/Day 2 of mini-camp).

**BW:** Compliments for effort, competitiveness and spirit at mini-camp. Remind players to perform the warm-up exercises with focus and attention to the technique of each movement. After ball skills, place soccer ball on the touchline to have the balls available (set the standard early for each player having access to a properly inflated ball).

**FL:**

- Individual: foot-skills — V, L moves; Foot juggle — low-low-high, low-high

- All players on touchline, facing coach and ready to jog backward over 20 yards; demonstrate position/ stance for individual defending (one foot slightly in front of the other, get low, knees bent, on balls of feet, eyes on ball), command players to begin going backwards on a jog, switching front foot on command — remind players not to drag their feet, players should move quickly with small steps; repeat.

- 2s/1 ball

  - Player A with ball at feet, Player B one yard away in defensive stance facing Player A. On command, Player A begins dribbling and Player B moves backward in defensive stance with eyes on the ball. Player A makes moves and cuts often to force Player B to change front foot. Player B is not trying to actually take the ball away, but instead, working on technique. After reaching far side, switch roles and return to start. Repeat, and allow attacking player to dribble faster.
  - Same as above, except this time, the attacker pushes the ball out a bit farther on occasion, which is a signal for the defender to briefly touch the ball with a hand, then both players continue moving. The idea is to teach timing of the tackle — tackle when the attacker's foot is off the ball, otherwise the attacker is likely to beat you with a move if their foot is on the ball. Repeat. Note: Placing the hand on the ball is to emphasize the player staying low and "pouncing" on the attacker's bad touch or brief moment of non-possession.
  - Review (or teach) block tackle, poke tackle.

**MR:** (My recommendation is to divide the team into two groups so that there is a team competitive element in addition to individual competition.) 2s/1 ball, keep score, 1v1 games are 90 seconds each; rotate after every game. Grids are 10 x 12. Emphasize 1st defender roles of "deny/dispossess (off of a bad touch), divide, delay," stance, decision-making and closing down speed/slowing down as appropriate. Continuous, intense play is expected, but also be sure to teach.

- Player A passes on ground to Player B across grid, Player B attacks and tries to stop ball on line to score. Player A may counterattack to score.

- Players begin on opposite diagonals of grid; begin as above. The attacker can only score by stopping the ball in either corner.

- Players begin on same corner of grid, one behind the other. Front player is attacker and self-passes anywhere while defender closes down the attacker. Attacker tries to turn and score in either corner on the side that play begins.

**MC:** Scrimmage unrestricted, extra points awarded for good tackles, dispossessions, and any 1st Defender roles. Immediately correct any player who gets caught "sticking" and is beaten 1v1.

FW: Players are in pairs sitting back-to-back. They spend one minute individually drawing what leadership looks like to them (no words, only a drawing). Then they spend the next two minutes trying to draw their partner's leadership drawing, interpreting their diagram via good communication by the respective partner (no peeking).

## SESSION 7

Session before team's first scrimmage, usually schedule a team such as an older team, a boys' team if coaching a girls team, a good HS team if permitted, and so forth.

Main topics: Passing and Receiving — ball stays on the ground; speed of play.

BW: Challenge of playing a "bigger team" is to defeat them with skill and play quickly so it is not a game of "clutch, grab and kick" or "bump, kick and run." I use examples such as Brazil, Spain, Barcelona or Arsenal (particularly in the final third) as examples of the style that we want to play — quick passing, mindset of possession to attack; the failure of many teams is that they cannot move the ball quickly in the final third nor can they maintain possession anywhere else but their back third. To develop the skill, we keep the ball on the ground and limit dribbling in today's session or aimless ("hopeful") balls launched from the back.

FL:

- Individual: foot skills — Cruyf, scissors; stationary — saw-see, triangle; toss and settle (inside/outside foot wedge, elevator, roof).

- 2 teams of nine players each (includes GKs), 2 balls per team; ordered passing/random movement (emphasize types of runs: check, slash, stretch, wide-high, support, etc. and continue to coach these in sessions).

  - Start balls at Player 1 and Player 5, pass and move sequentially without any restriction other than every pass is on the ground.
  - Repeat, except one ball is passed with 1-touch and the other is passed with 2-touches; this establishes rhythm and communication.

MR: Position-based possession — set up each team in a 1-3-3-2 and play directional, without any shooting on goal.

- First game is simply maximum 3-touch, first team to 21 passes wins.

- Second game is played so that both teams must complete 21 passes x 3 in the following order: forced 3-touch, forced 2-touch, then 1-touch.

MC: Brazilian-style scrimmage to full-sized goals — everything on the ground, 2-touch max, no square passes, play the way you face, add flair of hip/shoulder fake before passing, look past just the obvious first option pass (1st option is the one that is closest and most predictable, 2nd option is the medium-range option, 3rd option is the farthest and most unexpected). Then go to unrestricted.

FW: Communicate — be loud, but effective — understand the roles of the "giver" and "receiver" in communication situations; have fun.

The next day is usually a full 11v11 scrimmage; I give my team a restriction in the first half, such as 2-touch max on the ground (called "pineapple" in our code), and play two different formations. The scrimmage allows us to take the opportunity to train, rather than focus on a result.

## SESSION 8:

*Session one or two days after a scrimmage.*

Main topics: Support, role of 2nd attacker(s); Possession — speed of play; Technical — turning series (this exercise is a bit of fitness with a ball and involves technical speed).

BW: Review scrimmage, offering both positive comments and areas to improve. The season is upon us and we need to avoid getting too high or low after any one result; complacency and fear are weaknesses, whereas resolve to be better each day is powerful. "Excellence is performing ordinary tasks extraordinarily well and confidence comes from successfully executing skills under pressure." Thus, excellence and confidence are choices — will you choose them?

FL: Passing, receiving, turning

- 3s/1ball: pass on the ground and move all over the field, use drives for mid- and long-range passes, and work on technique; the run comes before the pass. Remember to accelerate to make a run, decelerate when making contact with the ball to make a "perfect" 1st touch then accelerate into space with ball.

  - Add in dynamic touch — big first touch into space at angles to change direction, speed dribble for 3-4 touches.
  - Throw in hip-swivel, head fake, shoulder shake for deception in one direction, take off in another direction.
  - Add in turn — player's choice.

- 3s/1 ball; turning series: half-turn (face-up), half-turn with drag (man-on), inside cross body, outside diagonal, glide turn, self-pass, leave, dummy. Teach difference between stretching and checking; encourage at least two looks, one while stretching and one before the ball arrives while checking; demand communication. Player A stretches slow/medium pace from Player B, then checks at speed to receive pass from Player B. Player A turns with the ball, looks up and plays Player C who is a high target, Player C lays ball off for Player A who now has taken Player C's place. Player C begins the pattern, receiving from Player A, turning and targeting Player B. Ratchet things up by adding agility figure 8 in the middle before receiving pass to turn. Teach players about angles of turns; even if this exercise is without pressure, it is critical that players train good habits.

MR: Possession games where the emphases are on the second attacker — must go over good support angles, showing closer than the 2nd defender to open up one-touch lanes, movement off the ball, staying open to the field with good body position, passing to proper foot, etc. Ideally, make this game competitive by dividing the team into groups to keep score and compete.

- 4v2: 16 x 12 yards, with markers at the midline; attack scores 1 point for every four consecutive passes, defenders score if they win ball and complete two passes. Must go over kite shape preference over diamond shape, flank support, how to play against the defenders that either press high or sit back, play vertical or horizontal. The four attackers illustrate high, wide and deep support — all elements in the big game. Be sure to use positional possession organization but also rotate players for understanding of all roles.

  - Variation: 2-touch forced by every player.
  - Variation: 2-touch max and mandatory 1-touch only if receiving a pass across the midline (this is excellent to set the standard for side support and work-rate overall).

- 5v3: keep ball rolling, look for up-back-through, play wide to go central and vice versa to imprint rhythm of play; variations would be restricting touches or varying touches such as challenging the attack to maintain a 3-2-1 touch rhythm as they maintain possession.

- Corner kick plays — attacking

MC: Scrimmage 9v9; first 10 minutes both teams play in a 1- then 2-touch rhythm; unrestricted.

FW: Pick five words that represent an ideal family and write about them in your journal — you will share these in a future team meeting.


## SESSION 9:

Main topics: Back-to-pressure (BTP) — this session covers the fundamentals of how players must deal with pressure from behind.

*Note:* *While it is good to teach players to "play the way you face," you must teach players how to deal with back-to-pressure situations. Even while playing back-passes, players must learn to deal with pressure, so teach this skill effectively.*

BW: Discussion — what it means to compete, ways to positively impact matches, the need to stay focused and tips on how to stay focused. Let us dictate the speed of play — when we possess the ball, we determine the rhythm and speed of the match, and when we defend, we make teams play a speed of play that they are uncomfortable with.

FL: Emphasize body position, vision, awareness, ball movement.

- 2s/1 ball: players begin approximately 2 yards apart, facing each other. The rhythm is pass-pass-pass through the legs, as the player (A) who lets the ball go through her/his own legs turns and goes after the ball. The partner who made the last pass (B) closes down space, in essence chasing down the player who is now between the ball and herself/himself. Player A shields, while Player B applies pressure on a count, "one thousand one, one thousand two." Make sure the pressure involves contact and basic arms-in hand checking that happens in real match play. As Player B ends the count, she/he chooses one side to pressure, forcing Player A to spin out with a sole role backward or forward, depending on which side the pressure is coming from. The players regroup, face each other and begin the sequence over again so that the next time, the roles are reversed. Make sure Player A shields with knees bent, low center of gravity, side-on, keeping the ball far enough away from the tackling leg of Player B. For beginning players, have the players pause for you to inspect, whereas advanced players can keep the ball moving and perform the exercises continuously.

- 4s/1 ball: players are paired, and the pairs face each other across a distance of approximately 25 yards. The rhythm is that one pair passes the ball on the ground to the other pair, who are coordinated by who is on attack and who is defending. Timing, body position, appropriate pressure, communication, and stance are critical to making the exercise run.

  - Early check — checking player checks to ball before ball is passed and leaves pressure on back early to create separation from defender on back, defender closes down space quickly, which does not allow player to turn, eventually creating the same BTP scenario as above.

*Note: In a match situation, a player checking early can be defined as checking before the passing player is ready to play and at a close distance; this is a signal to play over the top or through to a higher target. Such a situation is not what is going on in this exercise.*

- Late check — checking player indicates where ball is to be played by beginning movement but checks just after ball is actually passed, defender closes down space as above.
- No check — this is akin to "posting up" in basketball where the checking player is shielding in place, keeping a wide, broad stance and at the very last second, getting side on to shield and deal with pressure from behind. This helps keep the passing distance long and the attacking player closer to the goal to attack in real match play.

MR: Emphasize skills applied to match-related situations.

- Divide the team into half, where one team is on attack and one on defense. The team on attack is split to have a passer (A) and a receiver (B) who checks (early, late, or no check) while the defending team sends a defender to provide pressure on B's back. B deals with pressure and tries to spin the defender to get to goal; use a full-sized goal with live goalkeeper. Be sure to rotate where the pass and checking occurs, varying the angles and distance, but challenge players to keep score, compete, and play at match speed. Change roles so each team gets an even number of turns on attack and defense. Variations include building the numbers up from 1v1 to 2v2 and beyond.

*Note: This exercise is similar to "Bogies in the Sky," used by the women's soccer program at UNC.*

- Scrimmage 6v6, full-sized goals with live goalkeepers; use a 1-3-2 formation where the two forwards may not come back over a designated line so they are forced to work off of each other and create BTP game situations.

- Restarts — attacking goal kicks, kick-offs

MC: Scrimmage maximum 3-touch, no turning allowed unless it comes from a BTP situation. Move into scrimmage unrestricted.

FW: Praise effort and interconnectedness of teammates — continue to defend to our high standard in training sessions so the matches seem "easier." Offer specific and positive (not fluff) compliments to teammates when you see something worthy.


## SESSION 10:

Main topics: Transition and speed of play; perhaps the most important moment in most sports is that of transition. At the same time, as one moves up in competitive levels, speed of play increases.

BW: Fasten your seatbelts for an extra up-tempo training session!

FL:

- Individual: foot skills — step-over, hesitate; from sitting on the ground, toss ball high, get up quickly, jump in the air and settle with foot, thigh, chest, head and continue circuit.

- 3 teams of 6, each team is in a different color vest with two balls each, starting the balls off at players 1 and 4; random movement/ordered passing. Emphasize timing, touch, flow. Progression:

- Receive open to the field, move off against grain
- Maximum 2-touch, sprint four steps after passing
- Flighted ball (above head height in air) on every other pass
- 2 teams versus 1 team possession; team that loses ball goes on defense; CP: move ball, create options for each other; offer variations where players may not pass back to the same color that they receive from, touch restrictions overall or by team, make it competitive by keeping score (e.g., 5 passes = 1 point)

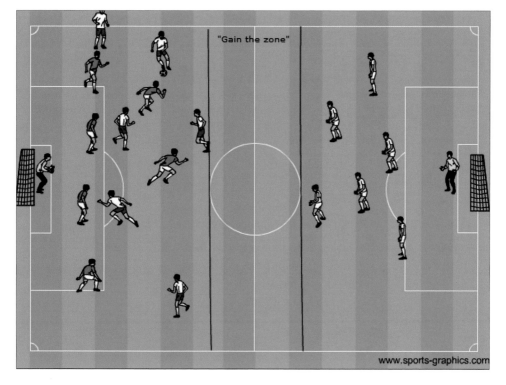

"Gain the zone"

www.sports-graphics.com

MR: Play to full-size goals, live GKs; vary restrictions per level and emphasis — if you are coaching the session effectively, speed of play increases and intentional play in moments of transition is elevated.

- 3 teams; B attacks A. A defends and tries to gain empty middle zone on-sides in order to attack C who awaits in own zone. Continuous play; advance to allow one defender to prevent free play in middle zone. CP: shape in transition to and from attack and defense, look for immediate counterattack opportunity high and how to make runs in support of the first pass, attacking a recovered defensive posture.

- 2 teams, play 6v6+2, 2-2-1-touch rhythm, followed by 3-2-1-touch rhythm

- Restarts: defensive corner kicks

MC: 2 teams, scrimmage unrestricted

FW: Write a letter of recommendation for yourself to a future coach — high school, ODP, DA, ECNL, college, pro, national team — a team that you have to try out for.

## SESSION 11:

Main topics: "Arsenal" games, attacking at speed

BW: Speed of play does not mean panic – requires technical speed, reading the game, 1st touch, speed of thought; decision-making, problem-solving

FL:

- Individual: foot skills in intervals – random, right foot only, left foot only, both feet, hook turn, chop; juggle (feet only) – high-high-low, high-low

- 4s/1 ball – turning series review (glide, inside cross-body, outside turn away, face up, man on turns)

- Take entire team to work on choreography. Train in your formation, begin ball with GK, distribute ball and move up the field as a team in attacking shape to finish in goal at far end – 10-second/4-passes, then move to timed shape. Everyone touches ball before shooting on goal (consequences for not meeting a set time such as 25 seconds). Be sure to make substitutions regularly to keep all players active and to get used to substitution patterns.

MR: 6v6 "Arsenal" attacking games, make it competitive by recording wins, losses, goals scored, assists, final passes, defensive transition pass. Play sequentially with the following restrictions:

- May only pass forward

- Upon winning possession, team must play in 1-2-touch rhythm (in that order) to goal

- May advance ball forward only by dribble or combination (e.g., 1-touch wall pass)

- Variation: one team must shoot within 10 seconds upon gaining possession while the other team must shoot after no more than 3 passes (switch roles)

MC: Scrimmage – unrestricted, but end with PK shootout

FW: Individually, then in pairs, then as a team – select 5 words that describe good leadership.


## SESSION 12:

Main topics: target play, longball/head, short-short-long rhythm

BW: Stretching, regeneration, rest; cutting out defending players with accurate long ball, noting that direct play does not mean "kickball"

FL: Focus on technique, preparation touch, striking below the midline for lift, follow-through, body position and stance when passing and receiving long balls.

- 2s/1 ball: pair up over 30-40 yard distance; keep scores on longball-settle, longball-head as in mini-camp; remember to serve user-friendly (back-spin) longballs, rotate partners

- 3s/1 ball: short-short-long; both short passes are on ground, long is in the air. Rhythm is that A passes to B in the middle, B returns pass to A, A strikes long over the top to C (B takes A's place, A moves into B's spot in the middle, creating a short-short-long rhythm with C)

- Whole team/5 balls: all over one-half of the field, move each ball in short-short-long rhythm (can perform this activity at random or by positions, but do this based on what the whole group and coach think are good choices). CP: pace of the pass increases over distance, but strive for accuracy of finding players on the run in one bounce or less.

MR:

- 3 teams of 5 (Blue, Red, Gray); Example: 5 Blue v 2 Red in a grid, Blue must complete 2-3 passes before serving into target grid where the Gray team awaits (the 3 other Red players in a middle zone may try to intercept any low or mis hit balls). If the Blue long ball successfully makes it into the target grid, then the Grays play 5v2 against two more reds (keep rotating defensively). The team that turns the ball over goes on defense; score 1 point for every successful long target pass.

- Scrimmage 9v9: divide field into thirds, playing a 1-3-3-2 shape, begin with the restriction that no players may come out of their third. Play to goal, but then add the restriction that they must complete a short-short-long rhythm before shooting (coach options such as backs to mids to backs to forwards).

- Functional: 11 versus 7, train defending against goal kicks/punts

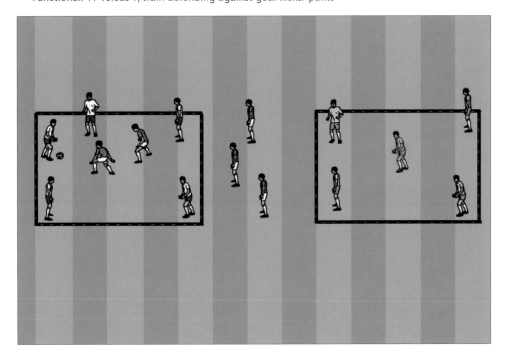

MC: Scrimmage unrestricted; CP: short-short-long rhythm, target play and making runs in support of the long ball played, review BTP, illustrate tight mark (space behind or withdraw) and loose mark (play feet). Don't force – maintain possession to move defense around in order to set up target play, defensively read serving space (small versus big) visual cues as to when long ball is on, rhythm, movement.

FW: Praise effort and encourage continued use of having more than one dimension in our play (indirect and direct styles of play).

## SESSION 13:

Main topics: Creating opportunities, finishing

BW: Analogy — Firehouse (used a *Sports Illustrated* article recalling 9/11 and sports leagues made of firemen and policemen in NYC). Explain how everyone has a role, some visible, more "fun," and interactive, while others more tedious and not glamorous, but everybody shares in the workload and the group is tight, loyal, and has each other's backs.

FL: Individual — foot skills to create imaginary finishing opportunities (drag, Matthews, zig-zig-zag), stop with a body part, trade balls on the dribble, knockout; speed training shuttles, agilities

- Divide team into 2 groups, each player has a ball and dribbles randomly using various moves and remembering to change pace, direction, size of touch, in a middle zone. On coach's command, each team dribbles out of their grid and attacks their target goal (since multiple shots are coming at the same time, use disc markers one yard in from either post on both goals to define target area. Reward 2 points for corner goal and 1 point for central goal, keep score for the entire practice.)

  - Power shooting (drives) off of a dribble — aggressive touch, move
  - Finesse shot off of a combination
  - Half-volley/Volley off of a combination in the air

MR:

- 6v6 in area approximately 30 x 50 yards with full-size goals, divide field in half so that each team plays with one goalkeeper and three players in defensive half and two players in the attacking half; progression:

  - Must play into attacking zone, then to defensive zone for a shot
  - Allow one player to come across into attacking zone by dribble or after a pass is played in
  - Must complete one pass in attacking zone before shot

- 5v5 unrestricted, extra team of 5 players scatters on outsides, playing as 1-touch neutral players. CP: shoot whenever an opportunity is there, create opportunities with the ball (drag, explosive touch for separation, finding a lane to the goal) and without the ball (overlap, separation from defender, loosely marked players)

- Restarts: free kicks — attacking

MC: Scrimmage 9v9 unrestricted

FW: Homework to watch and critique a match, focus on players in your position

## SESSION 14:

Main topics: Pressure-Cover-Balance (1st/2nd/3rd Defender roles); zonal defending

BW: Nutrition, hydration, rest

FL: Knock and move — 16 players/4 balls, whole team together, keeps the spirit and team camaraderie going; progression:

- After passing, if ball is passed into your area, immediately go to pressure the ball and communicate "ball!" (don't have to take away the ball, but work on stance, positioning, speed and angle of approach; pause, move on)

- Extend to two players reacting to pass and forming pressure-cover confrontation line, 1st defender (pressure) communicates "ball!" and the 2nd defender (cover) communicates "force left (or right)!"

MR:

- 2v2 grid training: stop on line to score, work on pressure-cover shape, stance, and communication, do not cross over each other's path on defense (use the analogy of a see-saw to move up and down as the ball enters your zone), review proper spacing, angle, and distance of the covering defender. The idea is to "get your guns," meaning one "gun" is pointed toward the ball and the other "gun" is pointed toward the opponent so that you see both.

*Note:* *The analogy is from the old American western days where gunslingers had guns in holsters on both hips.*

- 3 teams of four; 2 teams lined up across the end lines of a shallow rectangle while the third team is in the middle. All passes must be on the ground.

  The two teams on the outside may pass to each other sideways and ultimately they will try to pass across to the opposite team to score a point. The defending team in the middle must use good pressure-cover-balance-cover ("fishhook") shape that is tight, compact, and constantly adjust for "perfection" with intensity. CP: have one of the teams move the ball from player to player, showing how the middle team must react quickly to adjust, get into passing lanes, deny passes, and "be in the way." Keep score and rotate teams on 2-minute intervals (you will also remind the team about fitness through this exercise since this exercise is physically and psychologically demanding). The team allowing the fewest passes through wins.

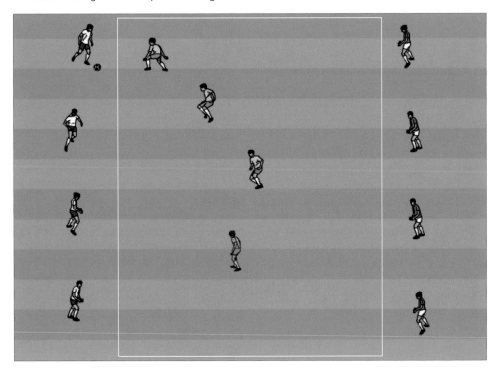

MC: Scrimmage, coaching each team to form pressure-cover "Vs" on the ball within the smaller game and good pressure-cover-balance lines in the bigger game.

*Note:* *Review the 11v11 formation of choice and how the P-C-B lines change in angle. Midfield — most diagonal; backs — least diagonal (more "flat"); and forwards — medium diagonal. Restarts — defending corner kicks.*

FW: Playing the way you think you are versus playing the way you actually are — impression, reality, honesty, expectation, standard; get "proof" (e.g., video) versus being one's own critic.

## SESSION 15:

Main topics: 2-player (wall pass, overlap, take-/fake-over, double-pass) and 3-player (3rd man run) combinations; bending balls (by-products of the session are change point of attack, speed of play, defending in groups)

BW: Picture of ducklings crossing the road — family, teamwork, interdependence

FL: Individual foot skills — scoop, pull-push; partner juggling — juggle-juggle-pass rhythm (meaning 2-touches then pass in the air to partner, no bounces)

- Whole team, half with a soccer ball and half without; those with ball dribble and those without move around and stay active; remember that the first pass of combo is to the feet, accelerate after the action. Keep this active and demand execution of proper technique. Be sure to switch roles, whereas some exercises will have natural switches going on:

  - Wall pass (give and go) — try some on the ground, playing to far foot of teammate, and also try some with a scoop (imagine lifting the ball over a defender's outstretched leg)
  - Overlap
  - Take-over, fake-over
  - Double-pass
  - Move on to 2s/1 ball: facing each other, partners will strike inside and outside of foot bending balls

- 3s/1 ball, 3-player combination ("third man run") — begin with two players on one end (A, B) and the third player (C) across from them approximately 25-30 yards. Ball starts with player on the left (A). C checks to A, A passes to C who plays ball back to B with left foot, simultaneously. C spins out (to his/her left, outside, creating space) and A makes bent run deep. B plays bent ball (inside right or outside left) into A's path on the run, A plays ball to C as they are now level. Now, A and C are together and B is the high player. Repeat several times. Switch so the ball starts on the right of the two players so that the deep bent ball is now played with the inside left or outside right. CP: Emphasize "wide-high" bent runs to stay onsides, play for the mis-struck ball, and to have vision; this is getting into the nuances of the game, but it is absolutely critical that the passing and running techniques are done well.

MR: Divide into 2 teams to play 8v8 on a rectangular field that has a 10 x 10 yard grid in each of the corners. The idea is to play possession (4 consecutive passes is a point) and create any of the 2- and 3- player combinations (2 points). Additional scoring of 1 point made by attacking the corner grids:

- Dribble in/dribble out

- Dribble in/pass out to teammate

- Pass in onsides/pass out to a teammate

- This exercise creates many teaching points, but it is also fun, lively, and entertaining as the play is naturally competitive, intense, and at a high level. CP: encourage team to imagine dividing the field into quadrants; on attack, change point of attack often to gain time/space/numbers advantages (think of a maximum of one or two passes in a quadrant), and on defense, try to force and keep ball in one quadrant as a group.

MC: Scrimmage 9v9 (11v11, if possible) to full-sized goals. CP: emphasize mid and final third tactics of moving the ball quickly, creating combos, playing with 1-2 touch rhythm, options, connectedness; end with PK shootout. For this training session, as with many training sessions (but not always documented in these sessions), we did fitness with a ball: 3s across the field — turning series, then "taffy pull" speed dribbling, moving closer for shorter sprints.

FW: Praise effort, proud to see team compete with intensity, skill, communication, and passion as they did in today's training session — this is how we play!

## SESSION 16:

Main topics: Circuit training, throw-ins, 4v4 tournament

BW: Spirit day — team is pre-divided to be in two teams, with each team subdivided into two sub-teams to form teams of four. Encourage spirit by wearing home/away uniform, each player wears a hat or "silly" socks, or just something different from the usual training kit. Encourage fun, teamwork, and competition — one way to show respect is to compete 100%, improving yourself, teammates, and opposition.

FL: Circuit training — 8 stations are laid out around the field. Spend 1 minute at each station, run to next station and begin on coach's command within 30 seconds; repeat. The stations are seal-walk (lie down on stomach, prop self up on forearms and toes, working on abs), juggling, side-bridge (lie down on side, prop self up by forearms, side of foot, switch side halfway through), toss and settle, push-ups, jump rope, crunches ("sit-ups"), speed ladder agility runs.

- 2s/ 1 ball: throw ball in to partner, settle with feet, and pass back to partner; switch roles.

- 4s/1 ball: practice three basic throw-in patterns. (The throw-in patterns are simply coach or team selected to generate movement; the team should be aware of roles and provide each other with high and medium support options. Our basic throw-in patterns are shown in chapter 8.)

MR: 4v4 tournament, one field has two full-size goals with live goalkeepers and is approximately 20 x 50 yards (narrow, long field). The other field has two full-size goals (because we don't have more than two GKs, the teams on that field can only score off of one-touch or hit the net on the fly, both in corners of goal only) and is 30 x 40. If out on touch lines, the restart can be a kick-in (indirect) or a throw-in (goals coming directly off of a throw-in are doubled).

Note:   If full-sized goals are unavailable for the second field then use small goals in the corner of the field and score by passing through gates, shin level or below. Keep score, add restrictions or have free play. Use a tournament format of first round (3 points win, 1 point tie, 0 points for a loss), advance to seeded semi-finals, then on to final and consolation. CP: Depth, width, support on attack, encourage 2- and 3-player combinations, movement, communication.

MC: 9v9 scrimmage

FW: Know the score

## SESSION 17:

**Main topics:** Finishing fundamentals plus competitive finishing

BW: Article on focus. Finishing low and why, rewarded throughout training session with finishes. Celebrate, and enjoy scoring. Note: The selected consequence may be 5 push-ups, 5 crunches/sit-ups, 5 burpees, 5 star jumps, or other brief exercise that perhaps the players may choose on occasion. This not a punishment, but a reminder to focus. The culture on our teams is highly competitive and demanding, yet positive, team-spirited and humorous, so much so that players understand the consequence and strive for a higher degree of focus on the task at hand.

*Note:   This is an individual penalty that we usually institute on day 1 and keep throughout the season. Goals are gold.*

FL: Individual: foot skills — fake shot cut, fake shot push, Cruyf. Juggling — feet only, emphasize "C" (or crunch) position, as in shooting technique. Two main finishing exercises:

* Two full-size goals facing each other, each with live GK, approximately 40 yards apart. Players are divided up into four groups, one group per post. Shooting occurs in both directions to minimize wait time and maximize repetitions. Individual scoring: 2 points for every goal scored in corner (marked off with disc 1 yard in from each post), 1 point any other goal. Work on finishing off of:
  * Dribble
  * Layoff
  * Back-pass
  * Wall-pass
  * Overlap
  * Turn
  * Volley/Half-volley

* 2 teams; one team on attack to full-size goal, live GK, and second team defends. Game goes in a rhythm of 1v1, 2v2, 3v3, 2v2, 1v1 in 60-second intervals. Teams switch roles and play again, keeping score.

MR: Emphasize fundamental technique, composure, desire.

* Two small-sided games, ideally have both fields equipped with full-size goals. Borrow GKs if necessary so that finishing is as realistic as possible.

* Two-thirds-field, 11v7. The 11 are working on attacking tactics, creating scoring chances, and shooting on one goal while the 7 work on defending as a group. If the 7 win the ball, they can finish in two counter goals on the sides or one full-size goal in the center (off of one touch or hit the net on the fly or live GK, if available).

* Restarts — attacking free kicks

MC: Scrimmage 11v11, if possible, otherwise play 9v9. Again, emphasize creating opportunities, properly weighted passes to lead to first time finish (final pass), preparation touch, and follow-through with both feet off of the ground.

FW: Stretching reminder, especially as season goes deeper, striking long balls, finishing, etc.

## SESSION 18:

Main topics: Final pass, revisit bending balls; positional, Zidane, and directional possession

BW: Leadership; final pass: pass leading to shot, the standard is the pass is textured so that the teammate can shoot on goal on first touch, or, the pass leading to the pass that leads to a shot on goal; we reward 1st and 2nd assists, in addition to the goal.

FL:

- Pass and move, add in bent balls, turns, flicks/settles, speed dribbling.

- 5v2 warm-up, review support closer then second defender to find a passing lane and to compromise defensive shape, stretch the field, as in 3rd attacker role; play 2-touch, forced 3-touch, 1-touch.

*Note: The 5v2 exercise is a core exercise used often, though not mentioned in these sessions.*

- 2 teams possession, divided up by position; one team is on the "outside" on attack in positions along with one or two teammates (center midfield types) on the inside, while the other team is on the "inside." May play directional along with GK's in formation. Teams switch roles when possession changes; if exercise is too advanced, then use two neutrals who always stay in the middle as plus players.

  - Force a restriction of "playing like Zidane" or "take it on the move," meaning a player cannot settle a ball where they are, but instead must touch to space on the first touch (away from defenders, into space, the way the great Zidane played).
  - Progress to maximum 2-touch, forced 3-touch (develop comfort on the ball and foot skills under pressure), 3 consecutive 1-touch pass incentives.

MR: Final pass, also known as "the Cone Game" in our team vocabulary; 2 teams play directional on a field approximately 50 wide by 30 long, with 10-yard end zones added onto each end. Discs are placed every 10 yards on the end lines leading into the end zones. Points are scored by getting the ball into the end zone in possession. CP: must coach correct surface final passing. Use restrictions of touches, as appropriate. Progression:

- Score by dribbling over end line into end zone and stopping ball with sole.

- Score by passing to attacker who is running onsides into end zone. Player must be able to stop ball with sole to score the point. The restriction is that the ball and player cannot enter the end zone through the same window, encouraging players to make slashing runs behind a flat back line. For advanced players, score extra points for each gate skipped as the final pass enters the end zone to the runner.

- Score as in above, but one attacker may enter the end zone (onsides) to join the runner who just got in onsides; one defender may enter the end zone. The two attackers try to complete one pass for a point.

- Extend by going to goal, two full-size goals with live GKs. First require the player who receives the onsides pass to finish on goal on his or her first-touch in the end zone, then progress to allowing one attacker and one defender to go into the end zone to add possible follow-up run for rebounds or a cross, but restrict to one pass at most. When GK plays ball out, defensive team may drop back into defensive end zone, but attackers may not.

- Other options can be added at the midline where any player receiving the ball in the front half has only 1-touch, or restrict touches by all, or must find 3 consecutive 1-touch passes before being allowed to attack the end zone/goal.

MC: Scrimmage 9v9. Emphasize the quality of final pass (texture, pace, correct surface), taking the ball on the move. Add in restarts — attacking corner kicks, unrestricted.

FW: Play the way we need versus only the way you want; the two should be harmonious and unified.

## SESSION 19:

Main topics: Longballs, Crossing/Finishing

BW: Warriors; artists and soldiers. Warriors — we need everyone to consistently compete with intensity (and doing so is a choice). The "how" that a teammate contributes to our cause may sometimes be represented by players who may be considered "artists" or "soldiers" or a blend of both. Know yourself and your teammates.

FL: Individual foot skills — Matthews and counter-Matthews, scissors and double-scissors; juggling — feet only, two high (approximately head height) and then do a 360-degree revolution and do one low; then, try foot-foot-head, adding in a 180-degree turn to head the ball.

- 2s/1 ball (keep score, rotate partners after each exercise):
  - Longball-settle
  - Longball-head
  - Longball off of a slow rolling ball-settle
  - Longball-clear
- 2 teams of 9 players each/3 balls per team: Pass and move — bend, long and lifted

MR: Set up field with two full-size goals on ends. Use discs to mark out a channel that curves toward the end lines at the six. At the midline, the channel is 2 yards wide. Each team plays a 1-2-3-1 and rotates two additional players into the channels to play as neutrals.

- Run through two patterns in which each GK distributes ball to outside player in channel (so both teams are working at once), form a combination in:
  - Defensive half — early cross to back post with flighted bent ball that bends away from the opposing GK (visual cue in game is that the opponent is flat and high, leaving space to cross into)
  - Attacking half — player goes end line and serves late cross back on the ground through a seam to the 6- to 12-yard marker (visual cue is that the opponent is defending low and defensive team has a 2nd defender in good position to prevent an early cross).

Note:  *Quality of service is critical. Cross with pace, runs into the box are near-far-slot to frame the goal (crossing runs for early cross and no crossing runs for late cross). Finish and rebound 1-touch only; demand players to go through patterns at match pace.*

- Scrimmage live

  - Designate neutrals in each half of each channel on both sides of the field. Maximum 3-touch in attacking half, maximum 2-touch in defending half. Players in the field are unrestricted, or may add 2-touch maximum restriction.
  - No neutrals; allow players to move into channel (but no defending) with touch restrictions as above.

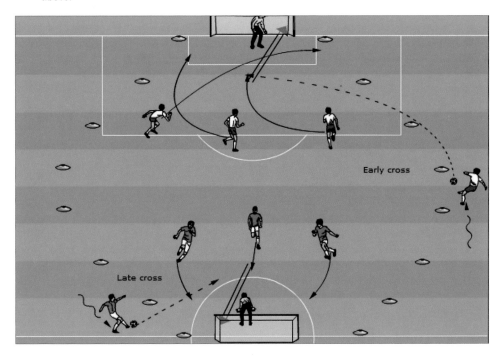

MC: Scrimmage 9v9 unrestricted. Add incentives, such as 3 points for a goal 1-touch off a cross (5 for a header). CP: cues, runs, type of service, demand at least three runs to frame plus one trailer run. Don't force the cross and avoid serving square crosses from outside the 18 but even with the 6-12 yard area since these crosses are easier for defenders to clear; serve away from the GK and out of the 6-yard box.

FW: Goal-setting, objectives, measure, assess, plan.


## SESSION 20:

Main topics: Possession; playing goal-up/goal-down

BW: Communication — receiver and giver of information, understanding each other's point of view; tone, attitude, clarity, get at the heart of the matter, follow-up. Go over non-verbal cues — facial expression, arm gesture, hands, head bobs, eyes, smile, etc.

FL: 6s/1 ball: shuttles, as in warm-up for matches — 2-touch, 1-touch, 3-touch, 1-touch wall pass rhythm, run-throughs and high ball settles and dribble from throw-ins. Players need to remember to pressure the next person in line to force the player to make a better touch under pressure.

- 6s then go to pass and move, 2 balls in each group. Progression: dynamic touch, aggressive touch into space, turning; groups are in different colors and intermixed so that through-passes and natural obstacles are a part of the fundamental passing series.

- 6v6 + 6 players around the outside who play as neutrals with one-touch; possession, emphasize maximum 2-touch, 5 passes = 1 point; do not allow neutral players to pass to other neutral players.

MR: 9v9, includes two live GKs in two full-size goals

- Directional possession with GKs as neutrals. Emphasize decision-making among players – are they passing to attack or passing for possession? Consider pressure on the ball (support must be closer), pressure on the teammate (serve proper foot), and generally, serve to the foot that puts teammate in the best position to either play 1-touch or to take a touch into space away from pressure (this is how we communicate with the pass).

- Scrimmage – team who scores cannot score again until the other team scores; the team keeping possession is up 1-0 and tries to maintain possession for the rest of the game (obviously encourage finishing opportunities if they present themselves), emphasize time and places to keep possession, especially wide to open up other team and create passing lanes. The team that is trying to score is down 1-0 and needs to be coached to send numbers forward, play more direct, and get numbers in the box.

*Note:* *Loss of possession will occur – remind the team of making good decisions in terms of if necessary, lose possession higher up the field, closer to the opponent's defensive third in the "channels" (space between sides of penalty area to the touch lines). Also when up 1-0, don't give up silly fouls or other obvious shooting opportunities to the opponent.*

MC: Scrimmage unrestricted; add in restarts – emphasize a review of attacking and defensive throw-ins

FW: Puzzle – problem-solving activity with goal to figure out which of three switches is connected to a light bulb that you cannot see.


## SESSION 21:

Main topics: Finishing – fundamental and match-related; combining midfield and forwards.

BW: Speed and its physical and mental importance.

FL: "Shooting carnival." Divide the team into four groups and have the shooting circuit laid out ahead of time. This part of the training session requires five full-sized goals that may or may not include portable "kick-back" type goals. Rotate stations after 6-8 minutes and be sure plenty of soccer balls are handy to maximize repetitions. As always, emphasize technique and make corrections promptly. Mark off corners of the goal, one yard in from each post. Penalize shots that miss over the goal as previously described. The stations:

- "Beckham" shooting on full-size goal, no goalkeeper and all players in the group may shoot at once. Players are 22-25 yards from goal and at their own choosing, they aim for each of the four corners of the goal (have markers with vests or other visible indicator for scoring). They must call out the corner before shooting, and they must strike at each of the four corners before repeating a corner. Use right and left feet to "bend it like Beckham."

- 2v2 using 2 balls, 2 full-size goals facing each other at approximately 50 yards apart. Players are paired up to try to score as many goals as possible (no GKs in the goals). Players may try to block shots with the body, but no hands allowed. In addition, they may dribble up to the midline to score, but have a maximum of four realistic touches before they have to shoot (includes passing or dribbling).

- Breakaway finishing on live GKs on full-size goal. Have two GKs for this one to rotate, as it will be fatiguing at the pace that we want to keep this exercise moving at.

- Crossing and finishing — two players in finishing positions, two players in crossing positions on the flank. Use full-size goal. Flank serves flighted ball to finisher farther away ("far post"), and finisher gets one touch to finish. Rotate roles and sides.

- Recommend fitness activity: could be pure fitness, fitness with a ball, or an active finishing exercise such as continuous 1v1v1 in the box.

- Bring full team together, set up two lines at the bottom of the circle.

*Note:* *Although I am not a fan of "line drills", these can be good after a round of fitness as rest, or to spend a brief amount of time on fundamentals. Work on finishing combinations: wall-pass, overlap, 3rd man run. Always send both attacking players to goal — allow 1-touch rebound finishes.*

MR: Half-field progression; attacking side goes to full-size goal with live GK, defending side goes to counter goals on sides or full-size goal in center with live GK. Begin with 5v4: 2 forwards and 3 midfield players attacking 1 GK, 2 backs, 1 midfield player. Review combination play and crossing using interpassing, movement, 1st/2nd/3rd options, and 1st/2nd/3rd runs. Increase numbers to 10v8.

MC: Scrimmage 9v9; restarts — attacking free kicks.

FW: Competing with and against friends, especially in big matches; focus on the task at hand, have an "ice" mentality as far as having a solid mentality, keep your focus, and stay cool under pressure.


## SESSION 22:

Main topics: Playing out of the back via wrapping (change point), using target and flank options; also technical 1st touch and passing repetitions

BW: Everyone counts; identify your role, be comfortable with it, but don't rest — strive to be better. Use the quilt analogy — everyone has a unique patch, but together it is really something special. Advanced topic today — need extra attentiveness.

FL: Focus on first touch, progress to passing patterns

- 2s/1 ball: Pingers — players stand approximately 1-2 yards apart and play one-touch back and forth, working on push pass ("punch" follow-through) technique, solid contact. Choose patterns — right to right, left to left, diagonals and straights, then move to 2-touch boxes (counterclockwise, clockwise).

- 3s/1 ball: Diamonds — one player works while two players actively rest. Player begins with ball, makes pass, then uses footwork to get to the adjacent side of the diamond (good agility work). Patterns:

- Pass short, receive long
- Pass long, receive short

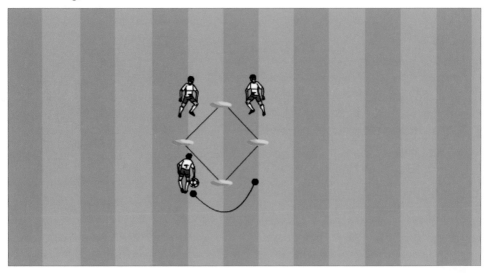

- 4s/1 ball: 2 players on outside, 2 players on inside; rhythm is player A long flighted serve to far inside player C, lay ball back to B, pass on ground to D. Repeat, rotate, and may compete by keeping track of successful cycles.

www.sports-graphics.com

- 4s/1 ball: wrapping — facing up field, players wrap, outside back to center back to outside back on opposite side, take space, spin, and repeat. There is the option is to skip a center back on way to wrap, but play near center back when dropping, vary options to train players to make good decisions based on spacing and pressure of opponent. Coach spacing, touch, distance, angles.

- 4s/1 ball: set up as a back, target forward, and outside flank player with one defending player on the flank. Make it continuous by alternating flank and defender roles, then switch back and target into those roles and vice versa. Coach options:

  - Defender applies medium coverage, flank player checks early but space to play ball is too small, so back plays to target forward while flank spins off of defender and gets ball from target.
  - Defender applies tight coverage and is cutting off the line, back plays to flank, flank flicks ball into space for target player, flank spins off opposite shoulder of defender to combine with target.

    - If defender cuts off middle, then flank lays ball back to the back, spins, and back can play flank player on run or to target.

  - Defender applies loose coverage — back passes to flank, flank player turns with the ball and plays to target player down line if defender cuts off middle or inside if defender cuts off line.

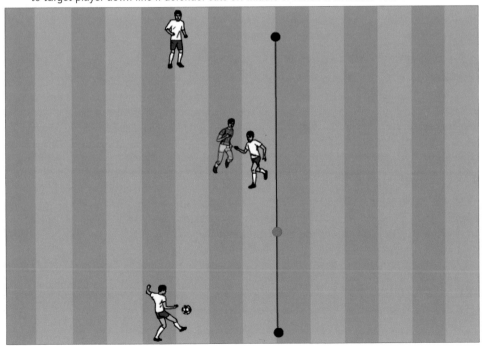

MR: Set up two-thirds field scrimmage (or at least to bottom of circle in opposite half) using full-size goals. Set up team in formation, using the outer two "diamond" formations, add in defenders to play 9v5 (includes GKs). Begin with wrap to outside back and create options as in above exercise. This is an advanced topic that needs coaching so that all players learn to read options.

MC: Scrimmage 9v9 unrestricted. Help "paint the picture" for players to read, understand, make a good decision, and execute skills. Restarts — defensive corner kicks.

FW: Praise effort, if applicable. Note that so many soccer matches are played between the 18s, but there is much more than that — most matches are won and lost in the penalty area and therefore, tomorrow's focus is the "battle in the box."

## SESSION 23:

Main topics: Clearing out of the box, finishing in the box. GK language — step up, slide (plus direction of right or left), side-on, and drop

BW: Communication in the "heat of the battle," intense competition or various surroundings can bring out communication that is loud (to be heard, but not personal). Communication is also brief since soccer is a fluid game with little stoppages. Thus, understand the importance of the fact that how we communicate on the field may not be the same as we communicate off of it. Note: The reader will notice that the area of communication is discussed frequently, as it is a critical part of any team construct.

FL: GKs lead movement of whole team. Put the team in formation, have coach and a few players oppose the team in formation and move the ball from side to side, sometimes dribbling at the team, sometimes making back passes away from the team. GKs must use appropriate language (see above), be loud, assertive, and precise in demanding good defensive shape.

* 2s/1 ball: longball series — settle, head, back pass, clear

MR: 5v5v5 game, "Battle of the Box." Rotation is as follows: team that defends goes to attack, attack goes to serve, servers come in to defend. GKs rotate after each game. Servers are scattered around touchlines to both corners and as far away as midline. Serve flighted, driven, bending, lofted balls into box. Attacking team attacks with all five members — 1st layer near-far-slot framing of goal plus 2nd layer trailers. Defending team defends with all 5 players, two cover post areas if GK comes out, three along the 6 and out (if working with beginning players, then defend or attack with only 3 players, depending on your objective). If ball gets cleared out toward servers, they serve ball back in the box 1st time. Encourage body shape, courage, seeing the ball not the player on contact, body up on players, run in front of the GK on attack (it is very typical to run behind and let the GK make the save, but on attack, you must not let this happen). The attacking players framing the posts should not let any ball go between them and the post they are framing. Defensively, focus on body position to clear high, far, and wide first time. Penalize whole team if any balls bounce in the box before being touched. GK communication, courage, and ownership of the 6-yard box is critical. In addition, after a clear, command team to clear box. Play until ball is scored, goes out of play, or is cleared satisfactorily. Penalize own goals and giving up of corner kicks with extra repetitions for the attacking team. Rotate after every 10-15 serves, but be consistent to keep score.

*Note:   This game is similar to team trains the GK used with the UNC Women's soccer program.*

MC: Scrimmage 9v9 on a shorter, wide field to encourage crossing opportunities that will give the team opportunities to win the battle in the box. Restarts — defending free kicks.

FW: Praise courage, but don't "embarrass" anyone. Be positive, but put the spotlight on the team, adding highlights of players if warranted. Illustrate courage as a team — faces, pose, etc., and use this in the upcoming match.

*Note:* *The reader will notice that some of the following training sessions revisit topics; this is not because I have run out of ideas, but more so because of the importance to emphasize and reinforce certain skill areas. I have also done this to show the reader how to include an overlap of skill exercises, advance the skill, and still make the training session different. In addition, the next set of training sessions include the use of halves or thirds in scrimmage situations. The coach will need to remind players on attack not to "camp out" on the edge of the grid hoping to receive the ball. Instead, players need to stretch the defense and create space for themselves to check into, working off of each other. You may also add an offsides line in the final attacking section or impose certain defensive constraints to help the exercises along, as appropriate. Lastly, readers should remember that the level of sophistication of exercises can be increased or decreased by adjusting time, space, and numbers to the appropriate challenge level.*

## SESSION 24:

Main topics: Driving balls in the air; application to driven balls to targets and secondary-range finishing

BW: Champion — compare and contrast what it means to win championships versus to be a champion. Physical versus mental mistakes/errors.

FL:

- Circle exercise — half of the team with soccer balls on the outside and half without on the inside. Progression: 1-touch return ball on ground, turn-dribble-find player on outside, headers, volley with instep/laces.

- Soccer tennis: singles and doubles in a 20 x 12 grid.

- 2s/1 ball: ball striking technical progression, begin with passes on the ground and develop to air, increasing distance to 35-40 yards. CPs: placement of non-kicking foot, angle of approach, point of contact to drive ball over distance in the air.

- Teach the "zinger" pass where the ball leaves the foot fast, has back-spin, and reaches the targeted player softly.

MR:

- 6v6v6 target/transition box game over distance (see Session 12 MR). Keep all players involved, emphasize driven ball in the air over distance (make the field appropriately longer since these types of passes are served with more pace).

  - 6v3 in the grids on the end, on completion of 3rd pass, drive ball successfully to the team waiting in the far grid for one point, then the three defending players in the middle zone go in to defend, repeat.
  - Turnovers cause rotation of teams to keep play continuous.
  - CPs: execution of technique under pressure, application of skill, rhythm, body position and preparation. Adjust size and limit number of touches depending on skill. You may also use target game (where the player serving the driven ball has to call out the name of the target who they are serving before serving, extra accuracy and vision).

- 7v7 (be sure to keep other players active and substitute frequently), field dimensions approximately 60 x 45; divide the field in half; full-size goals, live GKs, each team plays 1-4-2 formation.

- 4v2 in each half of the field (plus GK; field players play 3 in the back with 1 playing higher in the half as a CM); may not cross over into next zone.
- Backs look to drive ball into a forward, the other forward may score off of 1-touch or, the team may score from own half (long-range/secondary range finishing).
- Reward driven ball to target with 1 point and driven ball finish into goal with 2 points.

- Same as above, but now allow one player from the back half to join the attack off of any long driven ball from the back to the front half.

- Create numbers up. CPs: timing and angles of runs, rhythm of 3rd man run possibilities.

MC: 9v9 scrimmage unrestricted, field approximately 80 x 60. Encourage long driven ball at opportunities (to shoot, change the point of attack, target play), continue to focus on proper technique.

FW: Exit opportunity is a friendly juggling competition between the two teams. Find a way for each player to get a touch without repeating players until every player has touched the ball. Whole team juggle – same challenge.


## SESSION 25:

Main topics: Forwards receiving ball with back-to-goal. Focus is on the forwards' ability to deal with pressure from behind (and not on turning). Refer to Session 9: Back-to-pressure.

BW: *Braveheart* – the "Freedom" speech; "would you be willing....?" Medals, trophies, banners will eventually tarnish and fade, but the memories, feelings in your heart, sense of accomplishment, and unbelievable team connection will last forever. Go after being the best – don't assume or feel entitled, instead, you must work for it together.

FL: Repeat two warm-up exercises from the back-to-pressure fundamental exercises.

- 2s/1 ball: pass-pass-pass through the legs, turn, shield for at least two seconds. This time, through repetition, the players are sharper on execution and dealing with the pressure with cleaner technique. Advance the skill by adding a goal to get to after the turn (e.g., small gate or ball placed on top of a disc to knock over).

- 4s/1 ball: reminder that the emphasis is on controlling pressure initially and not on turning.

  - Early, late, no check progression. Make sure the defender pressures on both sides to encourage practice of sole rolling forward and back. CPs: body position and stance, checking speed and timing, quality of 1st touch.
  - Advance the skill by adding a goal for the attacker to get to after the turn (e.g., stop the ball on a designated line with the sole of the foot).

- Two teams shooting exercise to goal. Advance the skill by allowing the player to pass to options (simulate CM, OF, CF, etc., depending on start position), adding extra defenders for each pass made. Encourage the first player not to pass unless they have to and, if they do, both the attacking and defending teams must react quickly. Work on the "zinger" pass where the ball leaves the foot fast, has back-spin, and reaches the targeted player softly.

MR: 8v8 scrimmage. 60 x 50 with a midline. Each team plays a 1-4-3 (GK plus four in the back half (as in four "backs") and three in the front half (as three "forwards")). Progression:

- Forwards may not turn nor may they shoot (unless they effectively deal with back-to-pressure situations), all players must stay in their respective half of field.

- Same except maximum 2-touch; encourage early, late, no check decisions.
- Later on, one player from the defensive half may join the attack, but must return upon loss of possession.

MC: 9v9 scrimmage. Begin with the stipulation that no player can turn with the ball, emphasize back-to-pressure target play. As a result of this restriction, players will also learn to position bodies in attacking stance when possible. Reward points for successful BTP shield, spin/layoff rhythm. Then scrimmage unrestricted, adding in free kick restarts.

FW: Standards and expectations — how to assess, what it means to raise them. Momentum/rhythm in a match.

## SESSION 26:

Main topics: Early crossing — technique (bent, flighted balls) and application (final pass).

BW: Civil/Revolutionary War history — waves of attack, gaining territory, numbers, making use of resources.

FL:

- Triangle passing (adaptation from UNC) — set up 2 back-to-back triangles to create a diamond (approximately 40-60 yards across and wide, depending on skill level)

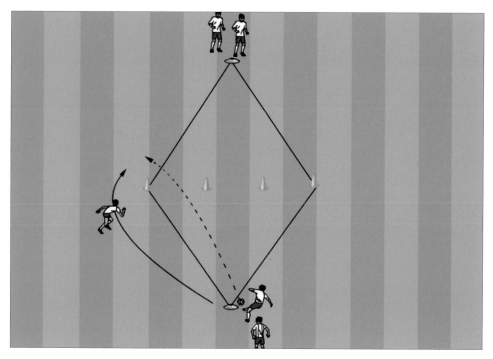

- Rhythm to remember is pass twice, receive twice, rotate out.
- Do this with maximum 4-5 players in each group for enough repetition.

- Change direction, offer targets in middle to simulate beating a flat back four; must serve correct surface, bent, flighted balls behind backs and into path of running teammate; be sure the runs are bent to stay onside, improve vision, and correct for any mis-served passes.
- Depending on level – increase distance, limit touches.
- Work up to flighted balls, keep points for successful serve and receive.

- Rehearse early crossing (see Session 19)

  - Visual cue is that the opponent's backs are stepped up and flat, leaving space to target early cross between the backs and their GK.
  - GK distributes ball to outside back, advance ball to midfield/forward who receives in attacking stance, cleans up and prepares ball, serves early bent cross behind opponent's backs and away from GK.
  - Target area is to the second "six" for attackers to run onto and finish. Review near-far-slot runs, timing, angles, and 1-touch finishes.
  - Run this simultaneously in both directions to reduce wait time.
  - To advance the skill, compete by having "chasers" on the flank players who cross, at least one defender in the box. Have the two teams compete.

MR: Play 7v7 in field plus 4 neutrals (2 in each channel; 1 in each half).

- Limit 2 touches in the channel.

- Can only score off cross from flank; watch for numbers up, cues.

- Extend to 9v9 (no neutrals), any player may go into channel and have maximum 2-3 touches. Allow one defending player to go in to channel so the cross is not free.

MC: 9v9 scrimmage. Reward 3 points for score off of early cross, 2 points for score off of any cross, 1 point for any other goal, incentive of 5 points for a goal off of 1-touch volley or head from flank cross. Move on to unrestricted scrimmage. Add in restarts.

FW: Understanding soccer in 3-D (length, width, height).


## SESSION 27:

Main topics: Counterattacking: emphasis on transition to attack; speed of play.

BW: Representing your self, family, team, club, state, region, nation.

FL: 3s/1 ball – short-short-long, 3rd man runs review (both feet, technique, surface, pace of service, bent passes, touch).

MR:

- Two teams of 4, 24 x 15 (midline at the 12); transition boxes, 4v2 in "home" half, 5 passes = 1 point, raise the level by limiting to two touches.

  - When the two defenders win the ball, they play to their teammates and join in the grid to create 4v2 in their "home" half. The opposing team sends in two players to defend.
  - Fast transitions.
  - Execution, position of 2 defenders to win ball in good shape, facing direction they want to counterattack in.

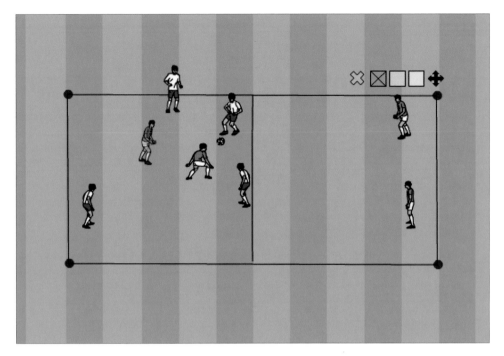

- Extend above game to 8v8 (8v4 in each half) transition boxes, approximately 30x40 space.

- 3 teams of 5 plus two GKs; scrimmage with full-size goals, live goalkeepers, regular rules except team sitting out are neutrals on the touchlines (not end lines) who have 1-touch.

  - Team that gets scored on rotates out and team that was on the outside rotates in. Meanwhile, the team that just scored stays on and immediately counterattacks in the opposite direction.
  - This is a particularly lively, energetic, competitive game where opportunities abound for decision-making and aspects beyond just counterattacking. Keep score and have consequences for how the teams finish first, second, and third.

MC: Scrimmage 9v9 (ideally 11v11). If necessary, coach can restrict shooting to less than or equal to four passes, no back passing, 1-touch after forward pass, or other restrictions to encourage more transition opportunities. Be sure to end up scrimmaging unrestricted. Work on defensive corner kicks and how to counterattack out of them. Base counterattack on the vertical half that the corner is cleared from.

FW: What do you do when no one is watching? Can be the difference between mediocrity and excellence — not a very complicated concept.

## SESSION 28:

Main topics: Opposed heading (heading under pressure on attack and defense), long flighted service.

*Note:*   *Consult medical personnel and latest research to train heading safely and within guidelines of the program.*

BW: Picture of intensity, competition, elation (bring in pictures from recent significant championships from any sport).

FL:

- Warm up with the heading game (advance ball by throw-in, roll, or bump/punch; must score with a header).

- 2s/1 ball — heading progression: from ground (cobra, crab walk, knees [dive forward]) to standing (alternate starting stance of each foot and both feet in addition to body angle to the ball) to jumping. Head juggle back and forth. Review attacking (downward) versus defensive (upward) headers.

- Circle drill (half the team on outside with a ball, half the team inside without a ball). Player on outside calls a name and that player must win the header back to the thrower, but the nearest player must try to jump in the way, creating a 1v1 heading duel.

- 4s/1 ball: Long service with heading duel in the middle. Set up so that two players are approximately 60 yards apart, with two additional players in the middle of them (approximately at 30 yards from either of the players on the ends). One player on end serves a long flighted ball to the two players. If the one farther away can win the ball and head it back toward the server then they receive one point. If the near player can flick the ball with the head past the far player then he or she earns the point.

MR: Live scrimmage with channels, total of four neutrals in the channels serve flighted balls in, win the 1v1 heading duels, 6v6 in middle. Points can be scored by winning attacking or defensive headers.

MC: 9v9 scrimmage (unrestricted). An extra point is awarded for any heading duel won in the run of play. Layer in attacking corner kick restarts.

FW: Journal — describe what "here to there" means to you via words, poem, or drawing.


## SESSION 29:

Main topics: Combination play — 2 player (see Session 15), possession; 1st touch; using maximum width/ depth.

BW: Periods of vulnerability — 2 minutes at the beginning and end of each half and immediately after a goal is scored. Restart moments. Magic moments may occur at any time during the match, stay and play in the moment one minute at a time, ideally one second at a time. Play free, but have a positive impact.

FL:

- Two teams of 9 (including GK). Pass and move to warm up, layering in basic combinations (emphasize technique), then build into possession (use whole-part-whole training concept in this session). Set up each team in a 1-3-2-1-2 by positions that players normally play. Play forced 3-touch and maximum 2-touch progressions, all on the ground. Five consecutive passes = 1 point, 3 consecutive 1-touch passes = 1 point, any 2-player combination = 2 points.

- 3s/1 ball: 1st touch exercises. A serves ball on the ground (progress to in the air) to B and C who alternate performing 1st touch passes back to A by executing skill and proper footwork around two markers. Work on push pass, volley and half-volley (inside and outside of foot, instep), header.

- 5v5 + 5 grid training. Approximately 40x40 grid. Two teams in the middle, third team is on the outside as neutral (1-touch for neutral players; maximum 3-touch for players on inside). The idea is to perform combinations with own team and neutrals (exploit the numbers up situation).

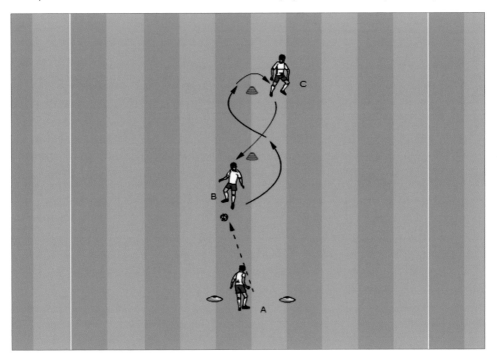

- Variation: use two teams, with each team providing players on the outside. Players on inside may pass to their teammate on the outside and take their place or overlap around the outside of them. Create decision-making opportunities as to when to make the switch with the outside player versus when not to.

*Note: We want to eliminate the "programming" that sometimes occurs in training. This game helps improve decision-making and problem-solving rather than forcing a combination just for the sake of doing one. We also get many good opportunities to look off of passes, perform "half-combinations," etc.*

MR: 9v9 scrimmage with 10x10 yard square grids in corners of the field. Use full-size goals, live GKs. Require players to get in and out of 2 grids (one in the defensive half and one in the attacking half) before going to goal. Use progression of dribble in-dribble out, pass in-dribble out, pass in-pass out; CPs: support, width, depth, change point. Encourage restrictions to maximum 2-touch, combination play, playing the ball on the ground (except for shots on goal) through use of points. With this set up, your GKs will also improve their foot skills and passing ability.

MC: 9v9 scrimmage unrestricted. Encourage maximum 3-touch and combination play, but do not restrict players. Encourage creativity and up-tempo speed of play. PKs to end the session.

FW: Community service – importance, what we are doing, everybody involved.

## SESSION 30:

Main topics: Pressure-cover-balance (refer to Session 14). Understand principles of defense and roles of 1st, 2nd, and 3rd defender; zonal defending.

BW: 2-up/2-down warm-up. Note: Recreational warm-up to keep beginning of the session light (again, a coach needs to know how to challenge the team, but also have enough variety to avoid monotony).

FL:

- 3s/1 ball: pass in a triangle. Every now and then, one player calls "ball" and goes to pressure the player who just received a pass, and the next player without the ball joins the pressuring player and communicates "force right" or "force left" to simulate the role of the second defender (cover).

- 3v3 in grids. To score, stop the ball on the opposing line. Go over zonal defending so that the defending team understands they should not cross over themselves; there should be a constant movement of up and back, sliding, along with communication amongst the three players. Help players see the picture of P-C-B line of defense and assist how to deal with an overlap by the attack; think of defending as one solid unit, communicating, moving, and adjusting together.

- 3 teams of four players — two teams on opposite sides of a rectangle. They try to pass a ball on the ground through the middle. They move the ball side-to-side before passing the ball across to try to unbalance the four in the middle who are moving in P-C-B-C line of defense. Although this is a review, emphasize urgency, intensity, competitiveness. Rotate teams and keep score.

MR: 6v6 in a wide, short field (approximately 35 long x 60 wide). Each team has four small goals to defend and consequently, four goals to attack (goals are 2-yard gates; score with a pass on the ground through any of the four goals). The formation for each team is a 4-2 to illustrate P-C-B-C shape and to emphasize P-C V-shaped defensive pods around the field when defending. Begin with the ball on the ground, then allow balls in the air. Limit touches to increase speed of play (and consequently, improve speed of "read and react" defensive adjustments). Players should anticipate and be proactive in getting into good positions to defend effectively. An extension of this exercise could be to use the four goals as gates to get through onsides before going to goal (adding in space on both sides of the rectangle and full-size goals with goalkeepers).

MC: 9v9 full scrimmage. Begin with 1-4-2-2 formation for both teams, then one team plays 1-3-2-3; unrestricted; layer in defensive free kicks.

FW: Connect with each player on the team and break down cliques (this was obviously worked on consistently throughout the season, but this is just a reminder and staying attentive to the need for connecting with each player.)

## SESSION 31:

Main topics: Finishing technique — finding shooting lanes; 1v1 lateral attack/defend.

BW: College recommendation forms for teachers and coaches; types of qualities sought after.

FL: Foot skills — add in small and big touches to the explosive step of fundamental moves (e.g., normally a Matthews goes inside to outside; instead, take a small outside touch immediately followed by a big outside touch to explode); practice with Matthews, scissors, V, and other moves along with see-saw and saw-see. Go on to instep/laces-only foot juggling; 2s/1 ball shooting progression.

- 4s/3-4 balls per group; set up two small gates (1 yard each) approximately 10 yards apart on a line.

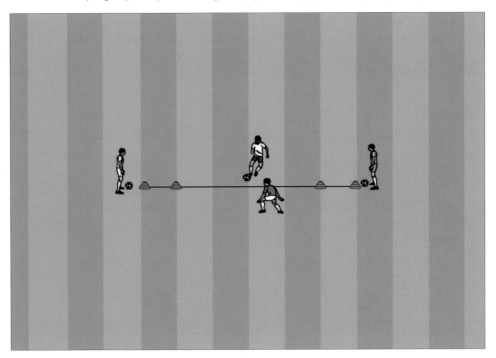

The game is a lateral 1v1 where one of the other players is designated attack and the other defense; neither player may cross the line. The attacker moves the ball laterally, trying to gain a step on the defender and score in either of the gates. The other two players are stationed one at each gate to help keep the supply of balls continuous. This is a terrific fitness exercise with a ball. Rotate so that each person plays all others in the group being on both attack and defense (60-second intervals).

- Set up 2 full-size goals with live GKs, divide the team into four groups, each at a post (see Session 21). Review shooting technique and work on finishes off of a dribble (use a move), off of a combo (wall, overlap), layoff, turn, short-short-long rhythm.

- 3v1 + GK: 3s begin at the bottom of the circle and go to goal at full speed, random movement, create any pattern so that all three players touch the ball before a shot is taken, follow up rebounds with 1-touch. Defender tries to counterattack to targets (use 3v2 for higher level players). Encourage the three to communicate ahead of time to be in charge of the pattern they want to execute, but point out cues based on where the defender adjusts and how the GK moves with each pass.

MR: 9v9 with each team playing a 1-2-4-2 or 1-3-3-2 depending on your emphases. The field is divided into thirds. Progression:

- Players must stay in their own third. Emphasize the need to take care of your roles on attack and defense (personal responsibility) and understand that your decisions with the ball on attack and without the ball on defense are critical for the team to succeed (team responsibility).

- Players may advance one third on attack (but must retreat to third on defense).

- Reward secondary range finishes, goals off of combinations and crosses depending on emphases.

MC: Scrimmage unrestricted, layer in attacking kick-offs.

FW: Review top 5 finishes of the day, of the season. Understand that the finishes result from good defending transitioning to attack (so that everyone is involved and understands the need for a sense of urgency from each player). Possession is a good defense.

## SESSION 32:

Main topics: Attacking runs in the box; refer to previous sessions on crossing and final pass.

BW: Goals, objectives — obstacles, temptations, landmarks, path to success.

FL:

- 1st touch exercise: 4s/2 balls — 2 players on ends, each with a ball, 2 players in the middle without a ball. The players on the inside alternate going to each of the end players but simultaneously to increase activity.

  - Skills to work on: passes on the ground, half-volleys, volleys, chest-volleys, headers, turns.
  - Ideas for agilities in the middle (inside player does these before receiving a ball): speed ladder, hurdles, crunches, forward roll (somersault), log roll, 7-count burpee, push-ups, sit and get up, or any other quick activity.

- Whole team — pass and move, similar to match warm-up. Emphasize that the types of runs dictate the type of pass: check, stretch, slash, wide-high, support; timing, angles, pace.

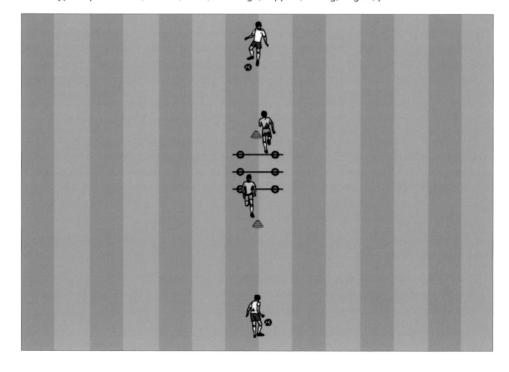

- Review early and late crossing, adding in pressure on the crossers and defenders in the box. Increase numbers from previous exercises emphasizing the need for 1st and 2nd layer near-far-slot runs. Teach this out of patterns for a full side, meaning train this actively on both sides and up the middle of a 1-4-3-3 or formation of choice.

MR: Scrimmage 8v8 + 2CM. The 2 center midfield players play with the team on attack, creating numbers-up situations and building opportunities for final pass and crossing situations. Emphasize quality of runs, and add an offsides line for each team, as appropriate.

MC: Scrimmage 9v9 unrestricted; PK shootout at end.

FW: Journal — write about the best moment in soccer you have ever had.

## SESSION 33:

Main topics: Goalkeeper distribution.

*Note:* *GKs are involved in every training session and they also have their own sessions; thus, I don't include GK-specific team focused sessions, except for this one. Review flank and target play via 6-goal game.*

BW: The beautiful game — soccer's challenges (e.g., playing with the feet, fitness demands, low scores) and beauty (e.g., skills, flow, rhythm, creativity, player-centered, teamwork of 11-plus, and much more).

FL: Pass and move, allow GKs to use feet and hands, encouraging various distribution techniques (roll, baseball throw, sling, over-head throw, drop kick, etc.). Encourage the GK to receive the ball from one direction and play to another direction. Extend to setting up two teams where the players are in positions they normally play. Simultaneous (two directions) choreography with GK distribution to outside back, outside midfielder, center back, center midfielder, and forwards. Start with a shot on goal to the GK from various distances and angles, encouraging the GK to look to change the point of attack upon making the save.

*Note:* *If appropriate, set up one direction and run 11v0, substituting players in so everyone goes over the various options and patterns of play. However, do not spend more than 5-7 minutes on this as players will get bored, and you will deny them touches that they could be getting on the ball instead.*

MR: 11v7: Playing out of the back; the 11 play in a 1-4-3-3 and the 7 play in a 1-2-2-2; play live, both teams going to full-size goals. Then, divide team into two groups:

- 6-goal game (credit UNC and USWNT); field is 70 wide by 40 long: score 1 point on wide goals, 2 points for a goal in the full-size goal; each team has three central players, two flank players and one goalkeeper, along with two high target players on the end lines. Use throw-ins, kick-ins, and corner kicks, as applicable. CPs:
  - GK distribution high target, central options, and wide-flat angles.
  - Flank play of creating loose and tight mark situations.
  - Combination play (2 and 3 player)
  - Finishing off of crosses
  - Finding seams (between players) and gaps (between lines).

MC: Scrimmage 9v9 unrestricted. Be sure to coach the GKs on distribution decisions and distribution techniques. In addition, place a high standard of starting position by players when the GK receives the ball (e.g., flank players must withdraw deep back toward own endline for improved passing angles from the GK). Layer in attacking goal-kicks and punts.

FW: Life skills of athletics — player-only discussion and summary.


## SESSION 34:

Main topics: Playing with numbers up, playing down from 0-2.

BW: Story of being down 4-0 in a match and coming back to tie 4-4.

FL: As a change of pace, set up an obstacle course for the team to go through in pairs. Include activities such as jumping over hurdles, sliding under bars, setting up rings for agility, soccer kick-back net, a path of "carrying the ball" without the use of any hands between the two players, and other activities that keep the players moving and working together.

• Shuttles, as in match warm-up: 2-, 3-, 1-touch passing.

• Possession numbers up games: divide team into two equal groups, for example, 8v8. Set up two adjacent grids where each team of 8 has a "home grid." Begin with one team playing with an 8v3 advantage, while the remaining 5 players wait in their adjoining "home grid." After every 4 passes completed, another defender enters, changing the numbers advantage to 8v4, then 8v5, and so on for as long as the team can maintain possession. If the 8 turn the ball over, then the other team begins with a ball in their "home grid" with an 8v3 advantage.

- Compete in adjoining grids again; 2 games of 5v3 or 3 games of 4v2. Tally up points for passes completed (e.g., 5 passes = 1 point) and defensive wins (stop ball on any side of the grid for one point).

MR: Divide team into two teams of 8 (not including the GKs). Set up a half-field scrimmage of 8v6 with one team going at the full-size goal and the other team going to two small counterattack goals. For the attacking team, they have a numbers-up advantage in their back half of 5v3, and a numbers-even situation in the front grid 3v3 (not including the GK; note that the defensive team has two players sitting out — provide them with active rest). After the attacking team completes five passes in their back half, they may pass to a player in their front half and then have two players join the attack in the front half, creating a 5v3 numbers-up situation. No defensive players may cross halves.

MC: Scrimmage unrestricted. Start one team down 0-2 (starting team, as applicable). Emphasize the need to get forward, move ball quickly, create options actively. PKs at end for likely penalty kick takers. The rest of the team can be a distraction behind the goal (on purpose).

FW: Faith, perseverance, patience, enduring spirit; also, revelation, karma, epiphany.


## SESSION 35:

Main topics: Playing out of the back — integrate longballs with backs-to-center mids-to-forwards and backs-to-forwards-drop back-to-center mids rhythm.

BW: Strategies — learning from mistakes, moving on. Pinch self for focus, pick up a blade of grass and throw it away (simulating throwing away the moment to forget and move on).

FL: Pass and move warm-up, progressing to long flighted and bending balls.

- 6s/2 balls: set up a 2v2 situation in a 12 x 12 yard grid. Approximately 20-30 yards away from either end, two additional players are each ready with a ball to serve. Servers alternate while the pairs begin ready at their own end of the grid. Servers serve to far pair, who then attack the near pair in a 2v2 battle. Score a point for stopping the ball on the line.

  *Note: The defending team cannot begin to move until the attacking team makes a first touch (or for advanced players, they can move when the ball is first struck).*

CPs: 1st touch, quality service, 2v2 principles of play. Can progress to 3v3 in the grid. Adjust the size of grid and length of service, as appropriate.

MR: Set up game in thirds, 9v9. Each team plays a 1-3-3-2; players begin with a restriction to stay in their own grid, and then progress to allowing one player to move up one grid on attack, as with past games in thirds exercises. Restriction: team may go to goal only after one of the two primary rhythms has been completed (B-CM-F or B-F-CM).

MC: Scrimmage unrestricted, layer in defensive corner kicks.

FW: Potluck analogy — what do you bring to the table?

## SESSION 36:

Main topics: Center-midfield play — train spacing and coordinated movement

BW: "Play hard, play smart, be alert, do your part." Players are to recite their favorite quote at the end of the training session.

FL:

- Foot skills — clock set up with discs, agilities with a ball. Dribble and turn, technical speed.

  *Note: The "clock" can have 6, 8, or 12 positions (coach can choose for variety).*

- Set up four 10x10 grids in the middle of a rectangle that is approximately 40 x 30. In the four grids, set up a 3v3 situation (ideally these are central midfield-type players versus forwards or other combination of players). In the end zones, set up 3v1 situations. The objective is for one team to begin with the ball at the back, find a central player who must find another central player and then find their target player on the opposite side. The key restriction is that on both attack and defense, only one player per grid of the same team may be in the center four grids. This helps the center midfield players to understand how their movement affects the movement of the other two players—two closer for support and the third further away to provide an outlet and opportunity to change the point of attack. Progress to various patterns, touch restrictions, and support along the flank.

MR: Add on to the previous exercise by going to full-size goals, live goal-keepers. Continue to play directional and keep central midfield play restricted to the grids. Then, maintain one rectangular grid (15 x 15) in the center of the field and only allow at most two players from the same team to be in it at any one time. Restrict touches in the central grid to two touches to emphasize quicker play.

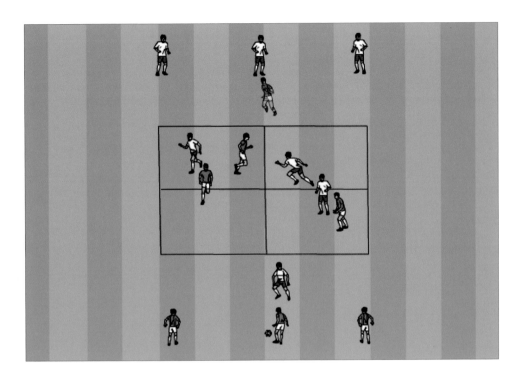

MC: Scrimmage 9v9 unrestricted; fitness with a ball—each player has a ball and goes back and forth 10 and then 5 yards with the ball at their feet, using different turns with the ball.

FW: Circle up, players recite their favorite quote.

## SESSION 37:

Main topics: 1v1 revisit, spacing, dividing the field vertically in thirds; fundamental foot skills.

BW: Soccer is a game of 1v1 duels — strive to win every one on attack and defense, but remember to respond effectively regardless of the outcome.

FL: Foot skills in a "square dance" set up — 4s, each player has a ball; players are positioned at the corners of 10 x 10 yard grids that have a disc in the middle to mark the center of the grid. Opposite diagonal players go at the same time.

- Turn away moves—players dribble to the center and turn away, ending at their original starting position: chop, spin, hook turn, step-over-turn, Cruyf, etc.

- Attacking moves—players dribble to center, perform a move to beat the center disc and player, ending up at the opposite diagonal from where they started: Matthews, L, scissors, step-over, V, fake-shot, etc.

- Active rest: all players at their own disc — "Brazilian" step-ups (or toe-taps) where the rhythm is touch (1st foot)-touch (2nd foot)-touch (1st foot) behind the 2nd foot; good agility, coordination.

MR: Set up 10 x 10 yard grids in a rectangular grid that is 40 x 30; extend the field in length by adding 10 x 30 yard end zones. Team is divided into 9v9.

- Each team is in the formation 1-3-3-2 or 1-4-2-2 depending on the emphases desired. GKs may control their respective end zones and field players have to stay in their respective grids (vary depending upon formation selected). For open grids, at most one player from each team may enter.

- Remove grids so that the field is divided into vertical thirds. Scrimmage, but allow at most one pass within a column of the field (i.e., ball has to zig-zag and change vertical thirds constantly).

MC: Scrimmage 9v9 unrestricted; end with an old MLS style shootout of 1 v GK breakaway to goal.

FW: Team dessert. Note: Food is a terrific motivator, so surprise the team with a treat as opposed to the usual lesson offered in the "Final Words" portion of training sessions.

*Note:* *Food is a terrific motivator so surprise the team with a treat as opposed to the usual lesson offered in the "Final Words" portion of training sessions.*

## SESSION 38:

Main topics: Understanding the triangle and "diamond" (or "kite") shape on attack — depth, width, support; possession, target play and counterattack.

BW: Rhetorical question, which is better, the number 3 or 4?

FL:

- 4s/1 ball: begin in "kite shape" (go over why the "diamond" is a poor choice), passing patterns with natural movements (forward and backward, side-to-side, up and back), keeping a natural connected shape.

- 4s/1 ball: play 3v1 in 10 x 10 yard grid, review support on both sides, body shape, angles — make players run all the way to the corners, don't let them all sag into the middle of the grid.

- 4v2 support exercise: emphasize "kite" shape and demand that flank players must run to half where the ball is in with good body position and stance; use a 20 x 12 yard grid (with markers at the 10 to indicate halves); advance to allowing only 1-touch after the ball crosses the midline, restrict touches to maximum two 2-touch.

- Possession 4v4 with 4 target (neutral) players on each end of a rectangular grid, approximately 40 x 30 yards. Earn points by completing 5 passes (may not pass from neutral to neutral) and by maintaining possession from one end to the other. Remind players not to make runs in front of the target players (obstructing passing lanes). Restrict touches, as appropriate. Be sure to rotate teams so each team plays the other two teams.

- 11v0 choreography; begin with GK and the team must play each line twice before shooting in the far goal down the field; illustrate triangles and diamonds. This type of player-chosen choreography is important, as it allows players to make decisions, problem-solve and communicate, rather than be dependent on having the coaching staff dictate where to play in a controlling manner.

MR: 7v7, extend above to have two full-size goals with live GKs and now, the target players are supplied by each team to their respective goal they shoot on. Players on the end line have one touch.

*Note:* *Generally, I do not prefer having players on the end line since that could be considered a "pass out of bounds," but the idea is to add immediate depth and encourage vision high up the field.*

*One may also add an off-sides line in front of the opposing GK as another option. In addition, if you want to work on width instead of depth, then place the neutral players on the sides of the playing area.*

MC: Scrimmage 9v9, unrestricted. PK shootout at the end. Instead of traditional alternating format, shoot in both ends (each team shoots on the opposing GK).

FW: The power of the mind: mental toughness, strength, focus, attitude.

## SESSION 39:

Main topics: Technical warm-up — foot skills, turns, 1st touch; possession to targets on border and outside players; no tackling on defense to emphasize getting into good position to intercept and counterattack.

BW: Communication, playing time, and substitutions.

FL: Technical warm-up. 2s/1 ball — set up two discs, players take turns with fundamental dribbling foot skills to far disc and back four times (one player works, one rests). Progress to turning, where one player passes to the teammate who turns and dribbles around far disc. Add in first touch exercises (half- and full-volleys): both feet, all surfaces (including heel, sides, sole — creativity, "expect the unexpected").

- 5v2: coach the support players, as they control movements by the defense to dictate play to their feet or to another player through a seam; progression—forced 3-touch, maximum 2-touch, 1-touch (defender wins ball and stops on the edge; "first-in-first-out" rotation for defenders) and in air only (defender can intercept with the head only). For the defense, emphasize communication and good positioning to win the ball in good position and stance.

- Set up two 30 x 30 adjoining grids so that the overall dimension is 60 x 30. Assign neutral players on both ends, middle, and on one side of the playing area.

  - Play 5v5 in one of the grids; when one of the teams completes at least 5 passes, including to the neutrals on the end and side, then they may pass to the neutral player who is on the border and enter into the second grid.
  - Once in the second grid, the team in possession tries to do the same. Award one point for each grid completed. Turnovers are dealt with as normal transitions in the grids that they occur in.
  - No tackling allowed; instead, players are encouraged to communicate, get into good shape, position body to win the ball so they can attack immediately (this is similar to a South American style where players win the ball standing up, facing the direction they want to attack, and can transition from defense to attack smoothly). If desired, keep this "restriction" on for the whole training session.
  - Advance the exercise by limiting touches to maximum 3-touch or other, as needed. Be sure to rotate neutral players regularly.

MR: Continue with above exercise, except take out the neutral players on the ends; play to full-size goals with live GKs. The restriction is that the team in possession must play all three neutrals in any order before taking a shot on goal. Progress to removing the neutral players, require a team to complete three consecutive 1-touch passes before going to goal (use the credit system where if the team loses possession before they take a shot on goal, they still keep the ability to shoot when they win the ball back).

MC: Scrimmage 9v9 unrestricted; attacking free kicks.

FW: "Lesser known" restarts such as back-pass or throw-in to GK who picks up the ball; GK stepping outside of the box or taking too long to release the ball.

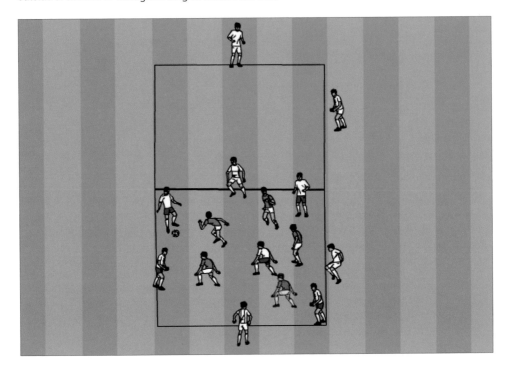

## SESSION 40:

Main topics: Finishing off of crosses; final-third finishing opportunities; choreography for playing out of the back; 1-touch passing technical warm-up.

BW: Review definitions—confidence: consistently executing skills under pressure with success, and excellence: performing ordinary tasks extraordinarily well.

FL:

- "Brazilian" one-touch agility with the ball exercise; 2s/1 ball: players are approximately 10-15 yards apart, depending on skill level (higher skill = shorter distance). Players are passing back and forth on the ground.
  - After passing, jog a few steps backward to touch the disc behind the player (touch with the hand), while still facing the ball and partner.
  - After striking one-touch pass, must use footwork to get around the disc placed behind the player ("pass in front, run behind"), make sure players keep a low center of gravity and always face the ball and their partner.
  - After passing, maneuver backwards and briefly sit, get back up, and be ready for the pass that is arriving to keep the 1-touch passing going (this one is very challenging so the coach may have to lengthen the distance).

- Divide team into two groups; pass and move with two balls per team, focus on movement off the ball (making good runs) and technique of ball striking with all surfaces, strive for medium, short, and long-range passes.

- Crossing/Finishing: Ideally, set up in both directions with full-size goals and live GKs with a total of four servers ("crossers"), two on each side, one in each half. The goals are approximately 36 yards apart ("double the 18") and use the full width of the field.

  - Two runners go at a time (in each direction); servers rotate between early and late crosses on both sides and in both directions.

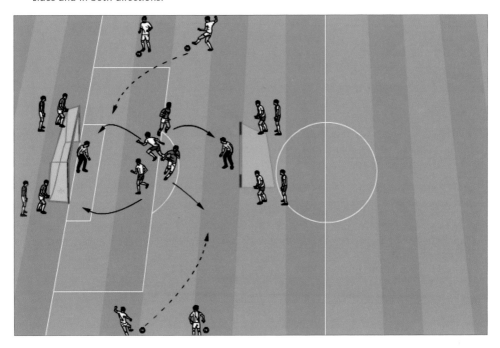

  - Driven ("worm burner") crosses on the ground for late crosses; driven crosses to back post in the air for early crosses.
  - Runners should try to adjust their footwork to strike ball first time whether from the ground, bounce (half-volley), or air (volley). Idea on the shot is to "knock the ball back where it comes from" to increase the chance of scoring (or at least creating a rebound or CK in a real match). If the ball arrives to the player nearer to the ball, allow that player to shoot or to set up the second runner with a shot.
    - Advance by reading touch of server- 1-touch versus 2-touch serves.

MR:

- Play 7v7 over halves, with each team playing a 1-4-2. There is a numbers up situation in the back for each team (4v2); shots may come from the back half (attackers frame and get rebounds from the crosses, or, if the attackers win a ball in their front half, they may go immediately to goal). Progress to the backs finding an attacking player and allowing one player to cross over into the front half.

- 11v5 choreography; set up a formation (e.g., 1-4-1-2-3), begin with a server shooting a ball through, over, or at the backs to the GK. GK plays ball to outside back and then train the following options:

- Play to near side checking forward
- Play to high forward
- Play underneath to attacking center midfielder or weakside forward (encourage the leave to advance ball to weakside for creativity)
- Combine with near attacking center mid

MC: Scrimmage 9v9 unrestricted (ideally, scrimmage 11v11); restarts-attacking CKs.

FW: Scouting—strengths and weaknesses, and why we limit its use. Social media—why it may motivate opponents unintentionally.

## SESSION 41:

Main topics: Playing with numbers up/down; passing and receiving; group defending.

BW: Picture—connectedness in nature.

FL:

- Dutch passing sequences: divide team into 6s or 8s with two players in the middle; work on 1- and 2-touch passing on the ground; movement, body stance, body position. Keep at least two balls moving, rotate directions and players.

- Diamond pass: players at each vertex of the diamond; pass in front of the discs on the longer side and pass behind on the shorter side.

- Functional passing: entire team, use 4-5 balls, get to a position on the field (give the team a direction, include the GK); pass and move, feel rhythm of the game (short-short-long, inside-outside flow); be active and move.

- 9v5 possession: speed of play, numbers up; group defending; may add gates as goals to score in (by passing through the gate to a teammate) or use a fixed number of passes for one point.

MR: 7v5 + 1GK; use one-half of the field and go to goal, divide the playing area in half so that the back half has a 4v3 numbers up advantage and the front half has a 3v2 numbers up advantage; must complete 3 passes in back half before advancing to front half; allow each team to go on attack for 2 minutes and keep score. May add variations such as allowing a defender to get into passing lanes along the border, restrict touches, allow one player to cross into attacking half (onsides).

MC: Scrimmage 9v9 unrestricted; end with fitness with a ball (3s/1 ball: turning series across the width of the field).

FW: Mental imagery training.

*Note:* *The last block of training sessions are brief on commentary and have a variety of topics as emphases, as opposed to simply training one or two ideas. At this point, it is later in the season and coaches will have to pick topics that address the needs identified in matches, review of topics, and ongoing player development.*

## SESSION 42:

Main topics: Technical: 1st touch, longball service/receive, 1v1; tactical: transition, decision-making (emphasis on vision), team defensive shape (several topics at once as team readied for a particular competition with limited number of training sessions).

BW: Be in the moment ("now") to connect past to future (past, present, future interconnectedness).

FL:

- Foot skills: moves plus toss and settles; remind players to see the ball early, cushion by relaxing the body, take the ball on the move (roof, elevator, inside/outside foot wedge, Cruyf).

- 4s/1 ball: two servers on ends of a 10 x 15 yard grid where two additional players are set up for a 1v1. Long serve to far player in grid, make a good 1st touch, take on other player in grid; stop the ball on the line to score.

- Two teams possession and shooting game; two GKs are in the middle of a triangle set up in the middle of the field. The other two teams try to score a goal by shooting (below shin level) through two sides of the central triangle; if the goal is scored, play continues with whichever team receives the ball, and if a GK makes a save, then the ball is distributed to the opposite team that just took the shot.

MR: Transition games with 3 teams (see Sessions 10 and 12); review team shape on defense— compression (horizontal) and compaction (vertical). Progress to 9v9 scrimmage with the separate restrictions of no forward passing, then no back passes.

MC: Scrimmage 9v9 unrestricted; PKs.

FW: *Lessons from Geese* team dynamics.


## SESSION 43:

Main topics: Midfield play—change point of attack and P-C-B line of defense; coming out of your line (F, M, B) to attack and defend.

BW: Poem or song lyric about perseverance.

FL: 4s/1ball—pass and move, create combos, drive, bend, chip, long balls; work on timing and accuracy (standard is to get it to teammate in "one bounce or less") and demand attentiveness to making runs off the ball. Make sure players are using both feet.

MR: Divide team into two groups of 8. Set up field 60 wide by 50 long, with midline to divide into two 25 x 60 fields, and four small goals.

- 2 simultaneous games of 4v4

  - Both red teams defend two small goals and attack the midline (stop ball on the line to score)
  - Both white teams attack two small goals and defend the midline
  - Keep score, rotate roles, play other teams, as appropriate

- Extend to 8v8 (remove midline) with each team playing in a 4-2-2 shape; each team has two small goals to attack and two small goals to defend

MC: Half-field scrimmage of 7 (1GK, 4B, 2CM) v 7 (4M, 3F); work on late and early crosses, review patterns, emphasize principles and playing quickly in each third of the field. Move on to 9v9 scrimmage, unrestricted.

FW: "Each day is a little life." (Arthur Schopenhauer)

## SESSION 44:

Main topics: Possession to change point, finishing off of runs, defensive clearing/tracking (from crosses and restarts), shape.

BW: Epiphany (revisited).

FL:

- 2s/1 ball, 3 discs (2 yards apart) in the middle: 1st touch/footskill technical exercises, weave between discs, alternate server and receiver roles to work on receiving balls from the ground, one-bounce (half-volley), no bounce (volley); extend to turning.

- Passing fundamental exercise (credit Hank Leung): 10 x 20 yard rectangle, 5s/3 balls, players on the end with two balls are ready (player in middle checks to one of the players) while the players on the other end with one ball are passing 1-touch back and forth; player in the middle turns with ball and finds "open" player in rhythm. This is a terrific exercise for vision, passing/receiving, 1st touch, and awareness.

- 9v9 "Possession" 4-goal game by positions; progression of forced 3-touch, then 2-touch max, all on the ground. Each team has two goals to attack and two to defend.

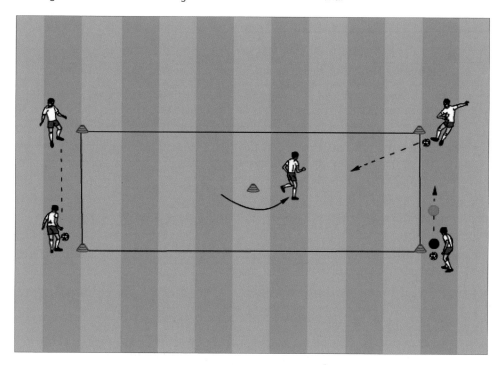

- Team divides into two training groups:

  - GKs, backs, holding midfielder—work on clearing (high, far, wide), communication, coverage, language (step up, slide [right or left], side-on, drop), coordinated movement, and defensive shape.
  - Midfielders and forwards- work on movement, first and second runs, finishing off of run (shot or pass to attack); defensively, don't allow ball to switch, keep the ball on one (vertical) side of the field.

MR: Bring the team together and set up a half-field scrimmage—GK, back 4 and midfield 3 versus forward 3 and attacking-midfield 2. Add in a neutral player at the midline who serves as support for the attacking team and as a target for the defending team. Start ball with attack (numbers down), encourage switching and early crosses to force defensive unit to execute training emphases. Work on defensive restarts (free kicks and corner kicks).

MC: Scrimmage 9v9, unrestricted.

FW: Attacking and defending interconnectedness—"all for one, one for all."

*SESSION 45:*

**Main topics:** Final-third tactics, speed of play, final pass.

**BW:** Set aside time for lines to get together to discuss goals and objectives (GKs go with backs).

**FL:**

- 3s/1 ball, pass and move, drive-aggressive touch, drive-turns, bending balls, flighted longballs

- 3 teams of 6 players each, send two away to defend so that there are now three grids of 4v2 possession; count number of completed passes for attack and number of intercepts (and stop on line) for defense. Play 2 minute games, rotate. CPs: support, movement, quality of passes.

- 9v9 possession: one team has 1-touch only (tries to complete 10 consecutive passes) and the other team has maximum 2-touch (tries to maintain possession); keep running time and time of possession.

**MR:** 9v9 final third passing; one team on attack (A)—after completing 3 passes, may send runner in onsides into zone to shoot, other team defends (B), tries to score with onsides stopping of ball into either side grid.

**MC:** 9v9 scrimmage unrestricted, end with PKs. Team did sprint intervals of 60, 45, 30, and 15 yards at 85-90% pace.

**FW:** Marketing—body language and the signals sent; this is particularly important regarding first impressions when trying out or "showcasing"; express my dislike of the term "showcase" and instead emphasize "compete-case."

## SESSION 46:

**Main topics:** Shape in attack for whole team, combination play, speed of play (numbers up); group defending (numbers down).

**BW:** Speaking with the media.

**FL:** Circle exercise—half of the players on outside with a ball, half of the players on the inside without a ball. Remember that players on the outside should serve, slide in either direction around the circle to provide a live target, and settle the ball without hands to make the exercise realistic. Rotate after every 2-3 skills to keep all players engaged and active. Progression:

- 1st touch return to same player

- 2-touch turn

- 5-touch, speed dribble, pass to an open player

- Half-volley, volley, headers (jump in the air to make contact, with both feet off of the ground)

- Use approximately 4-6 balls to start with inside players; execute combinations for 2 players (wall pass, overlap, take/fake-over, double pass) and 3 players (3rd man run). Be sure players are switching in and out regularly.

**MR:** 11v6 attacking shape; set up formation for the 11 to attack and defend full-size goals with live GKs. For the 11, begin with maximum 2-touch on ground, no square balls; encourage 2 combinations or 4 passes before going to goal. Then allow flighted balls on final passes and shots.

*Note:    If two GKs or two full-size goals are not available, let the 11 attack an end zone onsides. Force the defending group to shoot within 3 touches after winning the ball so that the attacking 11 get plenty of repetition. The defending group needs to remember to not stick, tackle when sure to win it and when cover is present, communicate, move as a group, and clog passing lanes.*

**MC:** Scrimmage 9v9 unrestricted, encourage rapid restarts (must put ball in play within a count of 2 seconds).

**FW:** Five words that describe our team. Ideally, the team has chosen these words and lived them throughout the season. So, discuss these words on a deeper level. This could be an appropriate time to discuss "senior," "retiring," or "veteran" players. Connect on emotion and depth.

## SESSION 47:

**Main topics:** 1v1 Defending. Footwork to avoid — "sticking" or "stabbing," manage "late arrivals."

**BW:** "The River of Leadership," by an NHL captain.

**FL:** Circuit training. Set up six stations around the field, all focused on footwork and agilities (e.g., speed ladders, jump rope, triangles, diamonds, 1-2-3-jump/landing repeats, clock).

- 1v1v1 continuous duels (do this with three players or with the team split into two groups for camaraderie and team spirit).
  - Emphasize body position and stance, "last foot forward is the first foot back" defending to close down space, but slow down two big steps away from the attacker with the ball

- If arriving "late," don't get caught "sticking" or "stabbing" for the ball. Be patient; wait for the attacker's foot to come off of the ball before tackling.

- 2v2 game. Divide team into four groups set up in a diamond. Opposite diagonals are on the same team. Play is continuous. Player who passes to teammate rotates out and another player comes in.

MR: Scrimmage 9v9 match-up game. Each player is paired with another player on the opposing team, which creates 1v1 duels within the bigger game. Only paired partners may defend their counterpart on the opposing team. If a player gives up a goal, then have a consequence ready such as sprinting a lap before returning while play continues.

- Set up 11v11 and review 1v1 duels, determine where players should take on (and not pass off responsibility of attacking), explain how to manage spacing and numbers, and how to turn 1v1 situations into 2v1 situations whether on attack or defense.

MC: Scrimmage 9v9, unrestricted. CKs — attack and defend.

FW: "Game 7" (give examples of national sport championships from the NBA, NHL, MLB won in game 7 of a best of 7 series).

## SESSION 48:

Main topics: Passing, receiving, finishing — power shots and off of crosses (credit to Chelsea FC for fundamental exercises).

BW: "Greatest fear" from *Coach Carter* (Nelson Mandela).

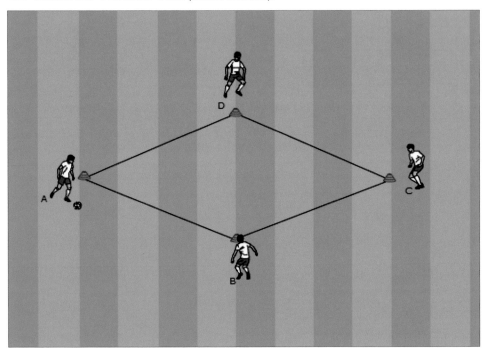

FL:

- Passing and receiving: 4s/2 balls. Players are set up in a diamond shape, keep two balls going. Two-touch pass and move (pass ball in front of discs on long end, pass ball behind on wide ends). Be sure to change directions. Progress to short-short-long rhythm, ABACDCA, in the diagram and repeat.

- Finishing: 4 stations beginning at the end line to a spot approximately 30 yards centrally from goal. Ball advances from end line while passing behind disc, front of disc, behind disc, receive and dribble, do a move, shoot and follow. Have the two teams compete (each team has a course on either side of the goal).

  - 2-touch as above
  - Extend to short-short-long rhythm (as with second progression of the diamond passing exercise)

- Finishing off of crosses: As with the above exercise, the players are in two teams, near the bottom of the circle, facing the goal. Flank players from both teams are outside of the 18, ready to receive pass, prepare, and cross. Where the teams are in the middle of the field, one player from each team steps up and they pass back and forth. On coach's command of "go," the player with the ball passes to a teammate out on the flank and goes to goal (the player that didn't get to pass chases back to defend). The flank player who receives the pass crosses, and the teammate on the opposite flank gets to join in to create 2v1 in the box. Keep score.

MR: Revisit 6-goal game (see Session 33). Emphasis on finishing!

MC: Scrimmage 9v9 unrestricted, layer in attacking free kicks.

FW: Assign "secret buddies."


## SESSION 49:

Main topics: Positional possession, turning/change direction with the ball (off of the dribble). Transition game with direction and positions.

BW: Picture of team when they were young (or picture of an old championship team of the club).

FL: 2s/1 ball — pingers, "Brazilians."

MR: Positional-possession with 2-plus players. When ball turns over, players on the outside switch with players on the inside (the teams basically switch so that the attacking team is on the outside and is more spread apart while the defensive team is on the inside and more compact). Include GKs in regular positions. CPs:

- 5 passes = 1 point

- Move ball quickly so opponent cannot set up

- Transition quickly — offensively expand and defensively compact

- Movement off of the ball

- Communication on defense (P-C-B)

- Keep the ball on attack!

MC: Progress from above exercise to scrimmaging. One team on attack to full-size goal, and the other team attacks to counterattack goals.

FW: "You are the best," please, and thank yous.

## SESSION 50:

**Main topics:** Longball/1st touch, possession, "Battle of the Box," Choreography/shadow play, final scrimmage.

*Note:* *This training session includes fundamental core exercises from our program. These are exercises the team especially enjoys, while at the same time, it gives the coach opportunities to emphasize technique, encourage focus on execution and effort, and inspire confidence in all players.*

BW: Share "secret buddies," and "this is our time."

FL:

• 5 v 2 ball on the ground, everyone moves, 2-touch max

• 2s/1 ball: longball — settle, head, off of slow rollers (back passes), clear.

• 5v5v5 + GK "Battle of the Box" serve, attack, defend flighted balls

MR: 11v0 to goal patterns of play. Emphasize moving as one unit — one heartbeat, one pulse. The "opponent" in this particular execution of the exercise is no one but ourselves (set a time standard for connecting every player and finishing on goal).

MC: Scrimmage 9v9 unrestricted, PKs for those who want it. Finish with light jog and agilities with everyone together. Note: As previously noted, we always begin and end with appropriate exercises to warm up and cool down, respectively. Especially on the day before, allow the team a bit of intentional extra time together with this cool-down.

FW: Believe in yourselves and in each other — *Let's go get 'em!*

Recall that coaches should be comfortable adapting and adjusting sessions as needed. Try creating your own, rather than only copy sessions verbatim; part of the process in designing training sessions keeps one engaged, learning, and actively improving. Ultimately, it makes one a better coach to both use time and tested sessions such as the ones in this book, and to treat training as a "work in progress" and a "soccer lab" where you design, experiment, test exercises and ideas. Make match-related adjustments in terms of size of playing area, number of players, restrictions, and all so that you are constantly monitoring the fundamentals of our game: time, space, executing skills under pressure, competitive energy, passion.

*Reflections*

- How do you plan training sessions?
- Do you focus on one topic, a couple of topics, or many at once?
- Do your training sessions have positive outcomes in the areas of technical skills, tactical skills, psychological, physical, social, emotional, individual, team?
- How do you make your sessions competitive?
- Do players commit fully to training with and without the team?
- What core skills do you revisit and how do you ratchet up the levels of challenge, competition, and intensity?
- How flexible is your training curriculum?
- Who decides topics for your training sessions? Is there an overall vision that has long-term player development as its goal?

# CHAPTER 10

## SUSTAINING EXCELLENCE, REMAINING RELEVANT, AND GIVING BACK TO THE GAME

*"Let me not pray to be sheltered from dangers but to be fearless in facing them. Let me not beg for the stilling of my pain, but for the heart to conquer it. Let me not look for allies in life's battlefield but to my own strength. Let me not crave in anxious fear to be saved but hope for the patience to win my freedom."*
— *Rabindranath Tagore*

### SUSTAINING EXCELLENCE AND REMAINING RELEVANT

There are several ways that coaches can continue to grow and develop. It is important to build resources and networks that consistently provide stimulation toward coaching ideas, methodologies, nuances, and philosophies. It's good to connect with coaches you can learn from, bounce ideas off of, and have discourse with, especially when it comes to player development. After all, if you expect players to grow and develop, so must you. To sustain excellence and remain relevant, consider the following points.

Whenever possible, watch quality matches live, online, and on TV. There are so many options available nowadays, be it World Cup, Olympics, European Cup, FA Cup, or professional leagues around the globe. Encourage your colleagues and players on your teams to do the same to support our game.

## Professional Development

Though coaches have access to several resources via books, DVDs, and online, the live interactive coaching education experience is very beneficial and irreplaceable. Such personal experiences are available through clubs, high schools, leagues, regions within states, and an array of other resources. Moving to organizations, there are several excellent coaching education opportunities available at all levels. I highly recommend that coaches pursue these, and hopefully they are supported at their respective local levels, too.

- National: United Soccer Coaches and US Soccer offer coaching courses, clinics, workshops and other sessions around the country that allow coaches to obtain credentials and enhance their overall coaching profile. The courses are available to anyone in the world, through an application process and associated fees, with the nice feature that anyone can become a member of such organizations. Both the United Soccer Coaches and US Soccer offer annual conventions in which coaching education is a significant part of the events. Just recently, Not long ago, the United Soccer Coaches absorbed US Soccer's smaller annual convention and thus, we finally have one central national convention for coaches. Other beneficial professional development by-products of the courses, clinics, and conventions also include networking, reuniting with friends in coaching, and the ability to interact with presenters of various levels, ages and experiences for both genders.

- Regional: The ODP, DA, and ECNL programs often hold regional symposiums for their members, sometimes at events and as separate coaching education sessions specifically for professional development. Obviously, these events are exclusive to their members, so while they are geared toward improving coaching education, they are doing so for a smaller segment of the population as compared to the United Soccer Coaches and US Soccer who try to reach across levels and genders.

- State: State organizations hold annual workshops that can be good opportunities to develop and network, though the level and variety of sessions varies from state to state. Given the smaller size of the workshops, there are fewer high-level sessions as compared to the national conventions. However, some state associations have some terrific coaches who are active promoters of coaching education, whether through the workshops, by hosting coaching courses, writing columns in state newsletters, or by serving as a good resource to approach ideas with.

- A note about international opportunities that focus on coaching education for professional development: There are a variety of international coaching education events available, but there does not seem to be as streamlined of an approach as there are with the national conventions and workshops indicated. Thus, coaches need to seek out opportunities offered by organizations such as the United Soccer Coaches (e.g., Algarve Cup), travel-abroad organizations (e.g., places include Brazil, England, Germany, Netherlands, Spain, etc.), and other resources. However, one should talk with other coaches about their experiences on such trips to see which opportunities cater to what the candidate is after.

## Creating Your Own Ways to Develop Professionally

Part of what has served me well in my coaching career has been my hunger to learn, as there is simply no substitute for knowledge. Thus, I've taken my coursework and attended my share of conventions and workshops, but I also attend matches, watch other sports, attend and work camps, and find any number of ways to develop as a coach, teacher, and person. Over the years, I have been grateful to some coaches who have let me watch their training sessions, visit them at camp for sessions, listen to their pre-match/half-time talks, observe their meetings and interactions with teams, pick their brains about coaching philosophy and methodology, or exchange ideas on player development, formations, training, match preparation, or just about any other topic. Certainly, these opportunities are much more interesting to me and give me something much more valuable than what taking formal courses and attending conventions and clinics can. Even after I had been awarded National Coach of the Year by both the USYSA and USOC, I continued to seek out additional opportunities for growth, as I never have been the type to think that I have arrived. Instead, I always want to be better, and I also want that from those with whom I work and coach. Especially in the area of finding my own opportunities, I regularly read articles, periodicals, and books. Some of these resources are about soccer while many are not, but instead, they provide terrific forays into coaching, teaching, psychology, management, leadership, adventure, and other useful concepts for leading teams. While there is no substitute for coaching to gain coaching experience, one's overall profile is enhanced that much more by taking such an active approach to gain knowledge. There are far too many articles to include, but I strongly suggest regularly reading articles on a variety of topics, many of which offer relevant and timely information to share with your teams and programs for their benefit. Good discussions can be had among your constituents regarding articles, periodicals, and books that you bring to their attention. Some of the books and periodicals I have read during my coaching career that I have found helpful include:

- Books

  - *America's BEST Classrooms* by Seymour & Seymour (Peterson's Guides, 1992)
  - *American Courage* by Herbert W. Warden III (HarperCollins, 2005)
  - *Annapurna* by Maurice Herzog (E.P. Dutton & Company, 1952)
  - *The Ball is Round* by David Goldblatt (Riverhead Books, 2006)
  - *The Beautiful Game* by Jonathan Littman (Avon Books, 1999)
  - *Blink* by Malcolm Gladwell (Little, Brown and Company, 2005)
  - *Bounce* by Matthew Syed (HarperCollins, 2010)
  - *Building a Moral System* by Ashmore (Prentice-Hall, 1987)
  - *The Carolina Way* by Dean Smith and Gerald Bell with John Kilgo (Penguin Press, 2004)
  - *Catch Them Being Good* by Tony DiCicco & Colleen Hacker (Penguin Books, 2002)
  - *The Champion Within* by Lauren Gregg with Tim Nash (JTC Sports, 1999)
  - *Classroom Management for Secondary Teachers* by Emmer et. al. (Prentice Hall 1989)
  - *Classroom Teaching Skills* by Cooper et. al. (D.C. Heath and Company, 1990)
  - *Coach: Lessons on the Game of Life* by Michael Lewis (W.W. Norton & Company, 2008)
  - *Coaching and Motivation* by William Warren (Prentice-Hall, 1983)
  - *Coaching Soccer* (by NSCAA) Edited by Tim Schum (Masters Press, 1996)
  - *Cold Mountain* by Charles Frazier (Vintage, 1997)
  - *Companions in Courage* by Pat LaFontaine with Larry Weisman, Ernie Valutis, Chas Griffin (Grand Central Publishing, 2001)
  - *Don't Sweat the Small Stuff* by Richard Carlson (Hyperion, 1997)
  - *The Edge* by Howard E. Ferguson (Getting the Edge Company, 1990)
  - *The Elements of Teaching* by Banner & Cannon (Yale University, 1997)
  - *Empires of the Mind* by Denis Waitley (William Morrow & Company, 1995)
  - *The Five People You Meet in Heaven* by Mitch Albom (Hyperion, 2003)
  - *For One More Day* by Mitch Albom (Hyperion, 2008)
  - *Free the Children* by Craig Kielburger (HarperCollins, 1998)

- *Getting to Yes* by Roger Fisher & William Ury (Penguin Books, 1991)
- *Go for the Goal* by Mia Hamm (HarperCollins, 1999)
- *Have a Little Faith* by Mitch Albom (Hyperion, 2009)
- *High Noon* by J.F. Rischard (Basic Books, 2002)
- *How Soccer Explains the World* by Franklin Foer (HarperCollins, 2004)
- *Ideas and Opinions* by Einstein (Crown Publishers, 1982)
- *If Winning Were Easy, Everyone Would Do It* by Kim Doren & Charlie Jones (Andrew McMeel Publishing, 2002)
- *In the Heart of the Sea* by Nathaniel Philbrick (Penguin Books, 2000)
- *In Pursuit of Excellence* by Terry Orlick (Leisure Press, 1990)
- *In These Girls, Hope is a Muscle* by Madeleine Blais (Warner Books, 1996)
- *The Last Lecture* by Randy Pausch (Hyperion, 2008)
- *The Leadership Moment* by Michael Useem (Three Rivers Press, 1998)
- *The Man Watching* by Tim Crothers (Sports Media Group, 2006)
- *Man's Search for Meaning* by Viktor Frankl (Pocket Books, 1959)
- *Mayflower* by Nathaniel Philbrick (Penguin Books, 2006)
- *Moneyball* by Michael Lewis (W.W. Norton & Company, 2011)
- *Morality & The Good Life* by Solomon (McGraw-Hill, 1984)
- *On the Move* by Bono (W Publishing Group, 2006)
- *Positive Coaching* by Jim Thompson (Warde Publishers, 1995)
- *Psychology Applied to Teaching* by Biehler/Snowman (Houghton Mifflin, 1986)
- *Sacred Hoops* by Phil Jackson & Hugh Delehanty (Hyperion, 1995)
- *The Second Family* by Ron Taffel (St. Martin's Press, 2001)
- *Soccer: How to Play the Game* (by US Soccer) Edited by Bobby Howe (Universe Publishing, 1999)
- *Social Intelligence* by Daniel Goleman (Bantam Books, 2006)
- *Standing Fast* by Michelle Akers & Tim Nash (JTC Sports, 1997)
- *Strive to Excel: Will & Wisdom of Vince Lombardi Compiled* by Jennifer Briggs (Rutledge Hill Press, 1997)
- *Success is a Choice* by Rick Pitino with Bill Reynolds (Broadway Books, 1997)
- *Success One Day at a Time* by John Maxwell (J. Countryman, 2001)
- *The Talent Code* by Daniel Coyle (Bantam Books, 2009)
- *They Call Me Coach* by John Wooden with Jack Tobin (Contemporary Books, 1988)
- *Training Soccer Champions* by Anson Dorrance (JTC Sports, 1996)
- *Tuesdays with Morrie* by Mitch Albom (Doubleday, 1997)
- Unlucky by Dave Ungrady (Sports Publishing International, 1999)
- *The Vision of a Champion* by Anson Dorrance & Gloria Averbuch (Sleeping Bear Press, 2002)
- *The Winner Within* by Pat Riley (Riles & Company, 1993)
- *Winning with Teamwork* Compiled by Katherine Karvelas (Successories, 1998)
- *You Just Don't Understand* by Deborah Tannen (Ballantine Books, 1990)

Note: *This list does not include all of the books that I have ever read, but instead books that have had an impact in my coaching career. I love analogies, and thus, some of the books of historical importance provide excellent perspectives that are indirectly related to team sports such as soccer. There are many other books not listed here that I would love to dabble in further, but they will have to wait. Some of the topics I would like to explore more of include a biography on Jose Mourinho, the history of Barcelona FC, and various books on psychology by Bill Beswick (I have attended several of his sessions in courses and conventions). Lastly, another book I am interested in is Soccer Coaching the NSCAA Way by Jay Martin (Meyer & Meyer, 2011). Please note that I have not added additional books to the second edition of this book; there are just too many good ones out there. By all means, ask your colleagues for suggestions if you are unable to locate some good ones as there are many!*

- Periodicals

  - *United Soccer Coaches Soccer Journal*
  - *Success in Soccer*
  - *World Class Coaching*

I am not a collector of videos, but I do like two of them made by Anson Dorrance and Tony DiCicco for Reed Swain, *Playing the 1-3-4-3* and *Playing the 1-4-3-3*, respectively. The latter is a video that Anson asked me to supply a few players for from a couple of my older teams from my coaching days in Virginia and in his words, they are "forever immortalized in DVD form." I am sure there are a lot of terrific videos available online and in traditional formats, and I strongly encourage coaches to use this medium on occasion since visuals are very helpful for coaching education. In just the same way, I have not included a formal coaching curriculum in this book, but coaches should consult resources to determine what is appropriate for specific situations.

Thus, to sustain excellence and remain relevant, coaches need to continue to grow and develop through any means possible. Coaches who are multi-dimensional, seek knowledge, use pop culture, improve teaching methods, adapt to various learning styles, expose themselves to various philosophies, and gain meaningful experiences are ultimately those who having lasting power and reach greater levels of success as compared to those who stagnate, assume they know everything, and show no interest in player development outside of their own team or program. In addition, one cannot simply take a course or observe a coach; there is so much more to it, and to be an excellent coach, one has to be willing to let go and accept ideas with an open mind, passion, intellect, and conviction. One cannot be a "yes-man" to any trend that comes along or for the sake of any political gain, but instead should be a person with vision, steadfast determination, drive to excel, and enduring effort to achieve. Soccer is an international game and its beauty is evident when coaches and players from all nations demonstrate the passion, enthusiasm, energy, and skills of this beautiful game.

## GIVING BACK TO THE GAME

Coaches do give back to the game simply by coaching. However, beyond that, they can encourage their players to also give back by helping them to serve as referees, coaches, and camp instructors. It is a great joy to see so many former players who are in the fields of coaching and teaching, passing on the legacy of good coaching and sharing positive coaching experiences with a variety of players and their families. By being a part of my programs over the years, players become excellent coaches and, likewise, parents become good advocates for player development. Though we have a long way to go in this country, progress is coming. In addition, coaches can give back to the game by: teaching courses (coaching other coaches how to coach); working at camps and clinics; widening the focus beyond local programs to state, regional and national levels; mentoring young coaches; and certainly in a variety of other ways. As an example, writing articles and a book serve as additional ways for me to contribute positively to soccer.

*Statement from a former soccer player:*

"Memorable Moment: One of the most memorable soccer moments I had was when we were playing at the Surf Cup in San Diego, CA. I was a senior in high school and we were playing one of the best teams in the nation and I was incredibly nervous in the match. I remember receiving a through-ball from a teammate and then beating the opposing team's keeper in a one-on-one situation and scoring. I honestly don't even remember if we won or lost the match (we won), but the feeling of scoring in a match, when we were the underdogs, was a reminder that our team could overcome any challenges that we faced. Giving back to the game: After graduating from college, I was openly accepted by my former club to be an assistant coach for two youth girls teams. I loved giving back the knowledge that I gained from Ashu and instilling life lessons, as well as the knowledge of the game of soccer. I then went on to be the head coach of a girls team for a year. Helping young players grow and learn to love soccer was just a small way that I could give back to my community. A good quality learned: Ashu also was a firm believer in good sportsmanship on and off the field. Before any big tournaments, I remember that he always used to email us and remind us that we not only represent ourselves and our family, but the team, club, and league. This was always important to me because it reminded me that I should think before I act. By showing good sportsmanship, I was also leading by example and that's an important characteristic that has stayed with me. "

– Jenn Bartucca, BRYC *Electra* U11-19 (UNC Wilmington)

*Statement from a former soccer family:*

"Teaching: When our daughter was looking for a new team, we selected the Electra because we thought the men in charge were teachers of the game over coaches of the game. It seemed subtle at the time but it proved to be a winning approach. Memorable moment: Leading the nationally ranked Torpedoes in the Raleigh Shootout, 1-0, at halftime in a snowstorm and having the match cancelled with the Electra declared tournament champions. Giving back to the game: Many of the Electra served as volunteer mentors and assistants for younger teams in Northern Virginia during their playing days. Some have been in soccer teaching videos and a number of them went on to become coaches at the youth level. Skills, tactics: The Electra team was a lot like the basketball team in the movie Hoosiers. Focusing on skills and tactics and not on winning at a young age proved to be successful. Winning championships was the end result. It's not how you start the journey but how you finish."

– The Bartucca Family (Jenn, BRYC *Electra* U11-U19, UNC Wilmington)

*Statement from a former soccer player:*

"Ashu understands the game to the utmost level. I never doubted his advice or coaching. He covered all aspects of the game such as skills, fitness, teamwork, leadership, and strategy. I always looked to Ashu to give me quality coaching points at practice and before, during, and after our matches. Ashu always made me see the improvements I could make to my game. If you were to ask me how I would describe Ashu, I would say he is honest, respectful, well-mannered, kind, considerate, even-tempered, caring, constructive, knowledgeable, and intelligent. Even after I finished club ball, he continued to support me and my career. He will be a lifetime coach and friend."

– Claire Zimmeck, BRYC Attack & WT Woodson (NSCAA All-American for High School and College, College of William & Mary, MAC Hermann semi-finalist x2, WPS player)

*Statement from former parents:*

*"Ashu is a winner and not just a developmental coach. On his teams, my daughter won two Virginia State Cups, a High School Championship, an Eastern Region Championship, and finished third in the US Youth National Tournament. Holding a club team together during the high school years is a true measure of a coach's abilities. Ashu's teams in Northern Virginia not only stayed together through high school but grew in quality. Ashu was always there for my daughter, on or off the field. He taught her new soccer tactics and skills, helped her with college coaches, and encouraged her to be super fit before starting college soccer. He is an outstanding coach, mentor, and friend. The parents of players on Ashu's club teams were supportive, cooperative, and fun unlike other clubs teams that we experienced. This is reflective of his leadership style and personality."*

— Steve Zimmeck (father of Claire, College of William & Mary)

## LESSONS LEARNED

Throughout my coaching career, which began in 1986, I have learned quite a bit. I look at each experience in life as an opportunity to learn, while at this point in my career, I look at this book as an opportunity to share some ideas that I have learned to help others. There is no doubt that I have opened the doors wide and let readers into my "secrets," "tricks of the trade," and coaching insights to so many facets of coaching soccer, specifically in the area of player development. Without a doubt, I am not perfect, nor do I have all of the answers. In addition, so much of soccer is about learning and extending this further. I have learned a lot of lessons about life through my experiences with the beautiful game.

There is no doubt that all of us coaches who are passionate about coaching and what it really means know that so much about coaching transcends wonderfully into life. We see players as people whom we can teach and learn from, rather than as sheer numbers. We understand our roles as teachers, coaches, and role models in professional ways, rather than seeking popularity and shirking the responsibility to do what is right. We see parents as allies in creating community, rather than simply as suppliers of transportation and finances. There are not many people who understand coaching to the depths that we do, nor do they understand the time on and off the field necessary to continually strive for coaching excellence. Throughout our careers, we may have chosen to reply to the phone calls and emails that we need to over dinner. We make personal sacrifices of money, time, and various life events to be there for the team, we do mundane tasks such as washing the training vests or picking up discs after training sessions. We meet with the team as a whole, individual players, parents, and just about anyone who demands of our time for their child. We often attend professional development opportunities on our own dime. We listen to critiques of our coaching even when we cannot retort back with criticisms of other's leadership and lack of parenting skills. We are the first to arrive and the last to leave, even when we have other things to do. We offer college advice, evaluations, and assessments even when some of them go ignored. We take a chance on a player when it seems to help them more even when it helps us less. We spend restless nights before or after a match analyzing our efforts and attention to detail, and so much more.

Of course, there are so many beautiful aspects of coaching and so many sources of pride, satisfaction, and comfort in knowing you had a positive impact on many other people's lives. Thus, through it all, I have learned a lot of lessons directly and indirectly from years of coaching experiences. I share some of these lessons here:

- Leave doors open — literally, the "office door," and metaphorically, opportunities.

- Every situation has a teachable moment — athletics is a tremendous platform on which to teach life skills.

- Find your passion and be passionate about things that matter — sometimes your interests may be divergent, sometimes convergent.

- Life is like a ride on the metro (subway, train, etc.) — one has people along for the journey for unpredictable periods of time, people will come and go and sometimes though you can't see them, they may be riding along in another train, but they are still with you while others will just leave, and that's okay, too; just enjoy and learn from each person you encounter.

*Statement from a former player upon my move from Virginia to North Carolina:*

*"Ashu,*
*It's hard for me to really express the gratitude I have for you having been my coach for nine years of my life (I still remember when we were sitting around the lower Frost fields deciding on a team name). I'll try my best to put it into words but the impact you've had on me as a player can't be fully expressed printed on paper. I wanted to start off with saying THANK YOU. Thank you for the time, effort, patience, perseverance, and faith you have put into this team. I knew how much of an impact you were while you were here, but after you announced you were leaving I realized how much greater of an influence you were on me as a person (and the team). You are truly the most influential person I have met in my lifetime (17 ½ years ... but it counts for something), and I say that with no hesitation.*

*I remember when we were younger (maybe U13?) and we ran the Cooper at the Woodson track. I, per usual, was lagging behind, but on the last curve you ran across the track to run with me until the timer hit 12 minutes. Why does this memory stand out so much? I think it's because it completely reflects how caring you are of the kids you coach, and how you wish for them to succeed in only the best. That memory jogs (no pun intended) my mind every so often because it shows me there are people to support me through every step of that last sprint, people who care every bit about my success as an individual, and in the big picture-as a teammate. So since then, whenever I've struggled to finish a fitness test, I think of how you made the effort to come out and support me (despite any knee problems you might've had) even if I felt like I wasn't going to make the team's goal of however many laps. I'm not sure if you even remember this, but to me this is one of the most memorable things you've created for me as a coach.*

*As a technical coach, I can't express how much you've taught me, as a goalkeeper and an athlete in general. Nine years is way too much to fit onto paper, but it can be completely reflected through me and the team's play. The climb from Division 5 to Division 1, three-peat Final Four, various tournament wins, etc., would all not have been able to have been accomplished without your detailed instruction and coaching. At this age, we should know the technicalities (although sometimes we don't show it), but to see how much we've improved and the skill-level we're at now, shows how much you've really taught us. As a leader, I also can't express how much you've taught me. You've inspired confidence with the seemingly insignificant comments or with the most important prematch speeches.*

*I write this as I also pack and prepare to leave for Dynasty Camp, and I can't help but think of the dynasty and legacy you've created with Blue Thunder and the BT Family. I am so proud of what we have accomplished, and how much of that is due to your will to help us improve as athletes and as individuals. Not many people can say they've been on a team for more than half their life and have been raised in this great of an environment by an outstanding coach, but I am incredibly proud to say that I have. None of this would've been possible if it wasn't for your faith in the team, so thank you for that, and thank you for everything. I could go on forever but as I said, let your impact be shown in our play and in our mentality. I am going to miss you SO much, but I wish you tons of luck in North Carolina. Being that we travel there at least twenty times a year, I'm sure we'll see you plenty. Thank you again."*

*Love,*

Erica Stein #1 (BRYC *Blue Thunder*, U9-U18, Emory University)

*Electra wins another state cup championship, completing its long youth career on top at U18.*

- Understanding, patience, perseverance — important life skills to pack along for the journey of coaching soccer and though others may have deficits in these areas, maintain them since they will serve you well in the "bigger picture."

- Connections — it is important to network. Do not use or step on people, but seek to help and be helped as appropriate. Stay connected to those who are loyal, trustworthy, supportive friends.

- Communication — strive to improve communication and be as effective as possible while at the same time, understand that you can ultimately only do and say so much. Misunderstandings are often the cause of conflict so try to encourage listening ("we're born with two ears and only one mouth") and empathy.

- Love and peace — ultimately, these make the world go around and give hope for humanity whereas soccer is just a game.

- Education — knowledge is something no one can ever take away from you. Therefore, support academics and encourage high standards in this area. Remember that you do not know it all — form good habits to excel.

- Be your own best supporter — as difficult as it can be some times, try not to listen to outsiders who do not understand your mission or vision. Especially as you achieve more at higher levels, there will always be people jealous and envious of your accomplishments and their reaction can sometimes be negative. Instead, surround yourself with positive life forces and continue to excel.

- Control the controllable — do your best to stay focused, as there are just some situations and circumstances beyond your control. Instead, expect change and manage adversity as best as you can.

- You are never alone — aspects of coaching can be very challenging, but seek out those who you respect and realize that you have understanding, supportive people who care. Reach out to your mentors wisely, just as they reach out to theirs.

- The team comes first — no one player is more important than the team. Don't play favorites. Strive to improve all players through constant effort, assessment, and evaluation. Players may come and go, but the core team values and the team culture that you lead must have greater importance than any individual.

- Help others, whether through coaching or community service, and make the world around you a better place.

- Coach from the heart and head — don't coach in absolutes, but teach and bring out each player's potential. Coach based on your personality rather than trying to be someone else.

- Keep things in perspective — never get too high or too low as results are simply not always going to go in your favor. Perfection is good to strive for, but it is unattainable. Instead, strive for excellence and keep moving forward.

- Take time for yourself — turn off the phone, stay off of email, and find time to enjoy life as you wish, responsibly, and with people in your life who don't look at you as a soccer coach, but as a special person who happens to coach soccer.

- Stand up for what you believe in — you have to have self-respect. Don't sell out your values or support faulty leadership situations that miss the key points of athletics. It is less about imagery and more about substance in the end.

- Avoid the status quo and "everyone does it" mentality — as a team player; still be your own person and be true to yourself. If you are working under a system that won't change for the better despite your efforts, then sometimes it may be better to walk away and move on. You deserve to coach in a healthy, supportive environment that is grounded with a vision and efforts toward player development over "business."

- Know your value system and frame of reference for making decisions/choices — although your value system may not always mesh with other people's, do the right thing and understand that some people are just not there yet.

- Strive for excellence by forming good habits. Be engaged in meaningful moments.

- Life before soccer — have your priorities in order.

- Remember the "big picture" — you have more to do than simply run training sessions and coach matches. Remember that it is a long journey to both reach and sustain success. Don't let the little speed bumps slow you down, but instead, continue to move forward, one step at a time.

Hopefully many of these lessons will provide support for you, my colleagues in coaching. Likewise, you are the main reason I have written this book, so I am hopeful that you have found several sections useful and immediately applicable to not just your life as a coach, but as a person, too.

Perhaps one of the strongest statements of credibility comes from one of my former players on that very special *Electra* team that I mentioned throughout the book:

*"What was special about being a member of the Braddock Road Electra was that it was the perfect combination of everything a girl wants and needs during the crazy years of middle school and high school: fun, friendship, a unique sense of acceptance and belonging, a challenging environment that rewarded hard work and commitment, and something to be proud of, something that set you apart. While some may argue these qualities could be found on any successful athletic team, what was unique about Electra was the uncompromising allegiance of the team members and families to the good and success of the entire team and the emphasis on the development of the person, not just the player. Electra was first and foremost a family with a unique team chemistry that made athletic success and personal growth inevitable. We learned not just the game of soccer but what it meant to be a part of something bigger than ourselves. Everyone worked tirelessly and consistently for the team because we all meant so much to each other and to give anything less would be to let down the people who believed in and cared about you the most. We held each other to a high standard and pushed each other harder than we thought we ever could but always with the understanding that what didn't kill us personally made the team collectively stronger. The unconditional love, support, respect and trust crucial to family dynamics were the same values that sustained and promoted the success of our team. This success was measured not only by wins and tournament championships but the personal growth of the players and the values and integrity the team demonstrated.*

*I think the best way to describe why Electra was such a unique and rewarding experience for me is to describe what I learned from my teammates and coaches, who were essentially my second family for ten years of my life. I learned what it means to be humble from Ashley, who was probably the most gifted athlete on the team but who never boasted or flaunted her remarkable successes. I learned what it means to be both a strong and assertive leader and a compassionate and thoughtful teammate from Erica, who was the team captain without ever having to be declared one. I learned what it means to have heart and grit from Laura, the smallest but toughest defender on our team. I learned what it means to work hard from Jenn, who lifted weights and played with the boys and redefined for me what it means to be a female athlete. I learned how to lead by example, both on and off the field, from Cassie, whose positive communication from the goal guided and comforted the team on the field and whose quiet faith and spirituality guides her life off of it. I learned what it means to persevere when confronted with obstacles from Christina, who suffered a torn ACL in the most important year of her soccer career but battled back and overcame. I learned what it means to be a loving person from Kenika, who always made sure that everyone was included and no one felt forgotten. I learned the value of humor and the importance of never taking anything too seriously from Keith, our coach who instilled in us a love of the game at an early age by making it fun. I learned the importance of maintaining a steadfast commitment to personal values and truth, even when people around you don't, from Ashu, our coach who made sure that we were developing as people first and players second and that our team success did not come at the price of our principles.*

*All of these people, and many more involved with Electra throughout the ten years I was blessed to be a part of it, taught me more about life and myself than I could ever learn in a classroom at school. Electra was pretty much an extension of my own family in those formidable years when we are desperately trying to find ourselves, fit in and grow into the person we want to be. The values instilled in me from my Catholic faith and my family were cultivated and strengthened throughout my years on Electra by the people who made up the Electra family.*

*Another thing that made Electra so special was the fact that it truly took the team to win. Often facing opponents loaded with national team players, we didn't have the luxury of relying on certain players to take over the match and win it for us. But the thing was, on Electra we didn't need or want that luxury. We trusted our training, believed in each other and desired to win as a team. There was something so rewarding in achieving wins, and even accepting the losses, when we knew that it was a team effort. We understood that collectively we would win or lose and that was what drove us to compete, not as individuals, but as a team. We embraced the underdog role we often found ourselves in because we never doubted that the intensity and uniqueness of our team chemistry, and the strength of our team training, would enable us to together confront and triumph over any challenge or opponent.*

*People say that it is not always the destination that matters but the journey, and this is an idea that I think truly applies to Electra. The value of my years on Electra is not judged by the number of wins and losses because for me the outcome is secondary to the overall experience, which is bigger and so much more meaningful and significant than tournament championships or a winning record. My involvement with Electra brought me to a greater understanding of myself, what it means to be a part of a team and the world around me. Club soccer gave me the unique opportunity to visit, not just soccer complexes but the idyllic beaches of San Diego, the American icon of Disneyworld in Orlando, the beautiful rocks of Sedona, Arizona, and the bustling Canadian city of Ottawa, just to name a few. It taught me how to work with other people to accomplish a goal and the incomparable benefits of teamwork."*

— **Katie Gallivan #11, BRYC** *Electra* **U9-U19 (Boston College)**

I repeat: you are a coach, coaching the world's most beautiful game — "is there anything better in the world?"

# ACKNOWLEDGMENTS

*"Every now and then, somewhere, some time, some place, you are going to have to make a point about who you are and what you believe in. When the time comes, you simply have to do it."*

— Lee Riley to his son Pat

Coaching soccer is a team effort, and it is a long journey. Through the years, I have had the good fortune of meeting many terrific people who have imparted some nugget of wisdom, offered assistance to my teams, supported my philosophy, or shared an exercise. It is impossible to list all of these people here. Below are just a few of the many friends in soccer who have contributed positively to my coaching career, whether indirectly or directly — I acknowledge their contributions, and I appreciate their support:

Anson Dorrance, M'Liss Dorrance, Natalie Dorrance, Bill Palladino, Chris Ducar, Tom Sander, Cindy Parlow Cone, Keith Wawrzyniak, Dave Banks, Ryan Spencer, Gene Mishalow, Jeff Tipping, Schellas Hyndman, Jay Martin, Barry Gorman, Peter Gooding, Marcia McDermott, Laura Kerrigan, Bill Steffen, Lew Atkinson, Hank Leung, Ken Krieger, Randy May, Richard Butler, Jim Abt, Dave Lombardo, Steve Swanson, Chris Petrucelli, Bill Hempen, Randy Waldrum, Hershey Strosberg, Nancy Feldman, Brian Pensky, Darren Marshall, Jim Riedel, Jan Federice, Betsy Drambour, Lynn King, Peter Clinton, Peter Downey, Jay D'Allesandro, Adele Dolansky, Michelle Shircliff, Mark Dolansky, Charlotte Moran, Sue Ryan, John Daly, Louise Waxler, Joe Pereira, Manoj Khettry, Stewart Pierce, Jeff Bowers, Mario Hurdle, Kevin Long, John Kenney, Amy Kiah, Beth Huber, Bettina Bernardi Fletcher, Susan Ellis, Angela Kelly, Staci Wilson, Tracey Leone, Curtis Freeman, Derek Greene, Nikki Izzo-Brown, Tony DaLuz, Denise Schilte-Brown, Brad Roos, Dave Greene, Kelly Cagle, Mike Yeatts, Peter Schreiner, Jeff Pill, Philip Poole, Gary Smerdzinski, Gig Mikell, Deb Dexter, Pat Reed, Susan Bach, Theresa Navaleiko, Larry Best, Sergei Stopek, Gary Rossi, Michael Ross, Troy Dayak, Sam Laity, Michele Clark, Jim Rike, Adam Denton, Brad Francis, Sam Okpodu, Joe Holt , Jason Sisneros, Thomas Phu.

I wish to support Bill Dooley, who was inspired by this book to write his own book to also improve player development: *Players 1st* (Meyer & Meyer, 2018).

In addition, there are many, many other coaches, officials, parents, and media personnel whom I have interacted with in positive ways along the journey. Most of all, I also acknowledge the many players whom I have been fortunate to coach — they allowed me to test out ideas, they inspired creation of various methods, exercises, innovations and strategies, and most of all, they gave me a chance; for that, I am forever grateful.

# APPENDIX

*"We are what we repeatedly do. Excellence, then, is not an act, but a habit."*

— Aristotle

*Evaluation tools: Standard mid- or post-season*

This is feedback to help give you ideas about where you can improve. This is for your eyes only, not anyone else's, nor for comparison with your teammates. The ratings are based on your play relative to both your teammates and age group in general terms. Use the information in a positive way: pick out areas you can fix on your own and work on them (even if that means away from training, perhaps with a teammate), try harder to learn how you can actively improve in our training sessions to impact matches and to improve overall. Feel free to discuss any areas that you are not sure how to improve. Remember that all players have areas to work on and that I keep standards very high. It is very rare that any player would get 1s in these categories since we all can reach for a higher level. Enjoy the game, have fun, and *Let's Go Get 'em!*

**1:** Excellent, **2:** Very Good, **3:** Satisfactory, **4:** Needs Improvement, **5:** Unsatisfactory

| PSYCHOLOGICAL | | | | | |
|---|---|---|---|---|---|
| COACHABLE/ATTITUDE | | | | | |
| CREATIVITY | | | | | |
| MOTIVATION TO COMPETE | | | | | |
| DETERMINATION/EFFORT | | | | | |
| MENTAL TOUGHNESS | | | | | |
| AGGRESSIVENESS | | | | | |
| LEADERSHIP | | | | | |
| IMPACT ON MATCH | | | | | |
| TECHNICAL SKILLS | | | | | |
| DRIBBLING/FOOT SKILLS | | | | | |
| PASSING | | | | | |
| RECEIVING | | | | | |
| FINISHING | | | | | |
| HEADING | | | | | |
| SHIELDING | | | | | |
| TURNING | | | | | |
| TACKLING | | | | | |
| TACTICAL AWARENESS | | | | | |
| MOVEMENT ON AND OFF THE BALL | | | | | |
| COMMUNICATION | | | | | |
| READING THE GAME | | | | | |
| UNDERSTANDS PRINCIPLES OF PLAY | | | | | |
| SPEED OF PLAY, RHYTHM, FLOW | | | | | |

| PHYSICAL COMPONENTS | | | | | |
|---|---|---|---|---|---|
| SPEED | | | | | |
| QUICKNESS | | | | | |
| ENDURANCE | | | | | |
| STRENGTH | | | | | |
| BALANCE, AGILITY, FLEXIBILITY | | | | | |
| ATTENDANCE | | | | | |

COMMENTS:

*Evaluation tools: Match data*

DATE:  TIME:  A/P  LOC:  OPPONENT:

| PLAYERS | POS | G | A | Shots | Possession | Restart T G C P F K | 50/ 50 | 1v1 att | 1v1 def | Head | Clear | Comm |
|---|---|---|---|---|---|---|---|---|---|---|---|---|
| FP 1* | | | | | | | | | | | | |
| FP 2* | | | | | | | | | | | | |
| FP 3* | | | | | | | | | | | | |
| FP 4* | | | | | | | | | | | | |
| FP 5* | | | | | | | | | | | | |
| FP 6* | | | | | | | | | | | | |
| FP 7* | | | | | | | | | | | | |
| FP 8* | | | | | | | | | | | | |
| FP 9* | | | | | | | | | | | | |
| FP 10* | | | | | | | | | | | | |
| FP 11 | | | | | | | | | | | | |
| FP 12 | | | | | | | | | | | | |
| FP 13 | | | | | | | | | | | | |
| FP 14 | | | | | | | | | | | | |
| FP 15 | | | | | | | | | | | | |
| FP 16 | | | | | | | | | | | | |

| | G | A | Saves | | Restart | Ch | Tp | Pn | Pr | Bx | Comm |
|---|---|---|---|---|---|---|---|---|---|---|---|
| GK 1* | | | | | | | | | | | |
| GK2 | | | | | | | | | | | |

KEY

**AM/PM: LOC:** Location, **FP#:** Field Player, **GK:** Goalkeeper , **POS:** Position, **\*:** Starting the match; **G:** Goal, **A:** Assist

**Restarts: T:** Throw-in, **G:** Goal kick, **C:** Corner kick, **P:** Penalty kick, **F:** Free kick, **K:** Kick-off; **Comm:** Communication

*Note: Coaches should adapt, as necessary, to assess what they feel is appropriate.*

*Evaluation tools: In-season feedback – Focus sheet 1 ("5-4-3-2-1")*

[TEAM NAME] FOCUS SHEET 1/COACH                           DATE:
NAME:

4 TEAM COMMENTS (2 impact + 2 to work on):
+                    +                    -                    -

SPECIFIC PLAYER:
"5 Ss FROM ASHU" (1:Excellent to 5: Unsatisfactory)
SPEED:              STRENGTH:                        SKILLS:

SENSE:              SPORTSMANSHIP:

"4 REASONS TO BE ON THE FIELD"
GOALS:              ASSISTS:         POSSESSION:         DEFENDING:

3 INDIVIDUAL COMMENTS (1 standout quality + 2 areas to focus on)
+                    -                    -

2 WOODEN "Pyramid of Success" WORDS

1 TEAM QUOTE (offer a quote to motivate the player's focus and effort for the week)

*Evaluation tools: In-season feedback – Focus sheet 2 ("Improving/Raising")*

[TEAM NAME] FOCUS SHEET 2/COACH              DATE:          NAME:

| Is improving... | Focus on raising skills in these areas... |
|---|---|
| (Be specific, accurate, offer examples) | (Be specific and end with measurable objectives) |

Also on this sheet, place the team motto, five words, or slogan and team logo. These should be on every document you use with the team.

*Note: They do not appear on all of the examples in the appendix.*

*Evaluation tools:* In-season feedback — Possession and self-rating

*Note:* Communicate with players (and parents, as applicable) to pick a fair-minded, soccer-knowledgeable resource in their support system to rate a match for the player.

[TEAM NAME]

COACH/POSSESSION AND SELF-RATING

Record the outcome of the player's touches in the grid using the coding system given below. Obviously, honesty and integrity are expected; all results are confidential and are to be shared only between the person recording and the player being recorded. The player can interpret their own results. A true, competitive, champion-minded athlete values objectivity far more than subjectivity. In addition, any attempts to misuse this rating system to "witch hunt" someone else on the team will be ignored — "responsibility of self brings about change in self," as I like to say.

**CODING:**

| | | |
|---|---|---|
| + | pass completed to teammate | **PLAYER:** |
| G | scores goal | **DATE:** |
| A | assists goal (first or second assist) | **FIELD/LOCATION:** |
| S | shot-on-goal (on frame) | **OPPONENT:** |
| 0 | touch/dribble/pass/shot out of bounds | **POSITION(S) PLAYED:** |
| x | touch/pass/dribble/ball stolen results in turn over to opponent | |

| | |
|---|---|
| FIRST HALF | |
| SECOND HALF | |

At the end of the match, hand this sheet to the player. Then, the player should self-rate on the five key team traits that we expect from our players, using the following rating system:

1. Excellent — could have not done any better and can point to examples of what the player did and said before/during/after the match that had a positive impact/result

2. Very good — tried hard and can point to examples of what the player did or said before/during/after the match that had a positive impact/result

3. Satisfactory — tried to be conscientious of the traits and engaged self before/during/after the match toward having an impact, though taking action or verbalizing constructive and positive comments was a challenge and not as impactful as it could have been

4. Unsatisfactory — although the player is aware of the desired five team traits, did not make an effort to engage self toward being active in pursuit of the team traits

5. May as well have not suited up — does not understand team expectations

| EFFORT | COMPETITIVENESS | FOCUS | COMMUNICATION | TEAM |
|--------|-----------------|-------|---------------|------|
|        |                 |       |               |      |

Additional thoughts and reflections by the player:

Sign and date this sheet (player):

*File this sheet in your soccer binder.*


*Evaluation tools: In-season feedback — Self-evaluation*

[TEAM NAME] SELF-EVALUATION
COACH/DATE

NAME: .............................................................................................................................................................

DIRECTIONS: Fill this sheet out now, on your own. Complete each statement without talking, avoid making any commentary about statements since it may influence others, and do not copy someone else's answer(s) in this process. Be honest when completing this self-evaluation; circle the answer that best describes you relative to where you are at present with the team. I will be the only person (other than you) to see this self-evaluation sheet, and it is to be used as a self-reflective learning process.

- **Use the following rating scale:** 1: Never; 2: Not often; 3: Sometimes; 4: Usually; 5: Always (Note that the numerical order varies from other evaluation tools)
- Answer every statement and circle only one answer for each statement (no double answers).

PART I: Attitude

01. I maintain a positive attitude toward my teammates.  1  2  3  4  5

02. I maintain a positive attitude toward my coach(es).  1  2  3  4  5

03. I maintain a positive attitude toward my club.  1  2  3  4  5

04. I maintain a positive attitude toward working on skills on off-days and in the off-season.  1  2  3  4  5

05. I maintain a positive attitude toward getting "fitter, faster, stronger" on off-days and in the off-season.  1  2  3  4  5

06. My attitude positively impacts the team in training sessions and in matches.  1  2  3  4  5

07. I display a consistent, competitive, never give up attitude in training sessions and in matches.  1  2  3  4  5

PART II: Performance

08. I am in attendance for training sessions, matches, team meals, and team meetings.

1    2    3    4    5

09. I execute skills with and without pressure well in training sessions.

1    2    3    4    5

10. I execute skills with and without pressure well in matches.

1    2    3    4    5

11. The team suffers without me on the field.

1    2    3    4    5

12. I get results (goals, assists, GK saves) in matches.

1    2    3    4    5

13. I hold possession of the ball well for the team.

1    2    3    4    5

14. I am a good 1v1 attacker and don't kick into legs.

1    2    3    4    5

15. I am a good 1v1 defender and don't stick.

1    2    3    4    5

16. I make good runs off the ball for the team.

1    2    3    4    5

17. I communicate positively and effectively on the field.

1    2    3    4    5

18. I know all of the attacking CKs and FKs and can effectively place players in the best positions for the team.

1    2    3    4    5

PART III: Character

19. I have a "team-first" not a "me-first" personality.

1    2    3    4    5

20. I display good sportsmanship toward officials and opponents in matches.

1    2    3    4    5

21. I give 100% effort in training sessions, from warm-up to exercises to team talks to cool-down.

1    2    3    4    5

22. I give 100% effort in matches, from pre-match through cool-down

1    2    3    4    5

| | 1 | 2 | 3 | 4 | 5 |
|---|---|---|---|---|---|
| **23.** I am focused – my teammates can count on me to pay attention and not distract the team from doing what needs to be done. | | | | | |
| **24.** I am reliable – my teammates can count on me to be present and give 100%. | | | | | |
| **25.** I am responsible – my teammates can count on me to read team emails, contact the coach directly when unable to attend a team event, and take care of team responsibilities. | | | | | |
| 26. I am loyal – I never talk badly about teammates, the team, the coach, the club. | | | | | |
| **27.** I am honest – I do not lie, blame others, or make excuses. | | | | | |
| **28.** I conduct myself to the team standards – wear the proper attire and equipment, help gather equipment, pick up trash before leaving training sessions and matches, am on-time for team events. | | | | | |
| **29.** I am confident in my ability to perform in matches. | | | | | |
| **30.** I do good things off the field to help my community. | | | | | |

PART IV: Discipline

| | 1 | 2 | 3 | 4 | 5 |
|---|---|---|---|---|---|
| **31.** I am one of the (physically) fastest players on the team. | | | | | |
| **32.** I can execute skills under pressure faster than my teammates. | | | | | |
| **33.** I am one of the fittest players on the team. | | | | | |
| **34.** I am one of the (physically) strongest players on the team. | | | | | |
| **35.** I am one of the (mentally) strongest players on the team. | | | | | |
| **36.** I am one of the (emotionally) strongest players on the team. | | | | | |

| | 1 | 2 | 3 | 4 | 5 |
|---|---|---|---|---|---|
| **37.** I pay attention to nutrition expectations – I eat appropriate foods at meal-time and snack-time, and I hydrate well. | | | | | |
| **38.** I get appropriate rest and make curfew when set. | | | | | |
| **39.** I display a competitive "will to win" during training sessions. | | | | | |
| **40.** I display a competitive "will to win" during matches. | | | | | |
| **41.** I watch soccer live or on television to try to improve. | | | | | |
| **42.** I take care of academics and maintain Bs or better. | | | | | |

**PART V: Team Values**

| | 1 | 2 | 3 | 4 | 5 |
|---|---|---|---|---|---|
| **43.** I want to develop as a player and a person on this team, regardless of just results. | | | | | |
| **44.** I understand and display passion on and off the field. | | | | | |
| **45.** I understand and display unity on and off the field. | | | | | |
| **46.** I understand and display discipline on and off the field. | | | | | |
| **47.** I understand and display dedication on and off | | | | | |
| **48.** I understand and display effort on and off the field. | | | | | |
| **49.** I understand and display "Lessons from Geese." | | | | | |
| **50.** I understand and display Wooden's "Pyramid of Success." | | | | | |

List areas of strength for you as a soccer player: ............................................................................

List areas of strength for you as a person: ..................................................................................

List areas of strength for you as a teammate:  ............................................................................

List areas you wish to improve in any of the above three areas:  ................................................

***Thank you for completing this self-evaluation.***

*Note:* *In statements 44-48, coaches should use the "five words" that apply to the specific team that they are working with.*

*"Creating Community" Peer evaluation/feedback*
*(credit for the idea goes to UNC Women's Soccer)*
Make a tabular grid listing each player and various qualities that your team values. Players grade each teammate, and they do not discuss their grades, nor do they have any time to communicate with teammates while filling these out (i.e., they fill this out on the spot as opposed to taking it home to work on). The coaching staff keeps this feedback and uses it in individual player conferences, as necessary. Below is a sample charting for a player's results:

**[TEAM NAME] PLAYER:**

A: Excellent, B: Good, C: Fair, D: Poor, N: no grade given

ATTITUDE

| | | |
|---|---|---|
| 1. | TEAMMATES | AAAABAA |
| 2. | COACHES | AAAAAAA |
| 3. | PROGRAM | AAAAAAA |
| 4. | SELF-DEVELOPMENT | AAAABAA |

PERFORMANCE

| | | |
|---|---|---|
| 5. | ATTENDANCE | BBAABAA |
| 6. | TRAINING | AAAACAA |
| 7. | MATCHES | AAAABAA |
| 8. | RESULTS | AAAABBA |

CHARACTER

| 9. MENTAL TOUGHNESS | AAAABBA |
|---|---|
| 10. RELIABILITY | AAAABBA |
| 11. LOYALTY | AAAAAAA |
| 12. CONDUCT | AAAAAAA |
| 13. STRENGTH | AAAANAA |
| 14. COMMUNITY | AAAABBN |
| 15. CONFIDENCE | ABAABAA |

DISCIPLINE

| 16. FITNESS | AAAACAA |
|---|---|
| 17. TRAINING | AAAABAA |
| 18. HARD-BODY/HEALTH | AAAABA |
| 19. SELF-DEVELOPMENT | AAAAB+AA |
| 20. THE WILL TO PREPARE TO WIN | AAAAB+AA |

**COMMENTS:** Extremely dedicated

*Pre-season mini-camp scoring grids:*
Numbers refer to the exercises – see descriptions. **T:** Total points. **R:** Rank

*Day 1- "Olympics"*

| PLAYER | FITNESS 1T  R | SKILLS (MISC) 2A+ 2B+ 2C+ 2D = 2T     R | SKILLS (W/PRESS) 3T     R | COMPETITIVE 4T    R | DAY RANK T  R | TOTAL RANK T  R |
|---|---|---|---|---|---|---|
| 1 | | | | | | |
| 2 | | | | | | |
| 3 | | | | | | |
| 4 | | | | | | |
| 5 | | | | | | |
| 6 | | | | | | |
| 7 | | | | | | |
| 8 | | | | | | |
| 9 | | | | | | |
| 10 | | | | | | |
| 11 | | | | | | |
| 12 | | | | | | |
| 13 | | | | | | |
| 14 | | | | | | |
| 15 | | | | | | |
| 16 | | | | | | |
| 17 | | | | | | |
| 18 | | | | | | |
| NOTES | | | | | | |

*Day 2 – Foot skills/Dribbling/1v1*

| PLAYER | FITNESS 1T R | SKILLS (MISC) 2A+ 2B+ = 2T R | SKILLS (W/PRESS) 3A+3B+3C= 3T R | COMPETITIVE 4A+4B=4T R | DAY RANK T R | TOTAL RANK T R |
|---|---|---|---|---|---|---|
| 1 | | | | | | |
| 2 | | | | | | |
| 3 | | | | | | |
| 4 | | | | | | |
| 5 | | | | | | |
| 6 | | | | | | |
| 7 | | | | | | |
| 8 | | | | | | |
| 9 | | | | | | |
| 10 | | | | | | |
| 11 | | | | | | |
| 12 | | | | | | |
| 13 | | | | | | |
| 14 | | | | | | |
| 15 | | | | | | |
| 16 | | | | | | |
| 17 | | | | | | |
| 18 | | | | | | |
| NOTES | | | | | | |

*Day 3 — Passing/Receiving*

| PLAYER | FITNESS 1T  R | SKILLS (MISC) 2A+ 2B+ = 2T  R | SKILLS (W/PRESS) 3A+3B = 3T  R | COMPETITIVE 4A+4B=4T  R | DAY RANK T  R | TOTAL RANK T  R |
|---|---|---|---|---|---|---|
| 1 | | | | | | |
| 2 | | | | | | |
| 3 | | | | | | |
| 4 | | | | | | |
| 5 | | | | | | |
| 6 | | | | | | |
| 7 | | | | | | |
| 8 | | | | | | |
| 9 | | | | | | |
| 10 | | | | | | |
| 11 | | | | | | |
| 12 | | | | | | |
| 13 | | | | | | |
| 14 | | | | | | |
| 15 | | | | | | |
| 16 | | | | | | |
| 17 | | | | | | |
| 18 | | | | | | |
| | | | | | | |
| NOTES | | | | | | |

*Day 4 – Longballs/Heading/Volleying*

| PLAYER | FITNESS<br><br>1T   R | SKILLS<br>(MISC)<br>2A+ 2B+ 2C+2D=<br>2T  R | SKILLS<br>(W/PRESS)<br>3A+3B=<br>3T  R | COMPETITIVE<br><br>4A+4B=4T  R | DAY<br>RANK<br>T   R | TOTAL<br>RANK<br>T   R |
|--------|---------|--------------------|-------------|--------------|----------|----------|
| 1 | | | | | | |
| 2 | | | | | | |
| 3 | | | | | | |
| 4 | | | | | | |
| 5 | | | | | | |
| 6 | | | | | | |
| 7 | | | | | | |
| 8 | | | | | | |
| 9 | | | | | | |
| 10 | | | | | | |
| 11 | | | | | | |
| 12 | | | | | | |
| 13 | | | | | | |
| 14 | | | | | | |
| 15 | | | | | | |
| 16 | | | | | | |
| 17 | | | | | | |
| 18 | | | | | | |
| NOTES | | | | | | |

*Day 5 – Finishing*

| PLAYER | FITNESS 1T R | SKILLS (MISC) 2A+ 2B+ 2C = 2T R | SKILLS (W/PRESS) 3T R | COMPETITIVE 4A+4B=4T R | DAY RANK T R | TOTAL RANK T R |
|---|---|---|---|---|---|---|
| 1 | | | | | | |
| 2 | | | | | | |
| 3 | | | | | | |
| 4 | | | | | | |
| 5 | | | | | | |
| 6 | | | | | | |
| 7 | | | | | | |
| 8 | | | | | | |
| 9 | | | | | | |
| 10 | | | | | | |
| 11 | | | | | | |
| 12 | | | | | | |
| 13 | | | | | | |
| 14 | | | | | | |
| 15 | | | | | | |
| 16 | | | | | | |
| 17 | | | | | | |
| 18 | | | | | | |
| NOTES | | | | | | |

*Pre-season mini-camp forms:*

(1) Sample individual feedback form for players, amend as appropriate:

**MINI-CAMP (Team/Dates/Year); PLAYER: Player 1**

If not in Top 10, then it's an area to improve in (suggestion: use a * if player is ranked below 10); t = tied; results discussed with team consider all comments. Please keep confidential — use results as positive feedback.

| | FITNESS | SKILLS (MISC) | SKILLS (PRESS) | COMPETITIVE | DAYS RANK | TOTAL RANK |
|---|---|---|---|---|---|---|
| **Day 1** | CooperRun | Jug/Lng/Ti/Sht | 4v4 | 8v8 | | |
| | 7t | 7 | 13t | 6t | | |
| **Day 2** | Cones | Fig8/1v1/Shield | 1v1side/goal | 4v4/8v8 | 1 | 2 |
| | 0 misses | 3t | 3t | 1 | | |
| **Day 3** | 120s | Pass/Rec-gates | 2v2 | 4v4/8v8 | 4 | 1 |
| | 0 misses | 4t | 4t | 10 | | |
| **Day 4** | SuperSets | Longball+ | 2v2Long/Head | 8v8 | 1t | 1 |
| | 3t | 1 | 3 | 5t | | |
| **Day 5** | 40s | Shoot/Finish | 4v4 | 8v8 | 4 | 1 |
| | 6 | 6 | 12 | 3 | | |

**FINAL: (Name/Ranking)**                                          *Let's Go Get 'em!*

(2) Sample team summary form for coach's use only.

## TEAM MINI-CAMP (Date/Year/Age group of team)

Considerations: Discuss with team to put results in perspective. Players missing days may not be in the cumulative ranks. If a player misses a certain section, then they get the lowest ranking and can still count toward cumulative rankings. Scores may be thrown off by players mis-counting, inaccurate measurements, etc. Results are just one component of evaluations. The sample below is that of a club team and modifications were made to include two non-ranked fitness sessions; fitness sessions were held in the morning and the soccer portion of mini-camp was held in the evening. Key: FP-Field Player, GK-Goalkeeper. Note how the mini-camp rankings offer each player opportunities to display their talents in various categories.

| FITNESS | SKILLS (MISC) | SKILLS (PRESS) | COMPETITIVE | DAYS RANK | TOTAL RANK |
|---|---|---|---|---|---|
| *DAY 1* | | | | | |
| CooperRun | Juggl/Lng/T-i/Sht | | 4v4 scrimmages | 8v8 scrimmage | |
| 1-FP7 | 1-FP13 | 1-FP1 | 1-FP13 | 1-FP13 | (same) |
| 2-FP4 | 2-FP5 | 2-FP16 | 2-FP4 | 2-FP4 | |
| 2-FP6 | 3-FP6 | 3-FP9 | 2-FP6 | 2-FP6 | |
| 4-FP13 | 4-FP2 | 3-FP7 | 4-FP10 | 4-FP12 | |
| 4-FP10 | 4-FP3 | 5-FP2 | 4-FP3 | 5-FP7 | |
| 4-FP12 | 6-GK1 | 6-FP11 | 6-FP5 | 6-FP5 | |
| 7-FP11 | 7-FP1 | 6-GK1 | 6-FP12 | 6-FP1 | |
| 7-FP1 | 8-FP12 | 8-FP12 | 6-FP8 | 8-FP2 | |
| 9-FP5 | 9-FP4 | 8-FP4 | 9-FP9 | 8-FP3 | |
| 9-FP14 | 10-FP10 | 8-FP14 | 9-FP11 | 10-FP11 | |
| 9-GK1 | 10-FP7 | 11-FP5 | 9-FP16 | 10-FP10 | |
| 9-FP3 | 12-FP11 | 12-FP13 | 9-FP2 | 10-GK1 | |
| 13-FP9 | 12-FP15 | 12-FP8 | 13-FP1 | 13-FP16 | |
| 13-FP16 | 14-FP16 | 14-FP3 | 13-FP14 | 14-FP9 | |
| 13FP-2 | 15-FP14 | 14-FP6 | 13-GK1 | 15-FP14 | |
| 13-FP8 | 16-FP9 | 16-FP10 | 13-FP7 | 16-FP8 | |
| (GK2- inj) | 17-FP8 | (GK2-inj) | (GK2-inj) | (GK2-inj) | |
| (FP15- inj) | (GK2-inj) | (FP15-inj) | (FP15-inj) | (FP15-inj) | |

*DAY 2*

| Cones | Fig8s/1v1 Shield | | 1v1side/goal | 4v4/8v8 scrimmages | |
|---|---|---|---|---|---|
| (No Sep Score) | 1-FP4 | 1-FP2 | 1-FP1 | 1-FP1 | 1-FP4 |
| | 2-FP2 | 2-FP5 | 2-FP4 | 2-FP4 | 2-FP1 |
| | 3-FP1 | 3-FP1 | 2-GK1 | 2-FP3 | 3-FP12 |
| | 3-FP3 | 3-FP3 | 2-FP3 | 4-FP2 | 3-FP3 |
| | 5-FP5 | 5-FP4 | 5-FP11 | 5-FP5 | 5-FP5 |
| | 6-GK1 | 5-FP8 | 6-FP12 | 6-FP12 | 6-FP2 |
| | 7-FP12 | 7-FP6 | 7-FP10 | 7-GK1 | 7-FP6 |
| | 8-FP7 | 8-FP12 | 7-FP14 | 8-FP8 | 8-FP7 |
| | 9-FP8 | 9-FP11 | 9-FP2 | 9-FP7 | 9-GK1 |
| | 10-FP9 | 10-FP9 | 9-FP7 | 10-FP11 | (9-FP13) |
| | 10-FP6 | 10-FP7 | 11-FP8 | 11-FP6 | 11-FP11 |
| | 12-FP14 | 12-FP10 | 12-FP6 | 12-FP10 | 12-FP10 |
| | 13-FP10 | 13-FP14 | 13-FP5 | 12-FP14 | 13-FP8 |
| | 14-FP11 | 14-GK1 | 14-FP9 | 14-FP9 | 14-FP14 |
| | (FP15-inj) | (FP15) | (FP15) | (16FP13) | 15-FP9 |
| | (FP16-abs) | (FP16) | (FP16) | (FP15) | (FP15) |
| | (FP13-abs) | (FP13) | (FP13) | (FP16) | (FP16) |
| | (GK2-abs) | (GK2) | (GK2) | (GK2) | (GK2) |

*DAY 3*

| 110s | Pass/Rec-gates | 2v2 | 4v4/8v8 scrimmages | | |
|---|---|---|---|---|---|
| (No Sep Score) | 1-FP9 | 1-FP11 | 1-FP5 | 1-FP2 | 1-FP1 |
| | 1-FP12 | 2-FP15 | 1-FP3 | 2-FP12 | 2-FP12 |
| | 1-FP7 | 2-GK1 | 3-FP2 | 3-FP5 | 3-FP2 |
| | 4-FP2 | 4-FP5 | 3-FP12 | 4-FP1 | 4-FP5 |
| | 4-FP1 | 4-FP2 | 5-FP13 | 5-FP15 | 5-FP3 |
| | 4-FP15 | 4-FP1 | 5-FP10 | 5-FP8 | 6-FP4 |
| | 7-GK1 | 4-FP8 | 7-FP8 | 7-GK1 | 7-FP7 |
| | 8-FP4 | 4-FP14 | 8-FP11 | 7-FP3 | 8-GK1 |
| | 9-FP13 | 9-FP10 | 8-FP7 | 7-FP7 | (9-FP13) |
| | 9-FP8 | 9-FP12 | 10-FP1 | 10-FP11 | 10-FP8 |
| | 11-FP3 | 9-FP3 | 11-FP14 | 10-FP13 | 10-FP6 |
| | 12-FP5 | 12-FP13 | 12-GK1 | 12-FP10 | 12-FP11 |
| | 12-FP6 | 12-FP7 | 12-FP6 | 13-FP14 | 13-FP10 |
| | 14-FP10 | 14-FP9 | 14-FP4 | 14-FP9 | 14-FP14 |
| | 15-FP14 | 15-FP4 | 14-FP15 | 15-FP4 | 15-FP9 |
| | (17-FP11-late) | 15-FP6 | 16-FP9 | 16-FP6 | (FP15) |
| | (FP16-abs) | (FP16) | (FP16) | (FP16) | (FP16) |
| | (GK2-abs) | (GK2) | (GK2) | (GK2) | (GK2) |

*DAY 4*

| Super Sets | Longballs | 2v2 Long/Head | 8v8 scrimmage | | |
|---|---|---|---|---|---|
| 1-FP4 | 1-FP1 | 1-FP2 | 1-FP9 | 1-FP13 | 1-FP1 |
| 2-FP13 | 2-FP2 | 2-FP9 | 2-FP13 | 1-FP1 | 2-FP2 |
| 3-FP1 | 3-FP6 | 3-FP1 | 2-FP15 | 3-FP2 | 3-FP3 |
| 3-FP3 | 4-FP13 | 4-FP13 | 4-FP4 | 4-FP9 | 4-FP5 |
| 5-FP16 | 5-FP11 | 4-FP5 | 5-FP10 | 5-FP6 | (5-FP12) |
| 6-FP6 | 6-FP9 | 4-FP10 | 5-FP2 | 6-FP3 | 5-FP4 |
| 7-FP14 | 6-GK1 | 4-FP4 | 5-FP1 | 7-FP4 | (7-FP13) |
| 8-FP5 | 8-FP12 | 4-FP8 | 5-FP8 | 8-FP10 | 8-FP7 |
| 9-FP2 | 9-FP3 | 4-FP3 | 5-FP6 | 9-FP11 | 9-FP6 |
| 10-FP11 | 10-FP7 | 10-FP11 | 10-FP12 | 10-FP8 | (10-FP11) |
| 11-FP7 | 11-FP10 | 10-FP12 | 10-FP7 | 11-FP5 | 10-FP8 |
| 12-FP9 | 12-FP5 | 10-FP14 | 12-FP11 | 12-FP14 | 10-GK1 |
| 13-GK1 | 12-FP14 | 10-FP6 | 12-FP14 | 12-FP7 | 13-FP10 |
| 14-FP8 | 14-FP15 | 10-FP7 | 12-FP3 | 14-FP12 | 14-FP9 |
| 15-FP10 | 15-FP8 | 15-FP15 | 15-GK1 | 15-GK1 | 15-FP14 |
| (17-FP12) | 16-FP4 | 16-GK1 | 16-FP5 | (FP15) | (FP15) |
| (GK2-inj) | (GK2-inj) | (GK2) | (GK2) | (GK2) | (GK2) |
| (FP15-inj) | (FP16-abs) | (FP16) | (FP16) | (FP16) | (FP16) |

*DAY 5*

| 40s | Shoot/Finish | 4v4 scrimmages | 8v8 scrimmage | | |
|---|---|---|---|---|---|
| 1-GK1 | 1-GK1 | 1-FP13 | 1-FP13 | 1-FP13 | 1-FP1 |
| 2-FP6 | 2-FP6 | 2-FP12 | 2-FP2 | 1-GK1 | 2-FP2 |
| 3-FP4 | 3-FP13 | 3-FP5 | 3-FP1 | 3-FP3 | 3-FP3 |
| 4-FP7 | 3-FP15 | 3-GK1 | 3-FP3 | 4-FP1 | (4-FP13) |
| 5-FP3 | 5-FP11 | 3-FP3 | 5-FP4 | 5-FP4 | 5-FP4 |
| 6-FP1 | 6-FP1 | 6-FP9 | 5-FP15 | 6-FP6 | 6-FP5 |
| 7-FP13 | 7-FP2 | 7-FP11 | 7-FP9 | 7-FP2 | (7-FP12) |
| 7-FP14 | 7-FP12 | 7-FP2 | 7-FP8 | 8-FP9 | 8-GK1 |
| 9-FP9 | 9-FP9 | 7-FP4 | 7-GK1 | 9-FP11 | 8-FP6 |
| 9-FP10 | 9-FP5 | 10-FP15 | 10-FP11 | 10-FP5 | 10-FP7 |
| 11-FP11 | 9-FP3 | 10-FP8 | 11-FP5 | 11-FP7 | (11-FP11) |
| 12-FP5 | 12-FP7 | 12-FP1 | 11-FP10 | 12-FP12 | 12-FP8 |
| 13-FP16 | 13-FP4 | 13-FP7 | 11-FP6 | 13-FP8 | 13-FP9 |
| 14-FP2 | 14-FP10 | 14-FP6 | 11-FP7 | 14-FP10 | 14-FP10 |
| 15-FP8 | 14-FP8 | 15-FP10 | 15-FP12 | (16-FP14) | (15-FP14) |
| (17-FP12) | (FP-14-abs) | (FP14) | (FP14) | (FP15) | (FP15) |
| (GK2-inj) | (GK2-abs) | (GK2) | (GK2) | (GK2) | (GK2) |
| (FP15-inj) | (FP16-abs) | (FP16) | (FP16) | (FP16) | (FP16) |

*FINAL*

| | | | | | |
|---|---|---|---|---|---|
| 1-FP1 | | | | | |
| 2-FP2 | | | | | |
| 3-FP3 | | | | | |
| 4-FP4 | | | | | |
| 5-FP5 | | | | | |
| 6-GK1 | | | | | |
| 6-FP6 | | | | | |
| 8-FP7 | | | | | |
| 9-FP8 | | | | | |
| 10-FP9 | | | | | |
| 11-FP10 | | | | | |
| (FP11) | | | | | |
| (FP12) | | | | | |
| (FP13) | | | | | |
| (FP14) | | | | | |
| (FP15) | | | | | |
| (GK2) | | | | | |
| (FP16) | | | | | |

\*    *These players competed in all sessions! Congratulations on another terrific mini-camp, everybody! Let's Go Get 'em!*

(3) Use the following feedback form for players after mini-camp and the team's first scrimmage in pre-season for evaluation and goal-setting:

This is feedback to offer ideas about where you can improve based primarily on the mini-camp week and first scrimmage. This is for your eyes only, not anyone else's nor for comparison with your teammates. The ratings are based on your play relative to your teammates in general terms. Use the information in a positive way: pick out areas you can fix on your own and work on them (even if that means away from training). Try harder to learn how you can actively improve in our training sessions, and feel free to discuss any areas that you are not sure how to improve. Have fun and *Let's Go Get 'em!*.

**1**: Excellent, **2**: Very Good; **3**: Satisfactory; **4**: Needs Improvement; **5**: Unsatisfactory — this area needs significant and dedicated improvement to be able to contribute to the team effectively.

| PSYCHOLOGICAL | | | | | |
|---|---|---|---|---|---|
| COACHABLE/ATTITUDE | | | | | |
| CREATIVITY | | | | | |
| MOTIVATION TO COMPETE | | | | | |
| DETERMINATION/EFFORT | | | | | |
| MENTAL TOUGHNESS | | | | | |
| AGGRESSIVENESS | | | | | |
| LEADERSHIP | | | | | |
| IMPACT ON MATCH | | | | | |

| TECHNICAL SKILLS | | | | | |
|---|---|---|---|---|---|
| DRIBBLING/FOOT SKILLS | | | | | |
| PASSING | | | | | |
| RECEIVING | | | | | |
| FINISHING | | | | | |
| HEADING | | | | | |
| SHIELDING | | | | | |
| TURNING | | | | | |
| TACKLING | | | | | |
| TACTICAL AWARENESS | | | | | |
| MOVEMENT ON AND OFF THE BALL | | | | | |
| COMMUNICATION | | | | | |
| READING THE GAME | | | | | |
| UNDERSTANDS PRINCIPLES OF PLAY | | | | | |
| SPEED OF PLAY, RHYTHM, FLOW | | | | | |
| PHYSICAL COMPONENTS | | | | | |
| SPEED | | | | | |
| QUICKNESS | | | | | |
| ENDURANCE | | | | | |
| STRENGTH | | | | | |
| BALANCE, AGILITY, FLEXIBILITY | | | | | |
| ATTENDANCE | | | | | |

GOALS FOR THE UPCOMING SEASON:

TEAM –

INDIVIDUAL –

WAYS COACHES CAN HELP YOU:

COMMENTS (ON ANYTHING ELSE):

*ASHU'S "FITTER, FASTER, STRONGER" TRAINING PACKET*

### *Dear [U15-U19 age team],*

*How are you? Welcome back to our returning players and a heartfelt welcome to players new to our program. I hope your spring seasons are finishing up well. As mentioned previously, now more than ever, it is important that we commit ourselves to summer training to return for the upcoming season "fitter, faster, stronger" than before. With ambitious goals and high expectations for our team and for what each player strives for in the long-term, it is important that we all commit to a rigorous strength training and fitness program.*

*Included is a packet of suggestions for training – this is created from a lot of excellent resources and contacts of mine. Ultimately, your physicians, athletic trainers, physical therapists, and other sports medical personnel can also assist you in planning for workouts. Remember, this packet of information has been put together by me for our team with suggested ways to get fitter, faster, and stronger. Please keep this somewhere so you have easy access to it. In addition, I am not mapping out a day-by-day plan since some of you are in positions where you have various competitions/camps, injury recovery, and other schedule challenges. Likewise, our program for regionals preparation or training/playing at camps suffices for workouts. Do not overtrain or double-up so we can avoid over-use injuries. Just know that I do not expect you to overdo it, and we need everyone healthy as soon as possible. So, do workouts that make sense for you individually and that will help us best as a team.*

*In general, the team expectation is that out of a seven-day week; you are active six days and resting completely for one day. Of the six days, you may consider the following: three high-intensity interval-type workouts, two medium-intensity workouts, and one low-intensity workout. For strength training (whole body), try to get three days in, two at a minimum, and again, consult a trainer*

*Note:    This means that you will run and strength train on the same day on two or three days per week.*

*Strength training does not have to be weights every time necessarily, either. Consider resistance strength training, such as plyometric exercises and other types of resistance strengthening/toning, or cross-training (swimming, cycling, inline skating, rowing, etc.) as part of your program, too. For example, one of the three strength-training days can consist of these resistance-type exercises. What I have provided for you is a plethora of running, intervals, agilities, strength training, and plyometric exercises. Work on agility/quickness exercises as part of your workouts two or three times per week. Note that some of these exercises can be used throughout the year, as fitness is a year-round commitment, not something one can gain in just a few weeks.*

*Remember to listen to your mind and body: you don't want to overdo it, yet you also want to challenge yourself appropriately. To improve even further and contribute to the team, work out with a teammate. By doing so, you can help challenge each other to a higher standard, yet also keep it fun knowing you have a teammate right there to support you. Remember to stretch well before and after working out, avoid working out at the hottest parts of the day or in the dark (i.e., be safe mentally and physically), and be sure to hydrate well. Vary the surfaces you run on – avoid hard surfaces (concrete, worn tracks, etc.), and be sure you have appropriate training gear. Pay attention to your nutrition habits, too. Lighten your workouts just before mini-camp, as we will come together to play and train appropriately. You will still need to work out on your own throughout the season, but we can go over those workouts in August.*

*Be sure to get touches on the ball – some of the best ways to improve technical skills are to play 1v1 and small-sided soccer, work on long balls, shoot on goal, practice heading, improve first-touch, do the*

UNCSSCP, and play pick-up. Watch higher-level soccer to improve your understanding and enjoyment of the game. Also, remember to reach out to your teammates throughout the summer. See, phone, email, text them, or do whatever it takes to stay connected. Let each other know you are working hard for them and that you support them. Reach out to someone that you normally don't chat with to make us even stronger as a team. Be bold, be thoughtful, and be a leader. Most importantly, be active, have fun and have a super summer! See you soon, and I probably don't say it often enough, but I am proud of your excellent efforts. Thank you for making the team what it is.

*Sincerely,*
*Enc/cc*                                                                      *Ashu*

## DEFINITIONS

### CARDIOVASCULAR ENDURANCE/AEROBIC FITNESS:

This type of running involves distance runs of one to three miles or 5-30 minutes in duration. This training allows the athlete to recover between high-intensity workouts and to sustain a low level of intensity for a long duration.

### LONG SPEED ENDURANCE/ANAEROBIC FITNESS:

This type of training involves running repeat 100-yard intervals with 45 seconds rest between repetitions. This type of running strengthens the anaerobic energy system and conditions the athlete for the shorter, more intense, and more specific conditioning work that usually follows.

### SHORT SPEED/ANAEROBIC FITNESS:

This type of training involves running short intervals (40 yards or less) with short recoveries (30 secs or less), which simulate the majority of sports recovery patterns.

### COMBINATION WORK:

This type of training involves the use of both long and short speed endurance workouts.

## RESOURCES FOR THIS PACKET

Though I have created some of these workouts, many of these workouts come from a variety of my contacts at United Soccer Coaches, US Soccer, Region One, UNC, athletic trainers, *Explosive Performance*, and other connections through years of coaching experiences. Also use the valuable information in the book, *Vision of a Champion* (Dorrance/Averbuch 2002). This book includes fitness with and without the ball (see UNC Skills Conditioning Program, Summer Speed Program, and other exercises in the appendix).

## SAMPLE FITNESS TESTS

An athlete ultimately wants to test her/himself to see where she/he stands in terms of their efforts to get "fitter, faster, stronger." Here are some sample tests (see tempo/interval runs that can also be tested):

- 2-mile run (under 14 minutes)

- 40-yard dash

- 6 x 200 meters (34 sec per each run plus 34 sec rest between)

- 15 x 120 meter shuttle (20 sec and 40 secs to return plus 20 sec rest)

- 3 x 300 meter shuttle (1 min plus 2 min rest)

- Vertical jump — 13-15 inches average

- Pro agility

- T-drill/T-test

- Cooper run (7.5 or more laps in 12 minutes). U18-U16: 7.5 laps (without rounding) in 12 minutes, with a preference toward 7.75 laps; U16-U14: decrease by 0.5 lap

- 120s — make 7+ (out of 10); sprint 120 yards in < 20 secs, return to start in 30 secs, rest at start for 30 secs (repeat 10x)

- Push-ups — number you can do in 60 secs

- Sit-ups — number you can do in 60 secs

- 8 x 20 yard sprints (20 secs stationary rest between reps), 8 x 40 yd sprints (30 secs rest between reps), 6 x 60 yd sprints (45 secs rest between reps), 5x 80 yd sprints (60 secs rest between reps), 4 x 100 yd sprints (75 secs rest between reps)

- Illinois agility test: start lying face down, sprint, weave, etc., 10 x 12 yard set-up

- 20-yard sprint, 20-yard agility

## SOCCER SKILLS TESTING

As any athlete would like to know areas that will be evaluated, here are some soccer skills topics and tests that we will record in the opening days of mini-camp.

DIRECT SOCCER-SPECIFIC DAY THEMES: 1v1, Passing/Receiving, Longballs/Heading, Shooting/Finishing, Turning/Back-to-Pressure, miscellaneous "Olympics" (various other skills)

*SKILLS:*
**Juggle** — 100+ (no specific body part more than two consecutive. Body parts include: head, chest, each shoulder, each quad, each of the following surfaces L and R: laces, inside, outside, heel).

*Note:   I have a separate juggling grid, and we are not really interested in long strings of juggles past 100 during training, however nice, due to time constraints at training and the need for an overall very active training philosophy. See sample training sessions and mini-camp models.*

**Longball for distance** — combined distance of 75+ yards, sum of one kick each with right foot and left foot (one chance each).

**Finishing** — start at 22, weave through two discs, finish from behind the 18, alternating posts. Make 7+ out of 10 (score if ball passes through space between post and disc one yard inside goal).

**Longball for accuracy/Heading** — with partner, serve ten each from at least 25 yards, head back 18+ yards, make 7+ times out of 10 (no extra chances).

*COMPETITIVE*
— win at least three-fourths of 1v1 games (cones, grids, to goal)

— win at least three-fourths of full-sided scrimmages

## PEP/AGILITY WARM-UP EXERCISES

(PEP: Prevent injury, Enhance Performance) Do these exercises at least three times per week. You can vary the exercises, but be sure to include some form of the following: warm-up shuttles, functional stretching, active warm-up runs — S, carioca, skip (forward/backward), alternate step and touch (lunge, touch foot with opposite hand), diagonal plant and cut (push off of outside leg), 360 runs, butt kicks, high knees (forward and backward), scissors, form running, bounding, sprint to backpedal, lateral shuffle to sprint, carioca to sprint, footwork/speed-ladder, jog and twist (forward/backward), backward run, power skip (for height), shoulder bumps, sprints with alternate starts (soccer start, staggered stance, balanced start off one leg, lateral start, crossover start, back step, etc.).

*Note:* *These exercises are modified from various resources with the main resource being Santa Monica Sports Medicine Program (smsmf.org).*

*Programmed warm-up:*

A. **General Warm-up Exercises — knees and feet straight ahead**

1. Jogging — touch line to touch line
2. Side shuffle — touch line to touch line (switch at mid field); keep hips low
3. Backwards jogging — keep hips low

B. **Stretching Exercises — each leg 30 seconds (except for inner thigh)**

1. Calf stretch
2. Quad stretch
3. Hamstring stretch
4. Inner thigh stretch — (a.) straight out; (b.) to the right; (c.) to the left (20 seconds each)
5. Hip flexor stretch — in the lunge position

C. **Strengthening Exercises**

1. Walking Lunge — 3 sets of 10 repetitions
2. Calf Raises — 30 repetitions on each leg
3. Kneeling Hamstring — 2 sets of 10 repetitions

**D.    Jumping Exercises – plyometrics – soft landings; bend the knees; keep knees from touching**

1.    Side to side jumps – side to side over disc cone jumps (20 repetitions)
2.    Front to back jumps – front to back over disc cone jumps (20 repetitions)
3.    Single leg vertical jumps – 20 repetitions each leg
4.    Vertical jumps – imaginary header vertical jumps (20 repetitions)
5.    Scissor jumps – 20 repetitions

**E.    Agility Exercises**

1.    Diagonal runs – zig-zag through 6 cones. Run through 3 times (set cones 5 yds X 5 yds apart).
2.    Shuttle runs – 10-yd forward – 10-yd backward – 10-yd forward jogging
3.    Bounds – bounding touch line to touch line

Note:    *As a reminder, several of the exercises listed in the following sections are geared toward getting players to be fitter, faster, stronger. Besides the benefits of cross-training, mental toughness, agility, and so much more, the exercises are challenging and keep players love for the game fresh. The common thought these days is "only soccer all year," but many people disagree. In addition, many "self-training" ideas with a soccer ball are also presented.*

## SAMPLE PLYOMETRIC DRILLS

- Jumps: squat, split squat (scissors), double leg tuck, pike, single leg vertical power, cycled split squat, box, in-depth box, double leg vertical power, standing triple; vertical, lateral, forward, backward, multiple

- Hops: single leg, single leg speed, lateral cone, double leg speed, double leg, single or double cone

- Medicine ball (or substitute with soccer ball): sit-up, plyo push-up, drop and catch push-up

- Bounding: combination, alternate leg

- Single leg knee tuck

    *There are numerous plyometric exercises available online, at your local gym, through athletic training personnel, etc. Use caution and consider ankles, knees, age, activity, injury and condition.*

## SAMPLE WEIGHT/RESISTANCE STRENGTHENING EXERCISES

See the strength training sheet designed for soccer athletes.

- High pulls
- Step-ups
- Squat
- Straight-leg jumps
- Press
- Wide-stance squats
- Reverse hypers

- Box hops
- Dips
- Ice skaters
- Straight bar curls
- RDL
- Russian twist
- Side bends
- Push press
- DB incline press
- Front squat
- Bent rows
- Box jumps
- Seated laterals
- Close grip bench press
- Bench press
- Pull-ups
- Push-ups
- Lunges — alternate forward, backward, side
- Leg curls
- Hang clean
- Weighted crunches

## ABS — MULTIPLE TECHNIQUES

Regular sit-ups, rock sit-ups, straight arm sit-ups, crossover sit-ups, crunches, quick crunches, side crunches, reverse crunches, stack crunches, twisting stack crunches, stack crunch combo, reach thrust, bicycle abs, straight leg crossover sit-ups, V-ups, leg raises, straight leg raises, hanging leg raises, standing side crunches, standing DB side crunches, standing twists, Big 40s, Super 60s, ABCs, Figure 8s, flutter kicks, "Chinese" thinker (seal walk or plank, plus extension), negative sit-ups, dying cockroach, three-man abs-assault, low cable abs, kneeling cable abs, band twists, triple medicine ball drop, two-man medicine ball sit-up pass, seated/standing medicine ball throw, back-to-back medicine ball pass, plyometric sit-ups, back-bridge (plus extension), side-bridge (plus extension), lateral sit-ups, hyperextension or back raises, leg hugs, Russian twist, hip curls, jackknives, reverse trunk twist, crunches.

Technique: sit-ups with weight in hands on chest, alternate leg twisted sit-ups, fixed feet/twisted sit-ups

## SAMPLE AGILITY/QUICKNESS DRILLS

- 3 cone drill
- 3 & 5 cone crazy 8s
- 45-degree drop square drills
- Cone chute
- Cross drill quick feet
- Hex drill quick feet

- 5 dot drill
- In & out agility drill
- Nebraska drill
- Illinois agility
- Pro agility
- Square drill
- Square drill quick feet
- Star drill
- Tag drill
- W drill
- Bag drills (like "speed ladder" drills)
- T drill
- 4 corner cone drill
- Rope-skipping (use various footwork – cross foot, heel-toe, straddle, toe-toe, etc.)
- Speed ladder: marching, high-knee running, high-knee lateral running, run in, sprint out, zig-zag, cross-over shuffle, zig-zag crossover shuffle, inside and outside cutting, 2 in 1 out ("Icky shuffle"), 2 in 2 out, 2 in 2 out hops, side right-in, side left-in, carioca, quick jumps and hops, ski jumps, slalom ski jumps, snake jump (pivot drill), 180-degree turn, etc.
- Wheel drill (8 spokes)
- Plant & cut (6 discs zig-zag)
- 4-cone 10x10 yard drill (sprint, shuffle, backward, carioca)
- 5-10-15 drill (variations: sprint-turn-sprint back, sprint out – backpedal back, backpedal out-sprint back, shuffle out – carioca back)
- 12 Cone Shuffle/Weave/Slalom drill
- Mirror drill (with partner) – move same direction, move opposite direction, incorporate ball
- 50-yard Ajax shuttle: 10 yards (there-back-there-back-there) repeat 5 times, working on form
- Clover leaf (5 cone cross)
- L-shuffle
- Partner ball drops

## SAMPLE INTERVAL/TEMPO RUNS

Remember that increasing or decreasing repetitions, distances, times, and rest can be adjusted to make these high, medium, or low intensity workouts. Add warm-up, middle run, and cool-down to these workouts to get the desired level of time/distance, as appropriate. Vary the surfaces you run on and be sure your running shoes have excellent support. The times listed are mostly top tier D1 women's soccer standards, so be realistic with your times. Be creative and have fun!

*Note: s = sprint; j = jog*

- "Large tempo": Sprint 100s on laps 1, 2, 3, 5, 7, 8, 11; 200s on 4, 6, 9, 10; rest by walking 50 or 100 between sprints; (100s 17secs, 200s 38 secs)
- "Giant tempo": 6 x 400s with 200 walk between sprints, extra 200 after the third 400 (1:30/400 sprint)
- "Small tempo": Run 100, Walk 50, R100, W50, R100, W100, R100, W50, R200, W50, R100, W100, R100, W50, R100, W50, R100, W100 (100s 17 secs, 200 38 secs)

- Liners — staggered (sprint to the marker, then sprint back to the starting line, sprint to the next marker, then sprint back to the starting line, etc.): 5, 20, 10, 40, 5, 30, 15, 25, 10, 20; rest 1 minute; 20, 5, 5, 25, 15, 40, 40, 15, 10, 30; rest 1 min; 20, 40, 10, 10, 30, 20, 30, 15, 5, 40
- Recall the 50, 100, 200 lap interval workouts — alternate sprint/jog
- 8x100 sprints w/100 jog recovery between each rep
- 2x400 sprints w/400 jog recovery between each rep
- Fartlek run — vary sprint/recovery lengths by sight or time
- 4x300 sprints w/300 recovery after each rep
- 4x (sprint 100/jog 100, s100/j100, s200/jog200)
- 8x 200 sprints w/200 recovery after each rep
- 2x 800 sprints w/400 recovery after each rep
- 6x (sprint 100/jog 100, s200/jog200)
- 16x 50 or 8x 100 or 4x 200 or 2x 400 hills w/rest between plus strides
- 4x 400 sprints w/400 recovery after each rep
- 2x (sprint 400, jog 100/sprint 300, j200/s200, j300/s100)
- "UCLA" (s100/j300, s200/j200, s300/j100, s400/j400, s400/j400, s300/j100, s200/j200, s100/j300)
- 8 "horseshoes" (8x s300/j100)
- 3x (s200/j200, s400/j400)
- 2x (s100/j100, s200/j200, s100/j100, s200/j200, s400/j400)
- Modify our "in-season" workouts from our trainings: cones, 100/120s, Rickey Marvins, Cooper run, Figure 8s, egg-timers/Roman 10s, horseshoes, railroad tracks, square dance, taffy-pull, repeat 100s, 10-20-30 sec sprints/30 sec jog, catch-the-pack, slalom, buffaloes, fartlek, stinkers (40 or 50 or 60 yard there-back-there), monsters (full or half-field)
- Caribbean Box
- UNC Summer Speed Program
- 12x 20s, 6x 40s with 20 stationary sec rest between reps
- 10x Cones: 5-10-15-20-25 yard liners; 35 or 40 seconds to complete each run (25 secs stationary rest after the 35 secs reps; 20 secs rest after the 40 secs reps)
- 10x 120s: sprint each 120 rep in 17-20 secs, jog back to starting line and rest within the next 30 secs, then repeat; extra 30 secs rest after the 4th and 7th reps
- 120s Supersets: alternate 120s and 50 yard shuttles; 120s are as above; 50 yard shuttles consist of running to the 50 yard line and back 3 times in one minute; rest 30 seconds between each rep. 10 of each is the workout — very high intensity workout.
- 40-yard shuttles: up and back three times (240 yds) within 45 secs, then rest 45 secs; start with 6 sets, work up to 10 sets; extra 15 secs rest after 3rd, 6th, 9th reps
- 50-yard cone drill: 10 and back, 20 and back, 30 and back, 40 and back, 50 and back (300 yds) within 1 minute; rest 1 minute; start with 6 sets, work up to 8 sets; extra 15 secs rest after 3rd and 6th reps
- Alternate Superset: 120-yd sprint in 18 secs, 120-yd jog back/rest in 30 secs, 25 secs rest on the line, 40-yard shuttle (see above) in 45-47 secs, rest 1:15; try 5 sets
- Jingle-Jangle: two markers 10 yards apart; up and back 10 times (200 yds) within 50-55 secs, rest 1 min; start with 8 sets, work up to 10 sets; extra 15 secs rest on 3rd, 6th, 9th reps
- Gauntlet: run 1 mile in 6:45, 1 min rest, run ½ mile in 3:30, 1 min rest, run ¼ mile in 90 secs, 1 min rest, run 200 yards in 45 secs
- Sides: use a soccer field. Begin in a corner. Sprint one side (longest side), jog one side for one lap. Sprint two, jog two. Sprint three, jog three. Sprint four, jog four. You can go "downward" as a variation (sprint is as fast as you can, jog is not a walk)

- "German" training: use a soccer field or set markers at 6, 18, 55 yards; first shuttle is to the 6 and back for 1 full minute, 1 min rest. Second shuttle is to the 18 and back for two full mins, 2 mins rest; third shuttle is to the 55 and back for three minutes, 6 mins rest; repeat
- 20-40-60-80-100 speed program (see UNC information in *Vision of a Champion*)
- Repeat 100s: 2-3 sets of 8x 100m sprints (20-24 secs each) with 30 secs rest between reps and 3 mins rest between sets
- 90 sec runs with 3 min rest between runs
- 30/30s: 10-12x (30 sec sprint/30 sec jog)
- 2 mins runs: 3-5x (2 min run/2 min rest)
- Power runs: 4x 30-45 secs all-out sprint with rest between reps; create your own variations
- 2x 200 sprint/200 jog, 6-8x s400/j200, 2x s200/j100
- 2x s200/j200, 1x s400/j200, 3-4x s800/j400, 1x s400/j200, 2x s200/j100
- 2x s200/j200, 1x s400/j200, 1x s800/j400, 1x s1200/j600, 1x s400/j200, 2x s200/j100
- Combo 100, 150, 200, 300, 400, 800 sprints by time with rest intervals
- "Killer 1s": sprint 100, jog back 50, sprint 100, jog back 50, sprint 400; rest 3 mins; repeat workout; rest 4 mins; repeat workout for a third time
- "Killer 2s": sprint 200 <36 secs, rest 30 secs, sprint 200, rest 3 mins; repeat two more times
- 100, 200, 400 combo sprints with rest intervals
- 120, 300 combo sprints with rest intervals

## TRAINING PACE

This is a handy reference guide for your own training pace for distance and interval running. Be sure to consult medical personnel regarding your condition, optimal heart rate, and other physiological considerations. To calculate your training pace, run one mile at your best pace and record the time in seconds. Calculate the following: Total seconds of your best mile x (100- % effort) + Total seconds = N. Then, take N / 60 and get a decimal. Take the whole number in your decimal and add that to the decimal portion of your answer x 60 to get your training pace.

Example: best mile is 6:30, which translates into 390 seconds. 60% pace is 390 x 0.4 + 390 = 546 seconds; 546/60 = 9.1; 9 + .1 x 60 = 9:06 training pace

Guide: 60% pace for easy, long run or recovery run; 80% for hard run between 1/2 and 2/3 of racing distance; 85% pace for intervals of 3/4ths to 1 mile; 90% pace for intervals of 1/2 mile; 95% pace for intervals of 1/4 mile.

## TRAINING LOGS

I strongly suggest coaches give players training logs to record their workouts. Writing down workouts is more likely to reap benefits of responsibility and accountability among your team. The format can be a coach-generated list of dates, noting key dates for team events, or the log can take the form of a calendar. Be sure that players describe their fitter, faster, stronger (FFS) workouts with appropriate detail.

# ADDITIONAL SELF-TRAINING IDEAS

Technical Skills

Be sure to always pick at least one core skill: 1v1, finishing, first-touch, serving and dealing with long balls, shielding. The following skills will help you in these areas.

## FOOT SKILLS
- "Stationary Touches": ping-pong, step-ups, "Brazilian" step-ups, drag-cut, triangles, see-saw, saw-see, U-V, pull-pushes with all combinations following, etc.
- "Moving Touches": pull-push (in/out-same/opposite), chop (in, out, Cruyff), pull-turn (+with drawing inside touches), Matthews (+counter-Matthews), zig-zag, step-over-turn, scissors/double scissors (lateral, breakaway), Figure 8s, in-in-out, out-out-in, hesitate, 360/"ballerina", sideways-drag (in, out), fake shot (push, turn, cut), double-touch, L, big-small, scoop, and many more!
- *Add the technical speed element: small then big touch to add explosiveness to these moves, quickness to your technical skill, agility to your physical construct. Play 1v1 (cone, grid, goal) to practice these moves, perform under pressure, compete, etc.*

## TURNS
- Inside of foot cross-body, outside of foot, half-turn/face-up, Chinaglia/man-on, self-pass, dummy, leave, drag cut, etc.; 2s, 3s, 4s; combine with moves, finishing.
- Consider back-to-pressure: early check, late check, no check.

## PASSING AND RECEIVING
- Longballs — long serve, settle, head, clear, chip, strike off of "slow rollers," etc.; late/early crosses (combine with finishing).
- Inside of foot, outside of foot, instep; bend, chip, loft, drive/power-shot, surface, triangle, etc. Consider pace versus distance.
- "Chinese Coervers" in partners — moving up and back together, using various three-touch combinations of inside and outside of feet.
- Receive with inside/touch across body/pass back with inside of opposite foot; receive with outside/touch outside/pass back with inside of same foot; "cradle"/inside-inside-inside, front-foot receive inside/pass outside, drag-cut, etc.
- "Brazilian" three touch — push away, bring back, pass with various combinations of inside and outside of foot surfaces.
- Diagonals and straights; rectangles — both directions.

## JUGGLING
- We do all types of juggling: foot-surfaces, thigh, chest, head, etc.; T-T-F, F-F-T, L-L-H, H-H-L, around the world, juggle-juggle-pass, Pill's "ladder" (F-T-H) and "circle" (T-T-F-F) and adding one touch on each cycle, make up your own, etc. Refer to the juggling grid.

## FINISHING
- Power, bend, drive, chip, surface. Pick from various situations, angles, distances — still ball, moving ball, off of a dribble, pass, turn, etc., coming from various directions (forward, back, side); off of crosses; volleys and half-volleys; in 1v1 and 2v2 and "in-the-box" pressure training.

## FIRST TOUCH

- Run-throughs, high-settles, lower-leg, "skips," triangle and diamond first-touch exercises, "Brazilians" up and back (moving up the body); circle drill with various exercises; toss 'n settles: roof, elevator, inside wedge, outside wedge, Cruyf.
- Consider shielding exercises: stationary versus moving ball; pass-pass-roll and shield.

## TRAINING TECHNICAL SKILLS UNDER PRESSURE/MATCH-RELATED CONDITIONS

- Play 1v1, 2v2, 3v3, 4v4, etc. up to 11v11, as appropriate. Start small-sided and work your way up to the full 11v11 game. There are numerous tactical games you can play, whether it is possession or to goals.

## OTHER SOURCES, COMMENTS, NOTES

- See our "FFS Training Log," UNCSSCP, *Vision of a Champion*, UNCGSC manual for camp coaches, United Soccer Coaches, DA, ECNL,, SIS, Region One ODP, US Soccer, VYSA, club, high school, and other resources.

A note to coaches and parents: This is plenty of material that our players know and should be used for self-training or at any time that I am not there and/or when you are looking for things for the players to work on. They have definitely benefited from training effectively on these and other skills. I obviously cannot put all that we do and all that is a part of our program here. We train these skills in a variety of settings (with/without pressure, with time/space pressure, individually, partners, groups, 1v1, competitive, purely technical, adding tactical concepts, etc.). Crossing, shooting/finishing, first-touch (run-throughs, high-traps, toss 'n settle, etc.) are also major parts of our curriculum. A heading series is also important to do every now and then. Tactically, we have obviously done so much that is not meant to be printed here! The key point is that players do not need an organized training session, a session with a trainer, or other pre-organized training environment. Players who supplement excellent training by constructing training environments on "off days," are the ones who will ultimately excel.

## *JUGGLING GRID*

| Exercise | Number: | 10 | 25 | 50 | 75 | 100 | 150 | 200 |
|---|---|---|---|---|---|---|---|---|
| *FEET ONLY* | | | | | | | | |
| Straight — laces/no spin | | | | | | | | |
| Right-Left (Alternate) | | | | | | | | |
| Low-Low-High | | | | | | | | |
| High-High-Low | | | | | | | | |
| Right-Left (Alt&Build) | | | | | | | | |
| All-surface (<=2) | | | | | | | | |
| *FOOT/THIGH* | | | | | | | | |
| Thigh-Thigh-Foot | | | | | | | | |
| Foot-Foot-Thigh | | | | | | | | |
| RtF,LfF,LfT,RtT | | | | | | | | |
| RtF,LfF,LfT,RtT Build | | | | | | | | |
| Thigh-Foot Alt | | | | | | | | |
| Thigh-Foot Alt&Build | | | | | | | | |

*COMBINATION*

Around the World (RtF, RtT, RtS, chest, head, chest, LfS, LfT, LfF)

Any part, but no more than 2 consecutive of same part

Same as above, but must complete each of the touches in Around the World before repeating a body part; add in Rt/Lf heel, inside/outside foot.

**Rt:** Right; **Lf:** Left; **F:** Foot; **T:** Thigh; **Low:** shin level or below; **High:** head height or above

## *RESTARTS: ATTACKING AND DEFENDING CORNER KICKS*

**Self-check:** How well do you know our attacking corner kick plays? Do you know which side is most effective for each attacking play depending on personnel of right-footed versus left-footed players?

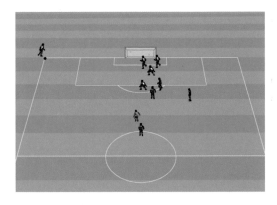

**Arm signal High** — far "triangle" of 6-12

**Arm signal Medium** — head height between 6-12

**Arm signal Low** — near "triangle" of 6-12

**Dorry** — timing of near run, angle of player and runner, execution of pass

**Back** — timing, delivery, execution of cross

**Blue** — timing, speed, preparation for shot

**2v1 (overlap, end line)** — short corner

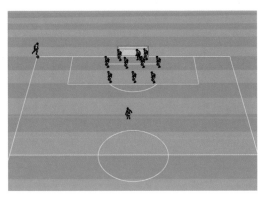

Do you know our defensive shape for corner kicks? Be sure you understand how the "zone" is set up and also know that you must defend relentlessly to deny your player an opportunity on goal. Zone does not mean passing off responsibility to someone else, but instead taking responsibility for defending and communicating. Note: We also use a combination of zone and "man-to-man," as we try to body up on specific opposing players.

### RESTARTS: AttackING FREE KICKS

Attacking restarts are excellent opportunities to score, especially if everyone is focused and executes their roles. Pay attention to the referee's arm signal — arm down means a direct kick is awarded; arm up means an indirect kick is awarded. Every player must know each play and get into position quickly. Players need to remember to frame the goal with first and second layer near-far-slot runs. Do your part, understand each play, and work together!

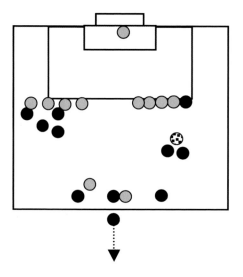

**OPTIONS:** Always look for a quick restart, but if it's not on, do not waste it. Read what the opponent is giving us — be sure you know where to run for each option and position.

**(1) Snake** — shot (this is the simplest — keep things simple!)

**(2) Cat** — chip far post

**(3) Dog** — drive far post

*Note: These are both served away from the opponent's GK with varied bend and pace depending on the distance away from goal, location of the opponent's wall, and ability of the player striking the kick*

**(4) Monkey** — "midfielder" spin out from outside edge of opponent's wall

**(5) Octopus** — "overlap" (players run in front or behind depends on what play we do; do not make the run for the Monkey or Bear plays)

**(6) Bear** — back overlaps ball down flank

**(7) Gorilla** — gap, ball played laterally into gap of opponent's wall and their marking players

**(8) Eagle** — edge, ball played diagonally to player posting up on inside edge of opponent's marking players

*Note: There are additional variations of all of these attacking restart plays, and we have additional plays not listed here.*

## MATCH DAY TEAM WARM-UP

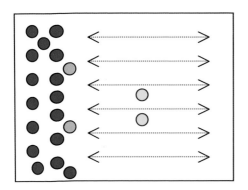

### PHASE ONE: Warm-up; Team motivation

- As a team, players jog back and forth across the field a few times; add agilities, dynamic stretching, followed by any other stretching; reach players — communicate roles and responsibilities

- As a team, each player has a ball: practice foot skills, moves, miscellaneous juggling

- Players pair off and warm-up with a ball — they choose the exercises: juggling, "Chinese Coervers," volleys, half-volleys, headers, etc.

*H20*

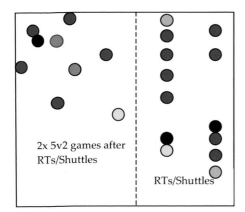

2x 5v2 games after RTs/Shuttles

RTs/Shuttles

### PHASE TWO: Fundamental First Touch, Passing, Receiving over "short" distance

- Divide the team into two groups —

  - A: shuttles — 2,3,1-touch +wall passing
  - B: run-throughs, lower-leg, abs and high-ball foot settles off of throw-ins

- After rotating, each group stays together and plays 5v2

*H20*

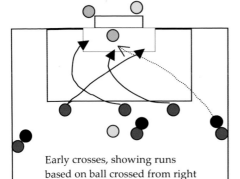

Early crosses, showing runs based on ball crossed from right side of field; alt with power shot.

### PHASE THREE: Pass, Receive, Cross, Finish

- 3s/1 ball — ordered passing/random movement: drives with aggressive touch receiving, add in Brazilian 3-touch receiving along with flicks 'n foot-settles (inside/outside wedge, elevator, roof, chop behind standing leg); stretch calves and hamstrings; turning series; stretch quads and any other; long balls — bend, drive, chip, loft, try to reach teammate on the run within one bounce or less

- Crossing and Finishing-early/late; finishing off dribble.

- 18-yard line to mid-line sprints plus short sprints just before the match

*H20*

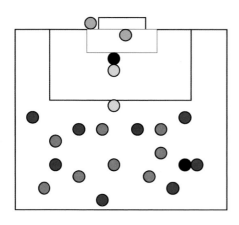

PHASE FOUR: Possession/Match-related (choose among the following based on time, space, etc.)

- 8v8 possession or game with goals

- 10v6 possession with rotating opposition (drop vest and person turning ball over picks up vest and becomes defender)

- 11v7 half-field game to large goal

- whole-team pass and move (unlimited) — drive, bend, chip, loft, combos, connect with every teammate

PHASE FIVE: Reminders, specific goals, inspire...
*Let's Go Get 'em!*

*Notes:*

- *See previous plans for more detailed descriptions of exercises.*

- *Coach players to higher standards, even on the fundamental exercises, as the warm-up is also an opportunity to improve and excel.*

- *Encourage communication, vision, intensity, effort, etc., throughout the warm-up; focus on effort and execution.*

- *Allow for water breaks, as indicated.*

- *This pre-match warm-up is designed for 45-60 minutes; adapt exercises, as necessary (e.g., second match's warm-up on consecutive days is usually only 30 mins, space limitations, etc.).*

- *Connect with every player; every player should connect with his/her teammates.*

# CREDITS

**Illustrations:** www.sports-graphics.com

**Interior Photos:** Courtesy of the Banks, Constantino, Dexter, Grose, and Reed families

**Author Photo:** © Greg Murray

**Cover Photos:** © Ken Huth, Melody Butts

**Cover and Interior Design and Layout:** Annika Naas

**Managing Editor:** Elizabeth Evans

*"In the Vision of a Champion, the book I wrote with Gloria Averbuch to help youth soccer players 'navigate all the treacherous waters' of their sport, I referenced Ashu as someone to contact who had mastered it. I stand by that now as you explore and apply his vision and his time-tested and practical ideas."*

–Anson Dorrance, University of North Carolina at Chapel Hill Women's Soccer Head Coach, former USWNT Head Coach; numerous elite coaching honors

*"Soccer is analogous to life. Our approach is determined by our knowledge, perspectives, beliefs, experiences, and insights—all of which add to the richness of the journey. I am confident this contribution from Ashu, on this subject will further add to the richness."*

–Hank Leung, Executive Director of Coaching, experienced college, youth and former USWNT programs coach

*"It is very clear that successful coaching means creating a positive environment in which the players can get better. The environment must be challenging, motivating and fun! That is how programs develop players. When you prioritize the duties of a coach, Xs and Os are way down the list. Creating the proper environment is at the top of the list.* The Well-Rounded Soccer Coach *is a road map to creating the right environment. I highly recommend this book to all coaches!"*

–Jay Martin, United Soccer Coaches Soccer Journal Editor and Ohio Wesleyan Men's Soccer Head Coach

*"I have been reading through this book and just wanted to say that Ashu has outdone himself! It is awesome! The perspectives coming from a quality person like him will give others a whole new look of how life is in the youth game and beyond!"*

–Ken Krieger, Executive Director of Coaching and long-time experienced boys and girls coach of highly competitive youth, HS, DA and ODP programs

*"I love re-reading Ashu's book. As a longtime (over 30 years) coach, I will pick up his book to find an exercise that I need for my session, and then I find something else that inspires me and my team to be the best. I also get to work side-by-side with Ashu at Durham Academy. I am the luckiest coach in the world."*

–Susan Ellis, veteran HS, youth, professional soccer coach; four-time NCAA champion at UNC-Chapel Hill; United Soccer Coaches HS Coach of Significance